BUILD YOUR RUNNING BODY

A TOTAL-BODY FITNESS PLAN FOR ALL DISTANCE RUNNERS, FROM MILERS TO ULTRAMARATHONERS

RUN FARTHER, FASTER,
AND INJURY-FREE

**Pete Magill, Thomas Schwartz
and Melissa Breyer**

PHOTOGRAPHS BY DIANA HERNANDEZ

Souvenir Press

This book is not intended as a substitute for the medical advice of physicians or other clinicians. Readers should consult with a physician, dietitian, or other health-care professional before beginning or making any changes to a diet, exercise, or health program. The authors and publisher expressly disclaim responsibility for any liability, loss, or risk—personal or otherwise—which is incurred, directly or indirectly, as a consequence of the use and application of any of the contents of this book.

Photograph on page 163 courtesy Roger Sayre
Photograph on page 161 courtesy of AquaJogger
Photographs on pages 295, 307, 317, 325, 335, and 347 courtesy of John Fell
Text design by Pauline Neuwirth, Neuwirth & Associates, Inc.

Printed and bound by Bell & Bain Ltd, Glasgow

BUILD YOUR RUNNING BODY

"This is so good. Honestly, I think this is the best running book ever."

—**Bob Anderson**, founder of *Runner's World* and of the
Double Road Race 15K Challenge and the Double Training Program

"*Build Your Running* Body represents something new and needed in sports literature. This is the 'right stuff' for runners who want to get faster, enjoy running more, and stay injury-free for a lifetime."

—**Bill Rodgers**, four-time winner of both the New York City
and Boston marathons

"At last, a running book that shows us how to enjoy running all through life, and that's as interesting as the sport we love so much."

—**Kathrine Switzer**, first woman to officially run the Boston Marathon
and author of *Marathon Woman*

"*Build Your Running Body* is the most useful, info-packed, and comprehensive training manual I've ever read. Coaches will find it invaluable, and runners of all levels will use it as a complete guide to reaching their goals."

—**Amby Burfoot**, 1968 Boston Marathon winner and
Runner's World editor-at-large

"I wish I'd had an encyclopedia on running like *Build Your Running Body* long ago. It's comprehensive—filled with relevant and valuable guidance—and articulated in a way that even the most novice runner can understand."

—**Jacqueline Hansen**, two-time world-record holder for the women's marathon,
Boston Marathon winner, and first woman to run
a sub-2:40 marathon

"A wonderful combination of running science with real-world wisdom for modern runners. When Pete Magill talks, smart runners listen."

—**Scott Douglas**, *Runner's World* senior content editor

"Coach Tom Schwartz possesses an understanding of training and racing that is world class. Utilizing an unconventional approach to training, Tom crafted a program that improved my endurance, my long-term development, and, most importantly, my confidence. Tom made me a champion."

—**Kevin Miller**, multiple times USA masters age-group and
age-graded national champion

"*Build Your Running Body* is nothing short of the Unified Theory of Running. Packed with delightfully fun-to-read advice and asides, it squeezes a century of technical research and coaching wisdom into a book of bite-sized lessons. Techniques and training, energy systems and recipes, race strategy and injury prevention—this book covers it all."

—**Ken Stone**, founder and editor of MastersTrack.com

"Pete Magill must have found the fountain of youth. I coach college students, and he consistently outruns half my team! He must know something the rest of us don't!"

—**Steve Scott**, former American record-holder in the mile (3:47.69),
3-time Olympian, 10 times ranked #1 American miler, and world record-holder
for most sub–4 minute miles (136)

"You will not want to put *Build Your Running Body* down. It's OK to miss a training day to learn from Pete Magill's knowledge and experience—runners of all ages and abilities will be smarter just by getting this book in their hands. It's filled with good, honest common sense gained from years of experience and results."

—**Rod Dixon**, winner of the 1983 New York City Marathon, Olympic Medalist,
two-time World Cross Country Championship Medalist,
and founder of KiDSMARATHON

"*Build Your Running Body* masterfully breaks down the essentials of running-specific training and will help bring you to the starting line of your next race happier, healthier, and faster than ever! Pete Magill is a master, and that's not just an age group designation! The wealth of knowledge in this book is truly remarkable—it shares much of what has allowed Pete to continue to thrive as an athlete and has something to teach every aspiring runner out there. It's truly a must have!"

—**Will Leer**, 2013 USA Champion, Indoor Mile & Indoor 3000 Meters

CONTENTS

PART FOUR: Build Your Running Diet—Protein, Carbs, Calories, and Nutrition

PART FIVE: Build Your Race Strategy

FOREWORD

I confess: When I was first asked to write the foreword for *Build Your Running Body*, I thought, "Oh no, not another training manual." Those of us who have been in the sport for years have seen these manuals come and go. I have read books that even I—a practicing physician, avid runner, and coach—have had trouble wading through, so burdened were they with complex running physiology. As every good physician and coach knows, the essence of communication is getting the message across. Would this book get its message across?

Pete Magill has been a friend of mine for almost three decades, going back to when we competed for Aztlan, a Southern California running club. I've made it a habit to read Pete's *Running Times* columns and have often discussed training with him. I continue to be amazed by his running prowess and achievements as a masters athlete and coach. When my own coaching was under the microscope—in the years when I coached Jordan Hasay, one of America's all-time high school distance running greats, at Mission College Preparatory High School—Pete asked me to explain my coaching philosophy in an article for his running website. I summed it up with the three things I tell all my athletes: "Let's be reasonable. Let's not get greedy. We can have fantastic things happen." Often, the way we train and race when we're young is the way we'll train and race as we get older. We develop habits that stay with us for a lifetime. A reasonable approach to training—one that relies on a long-term plan, patience, and resiliency in the face of unexpected obstacles, such as injury and illness—is the first habit runners should develop. It's the wellspring for success. Would this book offer runners such an approach, setting them on the path toward goal achievement and lifelong fitness?

Build Your Running Body offers an incredible amount of information, the depth of which may at first escape readers, since it's presented in a way that's so easy to understand. Part Two—the workout manual—presents information on running anatomy and physiology that is truly invaluable; I believe most novice and veteran runners could avoid the mishaps so many in the sport suffer with the knowledge embedded in these chapters alone. But *Build Your Running Body* goes further, teaching runners how to use this information to develop their own training schedules and equipping them with essential nutritional advice and go-to recipes for fueling their workouts. And lastly, it puts the whole package together with a practical approach to most runners' ultimate goal: race performance.

This book is unlike any I have seen. It borrows from the best and brightest in the sport—one chapter is devoted to the coaches and physiologists who have made major contributions to current training methods. As the book itself acknowledges, it "stands on the shoulders of giants." But it packages this information in a format that is unique and informed by decades of personal experience. Because of this easy-to-follow format, the material in the book is comprehensible and relevant for both beginners and forty-plus-year veterans like me.

Does *Build Your Running Body* succeed in getting the message across? And does it set runners of all ages on the path for a lifetime of running faster, farther, and injury-free?

I believe it does. Bravo to Pete, Melissa, and Thomas!

Armando Siqueiros, M.D., Internal Medicine
Coach of Cal Poly Distance Club
USA Track & Field 2009 National Developmental
Coach of the Year

INTRODUCTION

You opened this book for a reason.

Maybe you like the cover and wanted to see if there were more photos inside—there are, about four hundred of them, comprising the most comprehensive photo instruction guide for workouts, exercises, and drills available in a running book. That was by design. I've always wished that running—with its associated drills, plyometrics, resistance training, stretching, foam rolling, and other exercises—had an illustrated training manual like those for weightlifting, aerobics, martial arts, and practically every other sport on the planet. Now it does.

But I'm guessing that you opened this book for more than photos.

You want to get serious about a new running program (or improve an old one), and you're wondering if this book will help you achieve your fitness goals. You also want to know if there's something about *Build Your Running Body* that sets it apart from other running books. And you want to know if you can trust the training program in this book, if you can be confident that the authors aren't pushing yet another running fad or get-fit-quick scheme.

The answers are: Yes, yes, and yes.

Whether you're a beginner looking to train for the first time or an experienced runner hoping to improve a 5K or marathon PR, *Build Your Running Body*'s unique training approach will help carry you to your goal. That's because your authors recognize that every runner is different, that we all bring a slightly different body type, exercise history, and performance goal to our training. So instead of being asked to follow a generic prescription for mileage and speedwork (the top-down approach of most training programs), you'll build your fitness from the ground up, learning to target the individual components of your running body—your muscles, connective tissue, cardiovascular system, nervous system, hormones, and more—and to focus on those components that are most relevant to your goals. There is no guesswork. You will never be asked to train on faith.

When I began outlining *Build Your Running Body* in the spring of 2012, I envisioned a training manual for the twenty-first-century runner, a book that treats its readers like members of the fitness-savvy population we've become. Before 1972, before Frank Shorter broke the finish-line tape in the Munich Olympic Marathon and ignited the running boom, running was limited to a handful of perceived oddballs competing in cross country and track. But by 2013, fifty million Americans were lacing up their running shoes, while an equal number belonged to fitness clubs. And these days, we don't just run. We participate in weightlifting, aerobics, spinning, Pilates, yoga, swimming, kickboxing, and more. We utilize personal trainers, nutritionists, and physical therapists. We watch our cholesterol, choose sports drinks based on carbohydrate and protein content, and purchase supplements to the tune of $30 billion a year. We embrace studies on exercise, nutrition, health, and longevity, and we expect our training programs to reflect the cutting-edge science that drives innovation in the sport. But we also expect those programs to be tempered by the experience of coaches and athletes who've tested those innovations, who've embraced the good and weeded out the bad. It's this combination of science and experience that has fueled my own training and coaching. And it's what I wanted this book to convey.

Build Your Running Body will take you on an amazing journey through your running body. You'll begin with the microscopic fibers that comprise your running muscles, and then you'll tour every other running-related component of your body—traveling along the 60,000-mile superhighway of your body's blood vessels—before finally concluding your trip in the incorporeal mission control center that resides in your brain. You'll learn exactly how each component of your running body contributes to your running, and you'll be shown how to train those components on three different levels:

▶ First, you'll break down each separate component into its individual parts (e.g., your heart and blood vessels as parts of your cardiovascular system), and you'll learn specific training to target those parts in the "Training Recommendation" sections that appear in each chapter.

▶ Next, you'll find a photo instruction section at the end of every component chapter that offers a full array of training for the component as a whole (or lets you know where in the book to find the relevant workouts).

▶ Finally, you'll be advised on integrating

training for *all* your components into twelve-week programs, with Chapter 15 offering sample training schedules for all levels of runners (beginner, intermediate, and advanced).

Of course, *Build Your Running Body* offers more than workouts and schedules. As a runner and coach for four decades, I've learned firsthand that running is much more than exercise; it's a lifestyle. And successfully building that lifestyle requires practical, real-world advice on all aspects of our sport. That's why Part One of the book offers chapters on motivation, running's history (the better to understand and embrace the training innovations of the past century), running gear, and running vocabulary—this last chapter supplemented by an appendix glossary defining more than 250 running terms. And that's why Part Three includes a whole chapter devoted to injury prevention, and a corresponding table in the back of the book that lists exercise-specific prevention and rehabilitation guidance for more than forty common running injuries. And why Part Four offers six chapters on diet and nutrition. And why Part Five gets down to the nitty-gritty, detailing proper race preparation and tactics for the competitive runners among us. The book also includes pace tables for every conceivable run, calorie-burn charts for most workouts, and expert discussion throughout on topics from running fads to PEDs (performance-enhancing drugs) to sneaky sugars that manufacturers slip into your food.

You're encouraged to skim through the book as a prelude to reading it. Flip through the photo instruction. Read a few training recommendations. Glance at the tables. Check out the recipes in the diet and nutrition chapters. *Build Your Running Body* is designed to be a one-stop source for everything a twenty-first-century runner needs to know about training, the sport, and the running lifestyle. It will guide you from your first purchase of running shoes to your ultimate performance achievement.

Improved running performance and whole-body fitness aren't unsolved mysteries. Coaches, athletes, and exercise physiologists have been working on both for decades, and the giant leaps forward in fitness participation, race results, and health awareness speak for themselves. The trick lies in utilizing advances in training to achieve your own fitness goals. It's tempting to embrace magic-bullet solutions—to believe that running success can be had by filling your training log with a certain number of miles or by counting your strides per minute or by embracing a fad diet. But the truth is that your body is an incredibly complex biological machine with hundreds of working parts, and good training demands that you target all of them.

Build Your Running Body is dedicated to a simple principle: If you want to become a better runner, you must begin by building a better running body.

Good luck!

Pete Magill
January 16, 2014

PART

1

Build Your
Running
Knowledge

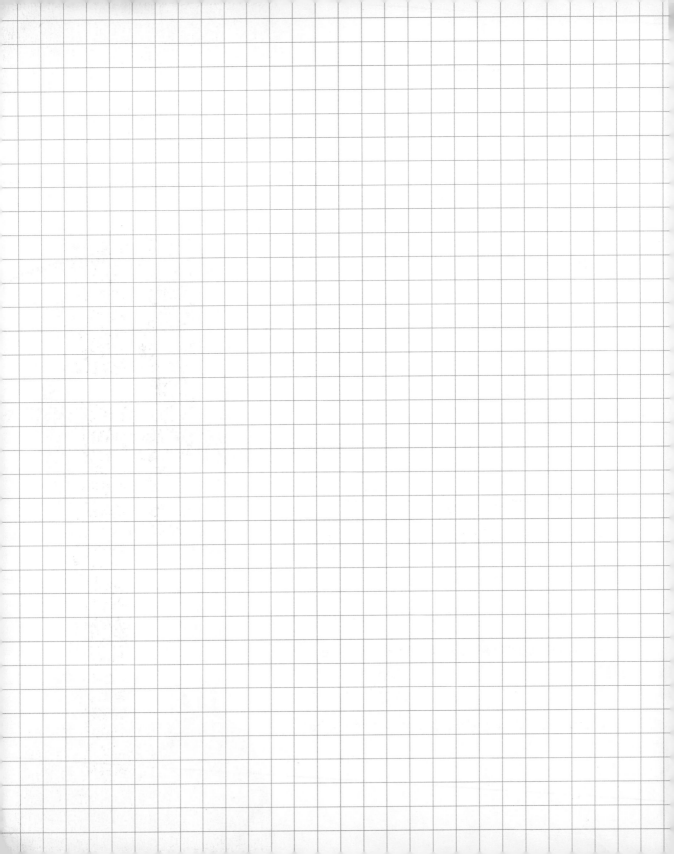

1

Build Your Running Motivation

Why do you run? What drives you to lace up your running shoes and head for the trails? We all need a reason. The simple motivations—such as better fitness and weight loss—are great for getting you out the door once. Or twice. Or for a few weeks. But to stick with a training regimen, to persevere when it's raining or cold, or you're tired, or (cross your fingers) you've already reached your original goal, you need more than simple reasons. You need great reasons. And this chapter has those to spare. First, you'll see that you aren't just improving your cardio or dropping a couple pounds; you're rebuilding every cell in your body to be better than it was before. Next, you'll be amazed at the lifelong benefits, both physical and psychological, that accrue with every workout. Finally, you'll discover what millions of runners have already found: just how much fun a good running program can be.

You are motivated. You proved that by opening this book. You crossed the threshold from thinking about a new fitness plan to putting that plan into action. That was the hardest step, and now that you've taken it, you're already on your way to building a better running body.

WHAT'S RUNNING MOTIVATION?

Running motivation is the daily impetus that keeps you moving forward in a training program. There is no single, universal motivation for all runners. Motivation is fluid; it is constantly changing. Most runners use whatever works for that day. And then whatever works for the next.

Today, you were motivated to open this book.

Tomorrow, what you read in these pages might spur you to lace up your running shoes and go for a short walk or jog, or to perform ten minutes of body exercises, or to prepare a healthier meal.

For more advanced runners, you may discover within these pages some aspect of training that you've overlooked—rewiring your nervous system or improving elastic recoil or increasing cardiac output—that may motivate you to try a few new workouts in the coming weeks.

Lao-tzu wrote, "A journey of a thousand miles begins with a single step." Your journey began with the motivation to open this book. It continues with the next step you take.

WHAT ARE SOME SPECIFIC SOURCES OF RUNNING MOTIVATION?

The first rule of running motivation is to take it one workout at a time. Successful runners understand two things:

1. There is never a perfect time to start a running program, so don't wait until you've mustered the motivation for long-term training before you begin any type of training.
2. The only workout you *must* perform is the next one, so that's where your motivation should be focused.

Today, you don't have to generate the motivation to accomplish all of your fitness goals. You don't have to complete an entire twelve-week training program. You don't need to lose ten pounds. Or race a 5K. Or conquer the marathon.

BEGINNER'S GUIDELINE

Use motivation to fuel your training, but don't become fixated on fueling motivation. Too many runners try to jump-start their enthusiasm by training too hard, going on crash diets, or buying expensive gear. *Slow down.* Fitness is a lifestyle, not a protein shake. The best way to maintain long-term motivation is through steady training success. Don't incinerate motivation with a onetime rocket blast to the moon.

You only need to complete today's workout. Tomorrow's workout can wait until tomorrow.

At the same time, understanding the enormous benefits of a long-term program will provide you with a bountiful source of motivation to drink from each day. Would-be runners are often shocked at just how extraordinary the benefits of a smart, well-rounded training program can be. It's not hyperbole to say that you won't just be building a better running body; you'll be building a better *you*.

Physical health

Every runner has heard the veiled admonition: "Aren't you afraid you're going to ruin your knees?" No, we're not. That's because running is good for your knees—and just about everything else. "Running improves your blood pressure," says Dr. James Fries, coauthor of a 2008 study from Stanford University that tracked 528 runners and 423 non-runners beginning in 1984. "You're less likely to get blood clots and varicose veins. Bones become stronger and denser. It's a treatment for osteoporosis. It prevents fractures of the hips and spine. The ligaments get bigger and stronger—they protect the joints from wobbling, which is one thing that causes joints to wear out. Lungs get stronger. Our physical reserve is greater." Other conclusions from the Stanford study include:

- ▶ Runners suffer fewer disabilities.
- ▶ Running delays age-related disabilities by almost two decades.
- ▶ Runners are seven times less likely to require knee replacements.
- ▶ Runners are less likely to suffer from cancer.
- ▶ Runners have fewer neurological problems.
- ▶ Running *doesn't* increase hip, back, or knee problems.

- ▶ Runners are half as likely as non-runners to die early.

Running isn't just good for your health; it will trigger a positive transformation of your body beyond anything you dreamed possible.

Weight loss

Don't believe reports that claim exercise won't help peel away the pounds. Running burns approximately 100 calories a mile—doesn't matter whether you jog, run, or race that mile. Generally speaking, if you burn 3,500 more calories than you eat, you'll lose a pound (see Chapter 23 for the ins and outs of weight loss). But here's what's amazing: Running leads to weight loss beyond what's predicted by calorie counting. A 2012 study from Lawrence Berkeley National Laboratory compared the weight loss of 32,216 runners and 15,237 walkers. Over six years, the runners averaged 90 percent more weight loss than walkers for the same amount of calories burned. And a lighter, leaner you isn't the only benefit of weight loss. Shedding pounds makes you a faster runner, and that's without having to improve any other aspect of your fitness. See Table 1.1 for some examples of just how much time you can drop in the 5K and marathon when you lose extra weight.

Stress Relief

They say stress kills. But before it kills, it does lots of damage along the way. Stress lowers immunity, increases inflammation, slows healing, decreases bone density, decreases muscle mass, increases blood pressure, increases fat, and intensifies blood sugar imbalances. So when we talk about "stress relief," we aren't merely referencing reduced anxiety. We're talking about a full-body protection plan. Think of stress as your body's version of termites. Think of running as

Table 1.1
The Influence of Healthy Weight Loss on Race Times

Starting Weight	Starting 5K Time: 15:00			Starting Marathon Time: 2:30:00		
(Pounds)	- 5 lbs	- 10 lbs	- 20 lbs	- 5 lbs	- 10 lbs	- 20 lbs
120	14:33	14:01	n/a	2:25:26	2:20:15	n/a
160	14:41	14:17	13:31	2:26:46	2:22:49	2:15:14
200	14:45	14:26	13:49	2:27:34	2:24:23	2:18:13
240*	14:49	14:33	14:01	2:28:07	2:25:26	2:20:15
280*	14:51	14:37	14:10	2:28:30	2:26:12	2:21:43

Starting Weight	Starting 5K Time: 20:00			Starting Marathon Time: 3:15:00		
(Pounds)	- 5 lbs	- 10 lbs	- 20 lbs	- 5 lbs	- 10 lbs	- 20 lbs
120	19:24	18:42	n/a	3:09:04	3:02:19	n/a
160	19:34	19:03	18:02	3:10:48	3:05:40	2:55:48
200	19:41	19:15	18:26	3:11:51	3:07:42	2:59:41
240	19:45	19:24	18:42	3:12:32	3:09:04	3:02:19
280	19:48	19:30	18:54	3:13:03	3:10:03	3:04:13

Starting Weight	Starting 5K Time: 25:00			Starting Marathon Time: 4:00:00		
(Pounds)	- 5 lbs	- 10 lbs	- 20 lbs	- 5 lbs	- 10 lbs	- 20 lbs
120	24:14	23:22	n/a	3:52:42	3:44:23	n/a
160	24:28	23:48	22:32	3:54:50	3:48:31	3:36:23
200	24:36	24:04	23:02	3:56:07	3:51:00	3:41:09
240	24:41	24:14	23:22	3:56:58	3:52:42	3:44:23
280	24:45	24:22	23:37	3:57:35	3:53:55	3:46:44

Starting Weight	Starting 5K Time: 30:00			Starting Marathon Time: 4:45:00		
(Pounds)	- 5 lbs	- 10 lbs	- 20 lbs	- 5 lbs	- 10 lbs	- 20 lbs
120	29:05	28:03	n/a	4:36:20	4:26:28	n/a
160	29:21	28:34	27:03	4:38:52	4:31:21	4:16:57
200	29:31	28:53	27:39	4:40:23	4:34:20	4:22:37
240	29:37	29:05	28:03	4:41:24	4:36:20	4:26:28
280	29:42	29:14	28:21	4:42:08	4:37:46	4:29:15

Starting Weight	Starting 5K Time: 35:00			Starting Marathon Time: 5:30:00		
(Pounds)	- 5 lbs	- 10 lbs	- 20 lbs	- 5 lbs	- 10 lbs	- 20 lbs
120	33:56	32:43	n/a	5:19:58	5:08:32	n/a
160	34:15	33:19	31:33	5:22:53	5:14:12	4:57:31
200	34:26	33:41	32:15	5:24:39	5:17:39	5:04:05
240	34:34	33:56	32:43	5:25:50	5:19:58	5:08:32
280	34:39	34:07	33:04	5:26:41	5:21:38	5:11:46

This table offers approximate performance improvements typical of healthy weight loss practices (see Chapter 23). For example, a 15:00 5K runner weighing 120 pounds who loses five pounds can expect to run 14:33. Note: In creating this chart's data, the authors used the American College of Sports Medicine formula for calculating VO$_2$ max.

*Listed times at these weight are highly unlikely.

BUILD YOUR RUNNING BODY

the exterminator. In addition, running increases endorphins (the source of the "runner's high"), improves sleep, and can serve as a time for tranquil reflection and meditation.

Smarts

Running stimulates the brain. A 2003 review of studies, conducted at the University of Georgia, concluded that submaximal aerobic exercise (e.g., easy distance runs) improves people's ability to process information. A 2004 study from UCLA showed that consistent exercise helps regenerate nerve function in the brain, and a 2011 paper from the Institute of Biomedical Research of Barcelona found that aerobic exercise can protect against neurodegeneration. A 2005 study from Sweden linked running to increased cell growth in the hippocampus, which plays a big role in both memory and depression. And for older runners, a 2010 study from the Medical University in Vienna found that endurance running helps maintain cognitive function into the golden years. Apparently, not only is it smart to run, but running makes you smart.

Use it or lose it

By age twenty-five, men and women begin to lose skeletal muscle mass (skeletal muscles are the muscles that move your body, such as biceps, abs, and hamstrings) at a rate of up to 1 percent per year. That adds up. And once a muscle cell is gone, it's gone forever. The same process occurs with your stride length (the distance each running stride carries you), which, barring intervention, will shorten up to 40 percent by the time you reach your seventies. Proper training can drastically curtail both these losses.

New friends

There are thousands of running clubs and hundreds of thousands of running-club members in the United States alone. And that doesn't include tens of thousands of local training groups—small gatherings of men and women who meet once or twice a week to exercise and socialize. Running is your invitation to one of the healthiest, friendliest, most all-inclusive peer groups in existence.

Nature

There are more than six million runners in the United States who regularly take to the trails. Trails not only reduce impact forces on your lower body, they give you the chance to commune with nature, and to indulge your nomadic instinct while temporarily escaping to a simpler world.

Competition

In 2012, there were more than 15 million finishers in American road races. A race provides a focal point for most runners. Whether your goal is to complete a race distance or to compete against other runners, race goals are a part of most long-term runners' training agenda.

Charity

Some runners find lacing up their shoes for charity to be a rewarding return on their training investment. Running for charity raises nearly two billion dollars per year, with the American Cancer Society's *Relay for Life* collecting more than four hundred million dollars by itself.

Eating

It's not true that endurance athletes can eat whatever they want. Most endurance athletes are lean *because* they watch what they eat. But with consistent training, you can indulge in occasional guilt-free, high-calorie splurges without dreading the impact on your waist, hips, or thighs.

IT'S GOTTA BE FUN

While discussing all the good reasons for runners to start a training program, let's not forget the two *most important* factors in determining whether runners keep training:

- ▶ Fun
- ▶ Results

Too many runners forget—or never realize—that training should be fun. If it's not fun, you'll quit. "It's gotta be fun," says Dr. Fries, discussing how the long-term runners in the almost four-decade-old Stanford study maintain their enthusiasm. "It has to really contribute to the evening of that day or to the next day. You've got to really be enjoying it. If you want to do cross-training or something else, do it if it's fun. Running's not a masochistic exercise program."

So how do you keep it fun? Let's count ten ways:

1. Run with friends.
2. Join a running club.
3. Vary the elements of your training.
4. Cross-train.
5. Change sports (e.g., to cycling) if you need a break from running.
6. Pick a goal race and train for it.
7. Volunteer to work at a local race.
8. Volunteer to coach kids, middle schoolers, or high school runners.
9. Keep a running log.
10. Most important, keep your training volume and intensity manageable.

Along with being fun, a running program must ultimately lead to improvement. Results count. At some point—hopefully sooner rather than later—you must get demonstrably fitter, faster, stronger, springier, thinner, healthier, and happier.

In the long run, it's the combination of fun and results that keeps your motivation from waning. When you're accomplishing your goals and having a blast, too, chances are good that you'll keep going.

2

Build Your Running History

Running is the oldest sport known to humanity (setting aside our competitive embrace of sex and fisticuffs). And endurance running is one of the few physical activities in which we humans are demonstrably superior to most earthbound species. In fact, among our bipedal peers, only the ostrich can run a faster marathon—forty-five minutes versus our top marks of just over two hours. And four-legged competition is limited to sled dogs, camels, and pronghorn antelope. Some researchers even suggest that endurance running drove human evolution, with Australopithecus padding shoeless out of Africa's forests and into its savannas four

Know your history. Almost every get-fit-quick scheme in running is rooted in the premise that the sport has never seen anything like it. Of course, almost invariably the scheme is nothing new. The history of running is a reliable guide to what's new, what's old, what works, and what doesn't.

million years ago, hungry for big game to supplement a diet of shrubs, ants, and termites.

But let's be honest: Although our mastery of distance running is admirable, it doesn't come naturally. Footraces can be traced to ancient Egypt, yet the majority of human performance improvement occurred during the past hundred years. There's a reason for this. For centuries, runners relied on walking and jogging as the centerpiece of their training. Then twentieth-century scientists turned their sights to running physiology, and their findings changed the sport forever. Knowing running's history is key to understanding the workouts you'll find in this book, because what sets us apart from other species isn't human evolution; it's our skill at innovation. While we may have been born to run, we weren't born to run well. We learned how to do that.

WHAT'S RUNNING HISTORY?

Running history is a mix of three elements:

- ▶ **Evolution**
- ▶ **Innovation**
- ▶ **Inspiration**

There's no question that human evolution produced adaptations that favor endurance running (we'll look at some important ones in a minute).

But that doesn't mean that these adaptations created a uniform species of distance runners. The majority of humankind is (take your pick) too tall, too muscular, too squat, too big-boned, too fat, or simply too uncoordinated to achieve much in the way of marathoning without good coaching and lots of training.

And that's where innovation comes into play. Competitive running can be traced to 3800 BC, yet most performance improvement has taken place in recent history, with world records in the mile and marathon dropping a stunning 20 percent and 30 percent, respectively, during the twentieth century. Evolution didn't create that improvement. Training innovation did—and most of that innovation continues to echo in the workouts you'll find in this book.

Finally, without inspirational performances, running wouldn't have garnered enough interest to compile a history. Would anyone run a marathon if Pheidippides hadn't run himself to death carrying news of Persia's defeat by the Greeks at the Battle of Marathon? If Roger Bannister hadn't broken the four-minute mile in 1954, would more than 1,300 runners have followed suit? Without inspiration, there would be no Olympics, Boston Marathon, or local 5Ks. Instead, there are now fifty million runners in the United States alone, a half-million of whom accomplished in 2012 what Pheidippides couldn't: They survived a marathon.

TRAINING DISCUSSION

"Running fads"

It's human nature to look for shortcuts. Why should runners be different? If someone says there's a way to run better without having to do all the hard work, we'll try it. The following ten fads either were or remain popular shortcuts. And while some of these fads have their place as a *part* of a good training program, taken alone they won't get you where you want to go.

1. **LSD (long slow distance):** In 1969, Joe Henderson, former editor-in-chief of *Runner's World,* introduced the phrase "long slow distance" to tout a regimen of high mileage run at a conversational pace, minus the "pain, torture, and agony" of traditional workouts. Lackluster performances soon led to the realization that LSD just makes you a "long slow distance runner."

2. **Barefoot and minimalist running:** Christopher McDougall's 2009 book *Born to Run* made minimalist shoes and no shoes the first great running fad of the twenty-first century. In 2013, however, evidence that injuries persist or increase with minimalism and that running economy declines led to a 30 percent drop in market share for minimalist shoes.

3. **Tabata intervals:** This extreme version of HIIT (high-intensity interval training) preaches short, all-out repetitions with even shorter rest periods (see page 145). Advocates claim improvements in VO_2 max. For decades, experienced runners have referred to these types of intervals as "speedwork"—training that leads to quick performance increases for six weeks, then equally quick performance decreases.

4. **Core training:** Another twenty-first-century magic bullet, core training promises better running through stabilization of the body's core (abs, pelvis, lower back, and other non-limb musculature). Of course, the best workout for core is—and always has been—running (to the tune of one thousand reps per mile). Some core work for muscle balance is great. More is just more.

5. **Pose Method and ChiRunning:** Pose Method teaches stride technique as a series of perfect "poses." ChiRunning emphasizes core strength, posture, relaxation, a midfoot strike, and the utilization of gravity. Both techniques reduce running economy (see page 27) and ignore the research consensus that the best stride—for performance and injury avoidance—is a "self-selected stride."

6. **Low mileage and high intensity:** Blame two-time Olympic 1500-meter champion Seb Coe for this one. Coe claimed that intensity, not high mileage, was the key to his success. It was later revealed that Coe didn't include warm-ups, warm-downs, or jogging in his reported mileage. Estimates of his actual mileage range from 70 to 100 miles per week. In other words, high mileage.

(continued)

7. **Ice baths:** Edwin Moses won 122 international 400-meter hurdle races in a row, as well as gold medals at the 1976 and 1984 Olympics. When Moses recommended ice baths three times a day to reduce inflammation, three decades of crowded whirlpools and chattering teeth followed. Unfortunately, reducing post-workout inflammation can slow recovery and limit fitness gains.

8. **Carbo-loading:** Carbo-loading is great for races longer than ninety minutes, the approximate point at which the human body runs low on glycogen (stored carbohydrate). But athletes figured what's good for the marathon must be good for the 5K, or even the 1500. Of course, loading up on pasta before short races just means more weight to carry—and potentially slower times.

9. **Nasal strips:** These small splints spread the nostrils and promise reduced airway obstruction during exercise. Two problems: One, humans breathe through their mouths during exercise; two, breathing more air doesn't affect performance—you already breathe enough air. The trouble lies in extracting oxygen from air, transporting it via blood to muscles, and turning it into energy.

10. **Streaking:** This wasn't a performance-enhancing fad, but boy was it ever a fad! In 1973, runners and non-runners alike decided en masse to run naked. The term "streaking" was coined following a nude run by 533 University of Maryland students. And Ray Stevens' song "The Streak" sold five million copies in 1974, spending three weeks atop *Billboard's Hot 100* chart.

Other fads have had their moment: ankle weights, motion-control shoes, DMSO (dimethyl sulfoxide), massages, salt tablets, backward running, holding your breath during intervals, and more. It's been suggested that running itself is a fad—just one that's been going strong for three million years.

RUNNING EVOLUTION

Roughly four million years ago, our immediate ancestor in the evolutionary tree (*Australopithecus*) climbed down from trees and began walking on two legs. The reason for this remains unclear. A couple of million years later, *Homo habilis* and *Homo erectus* evolved traits that allowed them to pick up the pace from walking to jogging. A 2004 study by Daniel E. Lieberman, a professor of human evolutionary biology at Harvard, and Dennis M. Bramble, a biologist at the University of Utah, identified some of these traits and the advantages they provided, including:

▶ **Better tendons:** Reduced energy requirements by acting like springs
▶ **The arch of the foot:** Absorbed and returned energy like a spring
▶ **Longer stride length:** Increased speed
▶ **Bigger butts:** Stabilized trunks during exercise

- ▶ **Better shoulder, arm, and hip rotation:** Allowed for counter-balancing movements while running
- ▶ **More sweat:** Increased dissipation of heat through the evaporation of sweat
- ▶ **Less body hair:** Increased convection rate (dissipation of heat from the body)

Lieberman and Bramble conclude: "It is reasonable to hypothesize that *Homo* evolved to travel long distances by both walking and running."

That may be true, but a 2008 study by Karen L. Steudel-Numbers, a zoologist at the University of Wisconsin, Madison, and Cara M. Wall-Scheffler, a biologist at Seattle Pacific University, attempted to pin down the speed of locomotion for our distance-running forebears and concluded that, most likely, *Homo* was restricted to long periods of walking combined with surges of slow running. Which begs the question: How did a species of walker-joggers become the fifth-fastest species on the planet at marathoning?

RUNNING INNOVATION

If you want to get a feel for how quickly running performances have improved in recent history, look no further than the mile. In 1855, Charles Westhall of Great Britain posted the first official mile world record of 4:28. Ninety-nine years later, Roger Bannister of Great Britain ran 3:59.4 to break the four-minute barrier. Thirty-five years after that, Hicham El Guerrouj of Morocco set the current world record of 3:43.12. And the mile isn't the only distance where records have plummeted. Since 1900, the men's world record in the 5000 meters has dropped from 15:29.8 to 12:37.35. The men's world record in the marathon went from 2:55:18 in 1908 to its current 2:03:23. Women's

records have dropped even more dramatically, but curbs on female participation until the latter twentieth century skew the validity of those comparisons.

So how did we get so fast?

It's not like runners prior to 1900 hadn't trained volume. Or run sprints. Or run barefoot. Or eaten all manner of diets. It's not that outcomes weren't viewed as important. In ancient Egypt, at the Heb Sed Festival, the pharaoh ran a race around ritual boundary markers to prove his fitness to continue ruling. In ancient Greece, the winner of the Olympic *stade* (the single race of the original Games, measuring about 200 meters) had his name given to the entire four-year calendar period (the *Olympiad*) before the next Olympics. And in seventeenth-century England, nobles wagered huge sums on races between their carriage footmen. Footrace outcomes have been important since the time of the pharaohs, yet good high school runners today regularly surpass the world records from one hundred years ago!

If you're looking for an explanation, look no further than the twentieth-century embrace of exercise physiology and its methods. Over the course of a single century, a series of training innovations transformed our species from just another plodding mammal into a bipedal endurance machine.

Archibald Vivian Hill, lactic acid, and VO$_2$ max

Archibald V. Hill was a runner-turned-physiologist whose early-twentieth-century experiments heralded the age of aerobic and anaerobic training. Hill's experiments linked lactic acid to anaerobic energy production, showed the importance of VO$_2$ max in performance, and proved that athletes could not only absorb more training stress than previously thought, they could thrive on it.

Paavo Nurmi, even-paced racing, and terrace training

Paavo Nurmi, the "Flying Finn," erupted onto the international running scene in 1920. He eventually set twenty-two world records (from 1500 meters to twenty kilometers), earned nine Olympic gold medals, and won 121 races in a row. Nurmi intuited the benefit of even-paced racing and carried a stopwatch during training and racing to stay on pace. He also practiced "terraced training," in which he ran various distances (including sprints) that were alternated with rest periods.

Gösta Holmér and fartlek

In the 1930s, Gösta Holmér mixed unstructured surges and sprints with less-intense continuous running in a workout called *fartlek* (or "speed play"). Fartlek emphasized both aerobic and anaerobic elements of training. As coach of the Swedish cross country team, Holmér created this new training approach after suffering lopsided losses to Nurmi's Finnish squads in the 1920s.

Woldemar Gerschler, Hans Reindell, and interval training

In the late 1930s, German coach Woldemar Gerschler, influenced by cardiologist Hans Reindell, introduced a workout that alternated multiple repetitions over short distances (designed to elevate the heart rate to 180 beats per minute) with rest "intervals." During the rest interval, pressure inside the heart increased momentarily from returning blood, stretching the heart's ventricles. A three-week experiment on three thousand subjects produced an average increase of 20 percent in heart volume, as well as an accompanying increase in cardiac output (the amount of blood pumped by the heart). Interval training immediately resulted in huge drops in the 400- and 800-meter world records. In the decades to come, Emil Zátopek (with workouts of up to 60 repetitions of 400 meters) and Mihaly Igloi (who introduced multiple sets of intense repetitions with short rest intervals) used variations of interval training to produce world records and world record-holders.

Arthur Lydiard and periodization

Arthur Lydiard conducted a famous "experiment of one," with himself as guinea pig, that resulted in a system of training emphasizing aerobic "base training" and *periodization*. Periodization broke training into phases: a conditioning base phase in which all athletes ran 100 miles per week; a strength phase (hills); a four-week anaerobic phase; and a race phase. New Zealand athletes coached by Lydiard were a dominant force in the 1960s and 1970s.

Bill Bowerman and the hard-easy approach

"Take a primitive organism, any weak, pitiful organism, say a freshman. Make it lift, or jump or run. Let it rest. What happens? A little miracle. It gets a little better," said Bill Bowerman, as quoted in Kenny Moore's book, *Bowerman and the Men of Oregon.* "Stress. Recover. Improve. You'd think any damn fool could do it." Only runners hadn't. With his hard-easy approach to training, Bowerman coached thirty-one Olympic athletes and twenty-four NCAA champions, won the NCAA track and field championship four times, and brought jogging to the United States. He also handcrafted shoes (using his wife's waffle iron to create the soles), which he marketed with Phil Knight as co-founder of Nike.

Jack Daniels and tempo training

Jack Daniels didn't invent the tempo run, but he wrote the book on it—or at least the book that popularized it. *Daniels' Running Formula* (1998) recommends "threshold (T) pace" to raise lactate threshold (the intensity level at which anaerobic energy production begins to negatively affect performance). He suggested running tempo and *cruise intervals* (he did introduce the latter workout, even though he borrowed the name from a swimming workout championed by Dick Bower) at a "comfortably hard" effort, representing a pace that can be maintained for roughly an hour.

RUNNING INSPIRATION

Innovation provided the training breakthroughs that made better performance possible. But it was inspiration that recruited a talent pool of hungry young runners looking to share in the fruits of those innovations. The influence and star power of runners like Nurmi, Zátopek, Bannister, Ron Clarke of Australia, Peter Snell of New Zealand, Abebe Bikila of Ethiopia, Kip Keino of Kenya, and Jim Ryun of the United States ensured that there'd be no lack of future stars from all corners of the globe.

And when Frank Shorter won the 1972 Munich Olympic Marathon, he started the running boom, which grew a tiny, niche activity into a sport with millions of participants, all eager to experience a level of fitness that had never before been possible in human history. Joan Benoit's 1984 victory in the inaugural women's Olympic marathon—completing an aggressive quest for female endurance running equality that had stepped out of the shadows two decades earlier, in 1967, with Kathrine Switzer's first-ever official women's finish at the Boston Marathon—confirmed that women would not be left behind in the fitness revolution.

While inspiration won't make Olympians out of all of us, it can make a better runner out of you, as long as you're willing to learn from history and embrace both the evolution that created your human form and the innovation that unleashed its potential. Better running isn't a guess. And it isn't a gimmick. It's not a fad or a get-fit-quick scheme. To borrow a phrase from Sir Isaac Newton, better running is a matter of "standing on the shoulders of giants." The road to your human endurance success has been paved. Now all you have to do is run it.

When *Runner's World* recently performed a minor overhaul of their website, they eliminated the longtime tool "What to Wear," which offered advice on running outfits based upon temperature, training intensity, and a number of other factors. The response was immediate. Runners wanted the tool back. Warm-weather runners weren't sure what to wear in cold weather. New runners needed gear advice for racing. Older runners were confused about new fabrics. The tool was quickly returned to the site (runnersworld.com/what-to-wear), averting a rerun of 1970s-type streaking.

Running-gear sales for 2013 totaled $4.5 billion in the United States alone. That's a lot of running gear. And it's not just shoes. Runners face a smorgasbord of apparel and equipment options every time they enter a sporting goods store, running specialty shop, or online site. It's only natural to wonder, *What do I really need?* To answer that question: It depends. It depends on where you live, what you do for workouts, how much you're willing to invest—oh, and how much you love nifty, high-tech gadgets.

WHAT'S RUNNING GEAR?

Running gear is a catch-all phrase for any items associated with your training. In this chapter, however, we'll limit "gear" to items that you can wear on your person during a run. With that in mind, we'll look at five different categories of gear:

1. Basic gear
2. Shoes
3. Environment-specific gear
4. Gadgets
5. Cinderella gear

We won't get into brand-name recommendations. Running-gear styles and models change so quickly that a book can't keep pace. Instead, check out Jeff Dengate's *Runner's World* reviews for up-to-the-minute advice (runnersworld.com/person/jeff-dengate) on this topic.

BASIC GEAR

The first decision runners have to make is what to wear. So before embarking on your first run, you'll need to acquire at least a basic running kit:

▶ **One pair of running shoes**
▶ **Two pairs of running shorts**
▶ **Two running shirts (cotton or technical fabric)**
▶ **(Women) Sports bra**

Beginning and lapsed runners can temporarily stop at this basic kit, as you'll want to make sure that both you and your body are committed to training before committing your wallet.

"There are so many gear options, it can get really expensive really fast," says Dengate, the shoes and gear editor for *Runner's World*, as well as a lifelong runner and gear geek, veteran of two dozen marathons, and lover of mountain runs and snowshoes. "Shoes are the one essential piece of gear that you should spend time on. It's the piece of protective gear that we have. Football players have pads, we have shoes."

For those runners who feel that buying lots of

BEGINNER'S GUIDELINE

As a beginner, keep your focus on the running. Don't spend all your enthusiasm on a shopping spree. Start with a single pair of shoes and two simple running outfits—shorts and shirts (either cotton T-shirts or Dri-FIT will do). When you're certain the sport's for you, that's the time to add more gear.

gear equates to a stronger training commitment, Dengate offers this advice: "More gear isn't going to make you run more often."

SHOES

Almost 50 million pairs of running shoes were sold in 2013. Dozens of brands. Hundreds of models. So how do you pick the right shoe for you? Most runners choose a running shoe by "fit." If it feels good, they buy it. Unfortunately, fit doesn't always translate into function, and not all retailers will allow you to take shoes out for test drives. That's where talking to other runners, reading online and magazine reviews, and learning from experience come into play. You'll also want to stay abreast of structural changes to your favorite shoes, as the model you bought last time—and loved—might be completely different by the time you're ready to purchase it again.

How many pairs do you need?

"If you're not doing a lot of racing," says Dengate, "have two pairs of shoes. That way, if you run in a rainstorm one day, you'll have a dry pair for the next."

If you do buy two pairs of *trainers* (see "training flats" to the right), alternate them. They'll last longer that way. Also, buy different brands. Different brands have different designs, creating a slightly different foot strike from day to day. That leads to better muscle balance and diminishes the negative impacts of a particular shoe's shortcomings.

More ambitious runners will need additional shoes. You'll need lightweight trainers or racing flats for tempo, repetition, and fartlek workouts—lightweight trainers if you're looking for a little more protection, racing flats if you're looking for a little faster running. If you like rugged trails, get

trail shoes. And for competition, you'll need racing flats for the roads and spikes for the track.

Training flats (trainers)

A training flat is the shoe you'll use for most (if not all) of your distance runs. It's a sturdy shoe that protects against the excessive impact forces that occur when your foot strikes the ground. This is particularly important during the latter miles of a run, when your muscles are too fatigued to absorb the pounding. Some runners prefer to run in lightweight trainers for the majority of their runs but utilize a heavier pair for recovery runs. Other runners have serious mechanical issues that require heavier, more stable running shoes. It's probably best to train in the lightest shoe that you can comfortably run in. There's no reason to carry around extra bulk.

Minimalist shoes

Minimalism has been a hot topic in running for the past few years, but it has existed in the sport since the late nineteenth century, when lightweight running shoes with rubber soles and cloth uppers were first released. Modern minimalist shoes are lightweight, have reduced disparity in height between the heel and forefoot, and have a wider toe box. Advocates claim that the shoes allow a more natural running stride. "A minimalist shoe puts your foot close to the ground," says Dengate. "That way you can really feel what's going on in your foot. You want something that doesn't have any foam and stability features. It's something to fasten to your foot that can protect the bottom of your foot from debris."

Trail shoes

With more than six million trail runners in the United States, it's no surprise that sales of shoes designed for steep, mountainous terrain have surged. Trail shoes have deeper lugs and aggressive tread patterns; they're designed for traction. "The first thing you want is to stay on your feet," says Dengate. "You also want overlays at the front and sides of the shoes, so that if you step on a stick or rock, it's not going to rip through the shoe and hurt your foot." Other features can include waterproof liners (think mud-running), protective plates to cushion the impact of sharp rocks and roots, and minimalist designs.

Racing flats and spikes

Racing flats are exceptionally lightweight, with some models registering only three to four ounces per shoe (versus ten to fifteen ounces for most trainers). Racing flats fit snugly and have minimal padding. They're all about speed. It's estimated that you run one second faster per mile for every ounce you shed from your shoes. And several studies have concluded that a four-ounce reduction in weight can knock about three minutes off your marathon time.

Spikes are specialized shoes most often used for running on the track. They are lightweight, sport low- or no heels, and contain spike plates beneath the forefoot. The spike plates hold "pins" (the name for the actual spikes in the shoes), which give traction. The number of pins can vary from as few as three to as many as eight. Distance runners generally prefer spikes with a tighter fit, some heel cushioning (since repetition workouts can involve many miles of volume), and four pins. Sprinters largely eschew heel padding and prefer more pins. Most all-weather tracks require the use of pins that are no longer than three sixteenths of an inch. For cross country running, longer spikes (three eighths of an inch to half an inch) are often used to combat mud and thick grass.

SHORTS

After shoes, shorts are the one item of your running wardrobe that you can't do without—mostly because cities have ordinances against running in your birthday suit. You'll want shorts made from technical fabrics (e.g., Nike Dri-FIT) that are lightweight and wick away moisture. While current fashion leans toward longer shorts, many runners prefer shorter lengths ("short-shorts") for faster training efforts and races; that's because longer shorts cling to your legs and impede your stride when you get sweaty. Heavier runners often prefer longer shorts—or even short tights—to protect against chafing on their inner thighs. Women sometimes opt for briefs ("bun huggers") and extra-short tights; they're comfortable, allow greater convection (dispersal of heat from your body to the air), and can make you *feel* faster (never underestimate this psychological advantage). Be forewarned that shorts with pockets can catch your thumbs during normal arm swings. Also make sure your shorts have a key pocket (or extra pockets for carrying gels during races and long runs, if that's important to you). Finally, some runners wear underwear with shorts; some don't. Go with whatever works best for you.

SHIRTS

Shirts are usually chosen on the basis of climate. While runners in Southern California can probably get away with cotton T-shirts year-round, most runners will opt for technical fabrics that both wick moisture away from the skin and help control body temperature by retaining heat during cold weather and dissipating it when the temperature rises.

SPORTS BRA (FOR WOMEN)

If you're a woman, you'll need a sports bra. Sports bras come in enough shapes and sizes to accommodate all women. There are compression bras, which utilize a solid band of tight, stretchy fabric to hold breasts in place while running. And there are encapsulation bras, which are more like traditional bras, providing a separate cup for each breast and support from below. While larger-breasted women seem to prefer encapsulation bras, you should try both. And don't be shy when trying them on. Jump up and down. Turn from side to side. Simulate running. Make sure the bra you're trying on will provide the support you're after. Finally, be very careful if you're considering a top with a built-in bra (shelf bra), as these often lack the contouring, cup support, and additional reinforcement of a sports bra.

ENVIRONMENT-SPECIFIC GEAR

Once you've picked your basic gear, you'll want to expand your ensemble to match the specifics of your training. What you wear will be largely determined by climate, the time of day you train, and how fast you intend to run.

Warm-weather running

In warm weather, you'll want materials that wick away sweat, as well as gear to protect you from the sun and help keep you hydrated. Some starter items include:

▸ **Polyester shirts**
▸ **Loose shorts**
▸ **Hat with a brim**
▸ **Sunglasses**
▸ **Sunscreen**
▸ **Handheld water bottles**

You can get away with a visor (instead of a hat) if you use sunscreen or have a full head of hair. If you don't want to hold a water bottle, try a hydration belt with a couple of ten-ounce water bottles.

Rain running

Choosing the correct gear for rain depends on temperature. In warmer weather:

▸ **Hat with a brim:** This will keep the rain off your face, allowing you to stay relaxed.
▸ **Jacket or vest:** You'll need one with a zipper down the front. That way, when the rain stops, you can adjust the zipper to vent your body heat. Use the zipper as your thermostat.

In cold weather, you'll need to add a few items:

▸ **Tights or pants:** These should have a waterproof panel down the front (there probably won't be one on the back) to shield you from the rain.
▸ **Technical running socks:** Try to use these all the time, but especially in the rain. Cotton socks are a recipe for blisters. Merino wool keeps your feet warmer and resists odor.

With the right outfit, there's no reason a rainy day should put a damper on your run.

Snow and extreme cold-weather running

The main mistake people make is to *overdress* for snow and cold. They end up overheating. Instead, dress in three thin layers of clothing:

▸ **First layer:** You want a synthetic layer (some kind of polyester) next to your skin that will wick away moisture.

- **Second layer:** This is your insulation. It should be a little heavier than your typical Dri-FIT shirt. A half-zip design, buoyed by a little spandex, works great.
- **Third layer:** Top off your outfit with a windproof jacket (a shell to cover your other layers). It should have zippers—under the arms or full-length—to serve as your thermostat.

You might also consider three layers for your lower body:

1. **Underwear:** Non-cotton, with a windproof panel for men (you'll be grateful for this).
2. **Tights:** Classic tights, with a polyester-and-spandex blend.
3. **Running pants:** Less clingy than tights, they can be used either as your second layer or as the third, over your tights, when it's freezing.

You'll also want a hat (merino wool is good) and gloves, although in really cold weather you might prefer mittens—or, better yet, gloves with built-in, fold-over mittens. In snowy conditions, look for a hybrid trail shoe with a Gore-Tex–type upper to keep your feet warm and dry.

Altitude running

The one thing you'll absolutely need for altitude training is a water bottle or hydration belt. At altitude, you'll get dehydrated faster. And as Dengate explains, "It's hard to find water at altitude. Water likes to run downhill."

GADGETS

Gadget lovers would have you believe that technology is the key to better running. So that you can be the judge, we'll look at three popular gadgets, plus an old low-tech standby.

GPS watch

Who *doesn't* want to know exactly how far they've run, their pace for each mile, their average pace overall, and the calories they've burned—all while mapping the run and receiving pacing alerts? GPS watches turn each run into a data-producing mother lode, which can be dangerous for runners who use their GPS less for feedback and more as a video game whose previous scores must be surpassed. On the other hand, if you can afford a GPS watch, it can be pretty amazing.

Heart rate monitor

Heart rate monitors allow you to monitor exercise intensity based upon your heart rate. Once you establish your training zones, a heart rate monitor tells you when you're training aerobically, at threshold, or anaerobically. If you're an elite runner who's been lab-tested, heart rate monitors help you reliably stick to your training zones. For beginners and less-advanced runners, however, it might be overkill. "Most runners don't need it," says Dengate. "It's a great tool, but most runners get bogged down in the data and have no idea what they're looking at."

MP3 player

No single issue divides the running community like the use of MP3 players while running. Advocates embrace music's ability to motivate, reduce perception of fatigue, and fight boredom. Opponents believe it sabotages pace and physiological feedback while also leaving runners dangerously unaware of their surroundings (including other runners). If you side with music, look for an MP3 player that's small enough to clip onto your clothes or stow in a pocket or armband, and which comes with a high-quality, sweat- and water-resistant pair of headphones.

Hydration belt

It's not high tech, but it can come in handy. Pick a belt that doesn't ride up and put pressure on your belly, which can leave some runners nauseated. You want a belt that sits low on your hips and doesn't bounce around.

CINDERELLA GEAR

In the folk tale that bears her name, Cinderella is warned by her fairy godmother to exit the palace ball by midnight. If she's late, the prince will see her coach transform into a pumpkin and her coachman turn into a rat. The same advice should be heeded by runners who hold onto their gear: Lose it before the clock strikes midnight, lest you find yourself running on dangerously compacted midsoles and in shorts that slide down to your knees. There comes a day when old gear must go. The trick is to know when that day has arrived.

Shoes

If you see excessive wear or you've burned through the rubber sole, it's time to part ways. Ditto if the upper is torn. Shoes used to last between three hundred and five hundred miles. Better manufacturing has made shoes more durable, so you'll need to evaluate on a shoe-by-shoe

basis. You should also monitor how your legs feel. "If you have unexplained aches and pains," says Dengate, "it might be time to consider getting a new pair." And that means throwing away or recycling the old pair. It's footwear, not a trophy.

Shorts, sports bras, and pants

If the elasticity is disappearing, it's probably time to retire this apparel. Split seams indicate that a fashion funeral is in order. Shorts used to last a few months. Now they can last a few years. Don't confuse that with forever.

Shirts

Like shorts, shirts last a lot longer than they used to. A good Dri-FIT shirt can weather the changing of many seasons. Still, at a certain point—hmm, how to put this?—the shirts start to stink. Dengate notes that companies are trying new treatments to give shirts antibacterial properties. In the meantime, if your shirts come out of the washer smelling the same as when they went in, it's time to replace them.

There's no denying that it's fun to collect running gear. But keep in mind that what makes you a better runner is smart training, not shopping. There is something to be said for simplicity. You need shoes. You need shorts. You need shirts. If you're a woman, you need a sports bra. More gear is a bonus, but it won't make you a better runner.

Build Your Running Vocabulary

Let's try a quick test. A runner says, "I think I should do some core work to increase my VO_2 max." Which of the following is the correct response?

A. "What's VO_2 max?"

B. "Sounds good."

C. "I don't think VO_2 max is as important a performance indicator as running economy."

The correct answer is "C." It illustrates your command of *two* running terms, and it negates having to explain why core work is, in fact, useless for increasing VO$_2$ max. Answer "A" scores points for honesty. Answer "B" will be taken as an admission that you don't know the jargon, and you may end up excluded from future running conversations.

All kidding aside, running jargon isn't just a grab-bag of fancy terminology. It's the sport's vocabulary. If you want to understand the sport, you'll need to speak its language.

WHAT'S RUNNING JARGON?

Running jargon includes the terms, phrases, and unique usage of words that you'll speak and hear when discussing the sport. While a full compilation of running jargon would fill many pages, we'll jump-start your education with twelve of the most commonly used terms.

Aerobic

Running "aerobically" means that you're running at an effort level (or pace) that is almost entirely fueled by *aerobic* energy. Aerobic energy is created within your cells and can't be produced without oxygen. Of course, aerobic energy production isn't just for exercise. You are constantly producing aerobic energy. When you're sitting down, almost all of your energy is produced this way. But get this: It's the same when you run the marathon, during which 99 percent of your energy production is aerobic. Even sprinting uses aerobic energy—up to 20 percent for the 100-meter dash. See Chapter 10, "Build Your Running Energy System," for more information.

Anaerobic

Anaerobic energy is created within your cells without using oxygen. This does *not* mean that there is no oxygen in your cells; there is always oxygen in your cells. Instead, anaerobic energy is produced when your body needs energy faster than your aerobic system can produce it. Depending upon how long it's used, your anaerobic system can create energy between one hundred and two hundred times faster than your aerobic system. The problem with anaerobic energy production is that it's short-lived, fizzling out after about a minute at full capacity. That's perfect for activities like jumping, lifting weights, or sprinting, but not so good for long runs or sports like soccer, biking, and swimming. See Chapter 10, "Build Your Running Energy System," for more information.

VO$_2$ max

Your VO$_2$ *max* is the maximum amount of oxygen that your body can "consume" in a minute. In other words, it's the maximum amount of oxygen that

BEGINNNER'S GUIDELINE

Embrace running jargon. It may sound complicated and science-y, but that's only because the words and terms are unfamiliar. Once you start using the sport's vocabulary, you'll realize that no other words adequately capture the workouts, concepts, and strategies of running. Jargon is your key to understanding the running world.

your aerobic system is capable of using to create energy. Any oxygen in your blood that isn't used to create energy doesn't count when calculating VO_2 max. You improve VO_2 max by improving your body's ability to transport oxygen (your cardiovascular system) and to use that oxygen at the cellular level. The higher your VO_2 max, the more aerobic energy you can produce. See Chapter 8, "Build Your Running Powerhouses," for more information.

Running economy

Running economy measures how efficiently you use oxygen at a given running speed. If one runner requires less oxygen to run the same pace as another runner, that first runner is said to have better running economy. It's analogous to a car getting better gas mileage. There's a debate in the running community over what is more important to performance, VO_2 max or running economy. The answer is that both are important. See Chapter 11, "Rewire Your Running Nervous System," for more information.

Lactic acid

Lactic acid has spent almost a century serving as the bogeyman of running. Long thought to be a by-product of anaerobic energy production, lactic acid was blamed for muscle fatigue and pain during hard running. There's now evidence, however, that lactic acid is never formed within muscles. Instead, two different substances—lactate and hydrogen ions—are created. Lactate is a fuel that muscles use to create aerobic energy. Hydrogen ions *do* lead to acidosis, a presumed cause of fatigue, but they aren't a factor in longer races. See Chapter 9, "Balance Your Running pH," for more information.

Repetitions/Intervals

Runners use the terms *repetitions* and *intervals* interchangeably, although purists will argue that they have different meanings. For most runners, repetition and interval training both refer to workouts in which you run several short segments (e.g., 8 x 200 meters, or 3 x 1 mile) at a given pace, separated by recovery periods during which you walk, jog, or just stand around. Technically, the "repetition" is the hard running segment, and the "interval" is the rest after each repetition. Interval training originated in the 1930s (building off similar workouts from the 1920s) as a way to increase stroke volume (how much blood your heart can pump with each beat). See Chapter 7, "Build Your Running Cardiovascular System," for more information.

Split

A *split* can mean two different things. First, it can refer to time recorded *en route* during a race, usually at evenly spaced junctures. For example, if you're running a 5K, you might want to know your time at the first mile, which would be your "mile split." Running "even splits" means you maintain the same pace for each split. A "negative split" means you picked up the pace over the final portion of the race. The second way runners use "split" is when dividing a workout into parts. On distance runs, you might want to check your splits at each mile using a GPS watch. And during an interval workout, you'll record a split for each repetition. Runners often target specific splits during repetition training as preparation for upcoming races, where they hope to hit the same split times on their way to the full race distance. See the tables in Chapter 7's photo instruction for examples of target splits.

Tempo

The *tempo run* is probably the most misunderstood workout in running. A tempo run is a sustained running effort lasting from ten to forty minutes (sometimes longer for advanced distance runners) at a pace you could maintain for at least an hour. Coach Jack Daniels popularized the workout in his book, *Daniels' Running Formula*, in which he described tempo effort as "comfortably hard." Because tempo stimulates training adaptations that are beneficial for both aerobic energy production *and* the removal of the detrimental by-products of anaerobic energy production, tempo is a favorite workout among long-distance runners. Unfortunately, many runners treat a tempo run as a time trial (simulated race), negating many of its benefits while leaving themselves exhausted for their next workout. See chapters 7, 8, and 9 for more information.

Fartlek

Fartlek is Swedish for "speed play." As a workout, it's an unstructured blend of different paces aimed at challenging both aerobic and anaerobic fitness. After an initial warm-up, runners alternate surges with recovery intervals. The surges can last anywhere from seconds to minutes. As initially conceived, fartlek included long repetitions, sprints, and hills, all with recoveries at easy running pace. But fartlek invites innovation. For example, Coach Joe Rubio of the ASICS Aggies recommends that runners alternate surges and recovery periods between telephone poles. Other runners prefer predetermined time repetitions over uneven terrain that includes hills, trails, grass, and/or roads, with the recovery improvised by feel. See Chapter 5's photo instruction for more information.

Age grading

If you're over age forty, you'll need to know about *age grading*. With age grading, each runner's finish time is scored as a percentage of the maximum performance expected at that runner's age, with 100 percent being the top predicted score. The maximum performance for each age is determined by a curve of all age-group world records for the race distance. For example, a forty-year-old man running a 16-minute 5K would earn an 85 percent age grade, but a fifty-year-old man running the same time would score 92 percent. A fifty-year-old woman would need to run 18:10 to achieve the same 92 percent. In age grading, your finish place is determined by your age-graded percentage, allowing runners of different ages to compete against one another.

Mitochondria

If there's one science-y term you should know, it's *mitochondria*. Mitochondria are microscopic structures within your cells that produce *all* of your aerobic energy—and around 90 percent of the energy that you use every day. It's mitochondria that use the oxygen you breathe. Training increases both the number and size of the mitochondria in your muscle cells. The more mitochondria you have, the more aerobic energy you can produce, allowing you to run farther faster. See Chapter 8, "Build Your Running Powerhouses," for more information.

Proprioception

Proprioception is a recent entry to popular running jargon. Proprioception refers to your brain's ability to track your body's position in space and to then adjust your body's movement accordingly. The brain receives sensory feedback from a network of nerves located in your muscles, ligaments, organs, and inner ear. Proprioceptive decision-making then guides your body through activities that vary from walking a straight line to reaching for your alarm clock in the dark. As a runner, you use proprioception to negotiate uneven terrain, run through soft sand, and land on your foot in a way that minimizes the possibility of a sprained ankle. Proprioceptive training improves posture, stride length, and foot strike, among other aspects of your running. See Chapter 11, "Rewire Your Running Nervous System," for more information.

Bonus jargon term: Elastic recoil

Elastic recoil is a term that rarely comes up in running circles, yet it is quite possibly the most important single contributor to running success that almost no runner knows about. Recoil refers to the ability of your connective tissue (e.g., tendons, fascia) to store energy each time it's stretched and then release that energy as your muscles contract, simultaneously shortening the connective tissue. The best example of this is your Achilles tendon, which is significantly stretched during every stride. Recoil provides up to 50 percent of the propulsive force for each running stride. See Chapter 6, "Build Your Running Connective Tissue," for more information.

Armed with this simple running vocabulary, you should be able to understand and contribute to most running conversations. For a more extensive vocabulary list, visit the glossary at the back of this book—or read the chapters that follow.

PART 2

Build Your Running Body— Components and Workouts

The first thing you need to understand about your running body is that everything is connected to everything else.

Muscles are connected to bones by tendons. Your lungs are connected to your cells by your bloodstream. Your brain is connected to your hamstrings, calves, and Achilles tendons by your nervous system. And fascia literally wraps almost every inch of your body in one continuous weave.

No part of your running body is an island.

Instead, your body is the ultimate team. And your team's players are your running "components": your muscles, connective tissue, cardiovascular system, powerhouses (mitochondria), pH control, nervous system, energy system, hormones, and brain. Each of these components contributes to every stride you take. And to run your best, you'll need to train each to its maximum potential. Unfortunately, there isn't a single workout (e.g., a long run) that benefits all of your components equally. Just as you wouldn't train an NFL lineman the same way you'd train a quarterback, you'll have to target each of your components with training specific to its role in your running.

Naturally, there will be overlap with workouts. Your goal isn't to completely isolate each component from every other. It's to train each component to 100 percent of its potential, then to integrate it into the working whole that is your running body in motion.

You'll note that the chapters of Part Two are further broken down into the physiological parts that make up each component. For instance, running muscles will be broken down into slow-twitch, intermediate fast-twitch, and fast-twitch muscle fibers (cells). You'll learn a little about the physiology of each part, including its function in your running. This will be followed by a "Training Recommendation" section that suggests specific workouts for targeting that physiological part—all the exercises, stretches, drills, etc. featured in these training recommendation sections will then appear in the photo instruction for that chapter (unless they've already appeared in another chapter, in which case you'll be directed to the appropriate page number).

TRAINING DISCUSSION

Guidelines for 5K effort and pace

Many times in the coming chapters, you'll be asked to train at 5K pace or to choose a workout effort level (e.g., your easy-distance-run pace) based on that 5K pace. "5K pace" refers to your most recent 5K race time. That's because a recent 5K race time is a very good indication of your current fitness. You can then use that time as a starting point for determining the pace for most of your running workouts. Your 5K race time can't come from your distance-running past. And it can't be a goal pace that you haven't run. If you don't have a recent 5K time, never fear. There are some simple strategies (not requiring a 5K time) for picking your pace.

For distance runs, ignore the suggested pace-per-mile recommendations and train at a "conversational pace"—a pace at which you can carry on a conversation, ensuring you're getting enough oxygen to keep your effort aerobic (manageable).

For repetition/interval workouts, use two guidelines:

1. "Guesstimate" an effort level that is equivalent to the proposed pace. Whether you're targeting 5K, mile, or some other race pace, pick an effort that you estimate is correct, then ask yourself during the rep, "If this were an actual race and not a rep, could I maintain this effort for the full distance?" If the answer is *yes*, maintain the pace. If *no*, slow down.
2. Use the rule of repetitions: When running repetitions, always finish the workout knowing you could have run one or possibly two more reps if required. You'll keep improving as long as you don't overdo it; running too hard (i.e., to exhaustion) is counterproductive.

If you stick to these sensible guidelines, you'll soon find yourself fit enough to race a 5K and, thereafter, to utilize the pace tables.

For sample training schedules incorporating workouts for all of your components, turn to Chapter 15.

Build Your Running Muscles

Few runners think of themselves as muscle-bound. That's a term we equate with football players, bodybuilders, and bullies who kick sand in the eyes of skinny runners at the beach. But the reality is that the human body has about 650 muscles, and we runners use most of them.

Of course, putting those 650 muscles to work isn't like driving a new car off the lot. With a new car, you turn the key and go. Try the same thing with untrained muscles—throw on some running shorts and shoes and head out the door for a hard trail run—and you'll be spending the next few days on the couch, aching so badly that trips to the kitchen for Tylenol will bring tears to your eyes.

On the other hand, your muscles have a distinct advantage over a new car. A new car's parts are as good as they're going to get. A four-cylinder engine won't suddenly transform into a V-8. Not so with your muscles, which get better with training. If your muscles were a four-cylinder engine, they *could* become a V-8. But you can't wish that transformation into existence. Your body's ability to improve through training is a marvel, but it's not a miracle. It's the result of targeting the correct muscles with the correct training.

WHAT'S A RUNNING MUSCLE?

Your body contains three different types of muscle. You have *cardiac muscle*, which is found in your heart. You have *smooth muscle*, which controls involuntary functions like digestion and blood pressure. And you have *skeletal muscle*, which moves your body and includes Muscle Beach favorites like biceps, triceps, abdominals, and pecs—and also includes all your running muscles. Skeletal muscle accounts for more than one-third of your body mass.

By "running muscles," we mean all the muscles you use while running—that's a lot of muscles! Training each individually would be a Herculean task. But lucky for you, we runners utilize a different strategy. Instead of targeting individual muscles when we run, we target our three

muscle fiber types. When we want to build endurance, we train *slow-twitch* muscle fibers. When we want to build speed, we target *fast-twitch* fibers. *Intermediate* fibers can go both ways. And since every skeletal muscle is comprised of the three fiber types, training each fiber type ultimately trains every one of our running muscles, too.

This doesn't mean that runners don't also use the term "muscle" the way everyone else does. A hamstring strain means the same thing to a runner as it does to a bodybuilder, aerobics instructor, or NFL lineman. And when we stretch or do resistance training, we revert to this more common understanding of muscles.

But when we run, it's all about our fibers.

MUSCLE FIBERS

A *muscle fiber* is the scientific term for a muscle cell (i.e., both terms mean the same thing). Muscle fibers are shaped like cylinders and grouped together in columns called *fascicles*. Think of packaged spaghetti, and you'll have an idea of how muscle fibers are stacked within fascicles. Fascicles are then banded together to form skeletal muscles.

Within each skeletal muscle, there are three distinct types of muscle fiber:

▶ **Slow-twitch (Type I):** These small muscle fibers contract more slowly and less forcefully

BEGINNER'S GUIDELINE

When it comes to building your running body, slower is faster. Anyone can run too fast, too far, or too hard. The result is usually injury, sickness, or burnout. Instead, you should gauge your workouts to ensure that you'll be running tomorrow—and the day after, and the day after that. Patience and long-term planning must be your guides. Slower gets you there faster. Faster seldom gets you there at all.

TRAINING DISCUSSION

"What is DOMS?"

DOMS (Delayed Onset Muscle Soreness) is the muscular pain that runners experience in the days following excessive exercise. For experienced runners, DOMS usually results from abrupt changes in training intensity or duration. For beginners, the culprit is training too hard in the first few days of a program. Typically peaking within twenty-four to seventy-two hours after exercise, its symptoms vary from slight muscle tenderness to acute, incapacitating pain.

DOMS is thought to result from damage caused by *eccentric muscle contractions*. Less-credible theories blame connective tissue damage and high muscle pH (an acidic state). There is likely a nervous system component, too, as demonstrated in a 2013 study from Denmark, which found that initial bouts of exercise caused an overreaction in the nervous system, while subsequent bouts triggered "inherent protective spinal mechanisms against the development of muscle soreness."

Eccentric muscle contractions occur when muscles are forced to contract and stretch (i.e., shorten and lengthen) at the same time. For example, when you run, your quadriceps (frontal thigh) muscles contract when your foot touches down. If they didn't contract, you'd collapse to the ground. But your quadriceps muscles also stretch so that your knee can bend. This simultaneous contracting and stretching creates enormous tension within your muscle fibers. If the tension becomes greater than your fibers are trained to withstand, the result is DOMS.

Preventive measures taken post-run might reduce the severity of DOMS. These include cold baths, icing, massage, and electrical stimulation. Ibuprofen and other anti-inflammatories can provide short-term relief, but reducing inflammation interrupts the body's normal healing process and can delay repair of muscle tissue and recovery. For some people, moderate exercise can reduce soreness. If all else fails, try complete rest—or not overdoing it in the first place! Symptoms disappear within five to seven days, and, best of all, episodes of DOMS seem to immunize runners against repeat episodes.

---

than the other two fibers, but distance runners love them for their aerobic (oxygen-utilizing) endurance potential. Like the Energizer Bunny, they just keep going.

▶ **Intermediate fast-twitch (Type IIa):** These fibers boast tremendous aerobic potential of their own, and they also produce more force and contract faster than slow-twitch fibers. The combination of good endurance

and good speed makes them perfect for middle-distance racing.

▶ **Fast-twitch (Type IIx):** These large fibers are the speed demons of muscle cells. They contract fastest and most forcefully of the three fiber types. (In the past, type IIx fibers in humans were misidentified as type IIb; while type IIb fibers exist in rodents, often the subjects of scientific studies, fast-twitch fibers in humans are actually IIx.) Their downside is limited aerobic potential. But they're great for short bursts, such as those required for sprints and jumps.

Although your running muscles contain all three types of fibers, not all runners possess the same percentage of each fiber type. Marathoners have muscles that are mostly slow-twitch fibers (80 percent or more), while sprinters are equally rich in fast-twitch fibers. Genetics determines the percentage of fiber types in your body, but training can alter how those fibers function.

MUSCLE TRAINING

In spite of runners' best intentions, most training programs end within the first thirty days. Many don't last a week. Too many runners think the first step of a running program is to breathe hard and get in some "cardio." They want to sweat. They want to feel the burn. But training too hard, too soon leads to sore legs (see sidebar, "What is DOMS?" on page 37) and fatigue, not fitness.

Until you've strengthened your muscles, until your weak fibers have been fortified and your stride stabilized and your muscles balanced, you aren't ready for hard training. Certainly not on the first day. Not even during the first week—or two or three weeks. Running isn't a sport of leaps and bounds. It's a sport of incremental steps. And the first step is to build the foundation, to strengthen the muscles that will support you in your training.

In this chapter, we'll explore three ways to achieve this goal:

▶ **Running**
▶ **Resistance Training**
▶ **Stretching and Flexibility**

You have limited adaptive energy, so it's important that you use it wisely, targeting areas that need the most improvement. For beginners, this means muscles. Beginners who ignore the maxim "Walk before you run" do so at their own peril. Experienced runners returning from injury or time off should likewise make basic muscle fitness a priority. And all runners should engage in training to ensure that their muscular foundation remains strong.

RUNNING

The beauty of running is its simplicity. You put on your running shoes, step out the door, and your sport is on! It doesn't require a basketball or a seven-iron. Doesn't require a team. Doesn't require you to memorize a martial arts kata or a complicated dance routine. Instead, it's a simple motion, repeated over and over, sometimes at a faster rate, sometimes slower, sometimes with greater effort, sometimes not, sometimes over a smooth plane, and sometimes over uneven terrain.

But just because it's a simple activity doesn't mean that your training can be simplistic.

The *rule of specificity* requires that you train specific muscle fibers in the exact way that you'll want to use them in your sport.

In other words, you can't train to be a runner by only swimming. And you can't train fast-twitch fibers for sprinting by running all slow distance. You can't even train slow-twitch fibers for one sport by training slow-twitch fibers for another. Competitors in the Boston Marathon and Tour de France both rely heavily upon slow-twitch muscle fibers, but training for the marathon won't make you a good cyclist, and vice versa.

The only way to successfully train your muscle

TRAINING DISCUSSION

"How do muscle fibers get stronger?"

Muscles don't magically swell up and get stronger, like a Magic GROW dinosaur toy that expands to 600 percent of its original size when tossed into water. Instead, muscle-fiber training is an incremental process that involves the breakdown and repair—or replacement—of elements within the fibers. Within each fiber, you have rod-like units called *myofibrils*. And within myofibrils you have *sarcomeres,* and within sarcomeres you have protein *myofilaments*, including *actin* and *myosin*. During muscle-fiber contractions, actin and myosin work together to shorten (contract) the fiber. Weak actin and myosin filaments become damaged when called upon too often or too forcefully, as occurs during training. This damage, combined with other stresses upon the fibers and associated tissue, signals your body to increase the size and number of myofilaments. In fast-twitch fibers, this increase mostly results from accelerated protein synthesis (creation of new proteins), while in slow-twitch fibers the process is driven by a decrease in the breakdown of already-existing proteins.

If a myofibril subsequently gets too big (due to an increase in the size and number of its myofilaments), it splits. Thus, the creation of new and bigger myofilaments leads to new and bigger myofibrils, which in turn increase the size of muscle fibers. Unlike myofibrils, muscle fibers don't split; they just grow larger. Finally, these bigger and stronger muscle fibers collectively result in bigger, stronger muscles (*hypertrophy*).

It's no secret that endurance-trained slow-twitch fibers don't increase in size as much as fast-twitch fibers. Just look at any group of top distance runners. This disparity is made more apparent because any increase in slow-twitch size is often offset by atrophy (shrinkage) of fast-twitch fibers within the same muscle; therefore, the muscle as a whole doesn't increase in size at all (see sidebar, "Why do my muscles get smaller from running?" on page 43 for more on this).

Bottom line: Muscle fibers get stronger when you fortify the myofilaments and myofibrils within the fibers.

fibers for endurance running is to train your muscle fibers *with* endurance running!

To complicate matters even more, your body will *recruit* (call into action) the *lowest* number of muscle fibers necessary to perform an activity. For example, if you're running an easy distance run to strengthen your slow-twitch fibers, chances are good you're only recruiting *some* of your slow-twitch fibers. The rest, along with your intermediate and fast-twitch fibers, are like those roadside crews where ten crew members stand around while two guys do all the work.

To train your muscle fibers correctly, you'll have to recruit all of them during your running. And to accomplish that, you need to understand the *muscle fiber ladder*.

Chart 5.1 Muscle Fiber Ladder

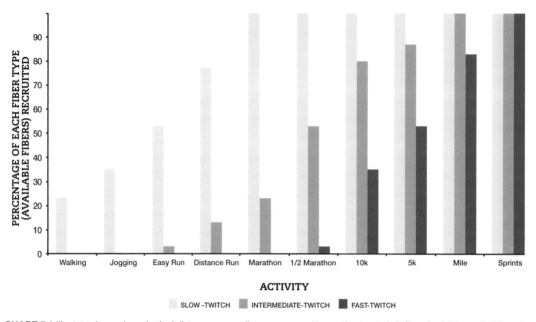

CHART 5.1 illustrates how a hypothetical distance runner (i.e., a runner with mostly slow-twitch fibers) might recruit different fiber types at different paces. At less intense efforts—like walking—almost all slow-twitch fibers are recruited. At increased efforts, more slow-twitch and some intermediate fibers are added. At half-marathon pace, the maximum available slow-twitch fibers, half the available intermediate fibers, and a few fast-twitch fibers are recruited. Sprints require 100 percent recruitment of all three fiber types. Of course, different runners have different muscle fiber makeups and will vary in their recruitment of fibers at different efforts and paces.

THE MUSCLE FIBER LADDER

When you run, you recruit your muscle fibers in a ladder. For low-intensity exercise (e.g., walking), a small percentage of your slow-twitch fibers provides all the force you need. That's the bottom rung of your ladder. As force requirements increase, you first add more slow-twitch fibers, and then (at about the time you transition from a slow jog to easy running) you begin to add intermediate fibers to the mix—you move up the muscle fiber ladder. If a combination of slow-twitch and intermediate fibers can't get the job done (e.g., mile race pace), you call in the big guns, your fast-twitch fibers. Fast-twitch fibers are the top rung of the ladder.

Recruiting up the ladder doesn't relieve slower fibers of duty. Instead, it adds additional fibers to the ones already working. When you recruit intermediate fibers, you're actually using both intermediate and slow-twitch fibers. Adding fast-twitch fibers means you're using all three fiber types. Chart 5.1 illustrates how this principle applies to different running efforts. An easy effort like jogging requires only a small percentage of your slow-twitch fibers, whereas an effort like the half marathon demands *all* of your available slow-twitch fibers and a large percentage of your intermediate fibers. Running sprints causes you to recruit 100 percent of available fibers from all three fiber types.

BUILD YOUR RUNNING BODY—COMPONENTS AND WORKOUTS

It's important to note that you never use *all* of the muscle fibers of any one type. Instead, you recruit "available" fibers—those fibers made accessible by your brain and nervous system. Your body has built-in safety mechanisms, and this is one of them. Using all of your fibers would generate *too much* force, damaging or even tearing your muscles.

Having a general idea of the fibers recruited at different paces is essential for successful training. For example, a runner who prepared for a 5K race by doing only easy- and regular-distance runs would fail to train the intermediate and fast-twitch fibers required for the race—leading to a disappointing performance and a few days of DOMS.

In general, movement up the muscle fiber ladder is triggered by two factors:

▶ **Force:** When your legs need to generate more power, you climb the ladder. Examples would be increasing your pace during a run or transitioning from flat running to a steep hill.

▶ **Fatigue:** When one fiber type runs low on energy (stored carbohydrate), you climb the ladder. For example, during two- to three-hour distance runs, slow-twitch energy stores can become depleted, forcing intermediate fibers to lend support—even fast-twitch fibers cycle in and out.

You should know that real-world running doesn't follow the strictly linear progression depicted in Chart 5.1. Faster fibers will cycle in and out as needed, unrelated to overall pace (although your fastest fibers can't stay on for long, because they fatigue easily). Some instances during runs that demand faster fiber input include:

1. The first steps of your run
2. Any time you accelerate
3. Any time you climb or descend, no matter the duration
4. Moments during each stride when faster fibers are required to support force demand

Still, these are exceptions to the rule. The best way to strengthen each fiber type is to design workouts that recruit a fiber type continuously, thereby maximizing the amount of training that the fiber type receives. For example, slow-twitch fibers need *lots* of endurance training, while fast-twitch fibers require shorter, high-intensity efforts—you can't train both fiber types with one approach. This is a big reason why runners train at different paces. It's the only effective way to train different fiber types to their maximum potential.

Training recommendation

To strengthen your muscle fibers through running, you'll need a multi-pace approach. For slow-twitch fibers, Distance Runs (see page 50) are your best bet. For intermediate fibers, more intense running that includes Strides (see page 51), hills (see pages 52 and 133), or fartlek (see page 49) does the trick. And for fast-twitch fibers, nothing beats short Hill Strides (see page 52). You'll continue strengthening your muscles as you incorporate workouts from coming chapters, but it's important to develop some base strength first.

RESISTANCE TRAINING

Resistance training increases your muscular strength by forcing you to work against an opposing force. Effective approaches include free weights, universal machines, and calisthenics (body-weight exercises). Resistance training builds your running body in five ways:

1. **Improves muscle balance:** When you strengthen opposing muscles (e.g., quadriceps and hamstrings), creating *muscle balance*, you reduce your risk of injury.

2. **Improves your stride:** Increased strength generates a longer, more efficient stride. Beginning runners are notoriously deficient in strength.

3. **Improves core strength:** A weak core leads to instability and decreased power production. It's hard to produce force when you're wobbling!

4. **Improves hip strength:** Weak hips contribute to instability and reduced power. A 2013 Australian research review found that first-time injured runners had significantly weaker hips than healthy runners.

5. **Improves neuromuscular control:** We'll cover this in Chapter 11.

Bottom Line: Resistance training improves your stride, stabilizes your form, increases your power, and reduces your chance of getting injured. What's not to like?

Training recommendation

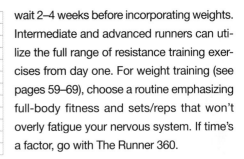

Beginners should focus on body exercises to improve all-around strength and stability (see The Runner 360, pages 53–58)—and should wait 2–4 weeks before incorporating weights. Intermediate and advanced runners can utilize the full range of resistance training exercises from day one. For weight training (see pages 59–69), choose a routine emphasizing full-body fitness and sets/reps that won't overly fatigue your nervous system. If time's a factor, go with The Runner 360.

STRETCHING

Stretching has recently gotten a bad reputation—a lot of it earned. For instance, a 2012 Croatian *meta-analysis*, which reviewed over one hundred studies, concluded that *static stretching* before exercise reduces strength by 5 percent and reduces explosive power by almost 3 percent—a great reason to avoid static stretches before hard workouts and races!

But not all stretching is static stretching (and even static stretching performed *post-workout* reduces stiffness for the next day's training). Effective stretching methods increase your range of motion, strengthen your muscles through that full range of motion, and reduce your injury risk. Four types of stretching you'll want to consider for your training routine are:

▶ **Static stretching:** You hold a position that stretches a muscle, which reduces lingering stiffness in the muscle.

▶ **Dynamic stretching:** You perform controlled leg and arm swings to increase your range of motion and activate your core muscles before running.

▶ **Proprioceptive Neuromuscular Facilitation (PNF) stretching:** After stretching a muscle to its maximum range of motion, you contract that muscle for 5–8 seconds, followed

TRAINING DISCUSSION

"Why do my muscles get smaller from running?"

Most people equate "strength" with bigger muscles. When you think of someone strong, your mind goes to Dwayne "The Rock" Johnson, not Justin Bieber. So if elite distance runners spend so much time strengthening their muscle fibers, why are they all so skinny? Shouldn't all those miles, hills, sprints, drills, and exercises be building Muscle Beach bodies?

In a word: No. And a good thing, too. Otherwise, New York would shake like a Southern California earthquake every time the marathon wound its way through the city's five boroughs. Instead, the world's top distance runners are defined by almost nonexistent upper bodies, slim thighs, and calves that are smaller than the norm.

When you run—and after you've fortified your muscle fibers by weeding out weak myofilaments—your muscle fiber DNA has to make a choice:

▶ Use the fiber's limited adaptive energy to create bigger muscles
▶ Harness the fiber's adaptive energy to forge more powerful aerobic power plants *(mitochondria)* within the fibers

If you want to be a top competitive distance runner, you can't have it both ways; the sheer volume of your training triggers a physiological response that shirks the big biceps and embraces increased aerobic power. On the other hand, if you want to be a fit, fast, but far-from-emaciated *good* runner, there are ways around this physiological roadblock.

For competitive distance runners, the choice is easy: Build those aerobic power plants! Greater volume (mileage) accomplishes that goal, and it also increases the number of capillaries (your smallest blood vessels) around your muscle fibers. More capillaries mean more oxygen and nutrient delivery for your improved power plants. And the combination of more power plants and more fuel means you'll be able to produce a lot more energy, which is the key to fatigue resistance. As your muscles budget less energy for maintaining mass, the fast-twitch fibers in your endurance-trained muscles begin to shrink; at the same time, your slow-twitch fibers do get bigger, but not enough to offset the loss of fast-twitch size. In this battle between fast-twitch atrophy (shrinkage) and slow-twitch hypertrophy (growth), atrophy wins, resulting in smaller, more physiologically efficient muscles.

Then again, you may not want to sacrifice a stronger build for a slightly faster time in your next 5K or marathon. Never fear. High-intensity training (e.g., weight training or hill sprints) spurs growth in muscle fiber size. As long as the high-intensity training is separated from

(continued)

BUILD YOUR RUNNING BODY

the endurance stimulus (e.g., instead of doing a weight workout after a distance run, you do it a few hours later) and as long as your endurance training volume isn't too high, you'll be able to live dual roles as road-running warrior and fitness club standout.

None of this means that high-volume competitive runners should skip the weights. Resistance training isn't just about sporting a ripped beach bod. Most strength gains in the first few weeks (sometimes months) of resistance training come from nervous system adaptations, not muscular growth. So competitive endurance athletes will get stronger regardless of whether they also get bigger.

Returning to the original question, your running muscles get smaller with high-volume endurance training for one simple reason: It's more efficient to run with smaller muscles. Your body is no dummy. It goes with what works.

by a period of relaxation during which the muscle exhibits decreased resistance; this decreased resistance allows you to move the muscle to a position of increased stretch. After another 5–8-second contraction, you can either end the stretch or hold it for up to 30 seconds, although the latter has been associated with the same decrease in strength and explosiveness attributed to static stretching. This is the most popular method for increasing range of motion.

▶ **Active Isolated Stretching (AIS):** AIS uses opposing muscles to move a muscle into a stretched position (e.g., contracting your quadriceps to stretch your hamstrings) and then increases that stretch for 1–2 seconds by gently pulling with a rope. You never "hold" a stretch in AIS, so you don't trigger your muscle's *stretch reflex* (see Muscle Spindles and the Stretch Reflex below), an involuntary muscular contraction that protects against overstretching. AIS increases range of motion significantly and is favored by

many of the world's top endurance athletes. Like static and PNF stretching, however, long-term use might lead to some decrease in strength and explosive power. And since the stretch reflex is avoided, you'll need to be careful not to overstretch.

Dynamic stretching is a great way to prepare your muscles pre-workout (after 10–15 minutes of easy jogging or running). Both AIS and PNF are good choices post-workout if increasing range of motion is your primary goal, although PNF works best with a partner. Static stretching is an option when you're short a rope, a partner, or a flat, dry, adequate location (e.g., no one wants to lie on a rocky trail in the rain for 15 minutes doing AIS). Static stretching is also a good alternative post-workout for runners who experience decreased power or explosive strength from long-term PNF or AIS stretching.

Muscle Spindles and the Stretch Reflex

Muscle spindles are stretch receptors located within your muscles and positioned parallel to your muscle fibers. They sense changes in the length of your muscles. When your muscles stretch (either through applied stretching or during exercise), your muscle spindles send messages to your spinal cord, which responds with orders for your muscles to contract. This contraction protects your muscles by ensuring that they aren't injured through overstretching. Muscle spindles also help define your stride length by gauging the optimal amount of stretch your muscles can endure while running.

Training recommendation

Beginners should start with a few static stretches post-run (see pages 76–78), then work up to dynamic stretches after two to three weeks. Intermediate and advanced runners can immediately incorporate dynamic stretching (see pages 75–76), AIS (Chapter 6, see pages 104–106, and PNF stretching (see pages 70–75) into their programs. Muscle spindle adaptations result from the thousands upon thousands of repetitions that occur during normal training. Runs over uneven terrain (e.g., trails and grassy parks) help muscle spindles adapt to variations in stride and direction, and faster runs during training are a must so that your muscle spindles can adapt to the stride lengths required for racing.

MUSCLE FIBER CONVERSION

There is an ongoing debate as to whether training can convert one type of muscle fiber into another (e.g., fast-twitch into intermediate). While the jury's still out on actual conversion, there is no doubt that faster fibers can be trained to take on the characteristics of slower fibers.

Table 5.2
Changes in Muscle Fibers Due to Training

Untrained Male	Training Focus	Fibers Post-training	
		Slow	Fast
Slow Fibers = 47% Fast Fibers = 53%	800m	48%	52%
	1500m	54%	46%
	3K	60%	40%
	5K	66%	34%
	10K	72%	28%
	Half-Marathon	78%	22%
	Marathon	84%	16%

Untrained Female	Training Focus	Fibers Post-training	
		Slow	Fast
Slow Fibers = 52% Fast Fibers = 48%	800m	53%	47%
	1500m	59%	41%
	3K	65%	35%
	5K	71%	29%
	10K	77%	23%
	Half-Marathon	83%	17%
	Marathon	89%	11%

TABLE 5.2 approximates the functional transformation of muscle fibers as a result of training. The left column gives the average percentage of fiber types in untrained runners. The "Fibers Post-training" columns show how fibers transform after long-term training geared toward the races listed in the "Training Focus" column. Note that "Fast" fibers include both intermediate and fast-twitch fibers.

The change in fiber function can be dramatic. For instance, heavy resistance training will cause a majority of fast-twitch (IIx) fibers to behave like intermediate (IIa) fibers in as little as a month. If you then cease resistance training, the new pseudo-intermediate fibers not only revert to fast-twitch, but *more* intermediate fibers begin (temporarily) to function as fast-twitch—good to know if you're a sprinter looking to increase your percentage of fast-twitch fibers. Conversely, it's theorized that if you'd never trained a day in your life—so that your muscle fibers represented a blank slate—and then you suddenly endurance-trained your right leg for eight to twelve weeks, while continuing to ignore your left, the fast-twitch fibers in your right leg would end up looking and acting quite a bit like the slow-twitch fibers in your left leg.

Of course, there's a limit to this type of pseudo-conversion. Usain Bolt, currently the fastest man alive, could run nothing but distance for the rest of his life and never end up with the slow-twitch function of an elite distance runner. That's because you can never fully alter a fast-twitch fiber so that it acts like a full-fledged slow-twitch fiber (intermediate fibers are more easily swayed). For one thing, fast-twitch fibers are controlled by bigger nerves (we'll discuss this in Chapter 11), a physiological fact that can't be changed by training. Secondly, fast-twitch fibers simply lack many of the cellular ingredients necessary for endurance that are plentiful in slow-twitch fibers.

Still, the ability to transform the functional characteristics of your muscle fibers is a key weapon in your training arsenal. Table 5.2 gives you an indication of just how much you can alter the function of your muscle fibers. Keep in mind, however, that this effect won't happen overnight. For most of us, it takes years of training to effect changes of this magnitude.

TRAINING RUNDOWN

Stronger muscle fibers are the foundation of any running program. Important training in this chapter's photo instruction includes:

- ▶ Walking
- ▶ Jogging
- ▶ Easy Running
- ▶ Beginner's Fartlek
- ▶ Distance Runs
- ▶ Strides
- ▶ Hill Runs
- ▶ Hill Strides
- ▶ Resistance Training
- ▶ Dynamic Stretching
- ▶ Static Stretching
- ▶ PNF Stretching

Training from other chapters that affects muscle strength gains includes:

- ▶ Resistance Band/Tubing Exercises (Chapter 6)
- ▶ AIS Stretching (Chapter 6)
- ▶ Repetition Workouts (Chapter 7)
- ▶ Cross Training (Chapter 9)
- ▶ Plyometrics (Chapter 11)

To see exactly how these workouts can be incorporated into your overall training program, skip directly to Chapter 15: Build Your Running Schedule, where sample schedules are available for runners of all fitness levels and abilities.

Chapter 5: Build Your Running Muscles—
PHOTO INSTRUCTION

RUNNING WORKOUTS

At this stage, you're working to fortify muscle fibers for each muscle fiber type. You'll weed out the weak myofilaments and replace them with stronger ones. Later, you'll use running workouts that target the cardiovascular, neuromuscular, and other systems to develop greater strength—and to develop parts of each fiber that contribute to energy production, balance, fatigue resistance, and more. For full benefits, your weekly training schedule will need to include at least three walking, running, or walking/running sessions—more if your goal is competitive fitness. Grace Padilla—a former American women's steeple-chase record-holder and current *masters* world record-holder—demonstrates the workouts.

Walking

The most fundamental exercise is the best way for beginners with no training background to start building the slow-twitch fibers in running muscles.

■ SKILL LEVEL: Beginner

① *Easy Walking:* It was Henry David Thoreau who said, "An early morning walk is a blessing for the day." If it's not a blessing, it's at least a good start. Easy walking prepares your slow-twitch fibers for jogging and running.

② *Brisk Walking:* Brisk walking recruits a slightly higher percentage of slow-twitch fibers, and it helps to reset your muscle spindles for longer strides to come. Whether your walk is easy or brisk, begin with 10–15 minutes and then gradually increase the length of your walk to at least 30 minutes.

Walk/Jog

Beginners ready for the next level and experienced runners returning from time off should ease into training with walk/jog workouts, which strengthen a fuller range of slow-twitch fibers.

■ SKILL LEVEL: **Beginner**

① *Walk:* Begin with the walk portion of walk/jog, then use walk breaks as recovery intervals from jogging. The walk should last as long as it takes to feel fully recovered.

② *Jog:* Your jog should be done at a comfortable pace. As soon as your breathing increases noticeably, slow to a walk. Your combined walk/jog workout should total 20–40 minutes.

Jog/Easy Run

Continuous jogging or easy running is a great way for fit beginners (coming from a different sport) or runners returning from time off to build running-specific slow-twitch strength.

■ SKILL LEVEL: **Beginner**

① *Jog:* For the beginner, it's not enough to "walk before you run." You should also jog before you run. Jogging is simply low-intensity running.

② *Easy Run:* Easy running means what it says—*run easy.* Resist the urge to feel the "burn." Before you run hard, you need to ensure that your muscles are strong enough to endure more-intense training. Otherwise, the only result will be DOMS. Whether you're jogging or running, your workout should last 15–40 minutes. Don't worry about pace. Just keep the legs moving.

Beginner's Fartlek

Alternating easy running with moderately hard surges allows you to recruit more slow-twitch fibers and begin strengthening intermediate fibers, too.

■ **SKILL LEVEL: Beginner; Intermediate**

① *Easy Run:* Begin by jogging 10–15 minutes, then use the jog/easy run portion of this workout for recovery intervals. It's essential that you recover fully from your fartlek surges, so don't start your next surge until you're rested and champing at the bit.

② *Fartlek Surge:* Fartlek is Swedish for "speed play." And that's what this is: Easy running alternates with surges lasting between 30 seconds and 3 minutes, depending upon your fitness level and effort. These are not sprints! Aim for what coach Jack Daniels calls a "comfortably hard" effort.

Easy Distance Run

The easy distance run is an extension of easy running, only now you'll base your effort loosely on a recommended pace for your fitness. These runs strengthen slow-twitch fibers while calling on a few intermediate fibers, too.

■ **SKILL LEVEL: All levels**

① New runners will explore fresh limits to their endurance at an "easy distance" effort. This effort is a notch above jogging, but still conversational (i.e., you shouldn't be breathing so hard that you can't carry on a conversation with a running partner). Intermediate and advanced runners use this effort for very easy days and for recovery runs. If you've recently raced a 5K, use Table 5.3 for suggested pace ranges based on your race finish time (the one you ran, *not* a goal time). If you don't have a current 5K time, stick with the conversational pace guideline. Either way, let feedback from your body be your final guide; you want to keep easy runs "easy."

Table 5.3 Easy Run Pace Guide

5K Time	Pace per Mile	Pace per Kilometer
14:00	6:53–8:05	4:17–5:01
14:30	7:06–8:20	4:25–5:11
15:00	7:20–8:36	4:33–5:20
15:30	7:33–8:51	4:41–5:30
16:00	7:46–9:06	4:49–5:39
16:30	7:59–9:20	4:57–5:48
17:00	8:12–9:35	5:06–5:57
17:30	8:25–9:50	5:14–6:06
18:00	8:37–10:04	5:21–6:16
18:30	8:50–10:19	5:29–6:25
19:00	9:03–10:33	5:37–6:33
19:30	9:15–10:48	5:45–6:42
20:00	9:28–11:02	5:53–6:51
20:30	9:41–11:16	6:01–7:00
21:00	9:53–11:30	6:08–7:09
21:30	10:05–11:44	6:16–7:17
22:00	10:18–11:58	6:24–7:26
22:30	10:30–12:12	6:32–7:35
23:00	10:42–12:26	6:39–7:43
23:30	10:55–12:39	6:47–7:52

24:00	11:07–12:53	6:54–8:00
24:30	11:19–13:06	7:02–8:09
25:00	11:31–13:20	7:09–8:17
26:00	11:55–13:47	7:24–8:34
27:00	12:19–14:13	7:39–8:50
28:00	12:42–14:39	7:54–9:06
29:00	13:06–15:05	8:08–9:23
30:00	13:29–15:31	8:23–9:38
31:00	13:52–15:56	8:37–9:54
32:00	14:15–16:22	8:51–10:10
33:00	14:38–16:46	9:05–10:25
34:00	15:00–17:11	9:19–10:41
35:00	15:23–17:36	9:33–10:56
36:00	15:45–18:00	9:47–11:11
37:00	16:07–18:24	10:01–11:26
38:00	16:29–18:48	10:14–11:41
39:00	16:51–19:11	10:28–11:55
40:00	17:12–19:35	10:41–12:10
41:00	17:34–19:58	10:55–12:24
42:00	17:55–20:21	11:08–12:39

TABLE 5.3 offers pace suggestions for easy runs based upon 5K performance. Find your 5K time in the left column; paces in the two right-hand columns are given as a range.

Distance Run

A normal distance run requires an effort quicker than an easy run but still conversational. You can exercise your nomadic spirit by covering more ground at this pace, and you'll work slow-twitch fibers and some intermediate fibers, too.

■ SKILL LEVEL: All levels

① The majority of your running will be completed at this effort. Distance runs form the backbone of any successful endurance running program. See Table 5.4 for suggested pace ranges based on your best (not goal) 5K race performance. Don't exceed the fast end of the range, as you'll risk excessive fatigue and an increased risk of injury. Remember that pace suggestions are just a guide. Adjust for variables like weather and fatigue. If you don't have a current 5K time, then stick to a conversational pace. All runners should let feedback from their bodies be the final guide; distance runs should remain comfortable (i.e., they aren't tempo or time trials).

Table 5.4 Regular Run Pace Guide

5K Time	Pace per Mile	Pace per Kilometer
14:00	6:00–6:53	3:44–4:17
14:30	6:11–7:06	3:51–4:25
15:00	6:23–7:20	3:58–4:33
15:30	6:35–7:33	4:05–4:41
16:00	6:46–7:46	4:13–4:49
16:30	6:58–7:59	4:20–4:57
17:00	7:09–8:12	4:27–5:06
17:30	7:21–8:25	4:34–5:14
18:00	7:32–8:37	4:41–5:21
18:30	7:44–8:50	4:48–5:29
19:00	7:55–9:03	4:55–5:37
19:30	8:06–9:15	5:02–5:45
20:00	8:18–9:28	5:09–5:53
20:30	8:29–9:41	5:16–6:01
21:00	8:40–9:53	5:23–6:08
21:30	8:51–10:05	5:30–6:16
22:00	9:02–10:18	5:37–6:24
22:30	9:13–10:30	5:44–6:32
23:00	9:24–10:42	5:51–6:39
23:30	9:35–10:55	5:57–6:47
24:00	9:46–11:07	6:04–6:54
24:30	9:57–11:19	6:11–7:02
25:00	10:08–11:31	6:18–7:09
26:00	10:30–11:55	6:31–7:24
27:00	10:51–12:19	6:45–7:39
28:00	11:13–12:42	6:58–7:54
29:00	11:34–13:06	7:11–8:08
30:00	11:55–13:29	7:24–8:23
31:00	12:16–13:52	7:37–8:37
32:00	12:37–14:15	7:51–8:51
33:00	12:58–14:38	8:03–9:05
34:00	13:19–15:00	8:16–9:19
35:00	13:39–15:23	8:29–9:33
36:00	14:00–15:45	8:42–9:47
37:00	14:20–16:07	8:54–10:01
38:00	14:40–16:29	9:07–10:14
39:00	15:01–16:52	9:20–10:29
40:00	15:22–17:14	9:33–10:42
41:00	15:42–17:36	9:45–10:56
42:00	16:03–17:58	9:58–11:10

TABLE 5.4 offers pace suggestions for regular runs based upon 5K performance. Find your 5K time in the left column; paces in the two right-hand columns are given as a range.

Strides

Strides are a safe and fun way for beginners to work intermediate fibers. They're also part of all runners' warm-ups before hard workouts and races.

■ SKILL LEVEL: All levels

① A stride is a brief acceleration to "fast" running. Fast doesn't mean all-out; it's not a sprint. Instead, it should build to the pace you might expect to maintain for a 5K race. As a warm-up for hard workouts or races, it should mimic the pace you expect to reach during the harder effort. A stride can cover anywhere from 40 to 150 meters (or yards—you shouldn't worry about exact distance for these), should last about 5–20 seconds, and should be run on flat, even surfaces.

BUILD YOUR RUNNING BODY

Hill Run

Hill runs are just distance runs that include a significant stretch of uphill. These runs not only build all fiber types, they also strengthen many other components of your running body.

■ SKILL LEVEL: Intermediate, Advanced

① The hill portion of the run should include a long stretch of continuous climbing. Depending upon your fitness—and the availability of hills in your area—this could mean anywhere from a quarter-mile to 2 miles. It's okay if the hill includes some level and downhill stretches. Just run the hill; don't race it. And always include 12–15 minutes of easy running before you start up the hill.

Downhill Running

Downhill running requires eccentric contractions from your recruited muscle fibers, increasing the load and leading to greater adaptations in strength, as well as protection from quad pain.

■ SKILL LEVEL: Intermediate, Advanced

① Running a hill isn't only about the climb. Downhill running at a comfortably hard effort (i.e., Beginner's Fartlek or tempo effort) creates an eccentric load on your quadriceps muscles. Eccentric loads recruit fewer fibers, create a greater training stimulus, and can help immunize you against quad pain. Start with about 3 minutes and then add minutes with each successive run (up to 12–15 minutes total). Always jog or run easy (i.e., warm up) for 12–15 minutes before attempting a downhill run.

Hill Strides

Short hill striding is the quickest and most efficient way to activate all your running muscle fibers, including fast-twitch.

■ SKILL LEVEL: Intermediate, Advanced

① For these strides, you'll need to find a fairly steep hill, although not so steep that you can't manage a good approximation of your normal running stride. You'll want to run 10–20 seconds at about the effort you'd race for a mile. Walk back down the hill and allow 1–3 minutes total between reps. Start with 4–5 reps your first time out, then build up to 8–10.

THE RUNNER 360

The Runner 360 is an all-around strength program for runners who prefer the outdoors or their own living rooms to the weight room. Best of all, fitness motivator and running yoga instructor Angie Stewart Goka, MPH, CSCS, has crafted a workout that can be completed in 12 minutes and that targets every muscle that runners need for strength and balance. Angie models the exercises to ensure proper form and offers a wide variety of workouts for runners who want more at angiestewartfitness.com. First, five quick rules for the workout:

1. Perform each exercise, in order, for one minute.
2. When the workout calls for left and right sides individually, perform each for 30 seconds.
3. Do as many reps as you can while maintaining good form (no cheating on form for more reps!).
4. Keep a log of reps as a way to track improvement.
5. For a more intense workout, repeat the entire set of exercises (up to a maximum of three times).

The following twelve exercises, from the Inchworm Plank to the Supergirl/Superman Plank, are all part of the same continuous workout.

■ **SKILL LEVEL: All levels**

Inchworm Plank

The inchworm plank helps to awaken your muscles, working both flexibility and strength. And if you're not very flexible, it's okay to bend your knees for this exercise.

① Begin in a standing position with your arms straight up. Be prepared to perform this exercise as quickly as you can without losing form.

② Come into a forward fold, dropping your hands to your feet.

③ Keep your legs straight (or bend them if you have to) and then walk your hands out into a plank position.

④ Perform one push-up. Then walk your hands back to your feet and return to your starting position. Repeat.

Squat-Thrust Climbers

Squat-thrust climbers are a great way to work your glutes (buttocks), quadriceps, and hamstrings.

① Stand with your feet close together and your arms at your sides.

② Squat down to the floor with your knees close together, placing your hands flat on the ground, shoulder-width apart.

③ Keeping your abs tight, jump your legs back to assume the push-up position.

④ For 5 seconds, "run" your legs under your chest, bringing your knees high and keeping your hips low. Then jump your legs back to the squat position, stand, and repeat.

Curtsy Lunge Hop

Curtsy lunge hops are the best calf-strengthener on the menu, so work them! You'll also target your hip abductors, glutes, quadriceps, and hamstrings.

① Start with your feet hip-width apart.

② Step backward, moving your right foot diagonally and to the left of your left hip. Simultaneously drop your right knee and bend your left knee.

③ Propel your right knee upward as you come off the ground with your left foot, and lift your left elbow by swinging it up and forward. Repeat for 30 seconds, then switch legs.

Scorpion Fighter

The scorpion fighter works your shoulders and core while stretching your obliques and hip flexors.

1. Start in the push-up position, with the balls of your feet on a bench or chair.
2. Bring your left knee beneath your body toward your right shoulder.
3. Now reverse directions, bringing your left knee back as you rotate your hips up and to the left, stretching your left foot toward your right shoulder. Repeat for 30 seconds, then switch legs.

Sidewinder Plank with Leg Lift

This exercise is great for your hip abductors and improving stabilization. It also targets your obliques, back, glutes, quadriceps, and hamstrings.

1. Start in the plank position with your arms in full extension.
2. Rotate your body to balance on the heel of your right hand and lift your opposite arm straight up (your wrist is directly beneath your shoulder).
3. Lift and lower your top leg, keeping your hips level. Repeat for 30 seconds, then switch legs.

Plank Pups

Plank pups will put the burn into your arms, shoulders, back, and core.

① Begin at the top of the push-up position.
② Bend your right elbow to lower onto your right forearm.
③ Bend your left elbow to lower onto your left forearm.
④ Lift your right elbow so that you can place your right hand flat on the ground, then do the same with your left elbow and hand. Return to original position, repeat for 30 seconds, then lead with your left arm for 30 seconds.

Lateral Speed Runners

Lateral speed runners work both your hip abductors and hip adductors, plus lots of core.

① Stand with your feet hip-width apart, your arms at your sides.
② Hop to your right, landing on your right foot while balancing your left foot behind your right leg. Simultaneously move your left arm forward and your right arm back in a runner's stance.
③ Repeat to the other side. Focus on speed and control.

Windshield Wipers

Windshield wipers target your full range of abs, and they're terrific for improving stability.

① Lie on your back with your arms spread wide, palms down, thighs perpendicular to the floor and knees bent 90 degrees.

② Maintaining the bend at your hips and knees, swing your legs to one side of your body. Make sure that your upper back maintains contact with the floor.

③ Bring your legs back to center, then repeat to the other side.

Plank Rotations

This variation on the traditional plank offers good core work while giving your shoulders a workout, too.

① Begin in the forearm plank position, except stack your forearms horizontally.

② Rotate onto your left side, elbow beneath your shoulder and right hand on your hip. Your feet should be stacked, your body straight. Rotate back to the center, then repeat on your right side.

Single-Leg Deadlift

Single-leg deadlifts are fantastic for improving balance and stability. They're great for your core, glutes, and hamstrings.

① Start from a standing position.

② Keeping your back straight, bend forward at the hips while lifting one leg straight behind you (in line with your spine) and reaching your hands toward the ground. Return to the starting position. Repeat for 30 seconds, then switch legs.

Marching Bridge

This exercise is great for your glutes and also works your hamstrings and lower back (it's often used to help relieve lower back pain).

1. Lie on your back with your knees bent and feet hip-width apart.
2. Lift your hips into a "bridge position."
3. March your knees toward your chest one at a time. Keep your back straight.

Supergirl/Superman Plank

The Supergirl/Superman plank finishes your workout with a tough challenge to your core, shoulders, and back.

1. Begin at the top of the push-up position.
2. Simultaneously extend your right arm in front of you and your left leg behind you. Stay level while balancing for 3 seconds.
3. After bringing your hand and foot back to push-up position, repeat on the opposite side. (As an easier alternative, perform this exercise from a "down on all fours" position, with hands and knees on the ground.)

RUNNER'S WEIGHT ROOM ROUTINE

Runners who prefer a traditional approach to resistance training can do a weight room routine. Eddie Andre, a former martial arts national champion who's made running a part of his fitness formula, leads you through some basic resistance training. Start with a few exercises representing different muscle groups (e.g., chest, shoulders, abdominals, quadriceps) and then add more (and more difficult) exercises as your fitness improves. Five quick rules for the workout:

1. Limit yourself to light weights and no more than 1–2 sets of 6–10 reps for new exercises the first two weeks.

2. Unless otherwise stated, limit weight training exercises to 1–3 sets of 6–12 reps.

3. Train on non-consecutive days (e.g., M, W, F).

4. Allow 2½–3 minutes of rest between sets.

5. Never lift to exhaustion during a set (or workout)—if you need a spot, go lighter next time.

TRAINING DISCUSSION

Building Your Weight Room Routine

If you're inexperienced in the weight room, you'll need to be careful choosing your workout routine so that you don't overload your nervous system and muscles.

Beginning runners with no weight-lifting experience should spend 2–6 weeks on the following routine (begin with one set per exercise, then add a second set after two weeks and a third set two weeks after that):

1. Leg Lifts
2. Russian Oblique Twist
3. Air Squat
4. Bodyweight Lunge
5. Heel Raises—Straight Knee
6. Push-Ups
7. Dumbbell Arm Swings

Runners with some resistance training background can begin with the following exercises and then either add exercises or increase the difficulty of the ones already being performed (e.g., swap air squats for squats with weights, or swap step-ups for step-ups with dumbbells):

1. Leg Lifts
2. Russian Oblique Twist
3. Push-Ups *or* Dumbbell Bench Press
4. Dumbbell Row
5. Dumbbell Arm Swings
6. Step-Ups *or* Step-Ups with Dumbbells
7. Air Squats
8. Bodyweight Lunge
9. Heel Raises—Straight Knee

(Continued)

TRAINING DISCUSSION

As you progress in your weight room routine, you'll want to add (or eliminate) exercises based on your training goals. Some general ideas, depending on your personal program:

All-around fitness: After a few sessions, try the other body exercises in this chapter. Eventually, you'll want to integrate weighted squats, lunges, and possibly cleans.

Sprinters and middle-distance runners: Include advanced lifts such as the squat, lunge, clean, and deadlift. Use fewer reps (3–5 reps) to target your nervous system and more reps to build muscle.

Distance runners: Many distance runners prefer circuit training to an exercise-by-exercise approach. Use high reps and move quickly from one exercise to the next.

Leg Lifts

■ SKILL LEVEL: **All levels**

Leg lifts help strengthen the abdominals, aiding core stability and knee lift.

1. Lie on your back with your knees bent, heels on the floor, hands behind your head.
2. Keeping the bend in your knees, raise your feet to 45°. Then lower them until your heels almost touch the floor. Repeat. Start with one set of 10–15 reps, then build up to 40–50 reps.

Russian Oblique Twist

■ SKILL LEVEL: All levels

This is a great exercise for strengthening your obliques (side abdominals). That means better posture, less lower back pain, and a more stable stride.

① Balance on your glutes, hands together and held in front of you, legs bent and lifted off the floor.

② Twist to one side, keeping legs steady while touching your hands to the floor.

③ Repeat on the other side. Start easy with 10–15 reps each side, then build up to 25–30.

Push-Ups

■ SKILL LEVEL: All levels

Push-ups are a great bodyweight exercise for increasing arm and shoulder strength while simultaneously working core, back, and quads for stability.

① Lie face-down on the floor with your hands spread slightly wider than shoulder width.

② Push against the floor to raise your body. Keep a straight line through your back and legs. Start with 10–15 reps, then work up to as many as you can do in a minute.

Variation If a full push-up is too difficult, let your knees rest on the floor and perform the exercise as previously described.

Dumbbell Bench Press

■ SKILL LEVEL: Intermediate, Advanced

This is a great exercise for building strength in your chest and triceps. Using dumbbells instead of a barbell allows you to develop balance and work both sides equally.

① Lie on a bench while holding dumbbells at shoulder width. The dumbbells should be to the sides of your chest.

② Lift the dumbbells, focusing on using your chest, until your arms are straight. Hold for a second, then slowly return to your starting position.

Dumbbell Row

■ SKILL LEVEL: Intermediate, Advanced

This exercise balances out the work you did with dumbbell bench press, strengthening your back and biceps.

① Place your right hand and right knee on the bench, your left leg angled away from the bench for stability. Grab the dumbbell (beneath your shoulder) with your left hand. Allow a slight arch in your lower back, keeping the rest of your spine straight—no bending your head up or down.

② Bring the dumbbell toward the outside of your lower rib cage, focusing on pulling your elbow upward. Then lower the dumbbell toward the start position, keeping a slight bend in your elbow. After 8–12 reps, repeat with the other arm.

Dumbbell Arm Swings

■ SKILL LEVEL: All levels

This simple exercise has been used by runners for decades. It mimics the running motion, which develops the upper body muscles that create balance in your arm swing.

① Stand with your feet hip-width apart. Position your arms as if you were running, while holding light dumbbells in each hand.

② Pump your arms, mimicking the normal arm swing of running. Stand tall—no slumping. Do at least 15 reps with each arm (there's really no upper limit).

Step-Ups

■ SKILL LEVEL: All levels

Step-ups are a great way to strengthen your quadriceps and glutes.

① Stand one foot away from a step, box, bench, or other platform. Keep your back straight throughout the exercise.

② Step onto the elevated platform, making sure that your entire foot is on the platform. The bend at your knee shouldn't exceed 90°—if it does, the platform's too high.

③ Step up onto the platform, generating force with the muscles of your bent leg. Use your opposite leg for balance only. Reverse the motion. After 8–12 reps, repeat with your other leg.

Step-Ups with Dumbbells

■ SKILL LEVEL: Intermediate, Advanced

Adding dumbbells to step-ups increases the difficulty—and the adaptation.

① Stand one foot away from a step, box, bench, or other platform. Keep your back straight and hold dumbbells (start with light weights) at your sides.

② Step onto the elevated platform, planting your entire foot on the platform. The bend at your knee shouldn't exceed 90°—if it does, the platform's too high.

③ Step up onto the platform, keeping the dumbbells at your sides; generate force with the muscles of your bent leg. Use your opposite leg for balance only—or place on platform if necessary to steady balance. Reverse the motion. After 8–12 reps, repeat with your other leg.

Bodyweight Lunge

■ SKILL LEVEL: All levels

Bodyweight lunges are a terrific way to strengthen your quadriceps, hamstrings, and glutes while mimicking a walking/running stride.

① Stand straight with your arms at your sides or hands on your hips. Your feet should be hip-width apart.

② Step forward, bending at the knee until your thigh is roughly parallel to the ground. Don't let your forward knee extend beyond the toes of the leading foot. Keep your front foot flat on the floor. Reverse your motion to return to your starting position. Start with 3–5 reps, then gradually build up to 10.

Air Squat

■ SKILL LEVEL: All levels

Air squats are the bodyweight version of squats, which are one of the best exercises for strengthening your quadriceps, hamstrings, and glutes.

① Stand straight with your feet hip-width apart, arms at your sides. Your toes should be pointed slightly out (keeps pressure off your knees during the squat).

② Bend your knees, pushing your hips back until your thighs are parallel to the floor. Simultaneously bring your arms up and extend them straight in front of your shoulders—this counterbalances the backward motion of your hips. Push upward with your quadriceps to return to your starting position. Start with 5 reps, then build up to 10–15.

Single-Leg Squat

■ SKILL LEVEL: Intermediate, Advanced

Single-leg squats offer more intensity and a better way to keep your hips and legs in balance than air squats.

① Balance on one leg with the opposite leg extended forward for balance. Hold your arms straight out in front of your shoulders, also for balance. If your balance is still shaky, it's okay to hold on to a secure object.

② Slowly lower yourself into the squat position (think of sitting in a chair). Keep your knee aligned over your foot. Don't squat

so far that you can't get back up! For single-leg squats, partial squats are fine. Do 5–10 reps, then repeat with the other leg.

Variation As an alternative, perform the single-leg squat on a bench. Hold a dumbbell extended in front of you for balance, and drop your non-weight-bearing leg to a level beneath the bench.

Wall Sit

■ SKILL LEVEL: All levels

This exercise may look like sitting down on the job, but it'll put the burn into your quads.

① Stand straight against a wall, then lower yourself until your knees form a 90° angle. Hold the position. Start with 30 seconds, then increase by 15-second intervals as you get stronger.

Variation For added difficulty, extend your arms directly out from your shoulders.

Heel Raises—Straight Knee

■ SKILL LEVEL: All levels

Straight-knee heel raises target your calves, especially the gastrocnemius (your largest calf muscle), and get you up on your toes during races—mandatory for middle-distance runners.

① Place the balls of your feet on a platform, heels hanging off, feet hip-width apart, while you lean into a wall or hold onto some other secure object for balance. Lower your heels so that they drop beneath the edge of the platform. (Just a mild stretch—don't shred your Achilles!) Beginning runners can perform this exercise on the floor, then work up to a platform.

② Raise your heels as high as you can, coming up on your toes. Pause at the top for 1–2 seconds, then lower your heels and repeat. 10–15 reps should do it, though up to 30 is okay.

Heel Raises—Bent Knee

■ **SKILL LEVEL: All levels**

Bent-knee heel raises also target your calves, only this version splits the work between your soleus (your deep calf muscle) and gastrocnemius. It also protects against lower hamstring strain.

① Place the balls of your feet on a platform, heels hanging off, feet hip-width apart, with your knees slightly bent, mimicking the bend in your leg while running. Lower your heels so that they drop beneath the edge of the platform. Beginners can perform this exercise on the floor, then work up to a platform.

② Raise your heels as high as you can, coming up on your toes. Keep the bend in your leg. Pause at the top for 1–2 seconds, then lower your heels and repeat. 10–15 reps should do it—don't overdo this version of the exercise!

Squat

■ **SKILL LEVEL: Intermediate, Advanced**

Squats are one of the best free-weight exercises for strengthening your quads, hamstrings, and glutes. Do 6–12 reps for your muscles. Do 5 or fewer reps if your focus is your nervous system.

① Stand straight with a barbell resting on your shoulders. Your feet should be hip-width apart, your toes pointed slightly outward. (It's best to start by taking the weight from a squat rack, with the bar racked at shoulder height.)

② Keeping your feet flat, move your hips back and bend your knees, lowering your torso until your thighs are roughly parallel to the floor. Resist arching your back or performing the exercise too quickly. Reverse the motion until you reach your starting position.

Lunge

■ SKILL LEVEL: Intermediate, Advanced

Weighted lunges recruit a wider range of muscle fibers (and muscle fiber types) as you mimic the walking/running motion. Do 6–12 reps for muscles, 5 or fewer reps for your nervous system.

① Stand straight with the barbell resting on your shoulders. Your feet should be hip-width apart. Use an overhand grip with your thumbs hooked around the bar for added stability.

② Take a big step forward, bending at the knee until your forward thigh is roughly parallel to the floor. Your forward knee shouldn't extend beyond your toes, and your front foot should remain flat on the floor. Pause, then reverse the motion until you reach your start position.

Variation As an alternative, hold dumbbells at your sides with your arms fully extended and your palms facing inward.

Clean

■ SKILL LEVEL: Intermediate, Advanced

Cleans are a fantastic full-body exercise, working muscles from your ankles to your shoulders. Do 6–12 reps for muscles, 5 or fewer reps for your nervous system.

① Grab a barbell on the floor with an overhand grip, hands at shoulder width or a little wider. Your back should be slightly arched, toes beneath the bar and shoulders over it.

② Pull (don't jerk!) the bar upward, keeping it close to your body so that it almost brushes your knees.

③ Accelerate the motion by jumping upward, simultaneously shrugging your shoulders.

④ Allow your elbows to angle outward, still keeping the barbell close to your body as you pull it to your shoulders.

⑤ Move your body under the bar, catch it on your shoulders, and then allow your legs to bend in order to absorb the force. From this semi-squat position (with heavier weights, you'll drop even lower than depicted in the photo), straighten your body. Then lower the bar to the floor in a smooth, controlled motion, and repeat. Begin with light weights for this exercise, since you'll need to get the form down before the weight can go up.

Deadlift

■ SKILL LEVEL: Intermediate, Advanced

Deadlifts work the lower back, spinal stabilizing muscles, glutes, quadriceps, hamstrings, and calves—boy, does it work them! This is a good exercise to finish with, since it's demanding on your central nervous system (see Chapter 11 on the nervous system). Do 6–12 reps for muscles, 5 or fewer reps for your nervous system.

① Use an alternate grip for this exercise—a mixed underhand-overhand grip—with your thumbs hooked around the bar. Start with the bar on the floor. Lower your hips until your thighs are roughly parallel to the floor, then flatten your back and look straight ahead. Your arms should be outside your knees. Your feet should be hip-width apart, toes angled slightly outward.

② Lift upward by standing up. Straighten your legs, hip, back, and shoulders at the same time. Don't "pull" with your arms. Bring the bar up straight (no swinging it). Then pause briefly before reversing the motion. Start with light reps, and never attempt a weight so heavy that you forfeit good form.

PROPRIOCEPTIVE NEUROMUSCULAR FACILITATION (PNF) STRETCHING

PNF stretching increases your range of motion and strengthens muscle, but it is best performed with a partner. In the photo instruction, Bianca Guzman, of CATZ Physical Therapy Institute in Pasadena, California, leads Tanya Zeferjahn, a two-time NCAA Division II national track champion (10,000 meters), through a PNF routine for runners. First, five quick rules for PNF:

1. Perform an easy cardio warm-up (e.g., 10–15 minutes of jogging) before stretching.
2. When performing a stretch, begin by moving the targeted muscle to its initial maximum range of motion (don't force this; instead, "find" this point).
3. Now contract the muscle you're stretching at 20–30 percent of maximal effort for 5–8 seconds.
4. Next, relax the muscle while your partner moves the stretched extremity to a slightly greater range of motion (small increments only)—or move the extremity yourself with a stretching strap. Now you have a choice: Hold this position for up to 30 seconds, or immediately begin with a new contraction. Holding the stretch is the traditional approach but risks the temporary decrease in strength and power associated with static stretching.
5. Repeat 4–5 times.

The following seven stretches, from the PNF Hamstring Stretch to the PNF Hip Flexors Stretch, can be performed individually or as part of one continuous session.

■ **SKILL LEVEL: All levels**

PNF Hamstring Stretch

This stretch is a great way to keep hamstrings loose and to avoid nasty hamstring strains—not to mention hamstring tightness during harder efforts.

① Lie down with one leg flat—or, for less-flexible runners, bent at 90°—and the other held straight by your partner at your initial maximum range of motion. Note that this is a gentle stretch. Once you've reached the end of your range of motion, pull (contract) with your hamstrings for 5–8 seconds at 20–30 percent of maximal effort. (Feel free to use a towel or small pillow under your neck.)

② Relax as your partner backs off stretching the hamstring to reduce the stretch.

③ Your partner moves your hamstring to a new maximum range of motion—this should only be an incremental

improvement! Hold for up to 30 seconds. Repeat steps 1 and 2. Repeat stretch 4–5 times.

Variation As an alternative, perform the stretch solo using a rope or stretching strap.

PNF Calf Stretch #1: Gastrocnemius

This calf stretch focuses on the gastrocnemius, the big muscle that gives your calves their shape.

① Lie on the floor while your partner rests your targeted leg over his or her thigh. Your partner cups your heel while using a forearm to press against the ball of your foot, moving your gastrocnemius to the end of its full range of motion. Now push your foot against your partner's forearm for 5–8 seconds at 20–30 percent of maximal effort.

② Relax as your partner backs off stretching the gastrocnemius.

③ Your partner moves your gastrocnemius to a new maximum range of motion—this should be an incremental improvement. Hold for up to 30 seconds. Repeat steps 1 and 2. Repeat stretch 4–5 times.

Variation As an alternative, sit on the floor, back straight, non-stretching leg bent to 90°, while you loop a rope or stretching strap around the ball/middle of your foot and perform the stretch solo (pull back on the rope, press against it for 5–8 seconds, relax, find new maximum, hold, and repeat).

PNF Calf Stretch #2: Soleus

This second calf stretch focuses on the soleus muscle, which lies deeper beneath the skin than the gastrocnemius and runs from below the knee to the heel.

① Lie facedown with a towel supporting the ankle of the leg resting on the ground. Your partner cups the heel of your raised leg (calf perpendicular to the floor) and uses his or her forearm to press down on your foot, finding your soleus muscle's maximum range of motion. Now push your foot against your partner's forearm for 5–8 seconds at 20–30 percent of maximal effort.

② Relax as your partner backs off stretching the soleus.

③ Your partner moves your soleus to a new maximum range of motion—this should be an incremental improvement. Hold for up to 30 seconds. Repeat steps 1 and 2. Repeat stretch 4–5 times.

Variation As an alternative, sit on the floor, back straight, your working leg bent to 90°, while you loop a rope or stretching strap around the ball/middle of your foot and perform the stretch solo, using the above instructions as guidelines.

PNF Glute Stretch

This stretch will take the tightness out of your glutes; if you're not very flexible, be careful not to over-stretch your glutes, as this can create strain for your lower back.

① Lie on your back while your partner gently moves your knee toward your chest. Your partner controls the motion with one hand below your knee and one on the bottom of your foot. When you reach your initial maximum range of motion, try to push your raised leg straight (5–8 seconds at 20–30 percent of maximal effort).

② Relax as your partner backs off stretching your glutes.

③ Your partner moves your glutes to a new maximum range of motion—this should be an incremental improvement. Hold for up to 30 seconds. Repeat steps 1 and 2. Repeat stretch 4–5 times.

Variation As an alternative without a partner, hug your own knee, repeating the process outlined above.

PNF Hip Adductor Stretch

Hip adductors bring your thighs toward the center of your body. Stretching them not only increases hip adductor range of motion but also reduces hamstring pain.

① Lie on your side with your head resting on a pillow and your hands comfortably in front of you. With your hips perpendicular to the floor, your partner raises one of your legs while placing a hand on your hip and the other hand under your knee. Your leg bends at the knee to rest across your partner's thigh. When you reach your initial maximum range of motion, contract your hip adductors (press your thigh down) for 5–8 seconds at 20–30 percent of maximal effort.

② Relax as your partner backs off stretching your hip adductors.

③ Your partner moves your hip adductors to a new maximum range of motion—this should be an incremental improvement. Hold for up to 30 seconds. Repeat steps 1 and 2. Repeat stretch 4–5 times.

Variation As an alternative without a partner, lie on your back, then loop a rope or stretching strap around the center of your foot. Swing the leg to the side and use pressure from the rope to mimic the stretch-contract-release-stretch action outlined in the above instructions.

PNF Quadriceps Stretch

This is a great stretch for the quadriceps, but it's important that you limit the "push" when moving the muscle through its full range of motion—you don't want to apply too much pressure to the knee.

① Lie facedown on a mat while your partner moves your heel toward your glutes. Your partner gently pushes with a hand on your ankle while stabilizing your position with a second hand on your hip. When your quadriceps muscles reach their initial maximum range of motion, press backwards against your partner's hand for 5–8 seconds at 20–30 percent of maximal effort.

② Relax as your partner backs off stretching your quadriceps.

③ Your partner pushes gently to move your quadriceps to a new maximum range of motion—this should be an incremental improvement. Hold for up to 30 seconds. Repeat steps 1 and 2. Repeat stretch 4–5 times.

Variation As an alternative, lie on your side and grasp your top ankle behind you (it's okay to have the lower leg bent also). Perform the exercise to mimic the above instructions.

PNF Hip Flexors Stretch

This hip flexors stretch is also great for relieving mild lower back tension—just don't overdo it!.

① Lie facedown while your partner grasps below your bent knee (about 90°) with one hand and uses the other hand to press on your hip to stabilize your position. Your partner lifts your thigh to its initial maximum range of motion. Then you press down for 5–8 seconds at 20–30 percent of maximal effort.

② Relax as your partner backs off stretching your hip flexors.

③ Your partner lifts your leg a little higher to move your hip flexors to a new maximum range of motion—this should be an incremental improvement. Hold for up to 30 seconds. Repeat steps 1 and 2. Repeat stretch 4–5 times.

DYNAMIC STRETCHING

Dynamic stretching is the best way to increase range of motion pre-workout or pre-race. Unlike static stretching, pre-run dynamic stretching improves performance! Below are a few simple dynamic stretches, but many athletes also include a few of the technique drills that you'll be learning in Chapter 11, which double as dynamic stretches. Always warm up for 10–15 minutes before doing any type of stretching.

The following two Leg Swings stretches can be performed individually or as part of one continuous session.

■ SKILL LEVEL: Intermediate, Advanced

Leg Swings: Forward and Backward

Forward and backward legs swings help activate your core and increase your range of motion.

① Balance against a wall, goal post, or other secure object. Standing tall, swing the leg on the same side as the supporting hand forward and backward from the hip.

② Allow your swinging leg to bend slightly (approximately 10 percent) at the knee and keep your upper body upright. Ten or more repetitions with each leg will help increase range of motion.

Leg Swings: Sideways

Sideways leg swings create a better range of motion in your hip abductors and hip adductors.

① Use both hands to balance against a wall, goal post, or other secure object. Lean slightly forward and swing your right leg across your body, pointing your toes upward as the leg rises. Keep your upper body still to isolate your adductors.

② Swing your leg back the other way, using your hip abductors to pull the leg as high as it will go. Ten or more repetitions with each leg will help increase range of motion.

STATIC STRETCHING

Static stretching has gotten a black eye in recent years. Studies show that it reduces strength and explosive power when performed immediately before a workout. On the other hand, runners who've consistently used static stretching pre-workout incur injuries more frequently if they stop stretching. For most runners, static stretching is best done post-workout and is used to reduce post-run stiffness that might otherwise linger until the following day's run. You should think of static stretching as "loosening"—you don't forcefully lengthen your muscles, you relax them.

The following six stretches, from Hamstring (static stretch) to Iliotibial (IT) Band Stretch (static stretch), can be performed individually or as part of one continuous session.

■ SKILL LEVEL: All levels

Hamstring (static stretch)

These are two variations of static hamstring stretching, both of which reduce tension in the hamstrings post-workout.

Variation 1 The seated variation of the hurdler's stretch has you sitting tall with one leg extended in front of you and the other folded with the bottom of your foot pressed against

BUILD YOUR RUNNING BODY—COMPONENTS AND WORKOUTS

the opposite inner thigh. Bend forward from the waist (don't hunch your back) and reach toward your toes. Don't overdo this stretch. When you reach the end of your range of motion, stop. Hold for 30 seconds.

Variation 2 Standing, hands on hips, prop the heel of your foot up on a platform. Now bend from your waist, sticking your butt out until you reach the end of your hamstrings' range of motion. Hold for 30 seconds.

Hip Flexor and Quadriceps (static stretch)

This simple stretch loosens your quadriceps and hip flexors.

① Standing straight, balance yourself against a wall (or other secure object). Bend your leg backward at the knee, grasping the top of your foot with your same-side hand. Pull back and up gently, until you reach the end of your range of motion for your quadriceps and hip flexors. The key to this exercise is to contract your glutes during the stretch. Hold for 30 seconds.

Quadriceps (static stretch)

This is the most effective static stretch for quadriceps and also doubles as a good hip flexor stretch.

① Kneel with your left knee forward. Rest your left hand on your front knee (or on a secure object if necessary for balance). Now grab your trailing foot with your other hand and lift upward. When you reach your quadriceps' initial maximum range of motion, you can adjust the stretch in either of two ways: You can move forward at the hips, increasing the stretch on your hip flexors, or you can pull up farther on your raised foot, increasing the stretch to your quadriceps. Hold for 30 seconds. Switch legs and repeat.

Calf (static stretch)

There are many different calf stretches, but the following one works great!

① Assume the push-up position, facedown, arms straight, back straight, legs extended behind you. Now cross one foot over the other as you allow your weight to move your lower foot into a dorsi-flexed (angled toward your shin) position. Keep your knees straight. Hold for 30 seconds.

Lower Back and Hip Abductors (static stretch)

This stretch will loosen both your lower back and your hip abductors, but inflexible runners should be careful not to push beyond their natural range of motion.

① Lie on your back, then let your knee fall over to the opposite side. Place your hand on your knee—don't push! Keep both shoulders against the floor, and keep your lower leg straight. Try not to pivot your hips in the direction of the stretch. Hold for 30 seconds.

Iliotibial (IT) Band Stretch (static stretch)

This stretch helps prevent and treat IT band syndrome. The IT band runs along the outside of the leg, from hip to knee, and tightness and inflammation can be felt as pain at either the hip or along the outside of the knee.

① This stretch utilizes a "revised" hurdler's stretch. Sit on the floor, one leg extended in front of you, one foot tucked back by your hip. Your knees should be separated by 1–2 inches (your thighs are almost parallel). Bring your head down toward the straightened knee. You should feel the "pull" along the outside of that leg. Hold for 60 seconds. Repeat with the opposite leg.

Build Your Running Connective Tissue

 **M**ost runners don't think about connective tissue until it hurts. We have a general awareness that our bodies contain support structures like bones and ligaments to prevent us from collapsing into blobs of Jell-O, but that's where our curiosity ends.

That's where it ends, that is, until our first case of Achilles tendinitis. Or plantar fasciitis. Or IT band syndrome. Or until we sprain an ankle, tear cartilage in our knee, or suffer a stress fracture. Then we become experts. Then we visit doctors or podiatrists, learn about the particular connective tissue we've injured, begin a lengthy course of physical therapy, and curse the day we overlooked the importance of strengthening this vital tissue. Because here's the scary truth: Once connective tissue damage is done, it's difficult—*sometimes impossible*—to undo.

WHAT'S CONNECTIVE TISSUE?

Connective tissue is exactly what it sounds like: tissue that connects your body's muscles, organs, blood vessels, nerves, and other parts to one another. It supports, surrounds, strengthens, stores energy for, cushions, and protects the components of your running body. It's the glue that holds you together.

Connective tissue is a catch-all phrase for tissues that take many forms, from the gel-like areolar tissue, which binds skin to muscle, to the rock-solid bones that comprise your skeleton. Whether connective tissue is gel-like or more solid is determined by the density of fibers in its *extracellular matrix*—the distinctive mix of fibers, proteins, carbohydrates, minerals, salts, fluids, and other elements that surrounds connective

tissue cells. Examples of connective tissue with densely compacted fibers are tendons and ligaments. An example of gel-like connective tissue with a looser fiber arrangement is fat.

In this chapter, you'll target five types of connective tissue:

- ▶ Bone
- ▶ Tendon
- ▶ Ligament
- ▶ Cartilage
- ▶ Fascia

Blood, fat, and skin are also connective tissues, but we'll save them for later chapters.

CT TRAINING

Most connective tissues adapt to training, but there's a catch: CT adapts at a much slower rate than muscle. When you allow your muscle development to outpace connective tissue adaptation, the result can be injury. Runners begin training, and their muscles improve rapidly. Encouraged, they increase the intensity and length of their workouts. Next thing they know, they've got Achilles tendinosis, tibial tendinitis, or a stress fracture in their foot. Their connective tissue couldn't cope with the increased workload, even though their muscles seemed fine.

BEGINNER'S GUIDELINE

Connective Tissue (CT) Rule #1: Do not injure your connective tissue! Seriously, don't do it. CT adapts more slowly than muscle, so you can't base your training on muscle fitness alone. You must strengthen CT and the muscles that affect it. Once CT damage is done, it can't always be undone.

TRAINING DISCUSSION

"Will running ruin my knees?"

We touched on this subject in Chapter 1, but it bears repeating: No, running will not ruin your knees. In fact, contrary to sedentary America's belief, running is good for your knees. We previously looked at Stanford University's three-decade study, published in 2008, which found that runners were seven times less likely to require knee replacement. But that's hardly where the data ends.

A 2013 study, published in *Medicine & Science in Sports & Exercise*, compared the incidence of osteoarthritis (a degenerative joint disease that leads to damage and loss of cartilage in the knees and hips) in runners and walkers. Of the nearly 75,000 runners in the study, 2.6 percent developed osteoarthritis during the seven-year study. Of the almost 15,000 walkers, 4.7 percent were diagnosed with osteoarthritis. Other non-running exercise was determined to increase the risk of developing osteoarthritis by 2.4 percent over running. In other words, running *reduced* the incidence of osteoarthritis when compared to less strenuous exercise. The authors speculate that running's beneficial association with weight loss (specifically a reduction in fat) was behind the study's results.

You're probably thinking, *But wait a minute, how can the increased pounding associated with running reduce knee damage when compared to the less-forceful impact of walking?* There's a simple reason, one illustrated in another 2013 study published in *Medicine & Science in Sports & Exercise*. Fourteen study participants were monitored during periods of both walking and running. The study found that while running results in more impact force per step, walking an equal distance requires so many more steps that the accumulation of impact force was the same. That's right, your knees get the same overall pounding whether you're running or walking.

Long-term knee damage usually results from osteoarthritis or ligament damage. Since running reduces osteoarthritis—and since it actually strengthens bone and tendon—you'll improve your knees; you won't damage them. So the next time someone asks about your knees, don't get annoyed. Have compassion. After all, *their* knees are seven times more likely to wear out, and their bodies aren't doing so great, either.

Some connective tissues won't ever improve much with training. For these tissues, such as cartilage and ligaments, your emphasis needs to be on injury prevention. You must strengthen muscles that directly affect the tissues (often smaller muscles overlooked in traditional strength training routines) and utilize stretching and massage to reduce tissue tension.

Most of all, training connective tissue requires patience. Get-fit-quick schemes rarely produce fast fitness; they produce injury. You can't get in shape from the couch.

"10 Foods for Happy Bones"

Most of us know we need calcium and vitamin D for healthy bones, but our skeletons are hungry for more than just a glass of milk. A good set of bones requires a constant and adequate supply of protein, magnesium, potassium, phosphorus, fluoride, and vitamin K. Each of the following ten foods is unusually abundant in at least several nutrients that give your bones a boost:

1. Almonds
2. Bananas
3. Canned sardines
4. Orange juice
5. Raisins
6. Roasted pumpkin seeds
7. Soy products
8. Spinach or broccoli
9. Wheat bran
10. Yogurt

BONE

Your adult body contains 206 different bones. These bones form a balanced and symmetrical skeletal structure that puts even the best Lego toys to shame. They're also your primary defense against gravity, with your *femur* (thigh bone) alone capable of supporting up to 30 times your weight.

Of course, we runners tend to push gravity-defiance to the limit. A single step during a distance run creates an impact force approximately two to three times your body weight. Let's put that into perspective. For a reasonably fit male runner weighing 150 pounds who logs one thousand steps per mile, that's 150 to 225 tons of impact force that his skeleton must endure each mile! Add extra tons for faster running (up to seven times body weight for sprinting), then multiply by weekly mileage, and it's no surprise that novice runners suffer injuries when they segue straight from a New Year's Eve resolution to a hard run on the roads.

It's alive!

Lucky for us, bone is a living tissue that undergoes constant renewal. Under normal conditions, about 4 percent of your bone is being broken down and replaced through a process called *remodeling*. When you run, this process goes into overdrive. Just as your body strengthens muscle fibers by replacing damaged myofilaments, it also uses remodeling and *modeling*—a separate process that fortifies bone with extra bone tissue—to create bigger, stronger, better bones.

But rebuilding and fortifying your bones takes time. At the beginning of remodeling, cells called *osteoclasts* dig out old, damaged bone tissue, leaving tiny cavities in your bones. It then takes three to four months for other cells called *osteoblasts* to fill those cavities with new bone. In the interim, you're left with porous bone that's susceptible to injury. During this phase, runners who push too hard for too long often end up with a stress fracture as their reward.

If you do get a stress fracture, the wait begins

again. It will take three to four months for your body to repair the fracture. Training too soon risks re-injury.

Training recommendation

Training bone begins with nutrition (see sidebar, "10 Foods for Happy Bones"). Poor nutrition leads to weak bones. In fact, deficient calcium in your diet can force your body to mine bones and teeth (which contain 99 percent of your body's stored calcium) for the mineral. In the event of a stress fracture, Pool Running (see page 161) is your best cross-training bet. Resistance training (Chapter 5) triggers improvements in bone strength, but intermediate and advanced runners might need to increase their usual volume of reps and sets by 25–50 percent to continue strengthening their CT.

TENDON

Tendons connect muscle to bone, transmitting the force generated by muscles to move your joints—and hence your body. But tendons are far more than organic cables. They are active, responsive, and vital partners with your muscles, so much so that the two tissues are regularly referred to as a muscle-tendon unit.

Muscles don't end where tendons begin. There is no line drawn in the sand. Instead, there is a transition area, the muscle-tendon zone (*musculotendinous zone*), where muscle gradually gives way to tendon. In this zone, muscle fibers and tendons merge, operating as a unit. It is only at the outskirts of this zone that tendons finally emerge as the glistening, white, fibrous cords that eventually connect to bone.

Tendon injury

The point at which individual muscle fibers meet tendon, the *myotendinous junction*, is your muscle's weak link. It's here that most muscle strains occur. Powerful eccentric contractions cause damage either at this junction or directly above it. If you're lucky, damage will be limited to a few fibers and short-lived soreness. If you're unlucky, a complete muscle tear might require surgery and physical therapy. The good news is that the muscle-tendon zone gets a rich blood supply from muscle fibers, resulting in a healing rate that almost parallels that of muscle.

Achilles tendon injuries, the plague of runners (especially runners age forty and over) range from mild tendinitis to complete *rupture*. *Achilles tendinitis* is an overuse injury that is accompanied by painful inflammation. *Achilles tendinosis*, on the other hand, involves degenerative damage at the cellular level that produces chronic pain without inflammation. Until the late 1990s, almost all Achilles pain was thought to result from tendinitis. Now, it's understood that most Achilles pain is generated by tendinosis. The treatment (and best prevention) for Achilles tendinosis is eccentric *Heel Dips* (see page 109), a remedy discovered by Swedish orthopedist Hakan Alfredson. Alfredson was a recreational runner who developed severe Achilles pain. In a podcast with the *British Journal of Sports Medicine*, he explained that he'd asked his boss to perform surgery on the tendon, only to have his boss reply, "If we operate on you, you need to be on sick leave. And we cannot afford that here at the clinic. . . I won't ever operate on your Achilles tendon." Desperate to get the operation, Alfredson attempted to rupture his Achilles with a high-volume bout of heel dips. Instead, he got better. A 2012 study published in the *British Journal of Sports Medicine* investigated the long-term effects of heel dips. Researchers questioned fifty-eight patients who'd previously treated their Achilles tendinosis with 180 heel dips per day for twelve weeks. The study reported that almost forty percent of the patients remained pain-free five years later. The researchers also noted that two similar studies on the long-term effect of heel dips showed even better results, with 88 percent and 65 percent of those patients reporting little or no pain. Interestingly, it's not calf strengthening that does the trick. It's stress on the tendon itself, and subsequent adaptations, that lead to healing.

In the absence of proactive treatment (like heel dips), damage done to tendons in the white fibrous zone—that bloodless stretch preceding the interface with bone—has a gloomy outlook. A 2013 study from Denmark tried to determine the tissue turnover rate (the time it takes to regenerate completely new tissue) for this zone. Previous estimates ranged from two months to two hundred years. The researchers chose subjects who'd lived during the nuclear bomb testing from 1955 to 1963, when atmospheric levels of carbon-14 were highest. They then measured existing levels of radioactive carbon-14 in the subjects' muscles and Achilles tendons. Tested muscle was clear of carbon-14. In contrast, tested tendon showed levels of carbon-14 that hadn't changed in the decades since atomic testing. So when can you expect damaged tendon tissue to regenerate? According to this study: Pretty much never.

Elastic recoil

If runners were superheroes, *elastic recoil* would be our superpower. Elastic recoil occurs during runs when you convert energy stored in your tendons and fascia (see "Fascia," page 88) into a free push. And not a little push—elastic recoil is more like a big shove that provides up to 50 percent of the propulsive force for each running stride.

The major driver of recoil is your tendons. Tendons aren't an elastic tissue, but they have elastic properties. They're like ropes that stretch under tension. At rest, their tough *collagen fibers* line up in parallel wavy lines. Under tension, these wavy patterns straighten to allow a stretch of 4–6 percent. Because your tendons are stiff, the act of stretching them requires a lot of energy. During runs, this energy is provided by the impact force each time your foot hits the ground. The impact force stretches your Achilles tendon as well as fascia in your legs. This impact energy is momentarily stored in your tendon and fascia. When your calf muscles contract, the energy is released, creating a catapult effect—elastic recoil—that multiplies the force produced by muscle alone. With proper training, it will feel like you're running on coiled springs!

Training recommendation

Running and resistance training exercises from Chapter 5 contribute to tendon stiffness—as will the workouts from chapters 8 and 11. Wobble board and resistance band/tubing exercises (see pages 91–99) further strengthen the entire kinetic chain (muscles, connective tissue, and nerves from hip to toe); this helps to prevent tendon inflammation and damage. Active Isolated Stretching (AIS) (see pages 104–106) is useful for working the muscle-tendon zone (since it sidesteps the stretch reflex that can lead to strains in this zone).

Best of all, elastic recoil costs nothing in terms of oxygen and calories. It's completely fueled by impact energy.

The amount of recoil depends upon a tendon's *stiffness*. Stiffness measures the amount of force it takes to stretch the tendon. The more force applied, the greater the recoil. That said, stretching a tendon beyond 4–6 percent is dangerous—beyond 8 percent risks rupture.

LIGAMENT

Ligaments connect bone to bone, and their prime directive is to stabilize joints. Tough and flexible, they're composed mainly of collagen fibers. These fibers are arranged in a crisscrossed pattern that improves your ligaments' ability to manage sideways forces. Just as bowling alley bumper rails prevent bowling balls from veering into the gutters, your ligaments guide bones—and the joints where they meet—through a normal range of motion.

Ligaments perform another essential function for your running body: They contain *proprioceptive* cells that signal the nervous system when the ligament is being overstretched. Not only does this keep you consciously aware of your leg's position in space (important for landing correctly and avoiding obstacles), it also cues your nervous system when to contract muscles in order to lessen stress on your ligaments. A 2011 study found that patients recovering from *anterior cruciate ligament* (ACL) surgery regained greater functional knee stability when ACL remnants were salvaged rather than shaved off during surgery. Salvaging ACL remnants allowed patients to retain proprioceptive cells, a major contributor to stability. Healthy, functioning ligaments don't just tell you where you're at; they allow you to get where you're going.

Lax ligaments

Runners usually suffer ligament injuries at the ankles and knees.

Most ankle injuries involve sprains, which occur when your foot lands awkwardly—rolled outward, bent inward, twisted, or tweaked by some other unnatural landing position. Sprains overstretch and tear ligaments, often leading to joint instability. Runners with poor ankle flexibility, inefficient neuromuscular activation, or any combination of weak muscles, tendons, or ligaments are more susceptible to ankle sprains. Running on uneven surfaces—or running steps or trails when overly fatigued—can increase your risk of injury.

This doesn't mean you should *never* run on uneven surfaces. While too much "wobbling," as occurs on trails, grass, and other natural surfaces, can lead to excessive stress on your ligaments and joints, some side-to-side motion can trigger strengthening in these same joints. At the opposite end of the spectrum, hard flat surfaces (e.g., sidewalks and asphalt streets) increase impact force, which can both stimulate strengthening or, in excess, lead to injury. Your best bet is to split your running between natural and manmade surfaces.

Knee injuries (that aren't cartilage damage) tend to strike two major pairs of ligaments: The *anterior cruciate ligament* (ACL) and *posterior cruciate ligament* (PCL), and the *medial collateral ligament* (MCL) and *lateral collateral ligament* (LCL). The cruciate ligaments sit in the middle of the knee, connecting the femur to the *tibia* (shin bone). They control forward and backward motion. The collateral ligaments stretch vertically along the inside and outside of your knee, controlling sideways motion. Damage to any of these ligaments can disrupt the stability of your knee.

Ligaments are capable of moderate stretching, but a prolonged or sudden, forceful stretch can cause ligaments to be overstretched or torn. Since ligaments have a poor blood and nutrient supply, they are slow to heal—just as they are slow to adapt. Full repair following injury can take anywhere from months to years. And even repaired, the new ligament tissue will be inferior. You'll be more likely to reinjure the ligament, which can lead to *ligament laxity*—"loose" joints (elongated ligaments) that create joint instability. It's wise to include exercises to prevent injury and imperative that you do so after injury has occurred.

Training recommendation

Wobble board and resistance band/tubing training (see pages 91–99) are important for both prevention and recovery from ligament damage (wobble board training has been shown to reduce the reoccurrence of ankle sprains by almost 50 percent). A good diet and regular stretching are also important. Balance drills (Chapter 11, see pages 217–219) help coordinate neuromuscular responses to avoid missteps that lead to injury.

CARTILAGE

Every bone in your body began as cartilage. In the womb, this tough connective tissue allowed for a more flexible skeleton, a huge plus given your cramped quarters at the time. As you grew, from toddler to teen to adult, most of your cartilage was transformed into the rigid tissue of bone, until finally the only cartilage left was in your ears, nose, bronchial tubes, and ribs—and, of greatest importance to runners, between your joints.

When runners talk cartilage, we usually mean *articular cartilage*. Articular cartilage forms the smooth coating on the surface ends of bones. This low-friction coating allows bones to glide over one another, and it provides a flexible cushion within the joint. The femur, tibia, and patella (kneecap) all have articular cartilage.

While studies confirm that physically active children can increase cartilage thickness, similar research on adults shows no difference in thickness between lifelong athletes and healthy non-athletes. In contrast, lifelong couch potatoes (and those otherwise immobilized) show decreased cartilage. Athletes tend to have larger knee joint surfaces than non-athletes, but it's unclear if this represents genetics (like height for a basketball player) or a training adaptation.

Damaged cartilage—just say no!

Damage to articular cartilage is bad news. Since cartilage lacks both nerves and blood supply, minor damage can go unnoticed and, more importantly, unrepaired. If the damage is allowed to progress, it can lead to significant disability. In the case of the degenerative joint disease osteoarthritis, the joint space can narrow to the point of bone-on-bone contact. The joint becomes inflamed, painful, less mobile, and partially disabled.

Most runners know someone who has suffered torn cartilage in the knee. This is usually an injury to the *meniscus*, not the articular cartilage. The lateral and medial menisci are two pads of *fibrocartilage* that provide shock absorption and structural support for your knee. In adults, treatment generally requires surgery to repair or remove the affected cartilage.

TRAINING DISCUSSION

"Does barefoot running reduce injury?"

Barefoot running is nothing new. Track and cross-country runners have made barefoot intervals around grass athletic fields and local golf courses a ritual of spring for decades. And Abebe Bikila of Ethiopia won the 1960 Rome Olympic Marathon running without shoes.

What's new is the claim that barefoot running is better for us than running shod.

In a 2010 study, Harvard anthropologist Daniel Lieberman proposed that our African ancestors' reliance upon persistence hunting (which involved walking and running long distances) created an evolutionary preference for endurance. The study indicated that barefoot runners who landed on their mid-foot or forefoot generated smaller collision forces than runners in shoes, who tended to be heel-strikers. His suggestion, taken up as a battle cry by barefoot and minimalist advocates, was that barefoot running, since it causes less impact and is more natural, might reduce injury. But does it?

The claim that barefoot running reduces injury relies upon the premise that the 80–85 percent of runners who heel-strike will transition to a mid-to-forefoot landing when barefoot. But the reality is that they don't. In fact, 80 percent of heel-strikers remain heel-strikers, only now they do it barefoot. As Ross Tucker, Ph.D., coauthor of the popular website *The Science of Sport*, points out in a post, "[The] result is an impact loading rate that is *seven* times greater than running in shoes with the same landing."

Barefoot and minimalist advocates would claim that these runners need more time to transition. But a ten-week study following nineteen runners who transitioned as instructed from shoes to Vibram FiveFingers (a minimalist shoe that mimics barefoot running) saw ten runners develop bone damage, including two stress fractures. Overall mileage dropped, too. Dr. Sarah Ridge, who conducted the experiment, suggested they ran less "because their feet hurt."

Barefoot advocates also claim that running without shoes is more economical (uses less oxygen and energy), giving a boost to endurance running performance. But data doesn't seem to support this claim, either.

A 2012 study from the University of Colorado compared the energy cost of running both barefoot and in lightweight running shoes. Twelve runners with "substantial barefoot running experience" alternated running barefoot and shod at the same pace on a treadmill. Running with lightweight shoes proved more economical. Strike one.

A 2013 University of Massachusetts study concluded that both natural rear-foot runners *and* forefoot runners who were forced to land rear-foot were more economical landing on their heels. Strike two.

(Continued)

TRAINING DISCUSSION

And Dr. Iain Hunter, a biomechanics instructor at Brigham Young University, filmed the 2012 USA 10,000-meter Olympic Trials, and then studied the way competitors landed. They landed heel first, forefoot first, mid-foot, twisted foot, and feet all over the place. For the best runners in the country, foot strike simply wasn't a factor. Strike three.

No one denies that runners get injured at an unusually high rate. But blaming either shoes or bare feet seems a little silly. Both lead to injury, so neither by itself can be the cause. Perhaps Tucker put it best: "I cannot stress enough that the reason for injury is training."

Training recommendation

Bottom line: There is no training mechanism for increasing the strength of cartilage at a rate that mirrors our targeted adaptation in other tissues. So remember Connective Tissue Rule #1: Don't injure it in the first place! Older runners with chronic knee pain or inflammation should consider getting an x-ray to rule out osteoarthritis.

FASCIA

Imagine that a spider with supernatural powers lives within you. And imagine that this spider spends its days spinning a single continuous web that cocoons your body beneath the skin, a web that spreads inward, surrounding and penetrating every muscle, nerve, organ, and bone—every structure, cavity, and tissue in your body. That'd be one heck of a web! Well, minus the spider, that web—a continuous weave of collagen and *elastin* fibers that grows thicker and thinner and that appears as membrane, sheet, cord, and gristle—is your *fascia*.

Once considered the Saran Wrap of the body,

fascia has recently been nominated for a status upgrade by some researchers. They view fascia as a reactive tissue. They believe it contracts and relaxes like muscles (albeit at a slower rate), recoils like tendons, provides sensory feedback like nerves, and links all 650 muscles into a single working unit. Oh, and they blame it for the vast majority of chronic pain and injury in runners.

Robert Schleip, Ph.D., head of the Fascia Research Project, in a 2009 interview for *Men's Health*, described fascia as an instrument for "structural compensation." In other words, fascia is responsible for posture. When we climb stairs or slouch at our desk, we create alterations in our posture that can become permanent. In this model, fascia is like a sweater. Tug on one part of the sweater, and the entire garment moves. Tension in one area can therefore affect every aspect of posture. Adhesions that build up between fascial surfaces due to injury can create chronic pain that radiates throughout our body. Seen this way, plantar fasciitis is no longer an injury of the foot; it could just as easily be caused by problems with the hips, back, or shoulders. Schleip and others in the field believe that myofascial release exercises and specific stretches can improve posture, reduce pain, and resolve injury.

Table 6.1
Connective Tissue Training & Effectiveness of Training Methods

Methods for Improvement	Types of Connective Tissue					
	Bone	Cartilage	Ligaments	Tendon (White Zone)	Muscle-Tendon	Fascia
Foam Roller	Ø	Ø	Very Low	Very Low	High	Very High
Nutrition	High	Very Low	Low	Low	High	High
Myofascial Release	Ø	Ø	Very Low	Very Low	High	High
Running Workouts (25% above normal routine)	Medium	Ø	Ø	Ø	Medium	High
Running Workouts (50% above normal routine)	Medium	Ø	Ø	Ø	High	Very High
Bodyweight Strength Training	Medium	Ø	Ø	Medium	High	High
Stretching	Ø	Ø	Low	Low	Very High	Very High
Resistance Bands/Tubing	Low	Low	Medium	Medium	High	Very High
Weight Training (25% above normal routine)	Medium	Ø	Ø	Ø	Medium	High
Weight Training (50% above normal routine)	Medium	Ø	Ø	Ø	High	Very High
Wobble Board	Ø	Ø	Medium	Medium	High	High

TABLE 6.1 estimates the effectiveness of different training approaches when it comes to stimulating adaptations in connective tissue. For example, while a foam roller will be very effective in both strengthening and loosening fascia, it will probably have no effect on bones or cartilage.

Training recommendation

You don't have to be a true believer like Schleip to recognize the value of stretching, foam rolling (see pages 101–103), and range-of-motion exercises. These exercises can range from resistance training to plyometrics and form drills (the latter two approaches are explained in Chapter 11).

TRAINING RUNDOWN

When it comes to training connective tissue, sometimes you can and sometimes you can't. See Table 6.1 for a breakdown of the value of different training approaches for connective tissues. Where running and weight workouts are listed, the percentage of increase above normal workout routine refers to total volume, not intensity, of single sessions (remember that you have to increase the training stress, in this case the volume of weight work, in order to trigger improvement in your body). Important photo-instruction training for CT includes:

▶ **Wobble board exercises**
▶ **Resistance band/tubing exercises**
▶ **Foam roller exercises (myofascial release)**
▶ **AIS (active isolated stretching)**
▶ **"Household props" injury prevention and rehab exercises**

Training from other chapters that affects connective tissue strengthening includes:

- ▶ **Running (Chapter 5)**
- ▶ **Strength training (Chapter 5)**
- ▶ **Plyometrics (Chapter 11)**
- ▶ **Technique and form drills (Chapter 11)**
- ▶ **Balance drills (Chapter 11)**

To see exactly how these workouts can be incorporated into your overall training program, skip directly to Chapter 15: Build Your Training Schedule, where sample schedules are available for runners of all fitness levels and abilities.

Chapter 6: Build Your Running Connective Tissue —
PHOTO INSTRUCTION

WOBBLE BOARD

This wobble board routine works your entire kinetic chain (the interconnected chain of muscles, nerves, CT, and other structural components of your running body). It helps immunize your lower legs against injuries like shin splints, plantar fasciitis, Achilles tendinosis and tendinitis, patellar tracking syndrome, and IT band syndrome. Wobble boards are supported by a round "ball" projecting from the base. While a smaller ball makes for easier rocking, the Thera-Band wobble board used in the workouts below features a slightly larger ball, which ensures stability throughout the exercise. Allow 2–3 minutes for recovery between sets. Sean Brosnan, a runner who's clocked 1:48 for 800 meters and 4:00 for the mile, demonstrates the exercises.

Wobble—Forward and Backward

This is a great exercise for strengthening and stabilizing both plantarflexion and dorsiflexion, which can protect against lower leg injuries and speed recovery from the same.

■ **SKILL LEVEL: Intermediate, Advanced**

① Hold on to a chair, counter, or other sturdy support structure. Center your weight over the middle of the wobble board (often, the best balance requires moving your heel closer to the center of the board). Rock forward and touch the front of the wobble board to the floor (or as close as you can get). Limit the bend at your knee. Focus on utilizing the ankle's range of motion.

② Rock backward until you touch the floor (or as close as you can get). One rep includes both the forward and backward rock. Start with 5–10 reps, then increase by no more than 10 reps per week to a maximum of 100.

Wobble—Side to Side

This exercise helps to stabilize against inversion and eversion (rotating the foot inward or outward).

■ SKILL LEVEL: Intermediate, Advanced

① Begin as you did the previous exercise. This time, rock inward and touch the side of the wobble board to the floor (or as close as you can get).

② Rock outward until you touch the floor (or as close as you can get). One rep includes both the inward and outward rock. Start with 5–10 reps, then increase by no more than 10 reps per week to a maximum of 100.

Wobble—Around the Clock

Wobbling both clockwise and counterclockwise builds on the strength and stability that you've developed from previous wobble board exercises.

■ SKILL LEVEL: Intermediate, Advanced

① For this wobble board exercise, rock forward to touch the front of the wobble board to the floor (or as close as you can get), then begin a clockwise rotation, keeping the edge of the wobble board against the floor.

After one full rotation, reverse direction, doing the same exercise counterclockwise. Use the same reps progression as with the previous wobble board exercises. One rep includes both a clockwise and a counterclockwise rotation.

RESISTANCE TUBING LOOP OR RESISTANCE BAND LOOP ROUTINE FOR CT

Resistance tubing (or resistance band) exercises for the hips and lower legs build strength to help runners maintain stability throughout the course of runs and races and provide protection for CT injuries from the hips to the toes. It's important to use tubing or bands that provide the correct resistance for your strength and fitness. The Thera-Band tubing and bands used in these exercises utilize eight color-coded levels of resistance. Always allow at least 2–3 minutes of recovery between exercises.

Side Steps

Side steps are a good workout for strengthening and stabilizing your hip abductors. Most chronic lower-leg connective tissue injuries have their genesis in weak hips. Either resistance tubing or a resistance band can be used for this exercise.

■ SKILL LEVEL: All Levels

① Loop the resistance tubing either above your knees (least resistance), below your knees (medium resistance), or around your ankles (greatest resistance, as shown). Bend your knees slightly with your feet hip-width apart.

② Step to the side until the tubing provides significant resistance (to the point you can reasonably go). Then slide your pivot foot over to recreate your original stance. Now repeat this sidestepping movement for 10–20 feet in one direction, and then reverse direction. Do one set for each direction. Gradually add distance.

Monster Walk

Monster walking works your hip flexors, extensors, and abductors, providing a great all-around strengthening workout for your hips. Either resistance tubing or a resistance band can be used for this exercise.

■ SKILL LEVEL: All levels

① Loop the resistance tubing either above your knees for less resistance or below your knees (as shown) for more resistance. Bend your knees slightly, with your feet hip-width apart. Hang your arms loosely at your sides.

② Step forward and to the side at a 45° angle, keeping the bend in your knees and your arms at your sides. Step forward and to the opposite side at a 45° angle. Keep walking for 10–20 feet, then gradually build up to longer distances.

Walkout/Jogout

Walkouts and jogouts provide good overall kinetic-chain training and are an integral part of knee (especially ACL) strengthening.

■ SKILL LEVEL: All levels

① Fasten low-resistance tubing to a door anchor, doorknob, or other secure object. Fasten the opposite ends to a belt looped around your waist. Face away from the anchor.

② Walk or jog a few strides forward, until the resistance interrupts your stride. Then allow the loop to pull you back as you walk/jog backward to your starting position. Repeat until fatigued (never push through pain with this exercise).

Backward Walkout/Jogout

Backward walkouts and jogouts continue the strengthening work for the knee (especially the ACL) begun with forward walkouts/jogouts.

■ **SKILL LEVEL: All levels**

① Fasten low-resistance tubing to a door anchor, doorknob, or some other secure object. Fasten the opposite ends to a belt looped around your waist. Face toward the anchor.

② Walk or jog a few strides backward, until the resistance interrupts your stride. Facing the same direction, allow the loop to pull you back to your starting position. Repeat until fatigued (never push through pain with this exercise).

Jumpouts

Jumpouts are a more explosive version of walkouts/jogouts. They contribute a greater stimulus to kinetic chain adaptation and knee strengthening (especially the ACL).

■ **SKILL LEVEL: Intermediate, Advanced**

① Fasten low-resistance tubing to a door anchor, doorknob, or other secure object. Fasten the opposite ends to a belt looped around your waist. Face away from the anchor.

② Bound (jump) forward explosively, pushing off one foot and landing on the other. Then hop backward off your same landing foot, returning to your starting position. Continue until fatigued (never push through pain with this exercise), then switch sides and repeat.

Jumpouts—Sideways

Sideways jumpouts are a more explosive version of side steps. As with other variations of this exercise, they build kinetic-chain adaptations and knee strength (especially the ACL).

■ **SKILL LEVEL: Intermediate, Advanced**

① Fasten low-resistance tubing to a door anchor, doorknob, or other secure object. Fasten the opposite ends to a belt looped around your waist. Stand sideways to the anchor.

② Leap sideways (away from the anchor) off the foot nearest the anchor, landing on your opposite foot. Then leap back to your starting position. Continue until fatigued (never push through pain with this exercise), then switch sides and repeat.

Hip Adduction

Hip adduction strengthening is often overlooked by runners, but it's important to balance hip abduction strength with adduction training. This exercise will help keep your hips stable through your full stride and during foot strike.

■ **SKILL LEVEL: All Levels**

① Secure a resistance band to an anchor or other secure object at ankle level. While standing, loop the band around your anchor-side leg, just above the ankle, with your opposite foot positioned slightly back. Hold on to a secure object for balance.

② Keeping your knee straight, pull your leg inward, across your opposite leg. Slowly return to the

start position. Continue until fatigued (never push through pain with this exercise), then switch sides and repeat.

Ankle Dorsiflexion

Ankle dorsiflexion (angling your foot toward your shin) training is great for preventing front shin splints (pain along the outside of your shins).

■ SKILL LEVEL: All levels

① Sit on the floor with one leg extended in front of you, the other bent at the knee. Attach the resistance band around the top of your foot and anchor to a secure object. If desired, place a towel beneath your Achilles. Start in the toe-forward position.

② Pull your foot backward toward your shin. When you reach maximum dorsiflexion, slowly return your foot to its original position. Continue until fatigued (never push through pain with this exercise), then switch sides and repeat.

Ankle Plantarflexion

Ankle plantarflexion (pushing your foot forward) training helps treat and prevent medial shin splints (pain along the inside of your shin, also known as posterior tibial tendinitis).

■ SKILL LEVEL: All levels

① Sit on the floor with one leg extended in front of you, the other bent at the knee. Loop the resistance band around your foot while holding on to the opposite end.

② Push your foot forward until your reach maximum plantarflexion, then slowly return your foot to its original position. Continue until fatigued (never push through pain with this exercise), then switch sides and repeat.

Ankle Inversion

This is the best exercise for preventing and treating medial shin splints (pain along the inside of your shin).

■ **SKILL LEVEL: All levels**

① Sit in a chair with one end of the resistance band secured to an anchor or other secure object at ankle level. Loop the band's other end around the arch side (inside) of your foot.

② Keep your knee straight as you pull your foot inward, limiting motion to your lower leg. When your foot reaches its maximum range of motion, slowly return to your starting position. Continue until fatigued (never push through pain with this exercise), then switch sides and repeat.

Variation As an alternative, cross your non-working leg over the leg being trained, then secure the band both by holding it with your hand and stabilizing it with your non-working foot (as pictured).

Ankle Eversion

Ankle eversion exercises are used to strengthen ankles post-sprain and can also be used as a preventive measure.

■ **SKILL LEVEL: All levels**

① Sit in a chair with one end of the resistance band secured to an anchor or other secure object at ankle level. Loop the band's other end around the little-toe side (outside) of your foot.

② Keep your knee straight as you pull outward with your foot, limiting motion to your lower leg. When your foot reaches its maximum range of motion, slowly return to your starting position. Continue until fatigued (never push through pain with this exercise), then switch sides and repeat.

Variation As an alternative, secure the band by stabilizing it with your non-working foot and holding the end of it with your hand (as pictured).

LUNGE WORK

While we included lunge exercises in the muscles chapter, two more lunge workouts serve as the perfect remedy for many hip and knee problems. Like much of our CT work, these exercises also work the whole kinetic chain. Always allow 2–3 minutes (or more, if necessary) of recovery between exercises.

Lunge Walk

Lunge walks build both endurance and strength, improving your stability during runs.

■ **SKILL LEVEL: Intermediate, Advanced**

① Start from a standing position, arms hanging at your sides.

② Take a big step forward, bending at the knee until your thigh is roughly parallel the ground, keeping your knee lined up over your foot. From this lunge position, step forward into another lunge with the opposite leg. Start with 20–30 feet of lunge walks, then gradually increase the distance (some athletes actually get up to 100 meters!).

Variation As an alternative, hold a medicine ball in front of you as you walk. This helps you to maintain form.

Lunge Clock

Lunge clock training provides strengthening and stability in all directions. A lunge clock is best performed on a prepared mat, with tape used as markers to mimic the hours of the clock.

■ SKILL LEVEL: Intermediate, Advanced

① Stand straight, arms hanging loosely at your sides, in the middle of the lunge clock.

② Step forward toward "12 o'clock," bending at the knee until your thigh is roughly parallel the floor (performing a lunge).

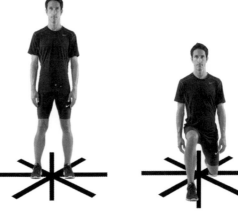

③ Step backward, assuming your original position.

④ Now step toward the various "hours" of the clock, lunging forward and to the side, sideways, backward and to the side, backward, etc. Never change the direction you're facing while lunging around the clock. Do 1–2 sets with each leg.

FOAM ROLLER ROUTINE

Foam rolling is about as close as you can get to a deep-tissue massage. It's a way to self-myofascial release—to release tension in the fascia and break down adhesions that are thought to form between fascia, muscle, and skin. All exercises are being performed on Thera-Band foam rollers, which allow gradual increases from extra-cushioned to stiff rollers. Roll each muscle group 60 to 90 seconds, 1–2 reps. These exercises are safe and effective for all training levels. Tanya shows how it's done.

Hamstring—Foam Roller

Begin your foam rolling with your hamstring, releasing tension that will free up your calves and lower back for better rolling in the next exercise.

① Sit on the floor with the foam roller beneath your knees. Place your hands behind you for support.

② Lift your glutes off the floor, extending your legs straight in front of you.

③ Roll all the way up to your glutes and then back toward your knees.

Variation As an alternative, increase pressure by stacking your legs. Do shorter, repetitive strokes in areas of greater tension.

Calf—Foam Roller

This is a great way to relieve the pain and pressure of knots, sore spots, and tension in your calves (both gastrocnemius and soleus muscles).

① Place the foam roller on the floor in front of you, then lay both calves over the roller. Keep your hands on the floor behind you for support.

② Lift your glutes off the floor and roll up toward your knees.

③ Reverse direction and roll down toward your ankles.

Variation As an alternative, stack your legs, then roll back and forth, working shorter strokes over tight areas. Rotate your leg outward and then inward to release different areas of the calf.

IT Band—Foam Roller

The IT band runs from your hip all the way down the outside of your leg and knee. Many runners experience tightness of the IT band, which leads to pain on the outside of the knee or hip, as well as snapping at the hip. This is a good way to keep the IT band loose.

① Lie sideways with the foam roller beneath your hip. Bend your top leg at the knee and drape it over your target leg; your top-leg foot should be flat on the floor. Your down-side forearm and opposite-side hand should also be on the floor.

② Using your foot, elbow, and hand to push and pull, gently roll back and forth over the outside of your leg from hip to knee. Maintain tight abs and straight alignment throughout.

Variation As an alternative, increase pressure by stacking your legs. Do shorter, repetitive strokes in areas of greater tension.

Quadriceps—Foam Roller

Your quadriceps (thigh muscles) take a beating from hill running (especially downhill running) and speed work. This is a nice way to reward them for all the impact they absorb.

① Lie facedown with your quads resting on your foam roller and your forearms on the floor.

② Use your forearms and elbows to power your roll from the top of your quadriceps to the top of your knees.

Variation As an alternative, increase pressure by stacking your legs. Do shorter, repetitive strokes in areas of greater tension.

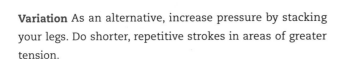

BUILD YOUR RUNNING BODY

Glutes—Foam Roller

Rolling your glutes is a good way to relieve pressure on your piriformis (a small muscle in your glutes that sits atop the sciatic nerve), which in turn releases pressure on your sciatic nerve.

   ① Sit on your foam roller with your legs extended in front of you. Place your hands behind you for support.

   ② Roll back and forth over your glutes.

Variation As an alternative, stack your legs and focus on one side at a time. Use the ridges of the foam roller (if yours has them) to mimic pressure point therapy to your piriformis.

Lower Back—Foam Roller

For many runners, lower-back tightness limits stride and stability. Finish your foam rolling session by working out the tension in your lower back.

   ① Sitting on the floor, lean back until your lower back is resting against the foam roller. Stabilize your position with your hands. Your feet should be flat on the floor.

   ② Press down with your heels to raise your glutes. Roll back onto your elbows if it helps stabilize your position, and then bend and straighten your knees to control movement as you roll back and forth over your lower back.

AIS

Active Isolated Stretching strengthens your muscles and increases your range of motion while avoiding the stretch reflex (a protective contraction that occurs when a muscle is stretched for more than 2–3 seconds), thereby providing a safer and more effective stretch for the muscle-tendon area. The following routine was created by Phil Wharton, who has worked with Olympians and world record holders including Shalane Flanagan, Bernard Lagat, Mo Farah, Khalid Khannouchi, Meb Keflezighi, and Moses Tanui. For more information and video demonstrations of stretches, visit Phil's website at whartonhealth.com. When performing AIS, remember these three rules:

1. **Activate:** Contract the opposing muscle to the one being stretched. Use that contraction to move the stretched muscle through its range of motion and to trigger relaxation in the muscle being stretched. Only use your rope to aid the final small increment of the stretch.
2. **Isolate:** Use proper form and technique to stretch the muscle being targeted.
3. **Don't Hold:** The first part of the AIS motion is usually quick, but the AIS movement slows down as you approach your full range of motion. Since the stretch reflex occurs after 2–3 seconds, it's important not to hold the stretch—release it and return to your starting position.

Ten reps on each side of the body should be enough for all of these AIS exercises, which are safe and effective for all training levels, although new runners should limit volume and intensity for the first 1–2 weeks.

The following five stretches, from Hamstring—AIS to Trunk Extensors (Lower Back)—AIS, can be performed individually or as part of one continuous session.

Hamstring—AIS

Focus on lifting your leg with your quadriceps during this stretch. Your rope should be used to facilitate no more than a small, incremental range-of-motion increase at the end of the stretch.

① Lie on your back with a pillow beneath your head. Bend your non-stretching leg, while keeping your exercising leg flat. Loop your rope around the arch of your foot (exercising leg).

② Inhale as you lift your exercising leg using your quadriceps. Keep your pelvis down during the stretch. Slow down as you near your full range of motion and use the rope to help reach that range. Don't hold the stretch. Exhale as you return your leg to the start position. Repeat for 10 reps, then switch sides.

Calves (Gastrocnemius)—AIS

Increasing range of motion in your calves is vital for preventing Achilles injuries and calf soreness. The gastrocnemius is the large muscle in your calf.

① Sit with one leg extended in front of you, the other bent. Loop the rope around the ball of your foot.

② Using the muscles on the front (outside) of your shins, pull your foot toward your shin (dorsiflexion). Use your rope to aid the last bit of the stretch and reach your full range of motion. Don't hold the stretch. Return to your starting position. Repeat for 10 reps, then switch sides.

Variation

① As an alternative, turn the foot inward to isolate the outer calf and repeat the exercise.

② To continue with this alternative stretching, turn the foot outward and repeat the exercise.

Quadriceps—AIS

Stretching your quadriceps increases your range of motion with each stride and decreases tension on connective tissue at your hips and knees.

① Lie on your side with your lower leg bent beneath you (stabilize with your rope, as pictured). Bend your lifted leg and grab the base of your shin.

② Use your glutes and hamstrings to pull your lifted leg backward. Use your hand to aid the last bit of the stretch (don't overstretch, as that can lead to lower abdominal soreness). Keep your pelvis forward to protect your back throughout the exercise. Return to the start position. Repeat for 10 reps, then switch sides.

Gluteals—AIS

Tight glutes and hips are two of the biggest impediments to stride length—and two major contributors to injuries up and down your legs. Work this exercise for stability and power.

① Lie on your back with one leg straight and the other bent.

② Use your abdominals to pull your knee toward the opposite shoulder. Grab your bent leg at the base of the outer shin (with your opposite-side arm) and on the outer thigh (with your same-side arm). Use your hands to aid the last bit of the stretch. Don't hold the stretch. Return to your starting position. Repeat for 10 reps, then switch sides.

Trunk Extensors (Lower Back)—AIS

Lower-back tightness will chop your stride, rob you of your speed, and take the joy out of easy distance running. Spend a minute reducing tension to ensure hours of enjoyable running.

① Sit with your knees bent, heels placed a little wider than shoulder width in front of you.

② Slide your hands to your ankles and tuck your chin to your chest as you use your abdominals to pull yourself forward, head aimed between your knees. Use your hands to facilitate no more than a small, incremental range-of-motion increase at the end of the stretch. Don't hold the stretch. Return to your starting position. Repeat for 10 reps, then switch sides.

HOUSEHOLD PROPS POST-RUN INJURY PREVENTION ROUTINE

Some runners have neither the time nor the props for more complex post-run CT exercises. For these runners, the following set of exercises might be the answer. This fast routine provides the ounce of prevention you'll need for plantar fasciitis, Achilles tendinosis, tibial tendinitis, lower back pain, and more. These exercises are safe and effective for all training levels. They're demonstrated here by Christian Cushing-murray, a former sub–four-minute miler and current masters national record-holder (age forty-five to forty-nine) for 1,500 meters.

The following seven exercises, from towel Toe Curls to The Daydreamer, are all part of the same continuous workout.

Towel Toe Curls

This exercise is a simple way to stave off plantar fasciitis, an injury that's usually felt as pain in your heel (often mistaken for a bruise) or your arch.

① Sit barefoot in a chair with a towel spread on the floor in front of you. Put a shoe or an item of similar weight on the towel's opposite end to create minor resistance. Keeping your heels on the floor, pull the towel toward you by scrunching your toes. Bunch the towel beneath your arch (or behind your heels) until you've reeled in its entire length. Repeat 1–2 times.

Foot Work

These simple foot exercises add stability to your ankles and help prevent both shin splints and plantar fasciitis. This foot work should be fluid and low exertion—don't strain.

① *Orbits:* Lie on your back with one leg straight, toes pointed upward, and one leg raised and bent 90° at the knee. Prop up the raised leg with your hands, then make circular orbits with your foot, doing 10 rotations clockwise and then 10 counterclockwise. Limit motion to the ankle and foot.

② *Gas Pedals:* From the same position, point your foot away from your shin (plantarflexion) and then pull it toward your shin (dorsiflexion). Perform 10 reps with each foot. As an alternative to both orbits and gas pedals, use your foot to draw the alphabet and write numbers from 1 to 10.

Big-Toe Taps

Big-toe taps are an easy way to build strength in your arch, which makes this exercise a frontline defense against plantar fasciitis.

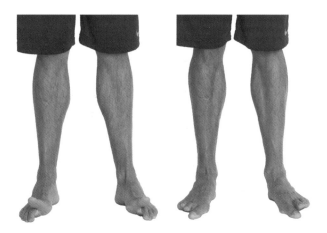

① Stand barefoot with feet hip-width apart. Lift your big toes as you simultaneously press down with the other four toes of each foot.

② Now reverse the motion, pressing down with your big toes as you raise your remaining toes. Start with a few repetitions and work up to 30 seconds or more.

Seated Toe Taps

Seated toe taps are a good defense against shin splints.

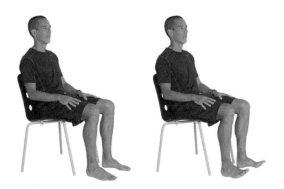

① Sit in a chair with your legs bent 90° at your knees, feet flat on the floor.

② Lift and lower your toes quickly and repeatedly, keeping your heels on the floor, until you feel a "burn" in the muscles outside your shins. This could take from a few seconds to 2–3 minutes. Do one or more sets.

Step-Downs

This exercise is great for strengthening hip flexors and building stability in the hips and knees. It's also great for preventing and rehabbing knee injuries.

① Balance on one foot, standing on a step or low platform. Your free leg should be bent slightly at the knee, with your knees aligned at the start of the exercise.

② Lower your hips, keeping all your weight on your front foot. To avoid injury, you *must* keep your weight-bearing knee in line with your front foot. The angle of your suspended lower leg should line up with your spine. Bend down just far enough to tap the ground behind you.

③ Now straighten your weight-bearing leg while bringing your suspended leg forward, lifting the knee in front of you (mimic the forward drive of your stride). Keep your down foot flat throughout the exercise. Do 5–10 reps with each leg.

Heel Dips

This is an eccentric exercise for the calves, and it's used to prevent and rehabilitate Achilles tendinosis. Although heel dips strengthen calves, their main benefit derives from creating movement within the tendons themselves (cells rubbing against cells).

① Use the balls of your feet to balance on a platform or step with your heels extending over the edge. Use a chair or other sturdy support for balance. Put all your weight on one foot and slowly lower the heel of that foot through its full range of motion.

② Use both feet to rise back up, then repeat. The benefit from this exercise doesn't come from rising on your toes; it comes from slowly lowering your heel. Start with 2–5 repetitions for each foot, then build up to 15–20. As an alternative for beginners (or for runners who are experiencing pain at the heel

rather than in the mid-range of the Achilles tendon), perform heel dips on a flat surface. For treating tendinosis, perform 3 sets of 15 reps (each heel) up to twice per day, up to three months; add weight (a backpack or weights) as your strength increases.

The Daydreamer

There's no better way to release tension in your lower back than to spend a few minutes in the day-dreamer position. This is a great way to finish your Household Props Post-Run Injury Prevention Routine.

① Lie on your back with your arms out to the side, hands at approximately waist level, with your lower legs and feet propped on a chair. Keep a 90° bend in your knees and try to prop your feet so that they don't roll outward. Take slow, deep breaths while relaxing. Don't "do" anything else. Hold for 5–10 minutes.

Build Your Running Cardiovascular System

The term "cardio" has become synonymous with endurance training. In fact, most runners think it's where conditioning begins. So you might be perplexed as to why we've waited until now to address the cardiovascular system. Don't be. First, you don't build your running body one component at a time; you build components simultaneously. Second, many improvements in cardio don't require you to target your cardiovascular system directly; instead, your cardiovascular system gets fit because you increase your body's demand for fuel, which the exercises in chapters 5 and 6 will certainly help you accomplish.

Cardio is the fuel delivery system for your running body. It supplies the steady stream of oxygen, energy (e.g., carbohydrates, proteins, and fats), water, and hormones that your body needs to function. But that's not all. It doubles as the garbage collector, carrying away waste products like carbon dioxide, acidic hydrogen ions, and even heat.

It should come as no surprise that improved running requires improved fuel service and increased garbage collection. Luckily for you, your cardiovascular system runs on supply and demand—if you increase demand from your running body, your cardiovascular system will increase supply. It will transform from the equivalent of an ancient Roman aqueduct into a high-performance twenty-first-century utility, complete with a powerful pumping station and miles of reinforced pipelines.

WHAT'S THE CARDIOVASCULAR SYSTEM?

At its simplest, the cardiovascular system is a blood-distribution network. But that's like saying the government is a rule-distribution network. The truth is that the cardiovascular system comprises a biological supply-and-demand infrastructure of almost unfathomable scope. It has your heart as its engine, beating one hundred thousand times per day to pump almost two thousand gallons of blood. It boasts approximately sixty thousand miles of blood vessels—enough to circumnavigate the globe two and a half times or to stretch a quarter of the way to the moon. And it utilizes twenty to thirty trillion red blood cells (RBCs) to carry oxygen to the one hundred trillion cells in your body.

And that's before you train. If you've played Monopoly, you can think of training as like plunking down houses and hotels on your cardiovascular "properties"—you're making an investment that will provide a substantial return, including a stronger heart, even more miles of blood vessels, and a higher volume of RBCs.

As a runner, you should think of your cardiovascular system as an *oxygen transport system*. Its number-one job during training and racing is to transport oxygen from your lungs to your skeletal and cardiac (heart) muscle cells.

In this chapter, we'll discuss three main features of the cardiovascular system:

▶ **Your heart**
▶ **You blood vessels**
▶ **Your blood volume**

Because lungs (part of the *respiratory system*) supply the oxygen transported by the cardiovascular system, we'll also do a quick drive-by and explore a training strategy for improving their strength.

BEGINNER'S GUIDELINE

You don't improve cardio by running until you're out of breath. You improve your cardiovascular system by increasing the long-term demand from its biggest customer, your muscles. When you run too hard—looking to feel the "burn"—you outrun your cardiovascular system's ability to deliver oxygen. You tire more quickly, and your cardiovascular system gets less work, meaning you'll see less improvement.

TRAINING DISCUSSION

"Will running lower my resting heart rate?"

Everyone knows that distance runners have low heart rates. Rates in the forties and the fifties (beats per minute) are considered normal for longtime runners, with a hearty few dipping into the thirties or upper twenties.

But does everyone's heart rate drop with training?

For most people, the answer is yes, but with a qualification: Genetics and the type of training you do will affect just how far your heart rate drops.

Compare two of running's all-time greats. Jim Ryun, America's last world-record holder in the mile, had a resting heart rate of sixty beats per minute. In contrast, Ron Clarke, an Australian distance runner who set seventeen world records in the 1960s, had a resting heart rate of twenty-eight. Both men were incredibly fit, but Clarke's heart rate was less than half that of Ryun!

To understand this disparity, you need to understand why your heart rate slows down. When you run, your heart's *left ventricle,* the lower-left chamber that pumps blood through your body, gets stronger (the way an aerobics instructor's abs get ripped from doing daily core work). And because it gets stronger, your heart pumps more blood with each heartbeat. At rest, everyone pumps about five liters of blood per minute. But when your heart pumps more blood with each heartbeat, it has to pump less often to move that five liters. While an untrained heart needs sixty to one hundred beats per minute to move that blood, a trained heart only requires forty-five to fifty-five beats.

Of course, you'll pump a lot more than five liters per minute when running. This brings a new factor into play: *Maximum heart rate*, the maximum number of times your heart can beat in a minute. The maximum amount of blood your heart can pump in a minute is determined by a simple formula: Take the amount of blood you pump with each heartbeat—known as your *stroke volume* (don't try to calculate this yourself, as you'll need a lab for that, but appreciate the concept)—and multiply it by your maximum heart rate. Or, written out:

Stroke volume × Maximum heart rate = Maximum blood volume per minute

Most people have a maximum heart rate equivalent to 220 beats per minute minus their age. For example, a thirty-year-old would have a predicted maximum heart rate of 190 (i.e., 220 minus 30). Maximum heart rate can't be trained; it's genetic. So if two 30-year-olds race each other, the one with the lower resting heart rate (i.e., greater stroke volume) would theoretically pump more blood, which would transport more oxygen to working muscles, and thereby gain an advantage.

Which brings us back to Ryun and Clarke. Ryun's heart didn't play by the rules. In his twenties, Ryun's reported maximum heart rate was an astounding 220–230, allowing him to

(Continued)

pump an enormous amount of blood with an average stroke volume. In contrast, Clarke had a normal maximum heart rate, so he had to increase his stroke volume in order to generate the blood flow necessary for world-class competition—especially since distance races require almost 100 percent aerobically produced energy. Clarke's heart was forced to adapt, big time. Ryun's, not so much.

Unless you're a genetic freak like Ryun, your heart rate will probably slow down. But unless you're a genetic freak like Clarke, it probably won't drop all the way to twenty-eight beats per minute.

CARDIO TRAINING

If you guessed that training your cardiovascular system involves a lot of running, you're right. And just as you utilized different paces to train different muscle fiber types in Chapter 5, you'll use multiple paces to target specific areas of cardiovascular fitness.

You actually began your cardiovascular training with the first runs (or walks) you did while strengthening your muscles. Now, it's time to build upon that base. You'll need to elevate both volume and intensity. Some of the workouts you can use to do that are:

▶ **Intervals:** Short, faster repetitions with rest intervals

▶ **5K/10K Trail and Track Training:** Repetitions run at 5K or 10K race effort, with rest intervals

▶ **Cruise Intervals:** Repetitions at a pace you could maintain for an hour, with rest intervals

▶ **Tempo:** A single sustained effort (10–40 minutes) at around half marathon to marathon pace

▶ **Long Run:** A distance run that can account for up to 20–25 percent of your weekly mileage

Each of these types of training has a specific effort level (often defined by pace) attached to it. Increasing the volume or intensity of any workout won't result in an advantage; more likely, it will sabotage the desired stimulus and adaptation.

THE HEART

The heart has captured the imaginations of poets and philosophers since we humans first felt its beat within our chests. The ancient Egyptians considered the heart to be a receptacle for the soul. Aristotle claimed that it was the seat of intelligence and sensation. The Catholic Church, at the Council of Vienna in 1311, dubbed it the wellspring for emotion, nutrition, and vitality. And a couple hundred years later, it was redefined as the cradle of love. It took Rene Descartes, the seventeenth-century philosopher and mathematician—"*Cogito ergo sum*" (I think; therefore, I am)—to declare the heart to be nothing more than a mechanical pump.

Modern runners—armed with a few hundred years of training experimentation—have transformed that simple pump, an organ composed of specialized cardiac muscle tissue that can beat nonstop for a lifetime, into the engine that's driven the fitness revolution.

Your heart is located near the middle of your chest, tucked between your lungs. About the size of your clenched fist, it has four chambers—two upper *atriums* and two lower *ventricles*—arranged like a duplex. On the right side of your heart, the upper atrium receives deoxygenated blood from your body, then transfers it into the lower ventricle, from which it's pumped to the lungs. On the left side of your heart, your left atrium receives newly oxygenated blood from the lungs, then transfers it to the left ventricle, from where it's pumped into the *aorta*, your largest artery, and then to the rest of your body. A normal, adult heart beats sixty to one hundred times per minute, making a "lub-dub" sound with each beat. The "lub" is the closing of the valves between the atriums and ventricles, after blood has been pumped into the ventricles. The "dub" is the sound of the ventricular valves closing after blood has been pumped toward the lungs and into the aorta. During your lifetime, your heart will pump approximately one million barrels of blood, enough to fill an average-size oil tanker!

Your training goal for the heart is simple: Increase its pumping capacity.

Cardiac output

The amount of blood your heart can pump in a minute is called your *cardiac output*. The more blood you pump, the more oxygen you send to your muscle fibers. This increases your fibers' ability to work aerobically, which is the key to endurance training and racing. Cardiac output is determined by two factors:

▶ **Stroke volume:** The amount of blood your heart pumps with each beat
▶ **Heart rate:** The number of times your heart beats in a minute

Table 7.1
Cardiac Output During 5K/10K

5K Time	10K Time	Cardiac Output (Liters/Minute)*
At Rest		4.5–5.5
14:00	29:10	30.5–36.5
15:00	31:15	28.3–34.0
16:00	33:20	26.4–31.7
17:00	35:25	24.8–29.8
18:00	37:30	23.4–28.0
19:00	39:35	22.1–26.5
20:00	41:40	20.9–25.1
21:00	43:45	19.8–23.8
22:00	45:50	18.9–22.7
23:00	47:55	18.0–21.6
24:00	49:60	17.2–20.7
25:00	52:05	16.5–19.8
26:00	54:10	15.8–19.0
28:00	58:20	14.6–17.6
30:00	1:02:30	13.6–16.3
32:00	1:06:40	12.7–15.3
34:00	1:10:50	11.9–14.3
36:00	1:14:60	11.2–13.5
38:00	1:19:10	10.6–12.7
40:00	1:23:20	10.0–12.0
42:00	1:27:30	9.5–11.4

TABLE 7.1 offers estimates of cardiac output associated with 5K/10K times. Find your 5K or 10K time in the columns on the left, then find your predicted cardiac output in the column on the right. Cardiac output measures the blood your heart pumps in liters per minute.
*Ranges allow for differences in body weight.

If you multiply stroke volume by heart rate, the result is your cardiac output. At rest, an average person will pump five liters of blood per minute. While running, your cardiac output increases significantly. Table 7.1 estimates the cardiac output required for different 5K/10K race efforts.

If you want to improve your running performance—either for workouts or races—you *must* improve your cardiac output. This means increasing your stroke volume or heart rate. Unfortunately, your *maximum heart rate* (the most times your heart can beat in a minute) is determined by genetics and can't be changed. That leaves stroke volume. Fortunately, stroke volume can be improved—*a lot!*

Stroke volume

Stroke volume can refer to the amount of blood being pumped from either ventricle, which in healthy adults is roughly equal. As a runner, however, you'll focus on your left ventricle, which pumps blood throughout your body (the right ventricle pumps blood along a short loop to the lungs and back). When you increase your stroke volume, you increase the amount of blood—hence, oxygen—that you can transport to your muscles. This is accomplished in two ways:

▶ **Enlarged ventricular chamber:** When you run, you increase the volume of blood filling your left ventricle, which causes it to stretch. The bigger the stretch, the more your body adapts by enlarging the ventricular chamber, which allows you to pump that much more blood with each heartbeat. This adaptation occurs to a greater extent in distance runners than middle-distance runners, probably because distance runners spend more time training.

▶ **Increased contraction strength:** The greater the stretch as blood fills your left ventricle, the greater the contraction strength when your heart beats. In some ways, this mirrors the elastic recoil in your Achilles tendon and fascia, with cardiac muscle and connective tissue rebounding from the ventricular stretch. But it's not all rebound. There's a neural component to contraction strength, and a muscular one, too (the thickness of your ventricle's muscular wall

will increase, although not on the scale seen in cyclists, rowers, and canoeists).

Interval training is the workout of choice for improving stroke volume. First introduced by Dr. Woldemar Gerschler and Dr. Hans Reindell in the 1930s, an interval workout includes short, fast repetitions followed by recovery "intervals," during which you jog or walk. The goal is to increase your heart rate during the repetition, then allow it to slow down during the recovery. While increased blood flow during the repetition is important, it's the recovery interval that's vital. During recovery, your heart rate drops more quickly than the corresponding drop in blood flow. This forces the ventricles to fill more fully, creating a brief increase in stroke volume. Repeated over multiple reps, this stimulus triggers an adaptation: Increased stroke volume.

Stroke volume is one of the greatest determinants of running performance. Unfit runners reach their maximum stroke volume while they're jogging. In contrast, trained runners increase stroke volume up to 5K pace or faster. That's a huge oxygen advantage.

When you train your heart, your heart does what human tissue does best: It adapts. Cardiac muscle fibers get bigger. Your heart's connective tissue gets stronger. Your ventricular chambers grow larger. Your stroke volume goes up. And your resting heart rate goes down (see sidebar, "Will running lower my resting heart rate?" page 113).

Training recommendation

Interval training is the best way to improve stroke volume. Intervals of 30–90 seconds at 1500-meter to 3K pace are very effective, as are slightly longer reps at 3K to 5K pace, even up to 10K pace (see pages 124–129). Hill repeats (see pages 133) also provide a great stimulus.

TRAINING DISCUSSION

"Heart Disease, Inflammation, and the Marathon"

When runners have heart attacks, like running-boom pioneer Jim Fixx's fatal heart attack following a training run, it's news. When runners die from heart attacks during marathons, as happened at the Chicago and London marathons in recent years, it's big news. And when a paper like the *Wall Street Journal* compares distance running to eating a cheeseburger, suggesting that "an increased vulnerability to atrial fibrillation and coronary-artery plaque" makes running a health risk, runners everywhere stand up and take notice. We know we're not immortal, but we like to believe we're healthy!

So how should we react to this latest Chicken Little assault on our sport? Should we stow our running shoes in the closet? Swear off running and take up less taxing pastimes — like reading the *Wall Street Journal*? First, let's see what the experts have to say.

A 2012 study published in *The New England Journal of Medicine* reviewed the incidence of heart attacks among 10.9 million competitors in marathons and half marathons run between 2000 and 2010. The study revealed that one out of every 184,000 participants had suffered a heart attack, with forty-two out of fifty-nine people dying in those incidents. That's tragic. But it's also low risk compared to other sports — one fifth the death rate for triathlons and a sixth that of college athletics.

If that doesn't reassure you, then a 2013 analysis by the National Runners Health Study will. It followed 32,073 runners and 14,734 walkers for six years and concluded that runners who logged more than twenty-four miles per week experienced fewer incidents of cardiac arrhythmia than those who exercised less.

The truth is that running makes us 50 percent less likely to experience a serious heart attack. That's because running doesn't cause heart attacks. Heart disease causes heart attacks. And what causes heart disease? While cholesterol has worn the black hat for years, a 2012 meta-analysis (170 researchers pooling data on 190,000 research participants) pinned a large part of the blame on inflammation. A 2006 study from Harvard Medical School and Brigham and Women's Hospital (Boston, MA) reached the same conclusion, declaring that there is "growing evidence that inflammation participates centrally in all stages of [cardiovascular disease], from the initial lesion to the end-stage thrombotic complications."

In other words, inflammation — *not intervals* — causes plaque buildup in arteries. And do you know what fights inflammation? That's right: running. Fast-moving blood shields arteries, staving off atherosclerosis. And a 2011 study from Scandinavia found that better physical fitness was associated with less overall inflammation.

So keep running. And if you're worried about the marathon, stick to 5Ks and 10Ks.

BLOOD VESSELS

Your blood vessels are your supply lines, allowing the 24/7 transport of oxygen, nutrients, hormones, and water to every cell in your body. Large blood vessels called *arteries* carry oxygen-rich blood away from your heart. This journey begins with your aorta, then branches into smaller arteries, then into even smaller arterioles, and finally into the tiniest blood vessels in your body, your *capillaries*. Capillaries are so small that red blood cells must pass through them in single file. It's your capillaries that bring blood to your muscle fibers, offloading oxygen and nutrients while picking up carbon dioxide and other waste products. Capillaries then guide blood into *venules*, which drain into veins, which finally steer blood back to your heart.

The capillary zone

Every warehouse has a loading bay—an area where goods are either loaded or unloaded—that's serviced by a steady fleet of cargo trucks. *Capillary beds* are your muscle fibers' loading bays, with RBCs serving as cargo trucks. These beds are the exchange zone for oxygen and carbon dioxide, for nutrients and wastes.

The most important thing for you to remember about capillaries is this: More is better.

The more capillaries you have serving each muscle fiber, the more oxygen you can bring to that fiber (and the more carbon dioxide and other waste products you can haul away). Table 7.2 estimates total capillaries for several runners of varying ability. You'll note that as runners get faster, their predicted capillary density for each fiber type increases.

New capillaries begin to develop during the first week of training, but they only grow for muscle fibers that are being recruited. Riding a bike

Table 7.2
Average Capillaries Per Fiber Type

5K Time	10K Time	Slow-Twitch	Intermediate	Fast-Twitch
14:00	29:10	5.6	4.2	2.8
15:00	31:15	5.4	4.0	2.7
18:00	37:30	4.5	3.4	2.2
21:00	43:45	3.6	2.7	1.8
24:00	50:00	2.8	2.1	1.4
27:00	56:15	1.9	1.4	0.9
30:00	1:02:30	2.2	1.7	1.1
34:00	1:10:50	1.9	1.5	1.0
38:00	1:19:10	1.7	1.3	0.8
42:00	1:27:30	1.5	1.1	0.8

TABLE 7.2 predicts the number of capillaries you'll have associated with each muscle fiber based upon your 5K/10K time. Find your 5K or 10K time in the columns on the left, then find your predicted number of capillaries for each fiber type in the columns on the right.

may be good for your heart, but it won't grow capillaries around non-biking muscle fibers. Similarly, if you run all slow distance, you'll develop capillaries around slow-twitch muscle fibers but not around faster fibers. There are five ways to stimulate capillary growth:

1. **Increase muscle fiber contraction:** You can increase the volume (number) of contractions, or you can increase the rate of contractions (the speed at which your fibers contract)—or you can do both. Long runs are an example of a workout that includes high-volume contractions. Intervals are an example of a workout that increases the rate of contractions. A tempo run would be an example of increasing both volume and rate.

2. **Increase blood flow:** Fast blood flow puts enormous stress on capillaries. When

the stress reaches a critical point, either your capillaries divide or you sprout new ones.

3. **Increase pressure on the capillary walls:** Constant tension against capillary walls can lead to increases in capillary diameter.

4. **Increase pace beyond aerobic threshold:** Running at a pace that demands slightly more energy than oxygen-fueled processes can provide stimulates capillary growth. Effective workouts are 5K pace intervals for advanced runners and 10K pace intervals for beginners.

5. **Increase lactate:** Raised *lactate* levels increase capillary growth. We'll discuss lactate in chapters 9 and 10.

Increased capillarization (capillary growth) is the only way to ensure delivery of the increased oxygen supply created by improved stroke volume.

Easy come, easy go

A common complaint among runners is that fitness takes forever to improve and no time at all to lose. Unfortunately, capillaries follow this pattern. When you stop training, you lose all your new hard-earned capillaries in as little as seven days. If you simply lower your training volume or intensity, you'll lose all capillary gains associated with the previous volume or intensity. Simply put, when you reduce blood flow, you reduce capillaries.

There's another thing worth mentioning when it comes to capillary growth: Exercising too hard sabotages it. Think of training as baking a cake. Putting in twice the flour and triple the salt does not a better cake make. Same goes for extra intervals and faster paces than prescribed.

Training recommendation

Training capillaries requires different volume and pace stimulus for different fiber types. Cruise Intervals (see page 129) and Tempo runs (see page 130) are great for slow-twitch capillaries. Faster intervals and Hill Repeats (see pages 124–128 and 133) are equally effective for faster-fiber capillaries. A bonus of training capillaries is that your *mitochondria* (Chapter 8) respond to exactly the same training stimuli—you kill two birds with one stone. All other blood vessels become more pliable with almost any type of training.

BLOOD

Like every other part of the cardiovascular system, your blood improves with training. The first improvement begins within hours or days of your first run: Your plasma volume increases. Increased plasma volume reduces your blood's *viscosity* (resistance), making it easier for blood to flow through blood vessels, especially the capillaries.

While all running improves blood volume, a 2012 study from New Zealand documented significantly increased plasma volume and performance following training in the heat, with the stipulation that mild dehydration (no more than 2 percent) must be allowed to occur to reap the full benefit. *Runner's World's* Alex Hutchinson noted in his blog, *Sweat Science*, that studies like this illustrate "the importance of allowing your body to undergo training-induced stresses, rather than making heroic efforts to cushion your body from discomfort . . . [Leaving] the water bottle at home may be a good call."

Table 7.3
Total Liters of Blood at Rest

Weight (Pounds)	Male			Female		
	Untrained	Trained	Elite	Untrained	Trained	Elite
250	8.9	10.5	12.2	6.7	7.8	9.1
225	8.0	9.4	11.0	6.0	7.1	8.2
200	7.1	8.4	9.7	5.3	6.3	7.3
175	6.2	7.3	8.5	4.7	5.5	6.4
150	5.3	6.3	7.3	4.0	4.7	5.5
125	4.4	5.2	6.1	3.3	3.9	4.6
100	3.6	4.2	4.9	2.7	3.1	3.7
75	2.7	3.1	3.7	2.0	2.4	2.7

TABLE 7.3 approximates the total liters of blood in your body based upon your weight and your relative level of fitness. Find the weight that is closest to your own in the column on the left, then find the associated blood volume based on your gender/fitness in the columns on the right.

The ABCs of RBCs

The other big adaptation in your blood is an increased number of red blood cells (RBCs). RBCs carry 98 percent of the oxygen that your body uses (and also participate heavily in the removal of carbon dioxide). Oxygen is picked up at the lungs, where it binds to RBCs' iron-rich hemoglobin molecules—it's iron that gives RBCs (and your blood) their red color. Increasing your volume of RBCs allows your blood to transport more oxygen.

RBC volume expands more slowly than plasma volume, taking weeks or even months to plasma's days. Eventual gains in overall RBC volume occur even as exercise-induced damage reduces their expected lifespan from 120 days to approximately 70. This damage is theorized to occur due to causes ranging from exposure to oxygen (causing oxidative stress) to "foot-strike hemolysis," in which RBCs are destroyed when your feet pound the pavement. Still, few runners end up suffering from true anemia (not counting the brief period when plasma expansion outpaces that of RBCs, sometimes called "sports anemia"), and RBC production soon exceeds its normal rate of production, which is 2 million RBCs per second. A 1995 study from the Australian Institute of Sport suggests that there's a benefit from the shorter lifespan of RBCs in runners: "[It] may be advantageous because young cells are more efficient in transporting oxygen."

Training recommendation

Some plasma volume increase occurs in response to all running. Greater plasma gains can be obtained by training in the heat (Chapter 10, see page 175). For red blood cell expansion, diet plays a large role; you need adequate iron intake (see Chapter 22 sidebar, "15 iron-packed food sources," page 340). Aerobic training triggers RBC volume increases, although the mechanism isn't well understood.

TRAINING DISCUSSION

"What is blood doping?"

In blood doping, distance runners receive a transfusion of blood for performance gain. The practice can elevate peak aerobic capacity

Traditional blood doping involves two methods. In the first, an athlete withdraws approximately two pints of his or her blood in the weeks or months before competition. The athlete's body then replenishes the lost blood. One or two days before competing, the athlete re-infuses the previously withdrawn blood, boosting his or her blood volume (including RBCs)—because this thickens the blood and increases blood volume, it increases the risk of blood clot, heart attack, and stroke. The second method is even riskier, involving a blood transfusion from a second athlete. While carrying all the risks of the first method, this method can also lead to viral infections or, worse yet, mismatched blood types. Both methods increase the oxygen-carrying capacity of the blood.

Dominant Finnish runners in the '70s and '80s were widely rumored to employ blood doping, with Kaarla Maaninka confessing, Martti Vainio testing positive for steroids at the 1984 Olympics after supposedly reinjecting tainted blood, and Olympic great Lasse Viren under suspicion to this day. More recently, disgraced cyclist Lance Armstrong admitted to a blood-doping scheme that included secret hotel-room transfusions, complete with taped-over windows and lookouts stationed in the hallways.

In recent years, synthetic versions of the hormone erythropoietin (EPO) and other RBC-boosting agents have replaced transfusions as the dopers' method of choice.

LUNGS

The lungs are part of the respiratory system, but they're also the portal through which oxygen enters the cardiovascular system—*and they're trainable.*

Your lungs are much more than balloons. They are not two hollow chambers that inflate and deflate with each breath. Instead, the interior of your lungs has the consistency of a sponge, filled with complex networks of bronchi and bronchioles (air passageways) that end in tiny air sacs called *alveoli*. How many alveoli? Anywhere from three hundred million to eight hundred million per lung. Alveoli are wrapped in capillaries, and it's here that your blood exchanges carbon dioxide for oxygen. The sheer number of alveoli, capillaries, and RBCs in the lungs explains why smokers can destroy so much lung tissue and still get oxygen into their blood.

You train your lungs by strengthening your respiratory muscles. To inhale, you contract your diaphragm and external intercostal muscles. This expands your chest, which lowers air pressure in your chest cavity and ultimately causes your lungs to fill with air. When you relax the same muscles, you exhale. When you're running like a maniac during hard workouts or races—what some runners joylessly refer to as *sucking wind*—you engage other respiratory muscles (abdominals and internal intercostals) to help you exhale faster.

Table 7.4
Training Effects of Workouts

Training	Stroke Volume	Blood Volume	Red Blood Cells	Lungs (Muscles)	Capillaries (Slow-Twitch)	Capillaries (Intermediate)
1500m Pace Intervals	Very High	Moderate	Moderate	Very High	Low	Very High
3K Pace Intervals	Very High	Very High	High	High	Moderate	High
5K Pace Intervals	High	Very High	High	High	Moderate	High
10K Pace Intervals	High	High	Moderate	Moderate	High	Moderate
Cruise Intervals	Moderate	High	Moderate	Moderate	Very High	Moderate
Fast Tempo	Moderate	High	Moderate	Moderate	Very High	Moderate
Slow Tempo	Moderate	High	Moderate	Moderate	Very High	Moderate
Long Run	Moderate	Moderate	Moderate	Moderate	High	Moderate
Hill Reps	High	Moderate	Moderate	Very High	Low	Very High
Regular Run	Moderate	Moderate	Moderate	Moderate	Moderate	Moderate
Easy Run	Low	Moderate	Low	Low	Moderate	Low
Lung Inspiration Devices	Very Low	NA	NA	Very High	NA	NA

TABLE 7.4 looks at the effect of various types of training on different aspects of your cardiovascular system. For example, hill repeats have a very high effect on capillaries in intermediate fibers, increasing the number of capillaries signifcantly. On the other hand, they have a low effect on slow-twitch capillaries, which require longer duration running, such as tempo runs, to stimulate similar increases in capillary density.

Stronger respiratory muscles not only lower the psychological stress from sucking wind, they also lower your energy use. At rest, breathing accounts for about 1 percent of your energy use. During hard running, this figure can rise to 9 percent. Cutting that down by a few percentage points leaves more energy for the rest of your running body. And training these muscles works. A 2011 study on endurance cyclists found that respiratory conditioning resulted in a 34 percent increase in respiratory muscle strength and a 38 percent increase in respiratory muscle endurance.

Training recommendation

Training respiratory muscles requires fast running (e.g., moderate- to high-intensity intervals) or special apparatus, such as respiratory performers (see page 135).

TRAINING RUNDOWN

Cardiovascular system training involves the interval and tempo running that most runners associate with race conditioning. Important training in this chapter's photo instruction includes:

- ▶ **Interval Training**
- ▶ **Hill Repetitions**
- ▶ **5K/10K Repetitions**
- ▶ **5K Effort Road and Trail Repetitions**
- ▶ **Cruise Intervals**
- ▶ **Fast Tempo**
- ▶ **Slow Tempo**
- ▶ **Long Run**
- ▶ **Respiratory Muscle Training Devices**

Training from other chapters that affects cardiovascular system improvements includes:

- ▶ **Easy Running (Chapter 5)**
- ▶ **Distance Runs (Chapter 5)**
- ▶ **Various Cross Training (Chapter 9)**

To see exactly how these workouts can be incorporated into your overall training program, skip directly to Chapter 15: Build Your Training Schedule, where sample schedules are available for runners of all fitness levels and abilities.

Chapter 7: Build Your Running Cardiovascular System
PHOTO INSTRUCTION

RUNNING WORKOUTS

In the chapter on muscles, you were introduced to some basic running workouts, from strides to easy running—even some hills. As you begin to tackle the challenge of developing your cardiovascular system, you'll need to engage in more-intense training. Grace returns to demonstrate proper stride and form for each workout. To aid in your understanding of this training, each running workout is accompanied by the following:

1. A pace table to help you find your correct intensity
2. Instructions for doing the workout
3. A rundown of the adaptations that you can expect
4. Recommended recovery—the recovery interval is given at the bottom of the table, measured in time (e.g., 1:1 indicates a recovery time that equals the rep time; 1:½ indicates a recovery time only half as long as the rep time)

1500-Meter Pace Training

1500-meter pace effort is equivalent to the effort you'd use to race a mile. Since most runners haven't raced the 1500 or the mile, the pace table uses your 5K race pace as a starting point, then estimates an equivalent 1500-meter performance. If you don't have a current 5K time, use the guidelines outlined on page 34. 1500-pace suggestions are given for repetitions at 200, 300, 400, and 600 meters. Repetitions longer than 600 meters are not advised. 1500-pace reps can improve:

▶ **Stroke Volume:** 1500-pace reps are a valuable workout for increasing your stroke volume. Run for 30 to 90 seconds to elevate your heart rate, then quickly slow down during the recovery interval (walking is acceptable). Begin with 8–10 reps of 30 seconds each, then add reps (and later duration) as fitness allows. Your upper limit is dictated by fatigue.

▶ **Capillarization:** 1500-pace reps increase the number of capillaries around intermediate and fast-twitch muscle fibers. Longer reps (400 to 600 meters) are best.

▶ **Non-cardiovascular adaptations:** 1500-pace reps increase respiratory muscle strength (lungs). Longer 1500-pace reps improve mitochondrial density (Chapter 8) in faster fibers and increase monocarboxylate transport proteins (MCTs;

see Chapter 9) in those same fibers. To improve running economy (Chapter 11) for 1500m/mile racing, run 400-meter reps with 1:2 recovery. To increase anaerobic capacity (Chapter 10), schedule 200–400 meter reps.

1500-Meter Pace Training Table

5K Time	1500m Time	Repetition Paces				
		600m	400m	300m	200m	100m
14:00	3:49	1:32	1:00	0:46	0:31	NA
14:30	3:57	1:35	1:03	0:47	0:32	NA
15:00	4:05	1:38	1:05	0:49	0:33	NA
15:30	4:13	1:41	1:08	0:51	0:34	NA
16:00	4:21	1:45	1:10	0:52	0:35	NA
16:30	4:30	1:48	1:12	0:54	0:36	NA
17:00	4:38	1:51	1:14	0:56	0:37	NA
17:30	4:46	1:54	1:16	0:57	0:38	NA
18:00	4:54	1:58	1:18	0:59	0:39	NA
18:30	5:02	2:00	1:21	1:01	0:40	NA
19:00	5:10	2:04	1:23	1:02	0:41	NA
19:30	5:19	2:07	1:25	1:04	0:43	NA
20:00	5:27	2:11	1:27	1:05	0:44	NA
20:30	5:35	2:14	1:29	1:07	0:45	NA
21:00	5:43	2:17	1:32	1:09	0:46	NA
21:30	5:51	2:21	1:34	1:10	0:47	NA
22:00	5:59	2:24	1:36	1:12	0:48	NA
22:30	6:08	2:27	1:38	1:14	0:49	NA
23:00	6:16	2:30	1:40	1:15	0:50	NA
23:30	6:24	2:34	1:42	1:17	0:51	NA
24:00	6:32	2:37	1:45	1:18	0:52	NA
24:30	6:40	2:40	1:47	1:20	0:53	NA
25:00	6:50	2:43	1:49	1:22	0:55	NA
26:00	7:05	2:50	1:53	1:25	0:57	NA
27:00	7:21	2:57	1:58	1:28	0:59	NA
28:00	7:38	NA	2:02	1:32	1:01	0:30
29:00	7:54	NA	2:06	1:35	1:03	0:32
30:00	8:10	NA	2:11	1:38	1:05	0:33
31:00	8:27	NA	2:15	1:41	1:08	0:34
32:00	8:43	NA	2:19	1:45	1:10	0:35
33:00	8:59	NA	2:24	1:48	1:12	0:36
34:00	9:16	NA	2:28	1:51	1:14	0:37
35:00	9:32	NA	2:33	1:54	1:16	0:38
36:00	9:48	NA	2:37	1:58	1:18	0:39
37:00	10:05	NA	2:41	2:01	1:21	0:40
38:00	10:21	NA	2:46	2:04	1:23	0:41
39:00	10:37	NA	2:50	2:07	1:25	0:42
40:00	10:54	NA	2:54	2:11	1:27	0:44
41:00	11:10	NA	2:59	2:14	1:29	0:45
42:00	11:26	NA	NA	2:17	1:32	0:46

Work:Recovery (Time) = 1:1 or 1:2
The maximum recommended duration of a repetition at 1500m pace is 3:00.

3K Pace Training

3K pace training is the closest most runners come to VO$_2$ max effort. The pace table uses your 5K race pace as a starting point and then estimates your equivalent 3K pace, offering suggestions for repetitions at 200, 400, 600, 800, and 1000 meters. If you don't have a current 5K time, use the guidelines outlined on page 34. Repetitions longer than 1000 meters are not advised. 3K pace reps can improve:

► **Stroke Volume:** Like 1500-pace intervals, 3K pace intervals improve stroke volume. Run for 30 to 90 seconds to elevate your heart rate, then quickly slow down during the

recovery interval (walking is acceptable). Begin with 8–10 reps, then add reps/duration as fitness allows. The upper limit is dictated by fatigue.

▶ **Capillaries:** 3K pace reps are great for increasing the number of capillaries around intermediate fibers. Longer reps (800–1000 meters) are best.

▶ **Blood:** 3K pace reps are also great for increasing blood volume, including your red blood cell count. Again, longer reps are advised.

▶ **Non-cardiovascular adaptations:** Longer 3K pace reps are good for increasing mitochondrial density (Chapter 8) in intermediate muscle fibers. 3K pace reps improve running economy (Chapter 11) for races from 1500m to 10K.

3K Pace Training Table

5K Time	3K Time	Repetition Paces				
		1000m	800m	600m	400m	200m
14:00	8:09	2:43	2:11	1:38	1:05	0:33
14:30	8:27	2:49	2:15	1:41	1:08	0:34
15:00	8:44	2:55	2:20	1:45	1:10	0:35
15:30	9:02	3:00	2:25	1:48	1:12	0:36
16:00	9:19	3:07	2:29	1:52	1:15	0:37
16:30	9:37	3:12	2:34	1:55	1:17	0:39
17:00	9:54	3:18	2:39	1:59	1:19	0:40
17:30	10:12	3:24	2:43	2:02	1:22	0:41
18:00	10:29	3:30	2:48	2:06	1:24	0:42
18:30	10:47	3:36	2:53	2:09	1:26	0:43
19:00	11:04	3:41	2:57	2:13	1:29	0:44
19:30	11:22	3:47	3:02	2:16	1:31	0:45
20:00	11:39	3:53	3:07	2:20	1:33	0:47
20:30	11:57	3:59	3:11	2:23	1:36	0:48
21:00	12:14	NA	3:16	2:27	1:38	0:49
21:30	12:32	NA	3:20	2:30	1:40	0:50
22:00	12:49	NA	3:25	2:34	1:43	0:51
22:30	13:07	NA	3:30	2:37	1:45	0:52
23:00	13:24	NA	3:34	2:41	1:47	0:54
23:30	13:42	NA	3:39	2:44	1:50	0:55
24:00	13:59	NA	3:44	2:48	1:52	0:56
24:30	14:17	NA	3:48	2:51	1:54	0:57
25:00	14:34	NA	3:53	2:55	1:57	0:58
26:00	15:09	NA	NA	3:02	2:01	1:00
27:00	15:44	NA	NA	3:09	2:06	1:03
28:00	16:19	NA	NA	3:16	2:11	1:05
29:00	16:54	NA	NA	3:23	2:15	1:08
30:00	17:29	NA	NA	3:30	2:20	1:10
31:00	18:04	NA	NA	3:37	2:25	1:12
32:00	18:39	NA	NA	3:44	2:29	1:15
33:00	19:14	NA	NA	3:51	2:34	1:17
34:00	19:49	NA	NA	3:58	2:39	1:19
35:00	20:24	NA	NA	NA	2:43	1:22
36:00	20:59	NA	NA	NA	2:48	1:24
37:00	21:34	NA	NA	NA	2:53	1:26
38:00	22:09	NA	NA	NA	2:57	1:29
39:00	22:43	NA	NA	NA	3:02	1:31
40:00	23:18	NA	NA	NA	3:07	1:33
41:00	23:53	NA	NA	NA	3:11	1:36
42:00	24:28	NA	NA	NA	3:16	1:38

Work:Recovery (Time) = 1:1
The maximum duration of a repetition at 3K pace is 4:00.

5K Pace Training Table

5K Time	Repetition Paces				
	1600m	1000m	800m	400m	200m
14:00	4:29	2:48	2:14	1:07	0:34
14:30	4:38	2:54	2:19	1:10	0:35
15:00	4:48	3:00	2:24	1:12	0:36
15:30	4:58	3:06	2:29	1:14	0:37
16:00	5:07	3:12	2:34	1:17	0:38
16:30	5:17	3:18	2:38	1:19	0:40
17:00	NA	3:24	2:43	1:22	0:41
17:30	NA	3:30	2:48	1:24	0:42
18:00	NA	3:36	2:53	1:26	0:43
18:30	NA	3:42	2:58	1:29	0:44
19:00	NA	3:48	3:02	1:31	0:46
19:30	NA	3:54	3:07	1:34	0:47
20:00	NA	4:00	3:12	1:36	0:48
20:30	NA	4:06	3:17	1:38	0:49
21:00	NA	4:12	3:22	1:41	0:50
21:30	NA	4:18	3:26	1:43	0:52
22:00	NA	4:24	3:31	1:46	0:53
22:30	NA	4:30	3:36	1:48	0:54
23:00	NA	4:36	3:41	1:50	0:55
23:30	NA	4:42	3:46	1:53	0:56
24:00	NA	4:48	3:50	1:55	0:58
24:30	NA	4:54	3:55	1:58	0:59
25:00	NA	5:00	4:00	2:00	1:00
26:00	NA	5:12	4:10	2:05	1:02
27:00	NA	NA	4:19	2:10	1:05
28:00	NA	NA	4:29	2:14	1:07
29:00	NA	NA	4:38	2:19	1:10
30:00	NA	NA	4:48	2:24	1:12
31:00	NA	NA	4:58	2:29	1:14
32:00	NA	NA	5:07	2:34	1:17
33:00	NA	NA	5:17	2:38	1:19
34:00	NA	NA	NA	2:43	1:22
35:00	NA	NA	NA	2:48	1:24
36:00	NA	NA	NA	2:53	1:26
37:00	NA	NA	NA	2:58	1:29
38:00	NA	NA	NA	3:02	1:31
39:00	NA	NA	NA	3:07	1:34
40:00	NA	NA	NA	3:12	1:36
41:00	NA	NA	NA	3:17	1:38
42:00	NA	NA	NA	3:22	1:41

Work:Recovery (Time) = 1:1 or 1:½
The maximum duration of a repetition at 5K pace is 5:20.

5K Pace Training

5K pace training is an essential part of every competitive runner's program. The pace table uses your 5K race pace to offer 5K pace suggestions for repetitions at 200, 400, 800, 1000, and 1600 meters (1600 meters is ten yards short of a mile). If you don't have a current 5K time, use the guidelines outlined on page 34. Repetitions longer than 1600 meters/1 mile are not advised. 5K reps can improve:

▶ **Stroke Volume:** 5K pace reps are effective if shorter repetitions are used. Both 16–20 × 200 and 16–20 × 400, with recovery intervals 50–100 percent the length (in time) of the repetition, create a good stroke-volume workout.

▶ **Capillaries:** 5K pace reps increase the number of capillaries around intermediate fibers. High volume or longer reps are best.

- ▶ **Blood:** 5K pace reps increase blood volume, including your red blood cell count. Again, longer reps are advised.
- ▶ **Non-cardiovascular adaptations:** 5K pace reps increase mitochondrial volume (Chapter 8) in intermediate fibers, as well as muscle fiber contraction velocity (Chapter 11). 5K pace reps also improve running economy (Chapter 11) for races from 3Ks to half marathons.

10K Pace Training Table

5K Time	10K Time	Repetition Paces				5K Time	10K Time	Repetition Paces			
		2000m	1600m	1000m	800m			2000m	1600m	1000m	800m
14:00	29:10	5:50	4:40	2:55	2:20	23:30	48:57	NA	NA	4:54	3:55
14:30	30:12	6:02	4:50	3:01	2:25	24:00	50:00	NA	NA	5:00	4:00
15:00	31:15	6:15	5:00	3:07	2:30	24:30	51:02	NA	NA	5:06	4:05
15:30	32:17	6:27	5:10	3:14	2:35	25:00	52:05	NA	NA	5:12	4:10
16:00	33:20	6:40	5:20	3:20	2:40	26:00	54:10	NA	NA	5:25	4:20
16:30	34:22	6:52	5:30	3:26	2:45	27:00	56:15	NA	NA	5:37	4:30
17:00	35:25	7:05	5:40	3:32	2:50	28:00	58:20	NA	NA	5:50	4:40
17:30	36:27	7:17	5:50	3:39	2:55	29:00	1:00:25	NA	NA	6:02	4:50
18:00	37:30	NA	6:00	3:45	3:00	30:00	1:02:30	NA	NA	6:15	5:00
18:30	38:32	NA	6:10	3:51	3:05	31:00	1:04:35	NA	NA	6:27	5:10
19:00	39:35	NA	6:20	3:57	3:10	32:00	1:06:40	NA	NA	6:40	5:20
19:30	40:37	NA	6:30	4:04	3:15	33:00	1:08:45	NA	NA	6:52	5:30
20:00	41:40	NA	6:40	4:10	3:20	34:00	1:10:50	NA	NA	7:05	5:40
20:30	42:42	NA	6:50	4:16	3:25	35:00	1:12:55	NA	NA	NA	5:50
21:00	43:45	NA	7:00	4:22	3:30	36:00	1:15:00	NA	NA	NA	6:00
21:30	44:47	NA	7:10	4:29	3:35	37:00	1:17:05	NA	NA	NA	6:10
22:00	45:50	NA	NA	4:35	3:40	38:00	1:19:10	NA	NA	Na	6:20
22:30	46:52	NA	NA	4:41	3:45	39:00	1:21:15	NA	NA	NA	6:30
23:00	47:55	NA	NA	4:47	3:50	40:00	1:23:20	NA	NA	NA	6:40
						41:00	1:25:25	NA	NA	NA	6:50
						42:00	1:27:30	NA	NA	NA	7:00

Work:Recovery (Time) = 1:½
*The maximum duration of a repetition at 10K pace is 7:07.

10K Pace Training

10K pace training is a less-intense alternative to 5K pace training. The pace table uses your 5K race pace as a starting point and then estimates your equivalent 10K pace (or just look for your 10K pace); it offers 10K pace suggestions for repetitions at 400, 800, 1000, and 1600 meters (1600 meters is ten yards short of a mile). If you don't have a current 5K time, use the guidelines outlined on page 34. Repetitions longer than 2000 meters (not shown in table) are not advised. 10K pace reps can improve:

- ▶ **Capillaries:** 10K pace reps build capillaries in intermediate and slow-twitch fibers. High volume or longer reps are best.
- ▶ **Blood:** 10K pace reps stimulate blood volume increase, including your red blood cell count.
- ▶ **Stroke Volume:** 10K pace reps are a lower-intensity alternative for building stroke volume, although not as effective as reps at 1500m–5K pace.
- ▶ **Non-cardiovascular adaptations:** 10K pace reps increase mitochondrial numbers (Chapter 8) in slow-twitch fibers (and, to a lesser extent, in intermediate fibers), MCTs in intermediate fibers (Chapter 9), and muscle fiber contraction velocity (Chapter 11). 10K pace reps also improve running economy (Chapter 11) for races from 5Ks to half marathons.

Cruise Interval Training

Cruise intervals can be viewed as a less intense version of 10K pace reps or a slightly more intense version of tempo. The pace table uses your 5K race pace as a starting point and then estimates cruise interval paces for repetitions at 400, 800, 1000, 1200, and 1600 meters. If you don't have a current 5K time, use the guidelines outlined on page 34. Repetitions longer than 8 minutes are not advised. Cruise intervals can improve:

- ▶ **Capillaries:** Cruise intervals increase the number of capillaries around slow-twitch and intermediate muscle fibers.
- ▶ **Blood:** These intervals are good for increasing blood volume, including red blood cell count.
- ▶ **Non-cardiovascular adaptations:** Cruise intervals increase mitochondrial volume in slow-twitch muscle fibers (Chapter 8) and MCTs in intermediate and slow-twitch fibers (Chapter 9). They often serve as the "slower" interval portion of blend intervals (Chapter 8 photo instruction).

Cruise Interval Training Table

5K Time	Repetition Paces				
	2000m	1600m	1200m	1000m	800m
14:00	6:07	4:54	3:40	3:04	2:27
14:30	6:20	5:04	3:48	3:10	2:32
15:00	6:32	5:13	3:55	3:16	2:37
15:30	6:44	5:23	4:02	3:22	2:42
16:00	6:56	5:33	4:10	3:28	2:47
16:30	7:09	5:43	4:17	3:34	2:51
17:00	7:21	5:53	4:25	3:40	2:56
17:30	7:33	6:02	4:32	3:47	3:01
18:00	7:45	6:12	4:39	3:53	3:06
18:30	7:57	6:22	4:46	3:59	3:11
19:00	8:09	6:32	4:54	4:05	3:16
19:30	8:22	6:41	5:00	4:11	3:21
20:00	8:34	6:51	5:08	4:17	3:25
20:30	8:46	7:00	5:15	4:23	3:30
21:00	8:58	7:10	5:23	4:29	3:35
21:30	9:10	7:20	5:30	4:35	3:40
22:00	9:22	7:29	5:37	4:41	3:45
22:30	9:34	7:39	5:44	4:47	3:50
23:00	9:46	7:49	5:51	4:53	3:54
23:30	9:58	7:58	5:59	4:59	3:59
24:00	10:10	8:08	6:06	5:05	4:04
24:30	10:22	8:17	6:13	5:11	4:09
25:00	10:34	8:27	6:20	5:17	4:13
26:00	10:57	8:46	6:34	5:29	4:23
27:00	11:21	9:05	6:49	5:41	4:32
28:00	11:45	9:24	7:03	5:52	4:42
29:00	12:08	9:43	7:17	6:04	4:51
30:00	12:32	10:01	7:31	6:16	5:00
31:00	12:55	10:20	7:45	6:28	5:10
32:00	13:19	10:39	7:59	6:39	5:20
33:00	13:42	10:58	8:13	6:51	5:29
34:00	14:06	11:16	8:27	7:03	5:38
35:00	14:29	11:35	8:41	7:14	5:48
36:00	14:52	11:54	8:55	7:26	5:57
37:00	15:15	12:12	9:09	7:38	6:06
38:00	15:39	12:31	9:23	7:49	6:15
39:00	16:02	12:49	9:37	8:00	6:25
40:00	16:25	13:08	9:51	8:12	6:34
41:00	16:48	13:26	10:05	8:24	6:43
42:00	17:11	13:45	10:19	8:35	6:52

Work:Recovery (Time) = 1:½

Find your 5K time in the left column. Then use repetition paces in the corresponding row to the right.

Tempo Training

Tempo runs are completed at an effort level that über-coach Jack Daniels defines as "comfortably hard." The tempo-training table offers tempo runs at two different paces: "fast" and "slow." The faster pace is roughly equivalent to half marathon pace; runs at this pace should last 15–25 minutes. The slower pace is roughly equivalent to marathon pace; runs at this pace should last 20–40 minutes (up to 60 minutes when prepping for a marathon). You can also break tempo efforts into tempo intervals (e.g., 2 × 10 minutes, or 3 × 10 minutes, with 3–4-minute jog recovery intervals). The table bases your tempo paces on your 5K race time. If you don't have a current 5K time, then choose a pace that, if pressed, you could maintain for an hour (e.g., you run 15 minutes at tempo for your workout, but you believe you could maintain that pace for an hour in a race). Tempo can improve:

▶ **Capillaries:** Tempo is the best workout for increasing the number of capillaries around slow-twitch muscle fibers, and it also increases capillarization around intermediate fibers.

BUILD YOUR RUNNING BODY—COMPONENTS AND WORKOUTS

Tempo Training Table

5K Time	Fast Tempo		Slow Tempo	
	Mile	1K	Mile	1K
14:00	5:01	3:07	5:19	3:18
14:30	5:11	3:13	5:29	3:24
15:00	5:21	3:20	5:40	3:31
15:30	5:31	3:26	5:50	3:37
16:00	5:41	3:32	6:00	3:44
16:30	5:51	3:38	6:11	3:50
17:00	6:00	3:44	6:21	3:57
17:30	6:11	3:50	6:31	4:03
18:00	6:21	3:56	6:42	4:10
18:30	6:30	4:03	6:52	4:16
19:00	6:40	4:09	7:02	4:22
19:30	6:50	4:15	7:12	4:29
20:00	6:59	4:21	7:23	4:35
20:30	7:09	4:27	7:33	4:41
21:00	7:19	4:33	7:43	4:48
21:30	7:28	4:39	7:53	4:54
22:00	7:38	4:45	8:03	5:00
22:30	7:48	4:51	8:13	5:06
23:00	7:57	4:57	8:23	5:13
23:30	8:07	5:03	8:33	5:19
24:00	8:16	5:08	8:43	5:25
24:30	8:26	5:14	8:53	5:31
25:00	8:35	5:20	9:03	5:37
26:00	8:54	5:32	9:23	5:50
27:00	9:13	5:44	9:42	6:02
28:00	9:32	5:55	10:02	6:14
29:00	9:51	6:07	10:22	6:26
30:00	10:09	6:19	10:41	6:38
31:00	10:28	6:30	11:00	6:50
32:00	10:46	6:42	11:20	7:02
33:00	11:05	6:53	11:39	7:14
34:00	11:23	7:05	11:58	7:26
35:00	11:42	7:16	12:17	7:38
36:00	12:00	7:27	12:36	7:50
37:00	12:18	7:39	12:55	8:01
38:00	12:36	7:50	13:13	8:13
39:00	12:54	8:01	13:32	8:25
40:00	13:12	8:12	13:51	8:36
41:00	13:30	8:23	14:09	8:48
42:00	13:48	8:35	14:28	8:59

Find your 5K time in the left column. Then use the tempo paces in the corresponding row to the right.

▶ **Blood:** Tempo increases blood volume, including RBC count.

▶ **Non-cardiovascular adaptations:** Tempo increases the volume of mitochondria, MCTs (Chapter 9), and aerobic enzymes (Chapter 10) in slow-twitch and intermediate fibers. It also increases the contraction velocity of slow-twitch fibers and improves running economy (Chapter 11) for distances between a 10K and a marathon.

Long Run Pace Table

5K Time	Pace per Mile	Pace per Kilometer
14:00	6:26–7:29	4:00–4:39
14:30	6:39–7:43	4:08 –4:48
15:00	6:51–7:58	4:16–4:57
15:30	7:04–8:12	4:23–5:05
16:00	7:16–8:26	4:31–5:14
16:30	7:28–8:40	4:39–5:23
17:00	7:41–8:53	4:46–5:31
17:30	7:53–9:07	4:54–5:40
18:00	8:05–9:21	5:01–5:49
18:30	8:17–9:34	5:09–5:57
19:00	8:29–9:48	5:16–6:05
19:30	8:41–10:02	5:24–6:14
20:00	8:53–10:15	5:31–6:22
20:30	9:05–10:28	5:38–6:30
21:00	9:16–10:42	5:46–6:39
21:30	9:28–10:55	5:53–6:47
22:00	9:40–11:08	6:00–6:55
22:30	9:52–11:21	6:08–7:03
23:00	10:03–11:34	6:15–7:11

23:30	10:15–11:47	6:22–7:19
24:00	10:27–12:00	6:29–7:27
24:30	10:38–12:13	6:36–7:35
25:00	10:50–12:25	6:44–7:43
26:00	11:12–12:51	6:58–7:59
27:00	11:35–13:16	7:12–8:15
28:00	11:58–13:41	7:26–8:30
29:00	12:20–14:05	7:40–8:45
30:00	12:42–14:30	7:54–9:00
31:00	13:04–14:54	8:07–9:16
32:00	13:26–15:18	8:21–9:31
33:00	13:48–15:42	8:34–9:45
34:00	14:09–16:06	8:48–10:00
35:00	14:31–16:29	9:01–10:15
36:00	14:52–16:52	9:14–10:29
37:00	15:14–17:15	9:28–10:43
38:00	15:35–17:38	9:41–10:58
39:00	15:56–18:00	9:54–11:12
40:00	16:16–18:23	10:07–11:26
41:00	16:37–18:46	10:20–11:40
42:00	16:58–19:08	10:32–11:53

Find your 5K time in the left column. Then use the long run paces in the corresponding row to the right.

The Long Run

The long run is a staple in every distance runner's diet. Run once or twice a week—or sometimes once every other week—a long run can account for 20–25 percent of a week's training volume and can be longer than regular distance runs by 50 percent or more. Use the "Long Run Pace Table" to determine pace, based on your current 5K race pace. If you don't have a current 5K time, then stick to a conversational pace. All runners should let feedback from their bodies be the final guide; long runs should remain comfortable (i.e., they aren't endurance competitions). The long run has multiple benefits, including improvements to:

▶ **Capillaries:** The long run builds capillaries around slow-twitch muscle fibers. Also, the duration of the workout ensures that most available slow-twitch fibers will be recruited at some point—meaning comprehensive capillary building.

► **Non-cardiovascular adaptations:** Long runs increase mitochondrial volume in slow-twitch fibers (Chapter 8) and MCTs for transporting lactate (Chapter 9). They also improve nervous system recruitment patterns (Chapter 11) and strengthen connective tissue, allowing you to absorb the impact of higher mileage and longer races. By significantly increasing the efficiency of your stride, the long run improves running economy for all paces.

Hill Repeats

Hill repeats build a combination of strength, power, and endurance that can't be replicated by any other training. Find a hill that is challenging but not so steep that you can't maintain a good stride. Rather than timing each repetition, many runners time the first rep and then mark the spot where that rep ends; on subsequent reps, runners refrain from measuring time and use the mark as a finish line. Proper effort is equivalent to 1500m–3K race effort (not pace, as running uphill slows your pace an indeterminate amount—as hill steepness, terrain, and other factors will vary—making it impossible and counterproductive to target actual pace). Use the "rule of repetitions" for this workout: Always finish knowing you could have run one or possibly two more reps if required. No more than once a week (2–3 times a month) is enough for this workout. Hill reps can improve:

► **Stroke Volume:** Short hill repeats (30–45 seconds) are great for building stroke volume—stop at the end of the rep, walk for 10–15 seconds, then jog down to the start.
► **Capillaries:** Longer hill repeats (90–120 seconds) are an excellent way to increase capillarization around intermediate fibers and fast-twitch fibers.
► **Non-cardiovascular adaptations:** Longer hill repeats (90–120 seconds) increase your volume of intermediate fiber mitochondria (Chapter 8), improve muscular strength (Chapter 5), and help rewire your nervous system (Chapter 11) for more powerful and efficient messaging.

Hill Repeats

Rep Length (seconds)	Rep Volume (number)	Recovery (minutes)
30	10–15	1–1.5
45	8–12	1.5–2
60	6–8	2–3
90	4–6	4–5
120	4–6	4–5

Correct effort level for hill reps is equivalent to 1500m–3K effort. Always finish a workout with 1–2 reps left in you.

5K Road and Trail Reps

Off-track 5K effort repetitions are a good alternative for runners looking to improve fitness without having to focus on pace or distance covered for each rep. These reps are run by minutes, not distance, at an effort that approximates the feel of 5K race effort. If you aren't sure what 5K effort feels like, use the guidelines outlined on page 34. Recovery is an easy jog, nothing harder. For runners who prefer to do preseason training—or *all* their training—off-track, this 10-week progression is for you. 5K Road and Trail Reps build:

▶ **Everything that 5K and 10K reps build:** See previous entries for 5K and 10K pace intervals for the full list of benefits.

▶ **Non-quantifiable adaptation:** Running repetitions based upon effort and time trains you to read feedback from your body. On the track, runners often ignore feedback in their determination to hit goal times, which can lead to overtraining syndrome. Road and trail reps put you in touch with your body, and runners often end up better racers for the experience.

5K Effort Road and Trail Repetitions

Progression (weeks)	Rep Length (minutes)	Rep Volume (number)	Recovery (minutes)	Max Stimulus (minutes)
1	1	6–8	2	0
2	2	8	3	0
3	3	6	3	6
4	4	4	3–4	8
5	4	5	3–4	10
6	5	4	3–4	12
7	Substitute 20–30 minutes of Tempo for reps during Week 7.	NA	NA	NA
8	3	8	3	8
9	4	6	3–4	12
10	*Mix: Tempo & 5K Reps	Variable	3–4	NA

*For mix workouts, you should alternate tempo reps and 5K effort reps with recovery periods (jogging). An example of a mix workout (by minutes per rep/pace) would be: 3/5K, Recovery, 5/5K, Recovery, 7/Tempo, Recovery, 3/5K, Recovery, 5/5K, Recovery, 8/Tempo.

Respiration Trainer

Respiratory training targets the muscles involved in inhalation and exhalation (e.g., diaphragm, external and internal intercostals, abdominals). Stronger respiratory muscles lower both psychological stress and energy consumption. The PowerLung trainer used by Grace (as pictured) comes in four different resistance levels (color-coded) and can be incorporated into running workouts or used in separate training sessions. Some rules for use:

1. Whatever your model, set both inhalation and exhalation control dials to "1."
2. Place the mouthpiece in your mouth with the lip guard outside your lips.
3. Breathe in, filling your lungs completely in about three seconds.
4. Pause for two seconds, then breathe out, using your abdominals to push out all the air in your lungs in about three seconds.
5. If you need to increase resistance (because the exercise has become too easy), turn the inhalation or exhalation control dials (or both) to the right until your find the correct resistance.
6. Begin with a few repetitions, then work up to 10.

Build Your Running Powerhouses

Your heart may be the engine that drives endurance training, but there are microscopic structures called *mitochondria* that provide the power. Floating within the gel-like universe that constitutes the interior of your muscle fibers, these structures are a few micrometers long (just barely big enough to be seen with a light microscope), yet they produce all of your aerobic energy. Known as the *powerhouses of the cell*, mitochondria are the reason you can run long distances—or stroll to the corner store—and increasing their number and size will plug you into a power grid that makes the energy source you've been using look like a pair of AAA batteries. Something else about these tiny powerhouses: They're not entirely human. As you'll see, their ancestors were bacterial invaders that took up residence more than a billion years ago.

WHAT'S THE POWERHOUSE?

The "powerhouse of the cell" is what we call a mitochondrion. That's because mitochondria provide about 90 percent of the energy needed by your body every day. Mitochondria-produced energy is known as *aerobic energy*—meaning it can't be created without using oxygen. So if you were wondering where all that oxygen goes once your cardiovascular system delivers it to your muscles, now you know: It goes to your mitochondria. (We'll take an in-depth look at your energy systems in Chapter 10.)

Think of mitochondria as busy industrial factories—a whole lot of factories, since there are anywhere from hundreds to thousands within every fiber—floating within your muscle fibers. These factories never shut down, producing energy around the clock. Now imagine building new factories, bigger and better factories. What if you had 50 percent more factories? What if you had twice that? Imagine the energy you could produce then! Well, you can stop imagining, because building more mitochondria is what you're going to do in this chapter.

POWERHOUSE TRAINING

Training mitochondria is a lot like training capillaries (Chapter 7). That's because mitochondria and capillaries develop at the same rate, often from the same stimulus. This makes sense when you think about it: Capillaries increase in number to deliver more oxygen; mitochondria increase in number and size in order to process this larger supply of oxygen.

Training for mitochondria includes:

▶ **High-intensity interval training**
▶ **800m pace repetitions**
▶ **5K/10K trail and track repetitions**
▶ **Tempo**
▶ **Alternation/Blend Intervals**
▶ **Mileage (long-term volume)**
▶ **The long run**

Training your mitochondria not only increases your ability to produce aerobic energy, it also represents the final piece of the puzzle for the most revered measurement in running: VO_2 *max*.

MITOCHONDRIA

Mitochondria are prized by runners because they produce all our aerobic energy. Of course, they have other functions, too. For instance, they help

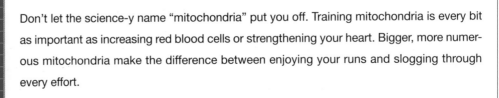

BEGINNER'S GUIDELINE

Don't let the science-y name "mitochondria" put you off. Training mitochondria is every bit as important as increasing red blood cells or strengthening your heart. Bigger, more numerous mitochondria make the difference between enjoying your runs and slogging through every effort.

TRAINING DISCUSSION

"Hitting the Mother Lode"

Don't get creeped out, but your mitochondria aren't even human—or, at least, they didn't start out that way. According to the *endosymbiotic theory*, your mitochondria are the result of an ancient bacterial invasion. More than a billion years ago, our young earth was buried in mounds of bacteria only just learning to breathe oxygen. Some of these bacteria (ancestors to our modern-day mitochondria) invaded or were eaten by larger cells—and lived to tell about it. In fact, the bacteria soon struck up a deal with their new hosts: "Allow us permanent residence, and we'll use our oxygen-breathing abilities to provide you with energy like you never dreamed possible!" A friendly handshake and eons of evolution later, mitochondria can no longer survive outside host cells.

Dr. Lynn Margulis and her son, science writer Dorion Sagan, proponents of the endosymbiotic theory, put it this way: "Life did not take over the globe by combat, but by networking."

Mitochondria are still about the size of bacteria. And unlike other *organelles* (tiny parts of cells, analogous to organs in the human body), they have their own DNA. This "mtDNA" allows mitochondria to produce their own enzymes and proteins. Still, they couldn't survive without fuel and oxygen provided by their host cells. For human distance runners, this tit for tat is a bargain that's paid big dividends; without aerobic energy, a marathon might as well be a race to the moon.

If you're queasy about playing host to evolved bacteria, don't blame this book. Blame your mother. Most experts believe mitochondrial DNA is inherited from your mother. That's because a mother's egg contains mitochondria that survive in offspring (that's you), while paternal sperm's relatively few mitochondria are marked for destruction as soon as sperm finish their long swim. So mom gets the credit—or blame—for your 5K and 10K PRs.

regulate cell death, supply enzymes to make hemoglobin, and detoxify ammonia in liver cells. But none of that matters when we runners toe the line for a 5K or marathon. At that point, it's all about the energy.

In Chapter 7, we discussed why the cardiovascular system is considered an oxygen transport system. Now, it's time to talk about the *oxygen uptake system*. This term refers to the process of extracting oxygen from capillaries, bringing it into your muscle fibers, and then using it to make aerobic energy. The stars of this system are

mitochondria, which import that oxygen and use it as one of the main ingredients when creating adenosine triphosphate (*ATP*), the energy that powers your muscles. The more mitochondria you have, the greater your oxygen uptake. Taken together, increased oxygen transport plus greater oxygen uptake increases a measurement known as your VO_2 max.

As you learned in Chapter 4, your VO_2 max is the maximum amount of oxygen you can "consume" in a minute. In other words, it's the total amount of oxygen transported by your cardiovascular system

TRAINING DISCUSSION

"What is VO_2 max?"

As runners, we hear a lot about VO_2 max. It's a favorite term of exercise physiologists, coaches, and running jargon-junkies. But what does it mean?

First, let's look at the term itself. "V" stands for "volume." "O_2" stands for "oxygen." And "max" stands for "maximum." Put together and given context, VO_2 max refers to the maximum volume (amount) of oxygen your body can consume in a minute.

At rest, you don't use anywhere near your VO_2 max. That's because your aerobic energy demands are low. But as you begin exercising, your energy requirements increase. Your cardiovascular system transports more oxygen-rich blood to your capillaries, your muscle fibers extract more oxygen, and your mitochondria use that oxygen to create a greater supply of aerobic energy. But this process has an upper limit. Only so much oxygen can be transported, and only so much of the transported oxygen can be used to create energy. When your body reaches that limit, you've reached your VO_2 max.

Most runners, depending on their fitness levels, reach their VO_2 max at the fastest effort they can sustain for five to seven laps on a track (2000 to 2800 meters). This means that any pace faster than VO_2 max (e.g., 800 meters or a mile) will require more energy than you can produce aerobically. You'll require an increased percentage of energy from anaerobic sources. On the other hand, any pace slower than VO_2 max (e.g., a 10K or marathon) can be fueled almost entirely from aerobic energy. In fact, marathons are 99 percent aerobic! VO_2 max is measured in two ways:

▶ **Consumption based on body weight:** Oxygen is measured in milliliters per kilogram per minute (mL/kg/min), with a kilogram equal to roughly 2.2 pounds. Three-time Tour de France winner Greg LeMond had a VO_2 max of 92.5 mL/kg/min. An untrained male would have a VO_2 max of about 40–45 mL/kg/min.

▶ **Absolute rate of consumption:** This is the total volume of oxygen consumed per minute. British rower Sir Matthew Pinsent, who won four consecutive Olympic gold medals, recorded a VO_2 max of 7.5 liters per minute—more than any cyclist, runner, or cross country skier in history—even as his VO_2 max based on body weight was a meager 68 mL/kg/min. At more than 240 pounds, Pinsent needed that level of overall oxygen consumption to compete in endurance rowing. An average untrained male would consume around 3 liters per minute.

Training typically improves VO_2 max in previously untrained runners by about 20–25 percent, although the actual range can vary from negative improvements to well over 50 percent. In highly trained runners, VO_2 max doesn't change much with training—it's already established. As an actual predictor of performance, VO_2 max takes a backseat to other factors (e.g., running economy), but it remains a valuable determinant of running potential.

that is subsequently absorbed by your cells. At rest, only 20–30 percent of the oxygen you breathe is absorbed. As you exercise, a far greater percentage of oxygen is extracted from your blood, until finally you reach the point where your mitochondria are producing aerobic energy at 100 percent capacity, meaning they can't process more oxygen. At that point, you've reached your VO_2 max. See the sidebar, "What is VO_2 max?" for a more in-depth look at VO_2 max.

MAXIMUM MITOCHONDRIA

Different muscle fiber types contain different volumes of mitochondria. Slow-twitch fibers boast the highest volume, while fast-twitch fibers have the lowest. But these numbers aren't written in stone. Just as the OSI (the fictional Office of Scientific Intelligence) rebuilt Steve Austin in *The Six Million Dollar Man* to be better, stronger, and faster than he was before, you can rebuild your mitochondria to be bigger, more powerful, and more plentiful than they were pre-training. There are two ways to increase mitochondrial volume:

▶ **Replication:** Mitochondria can split to form more mitochondria.
▶ **Size increase:** An individual mitochondrion can get bigger.

When your muscle fibers gain more mitochondria, it's like a community gaining extra power plants—it eases the burden on existing power plants and increases potential output. Ditto for bigger mitochondria, which can produce more energy.

You can build mitochondria quickly with proper training. In a 2008 paper on *mitochondrial biogenesis* (increase in mitochondrial volume),

Dr. John O. Holloszy writes that "studies have shown that a single bout of exercise induces a rapid increase in mitochondrial biogenesis." And Dr. David Costill (a giant in exercise physiology) and Dr. Scott Trappe write in their 2002 book *Running: The Athlete Within*, "Research has shown a progressive weekly increase of approximately 5% in the number of muscle mitochondria over a 27 week period of endurance training. At the same time, the average size of the mitochondria increased from 11.5 to 15.5 microns$^2 \times 10^{-2}$, a 35% increase in size."

Of course, improving your own mitochondrial volume will depend on several factors, including genetics, your current fitness, your training volume, and your training intensity. Predicting exactly when adaptations will occur is an inexact science. That said, Dr. Ronald L. Terjung, an exercise science researcher, has written that "muscle mitochondrial content appears to reach a steady-state after approximately 4-5 wk [sic] of training." Using Terjung and others' analysis of mitochondrial adaptations to training, Table 8.1 estimates the rate at which you can expect full adaptation to occur.

You should expect to experience four stages of mitochondrial adaptation:

Table 8.1
Mitochondrial Gains

Week Number	Mitochondrial Adaptation
1	44%
2	63%
3	77%
4	89%
5	100%

TABLE 8.1 details the length of time it takes for mitochondria to reach 100 percent adaptation in response to a sustained training stress (workout) like those outlined in this book.

1. **First Stimulus:** Within three hours of completing a workout that is sufficient in intensity and/or duration, mitochondrial adaptive activity kicks into overdrive.

2. **Half-time:** By the end of week one, mitochondrial adaptation reaches 40–50 percent.

3. **Aerobic boost:** Between days ten and thirteen, your adaptation passes the 50 percent threshold, and you experience a boost in energy production. Running gets easier!

4. **Full adaptation:** By the end of week five, your mitochondria reach full (or near-full) adaptation to the training stimulus.

To the above list, we need to attach a few stipulations:

▶ **Reinforcement:** During the adaptation period, you must reinforce the original training stimulus with equivalent workouts (e.g., weekly tempo, repetition, or high-volume sessions). You can't run a single workout and then sit on the couch, waiting for your mitochondria to bloom.

▶ **Staggered adaptation:** Not all mitochondria adapt at the same time. They can adapt singly or in groups, and while some are adapting, others continue to function normally.

▶ **Increased training stimulus:** If you increase the intensity or volume of the original training stimulus, you can trigger greater adaptation in your mitochondria.

The one drawback to mitochondrial adaptation is this: When mitochondria first begin adapting, they can't contribute to aerobic energy production. Dr. Bob Treffene, a PhD in bioenergetics and swim coach to Olympic multi–gold medalists Ian Thorpe,

Kieren Perkins, and Rebecca Adlington, has suggested that this phase lasts from ten to thirteen days and creates an "oxygen utilization problem." Since mitochondria often adapt in groups, a sizeable percentage of your mitochondria might go offline following a hard training stimulus. As a result, you can expect to feel sluggish doing workouts that were easy the previous week.

Don't panic. This is normal. In fact, it's good news. You've triggered an adaptation that will lead to improved performance within two weeks.

At the same time, be aware that training too hard in the weeks preceding a big race runs the risk of initiating mitochondrial adaptation. It's a good idea to forgo overly hard workouts during this period. This doesn't mean you should jog or do nothing. If you fail to reinforce your mitochondrial gains with further workouts, you'll lose about half of those gains in one week. Instead, include a long run, some 10K pace reps, or a little tempo while tapering.

High-Intensity Interval Training

In recent years, there's been a lot of chatter about high-intensity interval training (*HIIT*) serving as a shortcut to the demanding endurance programs traditionally favored by runners. Proponents claim the same type of mitochondrial gains from HIIT that have heretofore required tempo runs, long repetitions, and high mileage. Given the time constraints faced by many runners, programs that promise all the benefits in a third of the training time are going to generate some buzz.

So what, exactly, is HIIT? According to a 2012 paper by Martin J. Gibala, et al., of McMaster University in Ontario, Canada, "High-intensity interval training (HIIT) describes physical exercise that is characterized by brief, intermittent bursts of vigorous activity, interspersed by periods of rest or low-intensity exercise."

That sounds a whole lot like regular interval training, which runners have been using to achieve increases in stroke volume, capillarization, oxygen uptake, mitochondrial density, and anaerobic buffering (explained in the following chapter) since Gerschler and Reindell made it *de rigueur* way back in the late 1930s.

So most of HIIT is BTDT (been there, done that) for longtime runners.

On the other hand, what's new are studies that claim significant adaptations from super-short, ultra-speedy repetitions. How short? Try a half-dozen repetitions of thirty seconds each at maximum speed, with rest intervals of up to four minutes.

The recent obsession with HIIT got a big boost from CrossFit and other fitness programs' endorsement of "*Tabata intervals*"—twenty-second repetitions followed by rest intervals of only ten seconds, based on a 1996 study by exercise physiologist Izumi Tabata. The study compared two small groups who trained on a bicycle ergometer. One group trained only moderate-intensity endurance, while the other group did Tabata intervals. The study concluded that only the second group achieved improvements in *anaerobic capacity* (the amount of energy that can be produced anaerobically, which we'll discuss in Chapter 10), while both groups improved VO_2 max. The obvious flaw in this study is that moderate-intensity endurance training (the only kind performed by the non–Tabata interval group) has very little effect upon anaerobic capacity—*and no serious runner would train that way*. For comparing anaerobic capacity, you might as well pit Tabata's interval group against one that did nothing but eat pizza. And there's also this: Coaches and athletes have decades of real-world experience with high-intensity/short-recovery intervals, and the result is almost always short-term gain followed by

long-term burnout. That's because the training adaptations produced by Tabata-type intervals max out after 4–6 weeks (as you'll see in Chapter 9), damage mitochondrial enzymes (Chapter 10), and cause central nervous system (CNS) fatigue (Chapter 11). So while runners who do nothing more than moderate-paced distance will benefit from a few sessions of Tabata intervals, those who already include a variety of aerobic and anaerobic work in their programs would do well to steer clear.

Experiments that more closely compared HIIT with the well-rounded training practices of experienced runners were conducted by Martin Gibala and his group at McMaster. Gibala documented increases in mitochondrial adaptive activity from sessions of 7×30 seconds *all out*, separated by four minutes of recovery, that equaled or bested those of his control group (non HIIT athletes). Unlike Tabata, however, Gibala had his control group train at the equivalent of a fast tempo effort, which is proven to increase slow-twitch mitochondrial volume. So Gibala was able to show at least a short-term equivalency between HIIT and more time-intensive tempo training when it comes to building your mitochondrial powerhouses. Keep in mind, however, that these experiments were conducted on a bicycle ergometer. And biking isn't running. Runners deal with a whole host of variables that aren't replicated in biking. Runners change their stride to increase speed or intensity. They absorb increased impact forces with faster paces. There are differences in upper body motion, nervous system activity (including proprioception), elastic recoil, etc. In other words, what works in the lab for a bicycle ergometer won't necessarily translate to running.

Bottom line: Athletes looking for long-term performance improvements are better off sticking with traditional training concepts, while athletes pressed for time might find HIIT to be an effective *temporary* shortcut to improved fitness.

Training recommendation

Mitochondria in different muscle fiber types demand different training. For slow-twitch mitochondria, long-term Mileage is the answer (see page 150); think of the Colorado River carving out the Grand Canyon over eons. Long Runs (Chapter 7, see page 132) and Tempo workouts (Chapter 7, see page 130) also stimulate slow-twitch mitochondrial adaptations. For intermediate fibers, 2–5 minute reps at 5K/10K pace will do the trick (Chapter 7, see pages 127–129 and 134 for 5K, 10K, and 5K Effort Road and Trail Reps); fit runners can add long Hill Repeats (Chapter 7, see page 133). Fast-twitch mitochondria benefit from reps at 800-meter pace (see page 147), with reps as short as 100 meters and no longer than 60 seconds (and with rest periods equivalent to 2–4 times the duration of the repetition). Finally, for runners in a time crunch, HIIT can theoretically provide benefits for all three fiber types. Both all-out and 400m pace reps can be used for HIIT workouts (see pages 145–147 for HIIT and 400m pace intervals).

TRAINING RUNDOWN

Building your powerhouses (mitochondria) involves much of the same training that we used for improving capillaries, with the addition of faster repeats to stimulate mitochondrial gains in fast-twitch fiber. Important training in this chapter's photo instruction includes:

▶ **HIIT (High-Intensity Interval Training)**
▶ **400/800m Pace Intervals**
▶ **Alternation/Blend Intervals**
▶ **Mileage**

Training from other chapters that affects mitochondrial improvements includes:

▶ **5K/10K Training (Chapter 7)**
▶ **5K Effort Road and Trail Repetitions (Chapter 7)**
▶ **Tempo (Chapter 7)**
▶ **The Long Run (Chapter 7)**

To see exactly how these workouts can be incorporated into your overall training program, skip directly to Chapter 15: Build Your Training Schedule, where sample schedules are available for runners of all fitness levels and abilities.

PHOTO INSTRUCTION

RUNNING WORKOUTS

While much of the training for building your running powerhouses was covered in Chapter 7 (5K/10K pace training, long hill repeats, and tempo for intermediate muscle fiber mitochondria; long runs, 10K pace reps, tempo, and cruise intervals for slow-twitch mitochondria), we still have a few workouts up our sleeves—especially when it comes to fast-twitch mitochondria. However, remember that too much speed work can damage aerobic enzymes, overstress your nervous system, and lead to overtraining syndrome. Sean Brosnan illustrates five more ways to build mitochondria, the powerhouses of your cells.

HIIT (High-Intensity Interval Training)

Numerous variations of HIIT exist. Some champion all-out efforts of 30 seconds or less (see 400-Meter-Pace Training for estimations of pace) followed by extended rest. Others, like the Tabata Intervals, call for a 2:1 work-rest ratio. Less demanding variations utilize 30–60-second efforts at or below 100 percent of VO_2 max, followed by an approximately equal duration of rest. Recovery varies between complete rest and medium-intensity running (i.e., about 50 percent HIIT effort). Most runners will want to avoid extreme versions of HIIT, such as the Tabata and Wingate regimens. Runners with limited training time might include Gibala workouts. The Billat 30–30 session can produce big gains in VO_2 max, but it should be performed sparingly due to its intensity. The HIIT table for this workout lists six different HIIT routines, including:

▶ **Tabata:** Popular with CrossFit and fitness clubs, Tabata is derived from a study involving a handful of participants tested on a bicycle ergometer. While gains were achieved in mitochondrial volume, running variables such as impact force, fiber-specific development, aerobic enzyme effect, long-term viability, and nervous system fatigue make this routine a bad fit for runners.

▶ **Wingate:** Based on the Wingate Test, created in the 1970s to measure peak anaerobic power and anaerobic capacity, this HIIT variation builds both aerobic and anaerobic fitness. The downside is its long-term negative impact on the CNS and aerobic enzymes (not to mention that using it burns adaptive energy that could be used for more productive training approaches).

▶ **Gibala (two workouts):** If you think these two HIIT variations look a lot like a traditional miler's 300–400-meter workout … you're correct.

- **Timmons:** Interestingly, this method approximates the carbo-loading strategy championed by the University of Western Australia in 2002 (Chapter 10).
- **Billat:** The goal of Billat's 30–30 workout is to spend maximum time at VO_2 max. Since you remain at 100 percent of VO_2 max for the first 15–20 seconds of the recovery interval, this workout offers 45–50 seconds of VO_2 max work for every minute completed. When you can no longer continue at 100 percent of VO_2 max, the workout is over.

HIIT (High-Intensity Interval Training)

Type of HIIT	Rep Length (time)	Rep Volume (number of reps)	Recovery (time)	Weekly Sessions	Effort Level
Tabata	20 seconds	8	10 seconds	5	100%
Wingate	30 seconds	4–6	4 minutes	3–4	100%
Gibala (var. 1)	60 seconds	8–12	75 seconds	3	5K Effort
Gibala (var. 2)	60 seconds	10	60 seconds		90% max heart rate
Timmons	20 seconds	3	2 minutes easy running	3	100%
Billat	30 seconds	Until failure*	30 seconds at 50% VO_2 max	1	100% VO_2 max

* "Until failure" requires you to run until exhaustion forces you to discontinue the workout.

400-Meter-Pace Training

400-meter-pace workouts won't be a part of most distance runners' training programs, while most sprinters (100m to 800m) will incorporate reps up to 150m into their regimens. For runners who'd like to try Tabata, Wingate, or Timmons HIIT routines, 400-meter-pace reps will approximate the 100 percent effort required. (Although 400-meter-pace reps are not technically a 100 percent effort, running any faster risks injury for non-sprint-trained runners.) 400-meter-pace reps can improve:

- **Mitochondrial volume:** Reps of 50–100 meters produce increases in mitochondrial volume, especially in faster fibers.
- **Non-powerhouse adaptations:** Four to six weeks of training at 400-meter pace will increase buffers against acidosis (Chapter 9). 400-meter pace also helps muscle spindles (Chapter 5) adapt to longer, more forceful strides.

400-Meter-Pace Training Table

800m Time	400m Time	Repetition Paces			
		200m	150m	100m	50m
1:44	46.0	23.0	17.3	11.5	5.8
1:48	48.0	24.0	18.0	12.0	6.0
1:53	50.0	25.0	18.8	12.5	6.3
1:57	52.0	26.0	19.5	13.0	6.5
2:02	54.0	27.0	20.2	13.5	6.7
2:06	56.0	28.0	21.0	14.0	7.0
2:10	58.0	29.0	21.8	14.5	7.3
2:15	1:00.0	30.0	22.5	15.0	7.5
2:20	1:02.0	31.0	23.3	15.5	7.8
2:24	1:04.0	32.0	24.0	16.0	8.0
2:29	1:06.0	33.0	24.8	16.5	8.3
2:33	1:08.0	34.0	25.5	17.0	8.5
2:38	1:10.0	35.0	26.3	17.5	8.8
2:42	1:12.0	36.0	27.0	18.0	9.0
2:46	1:14.0	37.0	27.8	18.5	9.3
2:51	1:16.0	38.0	28.5	19.0	9.5
2:56	1:18.0	39.0	29.3	19.5	9.8
3:00	1:20.0	40.0	30.0	20.0	10.0
3:04	1:22.0	41.0	30.7	20.5	10.3
3:09	1:24.0	42.0	31.5	21.0	10.5
3:14	1:26.0	43.0	32.3	21.5	10.8
3:18	1:28.0	44.0	33.0	22.0	11.0
3:22	1:30.0	45.0	33.8	22.5	11.3
3:27	1:32.0	46.0	34.5	23.0	11.5
3:31	1:34.0	47.0	35.2	23.5	11.8
3:36	1:36.0	48.0	36.0	24.0	12.0
3:40	1:38.0	49.0	36.7	24.5	12.2
3:45	1:40.0	50.0	37.5	25.0	12.5
3:50	1:42.0	51.0	38.3	25.5	12.8
3:54	1:44.0	52.0	39.0	26.0	13.0
3:59	1:46.0	53.0	39.8	26.5	13.3
4:03	1:48.0	54.0	40.5	27.0	13.5
4:08	1:50.0	55.0	41.3	27.5	13.8
4:12	1:52.0	56.0	42.0	28.0	14.0
4:16	1:54.0	57.0	42.7	28.5	14.2
4:21	1:56.0	58.0	43.5	29.0	14.5
4:26	1:58.0	59.0	44.3	29.5	14.8
4:30	2:00.0	1:00.0	45.0	30.0	15.0
4:34	2:02.0	1:01.0	45.8	30.5	15.3
4:39	2:04.0	1:02.0	46.5	31.0	15.5
Recovery (minutes)		6–12	4–8	2–4	1–2
Typical Reps		2–3	3–6	4–10	8–20

The maximum recommended distance for a repetition at 400-meter pace is 200 meters. Note: Tenths of a second are listed as guidelines (i.e., 11.5 seconds indicates that any time from 11 to 12 seconds is acceptable).

800-Meter-Pace Training

800-meter-pace intervals are a staple for middle-distance runners, and they're about as fast as most endurance runners will train. The high intensity required for these reps can negatively impact both your CNS and aerobic enzymes, so it's best to limit yourself to 4–6 weeks of training at this pace, beginning a couple of months out from a goal race (benefits will last 2–4 weeks after you conclude "speed work"). 800m pace reps can improve:

▶ **Mitochondrial volume:** 800m pace reps increase mitochondrial volume in fast-twitch fibers.

▶ **Non-powerhouse adaptations:** 800m pace reps are also a terrific workout for increasing the number of transport proteins called MCTs (Chapter 9) in fast-twitch muscle fibers. And they'll increase anaerobic enzymes and buffers. 800m pace reps improve running economy (Chapter 11) for middle-distance runners by enhancing both muscle spindles and your nervous system.

800-Meter-Pace Training Table

1600m Time	800m Time	Repetition Paces			
		400m	300m	200m	100m
3:58	1:48	54.0	40.5	27.0	13.5
4:06	1:52	56.0	42.0	28.0	14.0
4:15	1:56	58.0	43.5	29.0	14.5
4:24	2:00	1:00.0	45.0	30.0	15.0
4:33	2:04	1:02.0	46.5	31.0	15.5
4:42	2:08	1:04.0	48.0	32.0	16.0
4:50	2:12	1:06.0	49.5	33.0	16.5
4:59	2:16	1:08.0	51.0	34.0	17.0
5:08	2:20	1:10.0	52.5	35.0	17.5
5:17	2:24	1:12.0	54.0	36.0	18.0
5:26	2:28	1:14.0	55.5	37.0	18.5
5:34	2:32	1:16.0	57.0	38.0	19.0
5:43	2:36	1:18.0	58.5	39.0	19.5
5:52	2:40	1:20.0	1:00.0	40.0	20.0
6:01	2:44	1:22.0	1:01.5	41.0	20.5
6:10	2:48	1:24.0	1:03.0	42.0	21.0
6:18	2:52	1:26.0	1:04.5	43.0	21.5
6:27	2:56	1:28.0	1:06.0	44.0	22.0
6:36	3:00	1:30.0	1:07.5	45.0	22.5
6:45	3:04	1:32.0	1:09.0	46.0	23.0
6:54	3:08	1:34.0	1:10.5	47.0	23.5
7:02	3:12	1:36.0	1:12.0	48.0	24.0
7:11	3:16	1:38.0	1:13.5	49.0	24.5
7:20	3:20	1:40.0	1:15.0	50.0	25.0
7:29	3:24	1:42.0	1:16.5	51.0	25.5
7:38	3:28	1:44.0	1:18.0	52.0	26.0
7:46	3:32	1:46.0	1:19.5	53.0	26.5
7:55	3:36	1:48.0	1:21.0	54.0	27.0
8:04	3:40	1:50.0	1:22.5	55.0	27.5
8:13	3:44	1:52.0	1:24.0	56.0	28.0
8:22	3:48	1:54.0	1:25.5	57.0	28.5
8:30	3:52	1:56.0	1:27.0	58.0	29.0
8:39	3:56	1:58.0	1:28.5	59.0	29.5
8:48	4:00	2:00.0	1:30.0	1:00.0	30.0
8:57	4:04	2:02.0	1:31.5	1:01.0	30.5
9:06	4:08	2:04.0	1:33.0	1:02.0	31.0
9:14	4:12	2:06.0	1:34.5	1:03.0	31.5
9:23	4:16	2:08.0	1:36.0	1:04.0	32.0
9:32	4:20	2:10.0	1:37.5	1:05.0	32.5
9:41	4:24	2:12.0	1:39.0	1:06.0	33.0
Recovery (minutes)		4–9	3–7	2–5	1–3
Typical Reps		2–4	3–6	4–10	8–20

The maximum recommended distance for a repetition at 800-meter pace is 400 meters. Note: Tenths of a second are listed as guidelines (i.e., 19.5 seconds indicates that any time from 19 to 20 seconds is acceptable).

Alternation and Blend Intervals

Rep	Alternation Intervals		Blend Intervals	
	Sample Workout 1	Sample Workout 2	Sample Workout 1	Sample Workout 2
1	Cruise Interval 400	Slow Tempo (-5 seconds) 800	1600 (5K pace)	Cruise Interval 1600
2	Slow Tempo 1200	Slow Tempo (+15 seconds) 800	Recovery 400	Recovery 400
3	Cruise Interval 400	Slow Tempo (-5 seconds) 800	300 (1500 pace)	1200 (5K pace)
4	Slow Tempo 1200	Slow Tempo (+15 seconds) 800	Recovery 400	Recovery 400
5	Cruise Interval 400	Slow Tempo (-5 seconds) 800	1600 (5K pace)	Cruise Interval 1600
6	Slow Tempo 1200	Slow Tempo (+15 seconds) 800	Recovery 400	Recovery 400
7	Cruise Interval 400	Slow Tempo (-5 seconds) 800	300 (1500 pace)	800 (3K pace)
8	Slow Tempo 1200	Slow Tempo (+15 seconds) 800	Recovery 400	Recovery 400
9	Cruise Interval 400	Slow Tempo (-5 seconds) 800	1600 (5K pace)	Cruise Interval 1600
10	Slow Tempo 1200	Slow Tempo (+15 seconds) 800	Recovery 400	Recovery 400
11	Cruise Interval 400	Slow Tempo (-5 seconds) 800	300 (1500 pace)	400 (1500 pace)
12	Slow Tempo 1200	Slow Tempo (+15 seconds) 800	Recovery 400	Recovery 400

Instructions: For each of the sample workouts above, follow the order of workout segments from 1 to 12 (left column). Alternation workouts have no rest interval, while the recovery interval for blend intervals should be a slow jog. Refer to pace charts in chapter 7 for pace guidance.

Alternation and Blend Intervals

Alternation and blend intervals are *only* for advanced runners. Both workouts trigger significant increases in slow-twitch mitochondrial volume, with blend intervals providing an equal stimulus for intermediate mitochondrial volume, too. The primary goal of these workouts, however, is to force your body to deal with increased *lactate* production (Chapter 9). Alternation intervals are a favorite of top marathon Coach Renato Canova, while blend intervals have been used by runners for decades. The corresponding table offers two sample workouts for each interval type—but creativity rules the day with this workout, and runners can fashion their own variations.

- **Alternation intervals:** There is no recovery period between the alternating intervals in this workout. You simply switch from one gear to another, then back to the first, back to the second, and so on. See the pace tables from Chapter 7 to determine correct repetition pace.
- **Blend intervals:** Blend intervals insert a recovery interval (e.g., a 400-meter jog) between repetitions. This allows for higher-intensity reps than alternation intervals. See the pace tables from Chapter 7 to determine correct repetition pace.

Mileage

Runners use the term "mileage" as a generic catchall for every running stride we take during the week. Jogging, hills, sprinting, pace work, distance—it all gets lumped into the week's "mileage." But when it comes to mileage, there is no magic number—no specific weekly target that guarantees success. In fact, runners are better off replacing the word "mileage" with "volume." That's because it's the amount of time—not miles—that you spend training at different intensities that's important. Think about it: An elite runner doing one hundred miles per week of distance at six minutes per mile would tally ten hours of work. A twenty-seven-minute 5K runner doing the same one hundred miles would require twenty hours. The elite runner would improve; the twenty-seven-minute 5K runner would break down. Remember: You're after the benefits of training, not bigger numbers in your running log. That said, increased volume is essential to improving your running. Long-term improvement is dependent upon the accumulation of volume over a long period of time (think months and years, not days and weeks). And higher volume also produces short-term improvement in slow-twitch mitochondrial density, MCTs (Chapter 9), running economy (Chapter 11), blood volume, muscle and connective tissue strength, and more. Simply put, you can't build your best running body without building a solid, substantial base of mileage—but "solid" and "substantial" will mean different things to different runners.

Balance Your Running pH

The term "acid rain" was coined in 1872 by Robert Angus Smith to describe the corrosive effect that atmospheric pollution was having upon the environment. Factories were pumping galactic clouds of sulfur dioxide and nitrous oxide into the air, which then mixed with rain, snow, fog, smoke, and dust, before falling back to the earth as an acidic rinse and soak. When you run hard—*really hard*—you create a similar atmospheric effect within your muscle fibers. As you rely more heavily upon anaerobic energy (energy that's produced outside the mitochondria without oxygen), you create an acidic pH, which in turn is believed to shut down muscle fibers, trigger nausea, and saturate your body with almost unbearable fatigue. While not a problem in longer runs and races, acidic pH can be a killer during high-intensity efforts.

WHAT'S RUNNING pH?

Your body's pH is a measurement of the *hydrogen ions* in your body. More hydrogen ions create an *acidic* pH, while fewer result in an *alkaline* pH. Your body prefers a slightly alkaline pH, measuring between 7.35 and 7.45 on a scale of 1–14. A pH below 7.0 is considered acidic, while anything above that is considered alkaline. The term "pH" has been variously reported to mean both "power of hydrogen" and "potential hydrogen."

So what does this have to do with running?

Running at an intensity that demands a large contribution from anaerobic energy—think shorter races and fast-paced workouts—results in an increased accumulation of hydrogen ions. When your pH drops below 7.0, you begin to suffer from *acidosis*. Acidosis is accompanied by fatigue, an inability to generate high muscle contraction force, and a burning sensation in affected muscles. If left unchecked, it can lead to a state of near-incapacitation, one that runners refer to as "rigging" (short for "rigor mortis"), "tying up," or having the "bear jump on your back." At a pH of roughly 6.4, your legs become dead weight. Cyclists have been tested with muscle pH as low as 6.4, and back in 1983, Dr. David Costill, et al., measured runners' leg-muscle pH at 6.63

following 400-meter sprints. Because fatigue at high intensities has traditionally been associated with lowered pH, runners train to lessen acidosis within muscle fibers (by exporting hydrogen ions from the fibers) and to buffer (explained in detail later in this chapter) the hydrogen ions within the fibers, thereby neutralizing them.

It's important to note, however, that this theory of fatigue has been challenged in recent years. Many researchers have discounted the effect of acidosis and proposed alternative theories. A major problem with much of the original research on acidosis was that tissue used in the studies (removed from rodents) was refrigerated, altering the results. When new studies were performed on warmed tissue—closer to normal body temperature—the effects of acidosis disappeared to a large degree. As often happens, however, these later studies were in turn contradicted. A 2006 experiment by Knuth, et al., tested the effect of acidosis upon warmed muscle tissue. Knuth concluded that "the fatigue-inducing effects of low pH … are still substantial and important at temperatures approaching those [in living tissue]." Stalemate.

Which leaves us with a bit of a conundrum. Should we reject the theory of acidosis? Maybe ignore alternative theories? The answer is that we'll cover both. We'll discuss alternative theories of fatigue in Chapter 13. As for this chapter, we'll take the advice of Dr. Ernest W. Maglischo, writing in a 2012 issue of the *Journal of the International Society of Swimming Coaching*: "I don't believe a

BEGINNER'S GUIDELINE

The best way to combat low pH in your muscle fibers is to avoid it. Don't go out too hard on runs. And stick to your prescribed paces for intervals and tempo.

TRAINING DISCUSSION

"Lactic acid—friend or foe?"

For years, *lactic acid* has served as the running community's bogeyman. It's been blamed for fatigue, pain, "rigging" at the end of races, and even DOMS (lingering muscle soreness).

This is the sum total of problems that lactic acid actually causes: None.

So how did lactic acid earn its skull-and-crossbones label? It began in the early twentieth century, when 1922 Nobel Prize winners Dr. Otto Meyerhof and Dr. Archibald Hill independently conducted experiments in which they administered electric shocks to severed frog legs. The frog legs would twitch at first, then go still. When inspected, the motionless legs were found to be covered in lactic acid. From this, it was deduced that anaerobic energy production—severed frog legs don't get much in the way of an oxygen supply—produces lactic acid, leading to a condition called "acidosis," which shuts down muscle fiber contraction. Runners and coaches accepted this finding, then spent the next six decades training to overcome the effects of lactic acid.

Attitudes toward lactic acid underwent a seismic shift in 1985, when Berkeley physiologist Dr. George A. Brooks demonstrated that lactate (for all practical purposes, lactic acid minus a hydrogen ion) is, in reality, a prized fuel for muscle fibers, not a contraction killer. Where it was previously accepted that lactic acid was the final by-product of anaerobic energy production, it was now assumed that lactic acid instantly splits to create both lactate and hydrogen ions. Lactate was good. Hydrogen ions—the culprit behind acidosis—were bad. And lactic acid remained a villain, if indirectly.

In a 2004 paper, Dr. Robert A. Robergs, et al., administered a second blow to the dwindling notoriety of lactic acid: Lactic acid, Robergs claimed, is *never* created during anaerobic energy production. Instead, hydrogen ions arise independently of lactate. What's more, lactate actually decreases acidosis, both by consuming hydrogen ions and by pairing with them and, guided by transport proteins, exiting the muscle fiber. Biochemist and textbook author Dr. Laurence A. Moran cheered this conclusion, writing on his blog, *Sandwalk*, "The important point is that lactic acid is not produced in muscles so it can't be the source of acidosis."

More recently, acidosis itself has been challenged as a cause of fatigue. In a 2008 paper, McKenna and Hargreaves write that "fatigue during exercise can be viewed as a cascade of events occurring at multi-organ, multi-cellular, and multi-molecular levels."

Whatever the final verdict on fatigue, one result is already in: Lactic acid isn't a bad guy. Instead, lactate is an energy source, hydrogen ions cause acidosis, and smart runners train to utilize the former and, until strong evidence appears to the contrary, avoid the latter.

BUILD YOUR RUNNING BODY

radical change [in training] is required. Our training methods have worked even though their reasons for doing so may be different than we once thought … [Until] we know for sure that acidosis is not involved, it would be wise to continue training to improve buffering capacity." In other words, if training based on low pH ain't broke, don't fix it.

pH TRAINING

Training pH began with building more mitochondria in Chapter 8. More mitochondria create more aerobic energy, a process that consumes hydrogen ions and decreases the required input from anaerobic energy production. In this chapter, we'll look at two other ways to improve performance while neutralizing acidosis:

▶ Buffers
▶ The lactate shuttle

For buffers, we'll try short sprints for a change of pace. Training the lactate shuttle will introduce an entirely new type of workout into your schedule: Cross training. You'll learn how riding an ElliptiGO or romping through the woods on snowshoes can offer big performance gains.

BUFFERS

Buffers are substances that neutralize the effects of hydrogen ions (acidic pH) within your muscle fibers. Examples of buffers are phosphates, bicarbonate, and some proteins.

If you never run harder than a jog, you don't have to worry about buffers. You have plenty already to neutralize the small level of hydrogen ions you'll generate. On the other hand, if you intend to run hard, you'll need to fortify your buffering system.

Runners are sometimes surprised to discover that the first thirty seconds of a race (at any distance) are more anaerobic than the remainder of the race, with the exception of the final gut-wrenching kick to the finish line. That's because it takes time for your aerobic system to get up to speed, at which point it provides the majority of energy for your effort. That makes the first thirty seconds the period when your buffers are most challenged. Since building more buffers requires overtaxing existing buffers, you'll need to run short-duration reps that tap into the high anaerobic load of those thirty seconds. That means repetitions at near-maximum speeds, followed by plenty of rest to ensure that you replenish your anaerobic energy supply for the next rep (so that it won't be fueled by your aerobic system).

Buffer training responds quickly, with maximum buffering capacity reached after only four to six weeks.

Training recommendation

Short reps at 400/800m pace (Chapter 8, see page 146–148) rev up your buffering capacity. But make sure to allow adequate recovery after each rep.

THE LACTATE SHUTTLE

The "lactate shuttle" refers to the combination of mechanisms through which your body moves lactate within your cells and between your cells, which invites the question: What does a lactate shuttle have to do with reducing the effect of hydrogen ions—hence, acidic pH—within your muscle fibers? After all, lactate is a fuel, not an acid. But the truth is that lactate and hydrogen ions are joined at the hip. In fact, for decades they were thought to be one entity, lactic acid (see sidebar, "Lactic acid—friend or foe?" page 153). Although we now know that hydrogen ions, and not lactate, are the problem, there are several reasons why we can't discuss acidosis without discussing lactate:

▶ Both lactate and hydrogen ions accumulate during anaerobic energy production.
▶ Lacate and hydrogen ions accumulate at roughly the same rate.
▶ Lactate and hydrogen ions leave the muscle fibers together, escorted out by specialized transport proteins called MCTs.
▶ It's easier to measure lactate than hydrogen ions.

Because lactate and hydrogen ions accumulate at about the same rate, we can test blood lactate levels (lactate that has exited muscle fibers and entered the bloodstream) as a way to estimate acidosis within the muscle fiber. The more lactate in the bloodstream, the more in the fiber. And the more lactate, the more acidosis. It's too expensive and difficult to measure fiber pH directly. As you can see in Table 9.1, some lactate accumulates at all running speeds. This is because both aerobic and anaerobic energy production are always ongoing (the percentage of each changes depending on your effort level).

When lactate levels within your muscle fibers get high—and as hydrogen ion levels simultaneously rise—your muscle fiber types respond differently. Slow-twitch fibers burn about 75–80 percent of produced lactate to fuel aerobic energy production in your mitochondria. Intermediate and fast-twitch fibers, however, lack similar lactate-burning capacity. So when lactate levels rise in faster fibers, these fibers go into the export business, shipping lactate to other muscle fibers, the brain, the heart, and the liver (where it's converted to glucose).

Your muscle fibers use specialized transport proteins called MCTs to move lactate. MCTs are to lactate what tugboats are to larger vessels. MCTs can tow lactate to mitochondria, where it's burned as fuel. Or they can push lactate—*accompanied by*

Table 9.1

Type of Training	% VO₂ Max	Blood Lactate (mmols)
Jogging	60	0.8
Easy Running	65	1.1
Moderate Running	70	1.4
Faster Running	75	1.9
Marathon/Slow Tempo	80	2.6
Half-Marathon/Fast Tempo	85	3.5
10K pace	90	4.6
5K pace	95	6.2
3K pace	100	8.2
1 mile/1500 meter pace	105	11
1200 meter pace	110	14.7
800 meter pace	115	19.6
600 meter pace	120	22.9
400 meter pace	135	26.1
200 meter pace	150	19.6
100 meter pace	155	11

TABLE 9.1 offers a comparison of average blood lactate levels at various running speeds (and roughly equivalent VO₂ max). Blood lactate levels give an indication of rising acidity within muscle fibers, which is theorized to lead to fatigue in shorter races. Note: "mmols" is the abbreviation for millimoles; a mole is a unit of measurement in chemistry.

hydrogen ions—out of the fiber. Or, when needed, they can import lactate from adjacent fibers and the bloodstream for use as fuel. Berkeley physiologist Dr. George A. Brooks dubbed this process the "lactate shuttle."

The lactate shuttle has two trainable limitations:

▶ **MCT volume:** You have a limited number of MCTs, which can be overwhelmed when lactate and hydrogen ion levels rise. Think of the taxi line at a busy airport.

▶ **Congestion:** Lactate and hydrogen ions leave the muscle fibers by *facilitated diffusion*, meaning they are transported across a cell membrane from an area of higher concentration to an area of lower concentration with the assistance of MCTs. As more lactate enters the bloodstream, blood lactate concentration rises, slowing facilitated diffusion. Think of trying to merge onto the freeway at rush hour.

The traditional solution to these limitations is simply to increase the number of MCTs, which escort lactate and hydrogen ions out of fibers and pull lactate from the bloodstream into non-working muscle fibers.

Increasing MCTs to export lactate requires different training for different fiber types:

▶ **Slow-twitch fibers:** High mileage and long runs

▶ **Intermediate fibers:** Workouts at 10K to tempo pace

▶ **Fast-twitch fibers:** Repetitions at 800-meters to mile pace

There's also an untraditional solution for dealing with the problem of congestion—of a rising blood lactate level that slows facilitated diffusion of lactate and hydrogen ions from muscle fibers. And that solution is cross training.

Cross training

Cross training (e.g., swimming, biking, snowshoeing, etc.) is loved by some runners and dismissed by others. The latter group correctly believes that cross training violates the *specificity-of-training rule*: Exercise you perform in practice must be as close as possible to the actual competition. But it's this very lack of specificity that makes cross training perfect for improving your body's ability to lower blood lactate levels while running.

Remember that a goal of training is to diminish blood lactate during hard running, thereby allowing hardworking muscle fibers to export more lactate and hydrogen ions through facilitated diffusion. What cross training accomplishes is to train muscle fibers that aren't used during running—that are specific to the cross training activity—to increase *their* MCT levels, thereby increasing their ability to import lactate. Then, when you run, these non-working fibers can act as lactate drop zones, gobbling up lactate from the bloodstream.

"[Decreasing blood lactate] is one of the reasons I started to insert a little more cross training into my athletes' training," says Steve Magness, the head cross country coach at the University of Houston, a former coach for the elite Nike Oregon Project, an exercise scientist, and author of *The Science of Running* (Origin Press, 2014). "It's not about replacing running. It's about getting adaptations that might help you while running."

To test his hypothesis, Magness did a basic lactate profile on himself. He then spent the next four weeks adding cross training and running circuits to his running schedule (see photo instruction in Chapter 12 for Jay Johnson's running circuits). His goal was to train new fibers to take up lactate. When he tested himself again after the four weeks, his lactate profile had improved at every training pace.

Cross training offers an untapped reservoir for offloading lactate, simultaneously lowering blood lactate levels and aiding the removal of hydrogen ions from muscle fibers. Not only will you balance your pH, you just might find that variety is, indeed, the spice of life—and of training.

Training recommendation

Training for the lactate shuttle includes traditional workouts like high Mileage (Chapter 8, see page 150) and Long Runs (Chapter 7, see page 132) for slow-twitch fiber, 10K or Tempo effort (Chapter 7, see pages 130 for 10K and tempo) workouts for intermediate fiber, and reps at 800m pace (Chapter 8, see page 147) or mile pace (Chapter 7, see page 124 for 1500-pace reps) for fast-twitch fibers. It also involves Cross Training (see page 158–163 range), which helps to keep blood lactate levels low during hard running.

TRAINING RUNDOWN

Developing your lactate shuttle and buffers involves much of the same training that we used for improving capillaries and mitochondria. At the same time, we're introducing cross training to create lactate drop zones in slow-twitch fibers. Important training in this chapter's photo instruction includes:

▶ **Cross Training (multiple sports)**

Training from other chapters that affects buffers and the lactate shuttle includes:

▶ **Tempo (Chapter 7)**
▶ **5K/10K Pace Road and Trail Intervals (Chapter 8)**
▶ **Mileage (Chapter 8)**
▶ **HIIT (Chapter 8)**
▶ **400/800m Pace Intervals (Chapter 8)**

To see exactly how these workouts can be incorporated into your overall training program, skip directly to Chapter 15: Build Your Training Schedule, where sample schedules are available for runners of all fitness levels and abilities.

BUILD YOUR RUNNING BODY

Chapter 9: Balance Your Running pH –
PHOTO INSTRUCTION

CROSS TRAINING

Cross training has long been a favorite form of alternative training for runners who are injured, interested in better all-around fitness, or simply looking for a change in their fitness routines. But now all runners have two very good reasons to make cross training a part of their programs:

1. It's a great way to combat acidosis within your muscle fibers.
2. It can turn your body into a giant, fully charged battery (see Chapter 10).

Cross training increases your MCT transport proteins (shuttle buses for lactate) within muscle fibers, allowing you to transport lactate/hydrogen ions (the cause of acidosis) out of those fibers and import lactate into non-working muscle fibers—those fibers become lactate drop zones when blood lactate levels are high. This photo instruction will highlight eleven cross training options, demonstrated by Christian (whom you met in Chapter 2's photo instruction); Emii, a martial arts athlete turned actress, pop entertainer, and runner; Roger Sayre, a former 2:30 marathoner and masters national cross country ski champion; and Callie Greene, a competitive cheerleader who uses running as base training, and who also builds all-around fitness with a mix of kickboxing, swimming, and stationary cycling.

Treadmill

The treadmill has existed as a popular indoor alternative to outdoor training since William Staub invented the PaceMaster 600 in the late 1960s, inspired by Dr. Kenneth H. Cooper's book, *Aerobics*. While treadmill running might look like outdoor running's indoor twin, it's not. It's different in several measur-

able ways. First, there's no air resistance on a treadmill; you use less energy to run. To counteract this, use a 1 percent incline. Second, research shows that runners use a shorter stride, faster cadence, and more flat-footed landing on the treadmill. This recruits a slightly different mix of fibers, reduces running economy, and requires a rewiring of your nervous system (see Chapter 11). Third, you'll run slower on the treadmill—studies show up to two minutes per mile slower than on the roads. So you'll want to choose your setting based on effort, not pace. The good news is that all these changes ensure the creation of new MCTs in a larger group of muscle fibers. Other than running a little slower, train like you would on the roads and trails.

Elliptical Machine

The elliptical machine was introduced in the 1990s and soon became a mainstay of fitness club cardio training. Elliptical machines have two foot-pedals (platforms) that move in an ellipse—meant to mimic the act of walking or running. You can adjust incline, resistance, and stride length (depending on the machine, stride length adjustments vary from just over a foot to almost three feet). Many models also include moveable handles, allowing you to work your upper body. For runners looking to improve upper body fitness, a must for developing the full range of MCT improvements, you'll need to increase resistance to slow down your stride rate (rpms); this allows you to grasp the handles more easily. For runners focused on lower body training, you might want to release the handles altogether and increase your stride rate to mimic normal running. Some runners hold light weights in their hands (e.g., 12-ounce fishing weights) to improve balance while running hands-free. To perform workouts like fartlek and repetitions, increase both stride length and resistance settings.

ElliptiGO Bicycle

The ElliptiGO is an elliptical bicycle, first marketed in 2010 and already gaining numerous adherents among elite open and masters runners. Like the elliptical machine, the ElliptiGO allows you to work muscle fibers beyond those recruited during running. Unlike the elliptical, the ElliptiGO doesn't have moveable handles for upper body training. Some quick rules for your first ride:

1. Pick a safe place (no traffic—cars, bike, or foot).
2. Wear a bike helmet, close-toed shoes (a firm toe box—the Keen McKenzie works great), and biking gloves.
3. Start in fifth gear.
4. Straddle the bike (both feet on the ground), then place your foot in the forward pedal platform and push off with your lower foot as you stand on your forward foot.
5. Stride out, shifting into a higher gear if the motion feels choppy.
6. Use both hand brakes to slow down, and drop your foot to one side when stopping.

Other than that, pick a duration and intensity that's equivalent to a running workout.

BUILD YOUR RUNNING BODY

Aerobics

Aerobics exploded onto the fitness club scene in the 1980s, fueled in large part by the 1982 release of Jane Fonda's exercise video, *Jane Fonda's Workout*. Given aerobics' emphasis on full body strength and endurance, it remains a fun and effective way to create the kind of training adaptations required for better MCT/lactate function. While "aerobics" can mean anything from spinning to martial arts to stair climbing to boot camp, two specific forms have remained the most popular classes at fitness clubs for three decades running:

- ▶ **Dance/Freestyle:** Includes both high- and low-intensity full-body movement. Often performed to music. Can include synchronized dance movements and strength exercises.
- ▶ **Step Aerobics:** Takes dance/freestyle and adds a low platform on which you step up and down. Like dance/freestyle, it recruits many muscle fibers not associated with running.

Aerobics is great for runners looking for a vibrant, social atmosphere for some of their training.

Kickboxing

Kickboxing (and other martial arts) provide a combination of endurance, strength, and nervous system training. But kickboxing isn't a sport you'll want to learn from a book or DVD. You'll need to find a local gym with either accredited personnel or instructors who are steeped in experience—instructors nationally ranked in kickboxing or other martial arts can be trusted to know their stuff. Also, realize that kickboxing isn't just about snapping kick/punch combinations at a sparring partner. A good training session begins with a cardio warm-up that might include running, stretching, resistance training, and form drills, among other elements. Actual kickboxing instruction will involve learning combinations of kicks and punches, aimed both at space and the heavy bag. You'll focus on form, balance, speed, strength, and endurance. Overall, the workout will challenge your body from head to toe, leaving you more fit than before you gloved up.

Cycling

Cycling holds the allure of allowing runners to go faster and farther than is possible in running shoes alone. Plus you get to coast down hills! With a bike (road or mountain), you can train muscle fibers in the legs that you barely touch with running. You'll need sunglasses or other eyewear for protection and either toe clips or clipless pedals and cycling shoes (both allow you to pull up as well as push down with each spin of the

pedals, which powers the full rotation of each pedal spin and increases the workload for your muscles). Before riding, adjust the seat height so that it's about 80 percent of your inseam, enough to allow a slight bend at the knees. Once you're pedaling, pay attention to cadence. Many runners start with higher gears and put more "mash" than "spin" into their effort. Instead, make 60 rpm (revolutions per minute with each leg) your absolute floor, and, as your fitness improves, shoot for 80 rpm or more (advanced cyclists maintain rates of 80–110 rpms). If you find yourself rocking from side to side when riding, readjust the seat height until you're more stable. Now ride fast, slow, up, down, far, and short until you've gotten a good all-around workout.

Stationary Bike

Riding the stationary bike—indoor cycling or "spinning"—garners most of the benefits of outdoor cycling, plus you can safely listen to music, control the weather, avoid run-ins with motorists (and annoying runners), and watch the latest episode of *Game of Thrones*, *True Blood*, or *American Idol*. As an extra bonus, you'll never have to change a flat tire! First, adjust the seat height and then set the bike's resistance, which is controlled by a knob/dial in some models and electronically in others. Begin your ride with moderate resistance, which equates to a flat outdoor ride. You can simulate acceleration or hill-climbing by increasing resistance. Or decrease resistance to enjoy the equivalent of a nice downhill ride. With some bikes, you can hook up to your computer and choose a virtual route or ride against a virtual competitor. To improve muscle fiber recruitment, try standing while pedaling during accelerations and climbs. And to combat rising body heat, set up a fan to help evaporate your sweat.

Pool Running

Pool running (along with the elliptical) is the preferred cross training activity for injured runners. It closely mimics your running motion and negates all landing impact. You only weigh about 10 percent of your normal body weight in water. By using an AquaJogger buoyancy belt (as pictured), you'll have no trouble keeping your head above water. You'll need a pool that's deep enough to ensure that your feet don't touch bottom. With some Aqua-Jogger foot gear, you'll literally be floating with every stride. This dramatically changes muscle fiber recruitment, as you no longer have to adjust for balance and weight distribution. Unlike running, your center of gravity—your hips in running—becomes a *center of buoyancy*, located at your lungs.

Use your abdominal and back muscles to maintain a straight line from your head through your trunk, with an overall forward lean of about 3 percent (or a lean that corresponds roughly to the lean you employ when running). Move your arms and legs as if you were running. Perform your normal running workouts in the pool—just go by effort and duration, not time and distance.

Swimming

Many runners avoid swimming for one simple reason: They sink. With their low body fat, elite runners fear ending up at the bottom of the pool. But even a runner with a little padding can find his or her hips and legs dragging through the pool like a boat's hull taking on water. What gives? What gives is a lack of form and balance. At sea level, water is 784 times denser than air. If you're not floating, you're doing something wrong. Imagine that you have an axis running from your head down your spine, and that you have another axis running from shoulder to shoulder. Where those two lines meet is the "T." You want to force the "T" downward into the water (known as "pressing the T"). This automatically brings your hips into position for kicking, while assuring a strong stroke. And you'll want that stroke. You get a third more propulsion from your pull than from your kick. Both freestyle and butterfly are good strokes for cross training.

Snowshoeing

Snowshoeing is a great cross training option for those who live where it snows. All you need are a pair of snowshoes (both Atlas and Redfeather are good brands) and a pair of waterproof boots—if not waterproof boots, then leather hiking boots, or even running shoes covered by neoprene overshoe booties (for the cost conscious, plastic baggies will do). For beginners or those navigating rough terrain, poles are also advisable. When training, it's best to find a packed trail (snowmobile trails are perfect). Because snowshoeing is more demanding than walking or running, you'll want to begin your snowshoe sessions with outings over relatively flat terrain. Treat snowshoeing like altitude training, where you hold back slightly on your effort, and don't be afraid to take walk or light jog breaks. Snowshoeing is similar in form to running, except that you lift your knees higher to clear the snow. For workouts that mimic tempo or 5K/10K repetitions, go by effort, not pace.

Cross Country Skiing

Cross country skiing is as good a VO_2 max workout as you're going to find. In fact, cross country skiers have recorded some of the highest VO_2 max scores in history. Espen Harald Bjerke and Bjørn Dæhlie both recorded 96.0 for VO_2 max, with Dæhlie's out-of-season score indicating the possibility of an unfathomable 100+ score when at peak fitness. You can choose from two popular styles, either classic skiing or skate skiing. For both, you'll need skis, boots, poles, and cold-weather gear.

▶ **Classic skiing:** This style is closest to running. You'll need to apply kick wax under the foot area of your skis to improve grip, as well as glide wax outside the kick zone. Then try to find a trail already set up with parallel grooves. You'll use the "kick and glide" technique, swinging your opposite leg and arm forward and planting your pole to add push to your kick. Don't shuffle. Start with all your weight on one foot, then shift to the other.

▶ **Skate Skiing:** Skate skiing is a lot like ice skating. While classic skiing utilizes forward and backward arm and leg movements, skate skiing relies on more forceful lateral movements. You'll utilize an outward kick and aim for higher speeds. Start by putting glide wax over the length of your skis. Use double poling for extra push, keeping a double pole/skate/double pole/skate rhythm. Avoid sitting back on your skis, and shift your weight—*boom*—from ski to ski with each kick. There are several techniques (e.g., V-1, V-2, V-2 alternate), so you'll need a little instruction before hitting the snow (there are numerous good videos on YouTube that demonstrate proper technique).

For workouts, mimic running using effort and duration as your guides.

Build Your Running Energy System

Your running is only as good as the fuel that powers it. Building a great running body and then providing it with inadequate energy is like having a Hennessey Venom GT (260 mph top speed, 0–60 mph in 2.5 seconds) and a full tank of lemonade. Building your energy system begins with the food you eat—with the carbs, fats, protein, and other nutrition that you choose to consume every day—and ends with your body's creation of ATP, the molecule that powers every movement you make, from the slightest twitch to the longest leap. Your favorite part about training your energy system will be picking healthy foods from the menu. But the most important part is teaching your body to turn bananas and pasta into faster, fitter running performances.

WHAT'S YOUR ENERGY SYSTEM?

Your body needs energy to run, just like kitchen appliances need electricity, a TV remote control needs batteries, and your car needs gasoline in the tank. Unlike electricity, batteries, or gasoline, however, the energy you need, as a runner, doesn't arrive ready to burn. You have to make it yourself—and that's the job of your energy system.

Human motion is powered by energy from the molecule ATP (adenosine triphosphate). You eat to harness food's energy (calories), but food doesn't directly provide energy for your running. Instead, your energy system breaks down carbohydrates, fats, and protein, and then uses that energy to create ATP. It's ATP that provides the energy you need to run.

In the grand scheme of things, you have one running energy system—the system that produces ATP—but it's easier to understand that energy system's function if we break it down into three systems, two that are anaerobic and one that's aerobic. Your two anaerobic systems don't require oxygen to produce energy and are limited in duration. Your aerobic system requires oxygen to function and can produce energy for the long haul. The three systems are:

- ▶ **Phosphagen (anaerobic)**
- ▶ **Glycolytic (anaerobic)**
- ▶ **Aerobic (aerobic)**

These three systems work together to ensure that you always have adequate ATP. In fact, they create fuels, enzymes, and other products that can be used by one another (e.g., your glycolytic system creates lactate, which is used by your aerobic system to make ATP). In other words, these systems are codependent. Keeping that in mind, here are four energy system principles:

1. All three energy systems work simultaneously.
2. Effort level and duration generally determine which energy system dominates energy production.
3. Oxygen is always present in your muscles, but its volume increases with aerobic energy demand.
4. Fatigue is caused by different factors in different energy systems.

In addition to describing the three energy systems, we'll discuss two other energy-related topics in this chapter: aerobic enzymes and body heat. Aerobic enzymes are an essential element in mitochondrial energy production, and body heat is created as a by-product of ATP production and use.

BEGINNER'S GUIDELINE

Never begin a new training program and a diet at the same time. Training adaptations require calories and nutrition. Starving yourself only delays recovery from workouts, depletes training energy, and lowers training enthusiasm. First, get fit. Then decide whether you need to get thinner.

TRAINING DISCUSSION

"How much ATP does it take to run a marathon?"

Evolution is no dummy. Speech, opposable thumbs, and our extraordinarily big brains prove that. So why don't our bodies store more than a couple minutes' supply of ATP, the energy molecule that powers all human movement? Since recycling ATP stocks requires around-the-clock fueling (eating), wouldn't we be better off with a longer-lasting ATP reserve? Maybe an hour's worth? Maybe enough for a whole day?

The answer is a resounding *No!*

If you think of ATP in terms of exercise, you'll understand why.

Two San Diego State University professors, Michael J. Buono and Fred W. Kolkhorst, have made it a practice to ask their physiology classes this question: "How much ATP does it take to run a marathon?" Using American record-holder Khalid Khannouchi's 2:05:42 marathon, they have their students compute the ATP that Khannouchi required to complete the race. Assuming a VO_2 max of 80 mL/kg/minute and a body weight of 121 pounds, then using the molar equation for the oxidation of carbohydrate … well, to make a long equation short, the answer is that Khannouchi used 132 pounds of ATP during his 2:05 marathon!

Try carrying that on your fuel and hydration belt.

As with so many things, Mother Nature knows best when it comes to ATP.

ENERGY SYSTEMS TRAINING

You train your energy systems by performing workouts that challenge the fuels (known as *substrate*), enzymes, buffers, and processes (e.g., the lactate shuttle) associated with each system. Because the workouts recommended in this chapter have already been demonstrated in the photo instruction for previous chapters, we'll use this chapter's photo instruction a little differently. To aid your fueling decisions, we'll break down a variety of workouts into their caloric requirements, as well as noting approximate contributions from carbohydrates and fats.

YOUR ENERGY SYSTEMS

You have three energy systems that are working twenty-four hours a day to provide you with the ATP you need. Of course, they're not working at full capacity twenty-four hours a day. And they're not making equal contributions to energy production for all activities. Your energy systems specialize, with each system best-suited for a different type of energy demand. Table 10.1 approximates the contributions from energy systems at different effort levels (represented by paces). Sprints are almost entirely anaerobic, with around 50 percent of energy contributed by the phosphagen system alone, while the marathon goes the opposite direction, deriving 99 percent of energy from your aerobic system. We'll look at each of your energy systems to see exactly how they work (and how best to train them), beginning with a brief overview of ATP itself.

Table 10.1
Aerobic/Anaerobic Energy Contribution

Run/Race Distance	Aerobic	Glycolytic (Anaerobic)	Phosphagen (Anaerobic)	Total Anaerobic
100m	20.0%	33.3%	46.7%	80.0%
200m	28.0%	51.3%	20.7%	72.0%
400m	41.0%	49.6%	9.4%	59.0%
800m	60.0%	35.9%	4.1%	40.0%
1500m	77.0%	21.0%	2.0%	23.0%
3K	86.0%	13.0%	1.0%	14.0%
5K	92.0%	7.5%	0.5%	8.0%
10K	96.0%	3.7%	0.3%	4.0%
Half Marathon	98.0%	1.9%	0.1%	2.0%
Fast Tempo	98.5%	1.4%	0.1%	1.5%
Slow Tempo	99.0%	1.0%	0.1%	1.0%
Marathon	99.5%	0.4%	0.1%	0.5%
Long Runs	99.7%	0.3%	0.0%	0.3%
Regular Distance Runs	99.8%	0.2%	0.0%	0.2%
Recovery Runs	99.9%	0.1%	0.0%	0.1%

TABLE 10.1 shows approximate contributions from all three energy systems—aerobic, glycolytic, and phosphagen—during various running efforts.

ATP

ATP has been called the "common currency" of energy. Whether you're sprinting, running distance, or just staring out the window thinking about going for a run, ATP is providing the energy that lets you do it. If muscle contractions were slot machines, ATP would be your coins.

You begin each day with about one hundred grams (roughly a quarter-pound) of ATP in your body and then recycle it as needed. But be forewarned: Those one hundred grams won't power more than a few minutes on the couch or a few seconds on the run. Just to meet daily energy demands, you'll recycle each ATP molecule approximately 500–750 times—a volume of ATP equal to your body weight! High-volume training increases demand up to

100 percent. (See sidebar, "How much ATP does it take to run a marathon?")

You always have a small supply of available ATP in your muscle fibers. If you didn't, you'd experience rigor mortis (muscles use ATP to contract *and* relax). But with your first running step, you start depleting that ATP. To continue running, you'll need to fire up the phosphagen system.

PHOSPHAGEN SYSTEM (*QUICK ENERGY*)

The phosphagen system is your first responder when muscle fiber ATP levels fall. Also called the ATP-CP system, it resides in your muscle fibers' sarcoplasm, relies upon *creatine phosphate* (CP or PCr) as its fuel source, and is anaerobic. Whether you're blasting out of the blocks in the Olympic 100-meter final or taking the first steps of a distance run, ATP levels will nosedive within seconds unless the phosphagen system comes to the rescue. And come to the rescue it does, in mere thousandths of a second, using CP to rapidly recycle ATP at twice the rate of your next-fastest energy system.

Your phosphagen system immediately arrests the fall in ATP levels until reinforcements arrive. For low-intensity exercise, your other energy systems will quickly take over ATP production. For high-intensity exercise like all-out sprints, which demand the kind of energy supply that only creatine phosphate can fuel, your phosphagen system will remain in the driver's seat, keeping your ATP levels at 80 percent of normal volume for up to ten seconds. Then, just as the nitro boost that rocketed Dominic Toretto's RX-7 to victory in *The Fast and the Furious* was short-lived, CP depletes rapidly. By fifteen to twenty seconds, it's mostly gone. That's enough energy for sprints, heavy lifts, plyometrics, or jumping a puddle, but not enough for a jog around the block—meaning you'll have to reduce your effort if you intend to keep running.

Training recommendation

Studies are mixed on how best to increase creatine phosphate stores. Some recommend aerobic training (endurance athletes resynthesize CP faster than non-endurance athletes). Others suggest that you can increase CP capacity by 10–20 percent with short sprints of 5–10 seconds, Short Hill Sprints (Chapter 11, see page 220), or high-intensity exercises like Plyometrics (Chapter 11, see pages 211–216). Creatine supplements have also been shown to increase CP stores up to 20 percent, but this benefit doesn't improve overall power (just a few seconds of duration) and doesn't provide an advantage to endurance athletes.

Whereas the phosphagen system produces energy anaerobically, rebuilding your CP stores requires oxygen. That's one reason you huff and puff after a sprint or heavy lift. It takes up to three minutes to restock your CP, so plan recovery from high-intensity activities accordingly.

GLYCOLYTIC SYSTEM

Like the phosphagen system, the glycolytic system resides in the sarcoplasm, is anaerobic, and ramps up as soon as you start exercising. During high-intensity exercise, the glycolytic system takes over as your primary energy source once the phosphagen system has run dry. It's also the perfect example of your individual energy systems working as branches of one big energy system. The centerpiece of the glycolytic system is a multi-step chemical reaction called *glycolysis*, which is the first step in *both* anaerobic and aerobic energy production.

Fueled by glucose and glycogen (carbohydrates), glycolysis quickly produces two or three ATP molecules anaerobically plus two very important molecules called *pyruvate*. If your muscle fibers' energy demand exceeds what can be produced aerobically, the pyruvate molecules will be cycled through "fast" glycolysis. If enough oxygen is available for aerobic energy production, most pyruvate molecules are shuttled to your mitochondria (if they aren't already at 100 percent capacity) through "slow" glycolysis.

Fast glycolysis (short-term energy)

Fast glycolysis is what most runners think of when they hear the term "anaerobic." Fast glycolysis can produce ATP up to one hundred times faster than your aerobic system. The drawback is that this production is short-lived. You'll get one minute max of full-capacity production, two minutes with a more conservative effort, and a longer-lasting dribble of energy if you throttle way back. Sprinters and middle-distance runners lean hard on this system (see Table 10.1).

Fast glycolysis begins with the pyruvate molecules created during glycolysis. The pyruvate enters a chemical reaction that produces lactate and the coenzyme NAD+. NAD+ is important because it allows glycolysis to cycle again immediately, producing another two to three ATP and two more pyruvate, which initiates yet another cycle, and another, going round and round at breakneck speed, until you've created an enormous volume of ATP.

Fast glycolysis occurs under three different conditions:

▶ **Continuously:** Even at rest, your muscle fibers produce some lactate.
▶ **Limited oxygen:** When there isn't enough oxygen to process all generated pyruvate in your mitochondria, fast glycolysis occurs. This includes the first thirty to forty seconds of a run, before adequate oxygen can be delivered to your muscle fibers for increased aerobic energy production.
▶ **Overloaded mitochondria:** When your mitochondria have enough oxygen but are already producing aerobic energy at 100 percent capacity, pyruvate gets backed up at the mitochondrial doors and undergoes fast glycolysis instead.

Training fast glycolysis requires *speed work*—repetitions of 200 to 400 meters at mile race pace or faster. Speed work increases *anaerobic enzymes*, and anaerobic enzymes break down the carbohydrates that fuel glycolysis. More anaerobic enzymes means faster energy production. But be forewarned that a byproduct of speed work is acidosis. And acidosis can damage or even destroy *aerobic enzymes* (we'll discuss these in a minute). For this reason, endurance athletes need to limit speed work by practicing these three rules:

1. Do the minimum speed work necessary to increase anaerobic enzymes and develop nervous system (Chapter 11) efficiency.
2. Employ work-to-rest ratios of between 1:2 and 1:12 (or more) for short, fast reps.
3. Limit speed work in the 2–3 weeks before an endurance competition.

Fast glycolysis will cycle in and out as needed during runs, and it's a major contributor when kicking to the finish line of a race.

A final note on fast glycolysis: If you do find yourself going out too fast in a run, race, or repetitions workout—and feel the unavoidable onset of acidosis—slow down to an easily held aerobic pace. Trained muscles are efficient at clearing both lactate and hydrogen ions, and while you won't be able to reverse the effects of acidosis completely, you'll recover enough to finish more strongly than if you hadn't backed off.

Training recommendation

For fast glycolysis, repetitions of 200–400 meters at 1500-meter (mile) pace or faster (Chapter 7, see page 124; Chapter 8, see pages 146–148) will increase anaerobic capacity. Allow the full recommended recovery between reps. These workouts increase anaerobic enzyme levels, which remain elevated for up to four weeks—meaning you don't have to risk high-intensity training during the couple of weeks before a big race.

Slow glycolysis

Slow glycolysis represents the other pathway for those two pyruvate molecules. Once adequate oxygen reaches your muscle fibers—and as long as your mitochondria aren't already producing energy at full capacity—most pyruvate will be shuttled to your mitochondria, there to be used as fuel for producing ATP aerobically.

AEROBIC SYSTEM (*LONG-TERM ENERGY*)

Aerobic energy production requires oxygen and takes place in your mitochondria. It produces the greatest volume of energy—*by far*—but takes time to get up to speed. While some oxygen is always present in your muscles, your cardiovascular system requires twenty-five to thirty seconds, and up to forty seconds for untrained runners, to deliver the volume of O_2 necessary for most running. Until then, unless you're running extremely easy, your anaerobic systems dominate energy production.

Once ample oxygen is available, your mitochondria shift into high gear. Utilizing two processes—the *Krebs cycle* and the *electron transport chain* (ETC)—your mitochondria will generate thirty-six ATP molecules from those original two pyruvate molecules, thirty-eight to thirty-nine if you include the ATP from glycolysis. Up to six of those ATP molecules are used by the mitochondria, leaving around thirty-two for your muscle fibers. As for oxygen, it waits at the end of the electron transport chain, ready to combine with electrons and protons to form water, a by-product of aerobic energy production.

Another well-known by-product of the aerobic system is carbon dioxide (CO_2). The rising CO_2 level in your bloodstream is the main reason your breathing rate increases during exercise (oxygen levels and acidosis play lesser roles). And offloading excess CO_2 is a big reason why you continue to breathe hard at the conclusion of a taxing run.

Fatigue during aerobic exercise can result from carbohydrate depletion, nervous system fatigue, electrolyte impairment, and free radical accumulation.

Lactate

When runners think of carbohydrate fuels for their muscle fibers, they tend to think of glucose and glycogen. They don't think of lactate. But they should, because lactate is an excellent carbohydrate source. In slow-twitch fibers, during exercise, your mitochondria use up to 80 percent of lactate produced by fast glycolysis to create aerobic energy—netting approximately fifteen ATP molecules per lactate molecule. Are you wondering how one glucose molecule could net thirty-two ATP molecules through slow glycolysis but only two through fast glycolysis? Now you know: It doesn't. It's just that the remaining energy in fast glycolysis gets temporarily stored as lactate. Again, this is a striking example of how your anaerobic system is linked to your aerobic system: Fast glycolysis simultaneously pumps out high-yield anaerobic energy while creating a fuel (lactate) for aerobic energy.

But lactate's role as a fuel source doesn't end there. Your muscle fibers can also export lactate to be used as fuel elsewhere. Exported lactate is not only the primary fuel source for your heart (cardiac muscle) during exercise, it's also a major fuel source for carbohydrate-depleted working muscles. Let's say you're running a demanding session of 5K pace repetitions. As the session continues, you deplete the muscle glycogen stores in your working slow-twitch fibers. Not to worry. In a properly trained runner, lactate from non-working muscle fibers can come to the rescue. A 1998 study

Training recommendation

Tempo runs and 5K/10K pace repetitions (Chapter 7, see pages 127–131) are great for training your mitochondria to burn all carbohydrates—glucose, glycogen, and lactate. Cross Training (Chapter 9, see pages 158–163) increases both MCTs and glycogen levels in a fuller range of muscle fibers, creating warehouses of available energy (once converted to lactate) during exercise. Runners can also increase their muscle glycogen stores (up to 150 percent in trained runners) by eating a diet high in carbohydrates.

by Rauch, Hawley, Noakes, and Dennis found that lactate can diffuse from adjacent inactive muscle fibers to provide an energy boost in active ones. And two studies by Ahlborg, et al. (1982, 1986) showed that glycogen stored in non-working muscles (e.g., the muscles of your arms when you're working your legs) can be converted to lactate, exported to the bloodstream, and thereafter converted into glucose, which fuels your working muscles. In other words, the ability of lactate to directly and indirectly fuel working muscles turns your entire body into one giant lactate battery!

Dr. Timothy Noakes, a South African professor of exercise and sports science at the University of Cape Town and author of the book *Lore of Running*, as well as an author of the 1998 study referenced above, writes that lactate might "be one of the most important energy fuels in the body." In the 1998 experiment, athletes exercised for six hours at 60 percent of VO_2 max. During the last few hours of exercise, lactate provided approximately one-sixth of total energy, with glucose (mostly ingested) and fat providing the remainder. The authors concluded that "there must have been a considerable diffusion of unlabelled lactate from glycogen breakdown in inactive muscle fibres to adjacent active muscle fibres."

Diffusion of lactate from nearby muscle fibers and export of lactate—and its subsequent conversion to glucose—from faraway fibers give you two more good reasons to engage in the cross training exercises illustrated in Chapter 9. Increasing MCTs in muscle fibers that can export lactate increases your available carbohydrate fuel supply.

Fat (lipolysis)

Fat is good. In fact, when it comes to distance running, fat is great! It's just that if carbohydrate-based aerobic energy production is slow, fat is glacial. Utilizing a multitude of steps, *lipolysis* (breakdown of fats to fuel aerobic energy production) delivers fatty acids to the mitochondria, which process them through the Krebs cycle and the electron transport chain. And if you've got the time, it's worth the wait. A single *palmitate* fatty acid produces 129 ATP molecules, four times the amount netted from glucose or glycogen. But because fat-based energy production is so slow, it can't keep up with the energy demands of races faster than 5K pace. That said, fat is a powerful fuel source for many occasions, including:

▶ **At rest:** The majority of your energy at rest is supplied by fat-fueled aerobic energy.

▶ **Below VO_2 max:** As long as your effort is below VO_2 max (about 3K pace or slower), fat will contribute energy—from roughly 10–15 percent at 5K pace up to 85 percent when walking.

▶ **Long duration exercise:** The longer you exercise, the more fat contributes to energy production. Noakes found that athletes training for three hours at 70 percent VO_2 max fueled 6 percent of their energy production through fat-burning at the start of exercise and 43 percent near its conclusion.

You can improve your fat-burning ability by increasing the number of fat-burning enzymes in your mitochondria and by training your body to become more efficient at using fat as a primary energy source. A study by E. Jansson and L. Kaijser found that trained athletes, exercising at 65 percent of VO_2 max, produce 53 percent of their aerobic energy from fat, while untrained subjects produced only 33 percent from fat.

Fatigue during fat-based energy production often results from the biomechanical fatigue of longer efforts—your connective tissues and muscles take a beating.

Training recommendation

The easiest way to train your body to burn more fat is to eat more fat (just don't ignore carbs completely). Training while glycogen-depleted also teaches your body to burn more fat. To burn fat more efficiently, high volume (mileage) and long runs will do the trick.

Protein

Protein is an oft-forgotten energy source. It's better known as the building block for muscle fibers and enzymes. But protein, once broken down into amino acids, can be converted to glucose by the liver. And broken down even further, it can even be converted to glucose within your muscle fibers, thereafter to be fed into the mitochondrial furnace. Ball State exercise physiologist David Costill estimates that up to 9 percent of the total energy expended during a marathon is fueled by protein. But that's not a route you want to travel on a daily basis. Protein breakdown generates toxic wastes

(e.g., ammonia). And protein provides structural and functional support for your cells—burning it is like having termites munching away at the support beams for your house.

Training recommendation

There's no advantage to training your body to burn more protein. Instead, keep your carbohydrate levels high. And ensure adequate restocking of any burned protein by making protein a part of your post-exercise fueling.

Taking your energy systems to the races

As mentioned in Chapter 9, most runners are surprised to discover that the first thirty to fifty seconds of a race—of *any race*—are the most anaerobic. We've grown accustomed to thinking that races become more anaerobic as they proceed, but this simply isn't the case. The reality is that all three energy systems kick in the second we launch ourselves off the start line. Because the sudden energy demand exceeds what can be produced aerobically—until enough oxygen is delivered to your muscle fibers and pyruvate is shuttled to your mitochondria—your anaerobic systems (phosphagen and glycolytic) must carry the early load. By about thirty seconds into longer races (e.g., 1500 meters or more), aerobic energy becomes the dominant energy source. But even in shorter races (e.g., 400 and 800 meters), aerobic energy starts to provide the majority of energy by forty to fifty-five seconds, as demonstrated in a 2003 Australian study by Duffield, Dawson, and Goodman. In races run at less than VO_2 max (e.g., 5K or longer), your aerobic system will take over almost all energy production. In shorter races, the energy demand exceeds what aerobic energy alone can provide, and anaerobic systems will

TRAINING DISCUSSION

"Do carbo-loading and fat-loading work?"

Runners are always looking for a performance edge. Some have turned to carbo-loading and fat-loading to ensure adequate fuel storage during endurance events. But do they work?

In a word: Absolutely.

But there are a few stipulations. Carbo-loading works great for races longer than ninety minutes. Fat-loading is the ticket for events extending beyond four hours. For anything shorter, not so much.

Carbo-loading dates to the 1960s, when athletes discovered that three to four days of carbohydrate restriction followed by three to four days of carbo-binging doubled muscle glycogen stores, which led to reduced fatigue during endurance races. Unfortunately, carbo-restriction also leads to irritability and gastrointestinal distress. So athletes kept looking for a better way. By the 1980s, athletes had found that a three-day taper accompanied by increased carb intake worked as well as the old seven- to eight-day routine—and with no side effects. In 2002, a University of Western Australia study showed that cyclists who pedaled hard for two and a half minutes, pedaled all-out for another thirty seconds, and then loaded up on carbs saw an 80 percent increase in glycogen stores within twenty-four hours. And a 2013 University of Minnesota School of Kinesiology study found that simply increasing carb intake during the twenty-four hours pre-race improved marathon times by 4 percent.

On the other hand, carbo-loading adds about four pounds to your weight, inhibits fat-burning, doesn't work well for women, and, as a race strategy, has been pretty much rendered obsolete by sports drinks, gels, and other glycogen-replacement strategies. Still, to ensure adequate glycogen levels, it's a good idea to increase carbs to 70 percent of all calories for three days before your race—and to taper.

Fat-loading is a performance-enhancing must for endurance events lasting four hours or more. Exercise scientist Dr. Timothy Noakes estimates that elite Ironman triathlon competitors burn fat at a rate of 50 percent above normal following a period of fat-loading.

There are two good fat-loading methods:

- ▶ **High-fat diet:** Stick to a high-fat diet for seven to ten days before your event. Your body learns to function at low glycogen levels that would stop a carbo-loaded athlete in his or her tracks.
- ▶ **Glycogen-deplete:** Train after fasting, or reduce carbs after the preceding workout. This teaches your body to burn more fat (an almost inexhaustible source of energy within your body) while running. In other words, this is a method of "fat-loading" by using your own fat stores.

(Continued)

All that said, anyone considering carbo-loading or fat-loading might be wise to remember the words of multiple-time USA masters champion and former 2:13 marathoner David Olds: "It's not a meal, it's a race."

continue to contribute until the buildup of acidosis and other fatigue factors force you to slow down or stop. But that pain you feel during the final portion of the race—the bear jumping on your back—is not the point at which you "go anaerobic"; instead, it's the point at which the increase of anaerobic by-products that began at the race start line has finally become too much to bear (pun intended).

AEROBIC ENZYMES

Aerobic enzymes are mitochondria's little helpers. These proteins improve your mitochondria's ability to provide aerobic energy by increasing the efficiency of chemical reactions inside your mitochondria. Within five seconds of commencing exercise, these enzymes go to work, and their activity level increases all the way up to marathon pace. In fact, training at marathon pace (tempo) is a good way to trigger creation of even more aerobic enzymes. At faster paces, acidosis can occur, and it negatively impacts and even destroys these enzymes.

Training recommendation

Aerobic enzymes flourish with tempo—fast tempo, slow tempo, and tempo intervals. On the other hand, speed kills when it comes to these enzymes, so don't overdo anaerobic work.

HEAT

Generating ATP also generates heat—about 98.6°F in most humans. You can't add energy to a system, in this case the human body, without creating heat. When you break down carbs and fats, you release energy to create ATP. When that ATP is used to power muscle contractions, you release more energy. But you don't capture all that energy, funneling every spark into your next quadriceps or calf contraction. Instead, you use as little as 25 percent of your produced energy, while the remaining energy escapes as heat. That heat is the source of your body temperature.

Have you ever wondered why you shiver when you're cold? It's because shivering requires muscles to contract and relax quickly, generating more ATP and heat. When you're hot, your body has two responses:

▶ **Increased blood flow to the skin:** This allows heat that was transferred from your muscles to your blood to be diffused into the air, a process called *convection*.
▶ **Sweat:** More than two million sweat glands help offload heat by secreting sweat. You lose heat energy when your sweat evaporates—sweating by itself doesn't cool you down.

But even with increased blood flow and sweating, your core body temperature rises during exercise. Normally, that's not a bad thing. Every runner knows that a warm-up aids performance. But when the air outside your body also heats up (especially if it's humid, too), problems arise.

If the air temperature is higher than 98.6°F, your body will *gain* heat from the air. In that situation, sweating is the only way to cool down. But, again, sweat has to evaporate for that to work. If it's humid, the air might not be able to absorb your sweat, and sweat dripping to the ground doesn't help you. You're left with no way to cool down except to jump in a pool, douse yourself with a hose, or stop exercising.

Steps you can take to mitigate the impact of hot and humid days include:

1. **Adjust your pace:** See "Air Temperature and Pace Adjustments" in Table 10.2.
2. **Stay hydrated:** Drink to thirst. Don't overhydrate, as that can lead to *hyponatremia*, a life-threatening condition in which sodium concentration in the blood is dangerously lowered.
3. **Wear light clothing:** Pick modern fabrics that allow heat to escape.
4. **Avoid hats:** Use visors and sunscreen to protect your skin.
5. **Slow down or stop:** If you're really feeling the heat, quit before *heat exhaustion* forces you to quit. Try pool running. Or maybe an elliptical machine in an air-conditioned fitness club.

Table 10.2
Air Temperature and Pace Adjustments

Temperature		Pace-per-Mile Adjustments Based on Heat*											
Fahrenheit	Celsius	4:30	5:00	5:30	6:00	6:30	7:00	7:30	8:00	8:30	9:00	9:30	10:00
120	48.9	5:23	5:59	6:34	7:10	7:46	8:22	8:58	9:34	10:10	10:45	11:21	11:57
110	43.3	5:07	5:41	6:15	6:49	7:32	7:57	8:31	9:05	9:40	10:13	10:48	11:22
100	37.8	4:55	5:27	6:00	6:33	7:05	7:38	8:11	8:44	9:17	9:49	10:22	10:55
90	32.2	4:45	5:17	5:49	6:20	6:52	7:24	7:55	8:27	8:59	9:30	10:02	10:34
80	26.7	4:38	5:09	5:40	6:11	6:42	7:13	7:44	8:15	8:46	9:17	9:48	10:19
70	21.1	4:34	5:04	5:34	6:05	6:35	7:06	7:36	8:06	8:37	9:07	9:38	10:08
*53	11.4	4:30	5:00	5:30	6:00	6:30	7:00	7:30	8:00	8:30	9:00	9:30	10:00
60	15.6	4:31	5:01	5:31	6:01	6:31	7:01	7:31	8:02	8:32	9:02	9:32	10:02
50	10.0	4:30	5:00	5:30	6:00	6:30	7:00	7:30	8:00	8:30	9:00	9:30	10:00
40	4.4	4:31	5:01	5:31	6:01	6:31	7:01	7:31	8:02	8:32	9:02	9:32	10:02
30	-1.1	4:34	5:04	5:34	6:05	6:35	7:06	7:36	8:06	8:37	9:07	9:38	10:08
20	-6.7	4:38	5:09	5:40	6:11	6:42	7:13	7:44	8:15	8:46	9:16	9:47	10:18
10	-12.2	4:45	5:17	5:48	6:20	6:52	7:23	7:55	8:27	8:58	9:30	10:02	10:33
0	-17.8	4:54	5:27	6:00	6:32	7:05	7:38	8:11	8:43	9:16	9:49	10:21	10:54
-10	-23.3	5:07	5:41	6:15	6:49	7:23	7:57	8:31	9:05	9:39	10:13	10:47	11:21
-20	-28.9	5:22	5:58	6:34	7:10	7:46	8:21	8:57	9:33	10:09	10:45	11:20	11:56

TABLE 10.2 shows pace adjustments for distance runs (or tempo, reps, etc.) in the heat. The chart assumes that *53 degrees is the optimal temperature; pace headings reflect pace/mile at this temperature. Find your optimal pace in the top row, then find pace adjustments in the column below that pace (associated with the temperature in the two left-hand columns).

BUILD YOUR RUNNING BODY—COMPONENTS AND WORKOUTS

The good news is that your body will adapt to hot weather within two weeks. According to an Australian review article by Saunders, et al., your blood plasma increases by up to 12 percent, your heart rate goes down, your ventilation goes up, you sweat more, and your energy requirements are reduced. In other words, your body gets better at running in the heat *by running in the heat*.

Training recommendation

It takes two weeks to acclimatize to the heat, and it requires sensible training. Run when it's coolest—early morning or in the evening. And adjust your effort and pace for the heat and humidity.

FUELING

The *Build Your Running Diet* section of this book will offer in-depth counseling on fuel choices, so for now we'll take a brief look at four areas of immediate concern:

1. **Pre-workout meals:** Workouts performed at 5K pace or faster require some pre-workout carbo-loading. A larger meal the night before or smaller meals during the day of the workout can do the trick. Success in these workouts is largely determined by the carbohydrate (glycogen) content in your muscle fibers.

2. **Supplementation:** Consider a carbohydrate/protein supplement in the 30 minutes post-workout. You'll elevate protein synthesis within the exercised muscle fibers, replace glycogen at an increased rate, and speed recovery.

3. **Ratio of carbs to protein:** For post-workout supplements, research favors a 4:1 ratio of carbohydrates to protein, although this can be adjusted to personal preference. Many runners consider chocolate milk to be the perfect post-run refreshment.

4. **Fueling during a race:** Fueling during races of 10K or shorter is unnecessary. For races of 70 minutes or longer, take approximately 30–60 grams of carbs (in fluid) per hour, with a carb concentration of no less than 2 percent and no more than 10 percent (4–8 percent is optimal). Sports drinks like Gatorade (6 percent) and Powerade (8 percent) fall squarely within this range. If you're using gels, drink adequate water to dilute the carb content.

For a better fueling rundown, turn to Part Four of this book.

TRAINING RUNDOWN

For this chapter's photo instruction, we're going to break down the caloric requirements of different workouts and tabulate approximate contributions from carbohydrates and fats. We'll also offer some fueling tips. Breakdowns include:

- ▶ **Walking**
- ▶ **Jogging**
- ▶ **Distance Run**
- ▶ **Sprints**
- ▶ **800-Pace Intervals**
- ▶ **Mile-Pace Intervals**
- ▶ **5K/10K Pace Intervals**
- ▶ **Tempo**
- ▶ **Resistance Training**
- ▶ **Cross Training**
- ▶ **Marathon Fueling**

Chapter 10: Build Your Running Energy Systems —
PHOTO INSTRUCTION

CALORIES, CARBS, FATS, AND THE NUTRITIONAL IMPACT OF TRAINING

It's one thing to know how to do the various workouts that are required to build your running body. It's another to properly fuel the effort. For this section, we'll break down workouts into calories, carbohydrates, and fats. You'll also find a meal or snack suggestion accompanying each workout. These suggestions are based on the specific caloric and nutritional requirements of each workout, but don't worry that they're your only choices. You'll find more recipes in Part Four of this book, and you probably have some favorites of your own. These examples are offered to help you get started. Also, remember that you burn calories around the clock (unless you're running one hundred miles per week or more, most of the calories you burn support your normal metabolism), so don't limit fueling to replacement of calories burned through exercise. To use the tables:

1. Find your approximate weight in the left-hand column.
2. Find your total calories (either per mile or per minute, depending upon the table), as well as approximate breakdown of those calories into carbs and fats, in the same row as your weight. Note that these numbers are averages and shouldn't be read as absolute values.
3. At the bottom of most tables, you'll find an additional line entry: "Actual % Carbs/Fats Range." This represents a more accurate range for the relative contributions of carbohydrates and fats to your workout, based on your body type, fitness, etc. For example, less-fit runners will burn less fat and more carbohydrate than fit runners during distance runs. These ranges should help you better plan your pre- and post-workout meals by alerting you to the energy sources you've depleted.
4. Note that values for protein are not given, as protein is a backup fuel that is only used when carbs are significantly depleted.
5. A pre-training or post-training meal/snack suggestion is given for each workout.

Because good fitness is a family affair, the Cushing-murrays will demonstrate the workouts. Christian, you've met. Wife Kathleen was a national junior age-group cross country champion and a scholarship athlete for UCLA. Son Nathaniel, now at UCLA, was a 9:15 high school 3200-meter runner. Daughter Jessica, still in high school, has run a 5:06 mile. Son Zachary was a sub-5:00 miler as a high school freshman. And daughter Rebecca ran a 5:27 mile in the sixth grade.

Walking

Walking recruits fewer muscle fibers at a less-intense effort than jogging or running, so it burns fewer calories. Most of the calories burned while walking come from fat, with carbs providing a smaller percentage. For "brisk walking," add 5–10 percent more calories per mile.

Calories Burned Per Mile: Walking Pace			
Weight (lbs.)	Total Calories	Calories from Carbs	Calories from Fats
50	27	5	22
75	40	7	33
100	53	9	44
110	58	10	48
120	64	11	52
130	69	12	57
140	74	13	61
150	80	14	66
160	85	15	70
170	90	16	74
180	95	17	79
190	101	18	83
200	106	19	87
210	111	19	92
220	117	20	96
230	122	21	101
240	127	22	105
250	133	23	109
275	146	26	120
300	159	28	131
Actual % Carbs/Fats Range		14–21%	86–79%

RECOVERY MEAL

Best Oats and Groats Ever

Oatmeal (made from healthy oat groats) is a great source of complex carbs and offers many other nutritional benefits. It's also not too high in calories, making it the perfect choice after a walk. This recipe uses an easy slow-cooking method that allows the added bananas and blueberries (or whatever fruit you have on hand) to meld into a luscious, fruity dessert-meal, with 42 grams of carbohydrates.

▶ **TOTAL CALORIES:** 227 per serving (including fruit)
▶ **RECIPE:** Page 303

Jogging

Jogging is more a matter of effort than pace. Sometimes jogging is performed at walking pace, while other times jogging can approach the effort of an easy run. Still, since the effort remains below that of a normal distance run, you'll rely most heavily on fat as an energy source.

Training: Energy and Nutrition Breakdown

Calories Burned Per Mile: Jogging Pace			
Weight (lbs.)	Total Calories	Calories from Carbs	Calories from Fats
50	38	12	26
75	57	17	40
100	76	23	53
110	84	26	58
120	91	28	63
130	99	30	69
140	106	32	74
150	114	35	79
160	122	37	85
170	129	39	90
180	137	42	95
190	144	44	100
200	152	46	106
210	160	49	111
220	167	51	116
230	175	53	122
240	182	56	126
250	190	58	132
275	209	64	145
300	228	70	158
Actual % Carbs/Fats Range		26–35%	74–65%

RECOVERY MEAL

Secret Healthy Pancakes

After a nice morning jog, you know you want to eat pancakes, right? Then by all means, do so. These have a sneaky swap of white whole wheat flour, which takes the guilt out of the guilty pleasure. Top with yogurt and berries, and eat as many as your calorie requirement allows, with each cake offering 8 grams of carbs, 1 gram of fat, and 2 grams of protein.

▶ **TOTAL CALORIES:** 53 per cake
▶ **RECIPE:** Page 314

Regular Runs

Regular runs include the full range of distance runs that you'll include in your training diet: easy, regular, and long. For easy runs, you'll probably burn near the lower end of the carbohydrate range. For long runs, you'll burn near the high end of the range.

Training: Energy and Nutrition Breakdown

Calories Burned Per Mile: Regular Run Pace			
Weight (lbs.)	Total Calories	Calories from Carbs	Calories from Fats
50	38	18	20
75	57	28	29
100	76	37	39
110	84	41	43
120	91	44	47
130	99	48	51
140	106	51	55
150	114	55	59
160	122	59	63
170	129	63	66
180	137	66	71
190	144	70	74
200	152	74	78
210	160	78	82
220	167	81	86
230	175	85	90
240	182	88	94
250	190	92	98
275	209	101	108
300	228	111	117
Actual % Carbs/Fats Range		43–54%	57–46%

RECOVERY MEAL

Lemon Risotto with Avocado and Salmon

A good mix of carbs and fats are the ticket for recovery after a distance run. This risotto offers healthy fats from the salmon, avocado, and olive oil, and an equal boost of complex carbs (36 grams) from the rice for balance. And pay no mind to risotto's bad reputation as a difficult dish to make—this is really easy!

▶ **TOTAL CALORIES:** 575 per serving
▶ **RECIPE:** Page 333

Tempo Runs

Tempo runs push the pace to an effort level that demands faster fueling from carbs. You'll still burn fat for a third of your calories—plus, the fact that you're covering ground faster means that you'll actually burn about the same amount of fat per minute as you did during regular runs.

Calories Burned Per Mile: Tempo Pace			
Weight (lbs.)	Total Calories	Calories from Carbs	Calories from Fats
50	38	25	13
75	57	38	19
100	76	51	25
110	84	56	28
120	91	61	30
130	99	66	33
140	106	71	35
150	114	76	38
160	122	82	40
170	129	86	43
180	137	92	45
190	144	96	48
200	152	102	50
210	160	107	53
220	167	112	55
230	175	117	58
240	182	122	60
250	190	127	63
275	209	140	69
300	228	153	75
Actual % Carbs/Fats Range		62–72%	38–28%

RECOVERY MEAL

Stuffed Tortilla Chiles with Feta, Corn, and Black Beans

For tempo run recovery, aim for a meal that doesn't skimp on calories and carbs, with a bit of protein and fat to round it out. This healthy spin on chiles rellenos offers up to 67 grams of carbs, which can be further boosted with a serving of rice.

▶ **TOTAL CALORIES:** 445 per serving
▶ **RECIPE:** Page 315

5K/10K Pace Running

Whether you're running 5K/10K pace for repetitions or during a race, your carbohydrate requirements just increased. The speed with which carbs are burned combined with the length of time you'll be running means you'll be going deep into the muscle glycogen well. You'll want to carboload the night before and follow the workout with a quick carb snack.

Training: Energy and Nutrition Breakdown

Calories Burned Per Mile: 5K/10K Pace			
Weight (lbs.)	Total Calories	Calories from Carbs	Calories from Fats
50	38	31	7
75	57	47	10
100	76	63	13
110	84	69	15
120	91	75	16
130	99	82	17
140	106	87	19
150	114	94	20
160	122	101	21
170	129	106	23
180	137	113	24
190	144	119	25
200	152	125	27
210	160	132	28
220	167	138	29
230	175	144	31
240	182	150	32
250	190	157	33
275	209	172	37
300	228	188	40
Actual % Carbs/Fats Range		77–88%	23–12%

DINNER-THE-NIGHT-BEFORE MEAL

Linguine with Anchovies and Things

Since carbs, carbs, and more carbs are the key to success here, indulging in pasta the night before should prepare you properly. This recipe relies on a fresh tomato, olive oil, and anchovy sauce—the main focus is on complex carbs (84 grams per serving), but the zesty sauce adds other important nutrients without too much fat.

▶ **TOTAL CALORIES:** 514 per serving
▶ **RECIPE:** Page 314

Mile-Pace Running

Most efforts at mile race pace—whether for a race or repetitions—don't burn fat. Above 100 percent of VO$_2$ max, most runners burn only carbohydrates. So the table for mile-paced running shows total calories without breaking down fat or carb content (note that slower runners will burn some fat). Also, the calories are given in "per minute" totals, since all reps are less than a mile. It has been theorized that high-intensity training might lead to an "afterburn" of 3–5 percent additional calories, much of it from fat.

Weight (lbs)	Mile Pace				
	4:00	6:00	8:00	10:00	12:00
50	9.5	6.3	4.8	3.8	3.2
75	14.3	9.5	7.1	5.7	4.8
100	19.0	12.7	9.5	7.6	6.3
110	21.0	14.0	10.5	8.4	7.0
120	22.8	15.2	11.4	9.1	7.6
130	24.8	16.5	12.4	9.9	8.3
140	26.5	17.7	13.3	10.6	8.8
150	28.5	19.0	14.3	11.4	9.5
160	30.5	20.3	15.3	12.2	10.2
170	32.3	21.5	16.1	12.9	10.8
180	34.3	22.8	17.1	13.7	11.4
190	36.0	24.0	18.0	14.4	12.0
200	38.0	25.3	19.0	15.2	12.7
210	40.0	26.7	20.0	16.0	13.3
220	41.8	27.8	20.9	16.7	13.9
230	43.8	29.2	21.9	17.5	14.6
240	45.5	30.3	22.8	18.2	15.2
250	47.5	31.7	23.8	19.0	15.8
275	52.3	34.8	26.1	20.9	17.4
300	57.0	38.0	28.5	22.8	19.0

Calories Burned Per Minute: 1-Mile Pace

Find your weight and mile pace; calories burned while sustaining that pace for a minute appear in the column beneath the pace. All values are approximate.

RECOVERY SNACK

Custom Homemade Hummus

This is the perfect time for a carb-heavy snack, with just a little fat. Hummus adds to the carbs, but it also provides a bit of healthy fat and other nutrients. One serving of hummus with a whole-wheat bagel will yield a dish with around 70 grams of carbs and 10 grams of fat. If you find post-run bagels tricky to consume, try a serving of hummus with a 300-calorie serving of pretzels.

▶ **TOTAL CALORIES:** 400 per serving (approximately 100 for hummus, 300 for bagel or pretzels)

▶ **RECIPE:** Page 355

800m Pace Running

Training or racing at 800m pace burns only carbohydrates. But it's hard to estimate the exact energy cost. When aerobically produced energy is your primary source, the energy cost is straightforward. But the moment that strength, speed, power, greater muscle fiber recruitment, and a primarily anaerobic energy supply become factors, the science becomes less clear, because studies to date haven't addressed those factors. Add to that a theorized 3–5 percent "afterburn" of additional calories, much from fat, and it'd be fair to say that calorie totals are partly guesswork. This book's best guess is that calorie totals are higher than those indicated.

Training: Energy and Nutrition Breakdown

Calories Burned Per Minute: 800m Pace					
Weight (lbs)	800m Pace				
	2:00	2:30	3:00	4:00	5:00
50	9.4	7.6	6.3	4.7	3.8
75	14.2	11.3	9.4	7.1	5.7
100	18.9	15.1	12.6	9.4	7.6
110	20.9	16.7	13.9	10.4	8.4
120	22.6	18.1	15.1	11.3	9.0
130	24.6	19.7	16.4	12.3	9.8
140	26.3	21.1	17.6	13.2	10.5
150	28.3	22.7	18.9	14.2	11.3
160	30.3	24.3	20.2	15.2	12.1
170	32.1	25.7	21.4	16.0	12.8
180	34.1	27.2	22.7	17.0	13.6
190	35.8	28.6	23.9	17.9	14.3
200	37.8	30.2	25.2	18.9	15.1
210	39.8	31.8	26.5	19.9	15.9
220	41.5	33.2	27.7	20.8	16.6
230	43.5	34.8	29.0	21.7	17.4
240	45.2	36.2	30.2	22.6	18.1
250	47.2	37.8	31.5	23.6	18.9
275	51.9	41.6	34.6	26.0	20.8
300	56.7	45.3	37.8	28.3	22.7

Find your weight and 800m pace; calories burned while sustaining that pace for a minute appear in the column beneath the pace. All values are approximate.

RECOVERY SNACK

Almond Cherry Pie Oat Bars

Since it's important to get carbs in your tank within 30 minutes of finishing an 800m pace run (the better to replace spent muscle glycogen stores more quickly), these bars are great to have on hand. They provide 41 grams of complex carbs, plus they're extra tasty topped with chocolate!

▶ **TOTAL CALORIES:** 265 per bar
▶ **RECIPE:** Page 345

Sprinting (400m Pace Running)

Few runners will run "sprints" at faster than 400-meter pace—and those who run HIIT can confidently use this same table. Again, it's nearly impossible to estimate accurate energy expenditures for primarily anaerobic activity, but this table should give you a ballpark idea. Sprint workouts won't burn a lot of calories, although there's a theorized 3–5 percent "afterburn" of additional calories, much from fat.

Training: Energy and Nutrition Breakdown

Weight (lbs)	Calories Burned Per Minute: 400m Pace				
	400m Pace				
	:50	1:00	1:20	1:40	2:00
50	11.3	9.4	7.1	5.7	4.7
75	17.0	14.2	10.6	8.5	7.1
100	22.7	18.9	14.2	11.3	9.4
110	25.1	20.9	15.7	12.5	10.4
120	27.1	22.6	17.0	13.6	11.3
130	29.5	24.6	18.5	14.8	12.3
140	31.6	26.3	19.8	15.8	13.2
150	34.0	28.3	21.3	17.0	14.2
160	36.4	30.3	22.7	18.2	15.2
170	38.5	32.1	24.0	19.2	16.0
180	40.9	34.1	25.5	20.4	17.0
190	42.9	35.8	26.8	21.5	17.9
200	45.3	37.8	28.3	22.7	18.9
210	47.7	39.8	29.8	23.9	19.9
220	49.8	41.5	31.1	24.9	20.8
230	52.2	43.5	32.6	26.1	21.7
240	54.3	45.2	33.9	27.1	22.6
250	56.7	47.2	35.4	28.3	23.6
275	62.3	51.9	39.0	31.2	26.0
300	68.0	56.7	42.5	34.0	28.3

Find your weight and 400m pace; calories burned while sustaining that pace for a minute appear in the column beneath the pace. All values are approximate.

RECOVERY SNACK

Top Ten Recovery Snacks

Since you need carbs but not a lot of calories following a 400m pace race or workout, refer to this list for suitable snack options.

► **TOTAL CALORIES:** varies by snack
► **RECIPE:** Page 309 (sidebar, "Top Ten Recovery Snacks" in Chapter 19)

Cross Training

Cross training encompasses a wide variety of sports and workouts and can't be broken down into calories burned across the board. Instead, this table attempts to give you an idea of how different cross training activities at different intensities stack up against one another.

Cross Training - Calories Burned per 60 Minutes		
Type	Intensity	Calories
Elliptical	Level-5 setting	550
ElliptiGO	15 mph	600
Treadmill	7 mph	650
Pool Running	Marathon effort	450
Cross Country Skiing	8 mph	675
Snow Shoeing	3 mph	625
Kickboxing	Medium effort	525
Cycling	14 mph	475
Stair Climbing	Level-5 setting	506
Swimming	75 meters/minute	375
Indoor Rowing	125 watts	550

Note: All values are approximate.

RECOVERY SNACK

Spicy Maple Hot Chocolate

All we can say is "thank you" to the researchers who determined that chocolate milk's balance of carbs and protein make for the optimal recovery drink—so drink it cold on hot days. But for days when you're training in a winter wonderland, try this spicy hot cocoa for postworkout. It has 47 grams of carbs and 10 grams of protein per serving.

▶ **TOTAL CALORIES:** 267 per serving
▶ **RECIPE:** Page 315

BUILD YOUR RUNNING BODY

Resistance Training

All resistance training is *not* created calorically equal. High-intensity endurance training workouts, like The Runner 360 (see page 53), burn lots of calories in 30 minutes (the factor used for determining calories in the table). Traditional weightlifting, with breaks between sets, burns fewer calories, although still a high percentage of carbs.

Training: Energy and Nutrition Breakdown

Weight (lbs.)	Weightlifting			The Runner 360		
	Cals	Carb Cals	Fat Cals	Cals	Carb Cals	Fat Cals
50	47	43	5	143	128	15
75	71	64	7	214	193	21
100	95	86	9	285	257	28
110	104	94	10	314	282	32
120	114	103	11	342	308	34
130	123	111	12	371	333	38
140	133	120	13	399	359	40
150	142	128	14	428	384	44
160	152	137	15	456	410	46
170	161	145	16	485	436	48
180	171	154	17	513	462	51
190	180	163	18	542	488	54
200	190	171	19	570	513	57
210	199	179	20	599	539	60
220	209	188	21	627	564	63
230	218	196	22	656	590	66
240	228	205	23	684	616	68
250	237	213	24	713	641	72
275	261	235	26	784	706	78
300	285	256	28	855	770	85

Resistance Training—Calories Burned per 30-Minute Workout

Note: All values are approximate.

RECOVERY MEAL

Peanut Butter Cup Smoothie

For help rebuilding muscles, protein is king after resistance training. This smoothie has a base of Greek yogurt and peanut butter, both great natural protein sources—plus banana and chocolate to make you happy! Per serving, it provides 22 grams of protein. Your muscles will thank you.

▶ **TOTAL CALORIES:** 343 per serving
▶ **RECIPE:** Page 322

Marathon Fueling

You won't need to worry about in-race fueling for 5Ks to 10Ks. But once races reach 70 minutes or longer, you can fuel with 30–60 grams of carbohydrate per hour (test yourself in training first, as different runners' needs and gastrointestinal reactions will vary). Since runners differ in how often—and how much—they want to fuel while racing, this table breaks down different fueling options in increments of 15–60 grams. For example, if you choose to consume 30 grams of carbs per hour, and Gatorade is your fuel of choice, you'll drink 8 ounces (the 15-gram equivalent) every 30 minutes. Many runners mix and match fueling sources during a race. Note that gels—a favored fueling source—come in 25-gram packets, but you probably wouldn't want to split those; you'll just take one every 30 minutes or hour, depending on your personal requirements. If you prefer chewy (rubbery) cubes or jelly beans to drinks and gels, then Clif Shot Bloks or sport beans might be the fueling option for you.

Training:
Energy and Nutrition Breakdown

Marathon Fueling					
Fuel Options	Options for 15–60 Grams of Carbohydrates per Hour				
	15 Grams	25 Grams	30 Grams	50 Grams	60 Grams
Clif Shot Bloks	2 pieces (16g)	3 pieces (24g)	4 pieces (32g)	6 pieces (48g)	8 pieces (64g)
Dates	1 date (18g)	1.5 dates (27g)	2 dates (36g)	3 dates (54g)	3.5 dates (63g)
Fig Newtons	0.5 cookies (11g)	1 cookie (22g)	1.5 cookies (33g)	2 cookies (44g)	3 cookies (66g)
Gatorade	8 oz (14g)	12 oz (20g)	16 oz (26g)	32 oz (52g)	36 oz (60g)
Gels	n/a	1 packet (25g)	n/a	2 packets (50g)	n/a
Honey	1 tbsp (17g)	n/a	2 tbsp (32g)	n/a	4 tbsp (64g)
Power Bar	0.25 bars (11g)	0.5 bars (22g)	0.75 bars (33g)	1 bar (44g)	1.5 bars (66g)
Pretzels (mini)	12 pretzels (15g)	20 pretzels (25g)	24 pretzels (30g)	40 pretzels (50g)	48 pretzels (60g)
Raisins	50 raisins (15g)	1 ounce box (22g)	100 raisins (30g)	2 boxes (44g)	200 raisins (60g)
Sport Beans	9 beans (15g)	1 ounce packet (25g)	18 beans (30g)	2 packets (50g)	36 beans (60g)

Rewire Your Running Nervous System

Good communication skills aren't just about conveying information to the outside world. They're also the key to utilizing your body's vast internal messaging network—the billions of *neurons* and trillions of *neural pathways* that comprise your nervous system. In the Mary Shelley novel *Frankenstein*, published in 1818, rogue scientist Victor Frankenstein jolts his monster to life with electrical current harnessed from a storm. In no less dramatic fashion, the electrochemical current of your nervous system animates your movements, delivers sensations, and constructs your thoughts. As a runner, you rely upon your nervous system to control every aspect of your running body. But this bioengineered software is only as good as your neural wiring, a network that stretches to the far reaches of your body and everywhere in between. Wiring this network for maximum efficiency—and then rewiring it to meet new challenges—is *your* job. And a properly trained nervous system makes the difference between good and great running.

WHAT'S YOUR NERVOUS SYSTEM?

Your nervous system is one of two principal communications networks within your body (your *endocrine system*, which produces *hormones*, is the other). It's comprised of the *central nervous system* (CNS), which includes your brain and spinal cord, and the *peripheral nervous system* (PNS), which contains all the nerves outside the CNS.

Your CNS is the command center of your nervous system. It's tasked with coordinating all physical activity and processing all sensory data. There are eighty-five billion neurons (nerve cells) in your brain and another billion in your spinal cord. Compare those numbers with the neurons possessed by a sponge (zero), a cockroach (one million), a cat (one billion), a chimpanzee (seven billion), and an elephant (twenty-three billion). That's right, elephants have more neurons than chimps. Don't forget that. You know elephants won't.

Motor neurons in your CNS send messages along *axons* (nerve fibers) to the muscles in your body, where the neurons trigger contraction and relaxation, as well as to organs and glands. In return, *sensory neurons* relay stimuli detected by your senses throughout your body via the PNS back to the CNS.

Neurons can fire off messages up to one thousand times per second, although most operate at a more manageable rate of between one and four hundred per second. These messages are called *impulses*, and they travel at varying speeds along different types of nerves. Kick your toe while running and you'll feel pressure almost immediately, since touch travels at 250 feet per second. Pain impulses, on the other hand, take twice as long because they travel on slower nerve fibers. Dull, throbbing pain inches along at two feet per second, giving you a two- to three-second delay before you'll need to start hopping on one foot and cursing your toe for its clumsiness.

As you can probably guess from those speeds, it's not electric current running through your nervous system. Instead, you have electrochemical impulses that travel several million times slower than the current feeding your television or toaster (see sidebar, "What's a nerve impulse?" for more on impulses).

On the other hand, your CNS can fire between 10^{13} and 10^{16} total impulses per second. That's roughly equivalent to the capability of the world's largest supercomputer, Oak Ridge National Laboratory's *Titan*, which covers 4,300 square feet, cost

BEGINNER'S GUIDELINE

The time to rewire your nervous system is sooner, not later. Both your stride and your running efficiency are largely dictated by your nervous system, and better wiring reduces the likelihood of injury, decreases fatigue, and improves performance.

TRAINING DISCUSSION

"What's a nerve impulse?"

So what, exactly, is a nerve impulse?

Is an impulse electrical? Is it chemical? Is it an unquantifiable spark of the ethereal soul?

If you've asked yourself those questions, you're not alone. Twenty-one Nobel Prize winners—from Camillo Golgi and Santiago Ramón y Cajal in 1906 to Arvid Carlsson, Paul Greengard, and Eric Kandel in 2000—earned the award for attempting to provide some answers.

Let's start with the nerve itself. A neuron (nerve cell) has a cell body, dendrites to receive messages from other neurons, a long fiber called an axon that transmits messages, and an axon terminal that marks the end of the nerve at the *synapse*, a small space (specifically the synaptic gap, or synaptic cleft) separating a neuron from other neurons and muscle cells. The neuron must communicate across the synapse if the message is to be delivered.

In the first half of the nineteenth century, nerve impulses were thought to travel at phenomenal speeds: Estimates ranged anywhere from eleven million miles per second to instantaneous transmission. Hermann von Helmholtz put the kibosh on that in 1849, calculating the speed of nerve impulses at twenty-five to thirty-nine meters per second—barely fast enough to outsprint a good racehorse.

By the twentieth century, work by Emil du Bois-Reymond, Julius Bernstein, Louis Lapicque, and others had ushered in the golden age of *electrophysiology*, in which nerve impulses were viewed as electrophysiological messages propagated by *action potentials*—exchanges of charged ions through the axon's membrane that could speed an impulse along an axon's length.

There was only one conundrum: What happened at the synapse, that tiny gap between a neuron and its target? Did electric sparks jump the gap? Or was some other mechanism at work? Two camps emerged in the debate. *Sparkers* believed it was all electrical, all the time. *Soupers* thought that chemical agents must be involved. As it turned out, Soupers were mostly right.

In 1921, Otto Loewi (who would share the Nobel Prize in 1936) harvested the still-beating hearts from two frogs, placed each in saline solution, and electrically stimulated one heart until its heartbeat slowed down. He then collected saline solution from around the affected heart and injected it into the second heart. The second heart slowed down, too—a result that could only be possible if there had been a chemical release into the saline. The chemical (acetylcholine) is now known to be a *neurotransmitter*, one of a group of chemicals released by neurons to communicate across the synapse.

But Sparkers weren't completely wrong, either. They earned a small victory in 1957 when David Potter and Edwin Furshpan showed that some electrical impulses jump the synapse by utilizing tiny cylindrical channels known as *gap junctions*.

So what is a nerve impulse? It's both electrical and chemical, and it communicates messages at limited speeds over the internal wiring known as your nervous system—awaiting further reassessment from future scientists and Nobel Prize winners.

$97 million to build, and performs 17.59 petaflops per second (more than seventeen quadrillion operations), a feat requiring enough energy to power seven thousand homes. That's some pretty impressive company your CNS is keeping.

NERVOUS SYSTEM TRAINING

When it comes to running, an untrained nervous system doesn't know what to do. Imagine if every time you switched on the light in your living room, the garbage disposal turned on in the kitchen. You'd call an electrician to rewire your house. An untrained nervous system is like that switch. You and your workouts must become the electrician. You'll need to rewire:

1. Motor-unit recruitment and coordination
2. Proprioception
3. Balance
4. Nervous system fatigue
5. Running economy

You'll accomplish this rewiring with a combination of traditional running workouts, technique drills, plyometrics, hill sprints, balance exercises, and more.

MOTOR-UNIT RECRUITMENT

Running begins when you "tell" your body to run. The message originates in your brain, travels to motor neurons in your spinal cord, and then is transmitted along the motor neurons' axons to your muscles. Each motor neuron controls a specific group of muscle fibers within a single muscle—together, the neuron and the fibers it controls are called a *motor unit*.

A motor unit might contain only a few fibers (ten to one hundred) if it's responsible for intricate

movement, such as control of your fingers while pinning a race bib to your shirt. Or it might boast up to two thousand muscle fibers for less coordinated movement, like contracting your quads as you blast off the start line.

All muscle fibers within a single motor unit must be the same fiber type (e.g., all slow-twitch), and a motor unit's fibers always fire simultaneously. Your CNS recruits groups of motor units within a muscle so that they can work together to contract the muscle. When contraction occurs, two mechanisms govern the force of that contraction:

▶ **Rate coding:** When you increase the rate at which impulses are sent from motor neurons to muscle fibers, you increase both force and duration of a muscle contraction. If a motor neuron sends a single impulse, the target muscle might only twitch (e.g., the blink of an eyelid). But if it sends a second impulse quickly enough, the muscle will twitch again before having a chance to relax. This adds the force of the second twitch to what force remains from the first, creating a contraction that is the sum of both—a process called *summation*. A cascade of impulses can piggyback one twitch on top of another until the twitches blur together, creating the type of smooth, sustained contractions required for everyday activities—from holding a toothbrush to stepping out the door for a run.

▶ **Recruitment:** The other way to increase force production is to increase the number and size of motor units recruited (see the muscle fiber ladder from Chapter 5). This is known as the *size principle.* Your motor units respond to signals sent from the brain. Slow-twitch motor units have small neurons that can be activated by weaker signals. Intermediate motor units have medium-sized neurons that require slightly bigger signals. Fast-twitch motor units have the biggest neurons and require the strongest signals. As the signal strength increases, you activate more and larger neurons—recruiting faster fibers and increasing the force of your muscle's contraction.

You use both rate coding and recruitment when you run—you generate force by increasing the rate of impulses (thereby increasing the strength and duration of your muscle fibers' contractions) *and* by recruiting larger motor units (and faster fibers), which produce more power.

Of course, there's more to muscle fiber recruitment than generating force. Let's look at a few other factors.

Recruitment patterns

To run efficiently, you need to coordinate contraction and relaxation of muscles across multiple joints. Hardwiring better neural pathways is the key. Think of a postal carrier with a new route. Until the carrier learns all the streets and homes on the route, delivery will be slow. But once the carrier has the route down pat, it takes less time to deliver the mail—and the letters and packages all go to the right addresses! It's the same with neuromuscular adaptation. Your nervous system learns the best new pathways for delivering impulses to muscle fibers in order to power a particular movement, and then these pathways get hardwired as *recruitment patterns*.

Strength gains

Nervous system adaptations are responsible for most early strength gains. While it's hard to measure strength gains in runners, it's easy to observe in weightlifters. Research suggests it takes between four to twenty weeks before muscle growth overtakes neural adaptations as the prime factor in strength gains from weightlifting. So important is neural adaptation that a 2007 study on *cross education* found an 8 percent strength increase in untrained limbs when opposite limbs are resistance trained. That's the nervous system applying what it's learned from one limb to another.

Reduced inhibition

When one muscle contracts, its opposing muscle must relax. When Popeye flexes his biceps, he relaxes his triceps. That's because a contracting muscle has to work harder when an opposing muscle doesn't fully relax. Try flexing your own biceps while simultaneously contracting your triceps—you can't do it! Untrained (and undertrained) muscles have a hard time coordinating contraction and relaxation. Training can change that. A 1992 study found that just one week of quad-burning knee extension exercises led to a 20 percent reduction in hamstring co-contraction.

Contraction velocity

Proper training can increase the *contraction velocity* of your muscle fibers. Contraction velocity measures the time it takes a muscle fiber to reach peak contraction (shortening). Average contraction velocities are:

▶ **Slow-twitch fiber:** 100–110 milliseconds
▶ **Intermediate fiber:** 60–70 milliseconds
▶ **Fast-twitch fibers:** 25–50 milliseconds

Faster contraction velocities allow you to generate more power, which translates to faster running. A 2008 study found that highly competitive distance runners had slow-twitch contraction velocities that were 70 percent faster than their couch-potato peers and intermediate rates that were 18 percent better. An earlier study at Ball

State found that marathon-type training increased slow-twitch contraction velocity up to 50 percent and intermediate velocity by 29 percent.

It's a cliché to say that "practice makes perfect." But it's a cliché with legs. By incorporating multiple paces, terrains, and exercises into your workout schedule, you'll increase your ability to recruit the full range of useful muscle fibers, increase the force of your contractions, coordinate different fiber types and muscles at varying pace and fatigue levels, and create the most efficient running movements possible.

Training recommendation

Training recruitment patterns demands varying the intensity, pace, terrain, and duration of your runs. Rate coding responds to heavy resistance training (Chapter 5, see pages 67–69) and Plyometrics (see pages 211–216). Reduced inhibition is improved by performing Technique Drills (see pages 203–210), Hill Sprints (see page 220, and other faster running. Contraction velocity improvements in slow-twitch fibers result from marathon-type training (volume, tempo, and longer intervals). And tapering (see page 364) by itself can lead to increases in intermediate contraction velocity.

PROPRIOCEPTION

Proprioception is your body's ability to track its position relative to the outside world and then to adjust accordingly. Think of an Olympic gymnast as she dismounts from the balance beam. Her nervous system must process a whir of motion as she rotates her trunk and hips, adjusts the bend in her limbs, and positions her feet for landing. It's proprioception that guides her movements.

You use proprioception every day. You use it to walk without watching your feet. Or to type at the computer without looking at the keys. Or when you run—a motion that requires your feet to leave the ground completely and then land safely time and time again.

Your proprioceptive system includes your inner ear and the nerves connecting your CNS to your muscles, tendons, and ligaments. Proprioceptive nerves relay position, tension, and stretch sensations to your CNS. Your CNS responds by triggering muscle contractions that hold or alter your body's position. These impulses travel on the fastest nerves in your body, reaching speeds up to 390 feet per second!

Your stride is governed by proprioceptors, which regulate posture, joint movement, balance, stride length, and foot strike. If you step awkwardly

TRAINING DISCUSSION

"Check your balance and proprioception"

Want to try an easy activity to learn the difference between balance and proprioception?

First, test your balance. Stand on one leg with your arms at your sides. Feel free to swing your arms, move the lifted leg, or do anything else to stay upright. That's balance.

Now for proprioception. Keep doing exactly what you've been doing for balance, only close your eyes. Feel the difference? That's proprioception. As you can see (or not, if you're still performing the activity), balance and proprioception are closely related, but they're also different.

BUILD YOUR RUNNING BODY

during a trail run, proprioceptors immediately inform your CNS, which instructs muscles to correct the problem before you roll an ankle.

Training recommendation

Wobble/balance board training (see pages 91–92) is an effective way to improve proprioception. Running (especially barefoot) on soft sand or grass can also improve your skills (see page 219). Playing court or field sports is another way to challenge proprioceptors.

BALANCE

Balance plays a far larger role in running that most runners realize. After all, balance is what keeps us on our feet instead of tumbling to the ground! Think that's easy? Then watch a child just learning to walk. Better yet, try the activities from the sidebar, "Check your balance and proprioception." In fact, every step you take as a runner is a challenge to your balance. While in motion, you have to land on one foot, stay upright, recruit the proper muscles to ensure stability, and then launch into another stride—often over uneven surfaces. That's an incredible feat! So incredible, in fact, that it took tens of millions of dollars and decades of research and experimentation before Boston Dynamic's 6'2", 330-pound *Atlas*, in 2013, became the first two-legged robot to walk over rough terrain.

Balance plays an especially large role every time you change direction or avoid obstacles. A 2013 study by Spanish researchers tested balance by having runners do strides that finished with a 90° sideways cut (change of direction) on a moveable platform. When the platform was allowed to wobble on the eleventh repetition, the runners

showed reduced activation of the muscles that stabilize the hips and knees—the runners' muscles were incapable of adjusting quickly to the unstable platform. They weren't able to balance.

Luckily, balance is easy to improve. A 2006 experiment had football players spend four weeks balancing on each leg for five minutes, five days a week. The result was 77 percent fewer ankle sprains during the season. And wobble board training (as mentioned in Chapter 5) reduces the reoccurrence of ankle sprains by 50 percent.

Training recommendation

Training balance can be as simple as standing on one leg (see pages 217–218) or using a wobble board (see pages 91–92)—or as complicated as walking a tightrope strung between two trees in your backyard. Exercises like Foot Work and Towel Toe Curls (both on page 107) can teach your body better recruitment and utilization of the small muscles that control your ankles and feet, which leads to an improved ability to react to uneven terrain, unforeseen obstacles, and turns (i.e., improved balance during real-world training).

NERVOUS SYSTEM FATIGUE

You can't learn new skills when your nervous system is run-down. Your CNS loses its capacity to efficiently deliver the brain's orders to your body. And your PNS likewise loses its ability to efficiently report the outcome of those orders, as well as relevant sensations. Acquiring new skills becomes impossible because your nervous system simply can't figure out how to perform them.

The only realistic way to deal with nervous system fatigue is to avoid it. You can't beat it. As the

TRAINING DISCUSSION

"Should I change my stride?"

These days, it seems that everyone wants to change your stride.

Form gurus tell you to shorten your stride. Or to lengthen it. To land on your mid-foot. Or to land barefoot. To pick up your stride rate. To use gravity. Not to use your calves. To pull with your hamstrings. To keep your feet behind your knees. Or to do a hundred other things you've never thought about in the past and aren't sure you should try now.

What's a runner to do?

For starters, stop listening to people who tell you to change your stride.

A highly touted 2004 review article out of Australia concluded that the best stride is "freely chosen over considerable training time." The authors note that "the aerobic demand of running at a given speed is lowest at a self-selected stride length," and that, in contrast, running economy (a measure of running efficiency) suffers when "stride length is either lengthened or shortened from that self-selected by the runner."

By "self-selected," the authors don't mean choosing a stride the way you'd pick an Easter bonnet. Instead, referencing a 1982 study by Cavanaugh and Williams, they suggest that we "naturally acquire an optimal stride length and stride rate over time."

This finding was reinforced by a 2005 study conducted by the Department of Exercise Physiology at Colorado State University. Researchers chronicled changes in the stride and running economy of triathletes who performed twelve weeks *of Pose Method* running. The triathletes' stride length shortened and, consequently, their running economy worsened.

The truth is that form gurus trying to sell you on a better stride in a few quick, easy lessons are making promises that they can't keep—and that will make you a less efficient runner.

This doesn't mean you should ignore form! You should simply avoid wholesale changes. Instead, work to improve the form you have. The best way to do that is through long-term mileage, drills, intervals, tempo, plyometrics, resistance training, stretching, and, above all, patience. It's proper and comprehensive training, not gimmicks, that creates a great stride.

Borg of *Star Trek: The Next Generation* always told soon-to-be assimilated races, "Resistance is futile."

Your goal should be to identify the signs of nervous system fatigue and then dial back your effort when you experience any of them. Symptoms include:

▶ **Trouble sleeping**

▶ **Difficulty concentrating**
▶ **Physical clumsiness**
▶ **Trembling hands**

Your grip strength is a good measurement of nervous system fatigue. You can test grip strength with a *dynamometer*. If your grip strength goes down, your nervous system fatigue has likely

Chart 11.1 A Comparison of Two Economy Curves

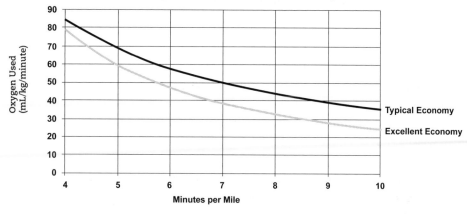

CHART 11.1 shows the performance curves of two runners, one with typical running economy, and one with excellent economy. The excellent-economy runner can maintain a faster pace at the same oxygen cost ("Oxygen Used") as the typical runner. For example, at 50 mL/kg, the excellent-economy runner runs under six-minute-mile pace, while the typical runner manages only seven-minute pace. In fact, the runner with excellent economy uses only 40 mL/kg of oxygen at the same seven-minute-mile pace that requires the typical runner to use 50 mL/kg. Since fatigue increases as runners approach VO_2 max, a runner using 40 mL/kg will feel far less fatigued than the one using 50 mL/kg at the same pace.

gone up. Decreased vertical jump is another good indicator, as is dropping your keys post-workout while trying to unlock your car.

Training recommendation

You don't train to improve nervous system fatigue; you avoid it. Limit volume and duration of high-intensity workouts, and allow at least three minutes between high-intensity sets (weights, running). Beginners should allow forty-eight hours between high-intensity workouts, while advanced runners should allow up to ten days and get a good night's sleep every night to ensure healthy neurotransmitters.

High-intensity, short-duration exercises are especially fatiguing for your nervous system. The closer to 100 percent effort you train at, the more stress your nervous system endures. For example, your nervous system is maxed out during sets of five reps or fewer for heavy lifts (weightlifting), where the reps represent a near-maximum effort, but you can shift the burden to your muscles by doing sets of six to twelve reps with lighter weights. The same principle holds true for running workouts.

RUNNING ECONOMY

Running economy measures how efficiently you use oxygen at a given running speed. This becomes extremely important at *submaximal running speeds*. A "submaximal speed" is a running effort below 100 percent of VO_2 max. All races of 5K and longer (and most workouts) are run at submaximal speeds. There are three things about VO_2 max and running economy that you should keep in mind:

1. Your VO_2 max represents the maximum amount of oxygen that your body can use in a minute.
2. Fatigue increases as you approach VO_2 max.

3. The less oxygen you need to maintain a given speed, the less fatigue you'll feel and the greater your advantage will be over someone with a similar VO$_2$ max but inferior running economy.

Confused? Then compare running economy to gas mileage in a car. The 2013 Chevrolet Cruz Eco and the 2013 Toyota Prius both have gas tanks that hold about twelve gallons. Traveling at fifty mph, the Cruz Eco gets forty-two miles per gallon, and the Prius gets forty-eight miles per gallon. So traveling at fifty mph, the Cruz Eco will run out of gas long before the Prius, even though both cars started with the same amount of fuel. Not only that, but the Prius can travel *faster* than fifty mph while still using a smaller amount (or the same amount, depending upon the speed) of gas than the Cruz Eco. If the cars were runners, the Toyota Prius would have better running economy. It can go farther at the same pace, or it can go faster using the same amount of fuel. See Chart 11.1 for a comparison of the running speeds that can be maintained by runners with different levels of running economy.

Running economy is determined by a variety of factors, with genetics and nervous system efficiency at the top of the list. Genetics can include, among other things, your height, percentage of slow-twitch fibers, calf size (smaller is better), and body type—an *ectomorph* body type, with long, thin limbs, flat chest, equal shoulder and hip width, and low body fat, tends to be most economical. But if that's not you, don't despair; runners come in all sizes and shapes. As for nervous system efficiency, that refers to trainable elements like recruitment, pace, and stride.

Becoming economical

Becoming economical involves a multi-pronged approach. There's no magic bullet, no single strategy, like doing sets of heavy curls when your goal is big biceps. Instead, you'll need to build better slow-twitch fibers, increase elastic recoil, re-wire your nervous system, and practice, practice, practice. It'll all part of the equation. Some types of training to focus on include:

▶ **Mileage:** Distance runners develop economy through high-volume running. Logging millions of steps per year allows your nervous system to hardwire optimal stride length, stride rate, and recruitment patterns. You learn to recruit *fewer* muscle fibers to perform the same workload, decreasing your energy requirements. And you level out the energy-wasting bounce that's exhibited in most runners' strides.

▶ **Tempo:** Tempo improves efficiency at race paces from 10K to the marathon—that's because training doesn't just improve your economy at the pace you're running, it improves it for paces roughly 10 percent faster or slower, too. That makes tempo a great workout for the 10K, since it's easier on your body than 10K-pace repetitions. As an example of how this works: If you do tempo at 6:00 per mile, you'll race economically at speeds from around 5:34 to 6:36 per mile.

▶ **Race pace repetitions:** Of course, there's no better way to improve economy at any race pace than to train at that pace. If you're too fatigued to run 5K or 10K repetitions, Cruise Intervals (see page 129) can be used as a substitution.

▶ **High-intensity workouts:** Short sprints, plyometrics, and heavy lifting (five or fewer reps per set) offer a quick return. A 2013 study from Italy on masters (ages forty and over) marathoners reported that maximal strength training increased running economy by 6 percent after only six weeks. And a 2003 study from the University of Texas showed that six weeks of plyometrics produced similar gains in regular (non-elite) distance runners. Finally, a 2010 study published in the *Journal of Strength and Conditioning* compared weight training and plyometrics, concluding that plyometrics was more effective for improving economy in "moderately to well-trained male endurance runners."

Training for better economy might sound like a lot of work, but the truth is that all of the above elements should be included in any solid, all-around training schedule.

Training recommendation

Training for better running economy requires training at different volumes and durations, including Mileage (Chapter 8, see page 150), tempo (Chapter 7, see page 130), and race pace intervals (Chapter 7, see pages 124–131). Quick improvements can be gained through high-intensity sessions of Short Hill Sprints (see page 220), Plyometrics (see pages 211–216), and heavy weight training (e.g., Squats, Lunges, Cleans, and Dead Lifts from Chapter 5, see pages 67–69). Remember that you can't teach your nervous system new tricks when your CNS is fatigued, so plan high-intensity sessions for when you're rested.

Table 11.2
The Effect of Running Economy on 10K Performance

Runner's VO_2 max	*Projected 10K Time Based Upon Running Economy			
(mL of O_2/kg/minute)	Poor Economy	Average Economy	Good Economy	Excellent Economy
30	1:05:24	1:02:13	1:00:37	59:21
35	58:46	55:54	54:28	53:19
40	53:09	50:33	49:16	48:13
45	48:25	46:04	44:53	43:56
50	44:28	42:18	41:13	40:21
55	41:11	39:10	38:10	37:22
60	38:25	36:33	35:37	34:52
65	36:05	34:19	33:27	32:44
70	34:03	32:23	31:33	30:53
75	32:11	30:37	29:50	29:12
80	30:23	28:54	28:09	27:34
85	28:31	27:08	26:26	25:53
90	26:29	25:12	24:33	24:02

TABLE 11.2 compares the predicted time for a runner based on VO_2 max and running economy. It also illustrates how runners with lower VO_2 max scores but good/excellent economy can defeat runners with higher VO_2 max scores but poor/average economy. For example, a runner with a VO_2 max of 70 mg/kg and good economy is predicted to run 31:33 for 10K, a time that beats a runner with a higher VO_2 max of 75 mg/kg but poor economy (estimated time of 32:11). All times in the table represent 10K race times. *Times are approximations and will vary from runner to runner.

VO$_2$ MAX VS. RUNNING ECONOMY

Recently, there's been a big debate over whether VO$_2$ max or running economy plays a bigger role in performance. The answer is that they each play a big role, so you shouldn't ignore either. Within groups of runners with similar VO$_2$ max measurements, the runner with the best running economy will theoretically run faster. But this doesn't mean that an elite runner with a high VO$_2$ max and average economy will lose to a runner with an average VO$_2$ max and excellent economy. Table 11.2 offers approximations for what runners with different VO$_2$ max measurements can expect to run for 10K based on their running economy.

TRAINING RUNDOWN

Developing your nervous system involves exercises to improve form, balance, proprioception, and the development of neural pathways that aid muscle fiber recruitment. Important training in this chapter's photo instruction includes:

► Technique drills
► Plyometrics
► Balance and proprioception
► Hill sprints
► Barefoot running (sand and grass)

Training from other chapters that affects the nervous system includes:

► **Heavy resistance training (Chapter 5)**
► **Tempo (Chapter 7)**
► **Race pace training (Chapter 7)**
► **Mileage (Chapter 8)**
► **HIIT (Chapter 8)**

To see exactly how these workouts can be incorporated into your overall training program, skip directly to Chapter 15: Build Your Training Schedule, where sample schedules are available for runners of all fitness levels and abilities.

Chapter 11: Rewire Your Running Nervous System –
PHOTO INSTRUCTION

TECHNIQUE DRILLS

Technique drills train your nervous system to recruit your maximum amount of available muscle fibers rapidly and explosively. They train opposing muscles to relax and contract in unison. Drills with a plyometric component improve running economy for all races. They also contribute to tendon stiffness and fascia strength, increasing elastic recoil. You don't have to do all the following technique drills every session. Find a routine that works for you, and repeat often (at least once every week or two) during base building, pre-season, or even off-season. Do 1–3 repetitions of each drill per workout. There are two ways to do drills:

1. Do drills only, with 1–3 minutes of rest between reps and 3–5 minutes between sets (if you're doing multiple reps of each drill).
2. Perform the drill, then jog back to the start line and immediately launch into a 50–70 meter stride, then walk back to the start line and perform the next rep/drill. This helps hardwire the nervous system adaptations into your normal stride.

Remember that your CNS can't learn new skills when it's tired. So don't add drills to a hard workout. Follow drills with a short distance run (3–7 miles). Jessica Ng, a triple jumper currently competing for Claremont McKenna College in Claremont, California, demonstrates all drills.

A March

This drill is performed on the balls of your feet. For this drill, as with most in this chapter, get used to keeping your heels off the ground. When you've mastered this drill, you can move on to the A Skip.

■ **SKILL LEVEL: Beginner**

① Walk forward on the balls of your feet, taking short strides while lifting your knee to hip level and swinging your opposite arm in a running motion. Your lifted knee should be at approximately 90°, with your lifted foot parallel to the floor.

② Alternate knees for 20–50 meters.

A Skip

This drill works the hip flexors and quadriceps, developing range of motion, power, and coordination during quick movements.

■ SKILL LEVEL: Intermediate, Advanced

  ① Move forward on the balls of your feet (note: the goal is not the speed of forward movement but rather correct form), lifting your knee to 90° or more and swinging the opposite arm in a running motion. Look ahead, not down at your feet.

  ② Keep your arm and knee raised as you execute a short skip with your lower foot.

  ③ Drive down the raised leg, landing on the ball of your foot.

  ④ Simultaneously raise the opposite knee and the arm on the same side as your landing foot, then perform another short skip with the lower foot. Repeat for 20–50 meters.

B March

This drill finishes what the A March started, adding leg extension into the motion. Runners with tight hamstrings should exercise caution. When you've mastered this drill, move on to the B Skip.

■ SKILL LEVEL: Beginner

  ① Walk forward on the balls of your feet, lifting your knee to hip level. Your lifted knee should be at approximately 90° (more if you're flexible).

  ② Extend your lower leg (of the lifted leg), swinging it forward.

③ Then actively pull your extended leg and foot to the ground, using your glutes and hamstrings to create a gentle pawing motion (as of a horse pawing the ground with its hoof in a digging motion) with your foot. Repeat with your opposite leg, then continue for 20–50 meters.

B Skip

This drill finishes what the A Skip started, adding a forceful glute- and hamstring-driven pawing motion to the end of each skip. Runners with tight hamstrings should exercise caution.

■ **SKILL LEVEL: Intermediate, Advanced**

① Move forward on the balls of your feet, lifting your knee to hip level. Your lifted knee should be 90° or more. Execute a short skip, as in the second step of the A Skip.

② Extend your lower leg (of the lifted leg), swinging it forward.

③ Use your glutes and hamstrings to forcefully pull your foot back toward the ground in a pawing motion. Repeat with the opposite leg, then continue for 20–50 meters.

REWIRE YOUR RUNNING NERVOUS SYSTEM

Butt Kicks—Trigger Action

This drill exaggerates the trigger motion of your stride, when you cock your heel high, near your glutes, before extending your leg forward.

■ **SKILL LEVEL: All levels**

① Stay on the balls of your feet while kicking your heels up underneath your buttocks. Don't worry if you don't touch, as less-flexible runners have trouble accomplishing this.

② Make sure to pull your heels straight up to your buttocks while lifting the knee of your same leg in front of you. Move forward at a slow, steady pace for 20–50 meters.

Butt Kicks—Dynamic Flexibility

In this version of butt kicks, you're actually trying to kick the back of your butt. It's a great way to stretch out and warm up the quadriceps, but don't work the drill too hard.

■ **SKILL LEVEL: All levels**

① Stay on the balls of your feet. Stand tall and keep your thighs relatively perpendicular to the ground as you kick one heel back toward your buttocks. Move your arms in a running motion.

② Kick your other heel backward. Don't worry if you can't touch your buttocks, as less flexible runners have trouble accomplishing this. Focus on the kicks, not forward motion, and do 20–50 meters.

BUILD YOUR RUNNING BODY—COMPONENTS AND WORKOUTS

Carioca

It's a good idea to try walking through this drill before doing it at full speed. This drill is great for developing hip abductors and adductors, as well as better coordination for your lower body.

■ **SKILL LEVEL: All levels**

① Start by bringing one leg across and behind the other leg. Move your arms in a motion that mimics a slightly wider version of your running arm movement.

② Use a hopping motion and lift the knee of your forward leg as you step laterally.

③ Bring your other leg across the front of your body, this time using a slight jump to help lift your knee high.

④ Land laterally to your back foot.

⑤ Step out with the back foot and begin the drill again. Do 20–60 meters, then switch legs.

Quick Feet

This is a simple drill for developing neuromuscular coordination associated with foot plant—it generates faster foot speed and reduced foot-plant time. It also gives your tibialis anterior and peroneal group (both outside shin muscles) a good burn.

■ **SKILL LEVEL: All levels**

① Stay on the balls of your feet and take quick "steps" forward, lifting your foot 1–3 inches off the ground. Use an abbreviated running arm motion (and don't worry if your arms don't match pace with your feet).

② Move forward 2–4 inches per step. Lift and plant quickly, but not so quickly that you lose control. To increase speed, drive the ball of your foot into the ground. 20–40 meters is good.

BUILD YOUR RUNNING BODY

Skipping

This simple version of skipping—think of skipping back in the schoolyard—begins an alternative trio of skipping drills to the A/B Skip routine. The focus of these skips is more on calves, quadriceps, and explosion (rather than the glute/hamstring emphasis of A/B Skip).

■ **SKILL LEVEL: All levels**

① Begin skipping forward. Take off on one foot . . .

② . . . then land on the same foot, after which you switch to the opposite foot . . .

③ . . . and skip off that foot, too. Skip for 20–60 meters.

High Skipping

This is a variation of normal skipping, working your calves, elastic recoil in your Achilles tendons, and lower-leg fascia. It trains your body to explode off your toes.

■ **SKILL LEVEL: Intermediate, Advanced**

① Begin your skip as in normal skipping, only this time . . .

② . . . spring upward, driving off your toes while lifting the opposite knee high. Swing your arms in an exaggerated motion.

③ Land on your takeoff foot.

④ Step forward into a similar spring/skip off the opposite foot. The object is to spring high, not to move forward quickly. Do 20–60 meters.

BUILD YOUR RUNNING BODY—COMPONENTS AND WORKOUTS

Long Skipping

In this variation of skipping, you'll skip for distance. This is like the "hop" part of the triple jump (the "hop, skip, and jump"). You'll take off with one foot, land on the same foot, then quickly step into a similar takeoff and landing with the opposite foot. This drill is not for beginners.

■ **SKILL LEVEL: Advanced**

① You'll need to initiate your skip with a forceful drive forward off one foot.

② Extend your back leg as you get air. Some runners find that a quick double-pump of the arms while in flight helps to align the hips (facing forward) for the imminent landing.

③ Land on your same takeoff leg, then do a quick stride forward into a skip on the opposite side. This in-between stride is not for length; it's just a switchover. Do 30–80 meters.

Flat-Footed Marching

Flat-footed marching takes your calves out of the picture, forcing your nervous system to focus on contributions from your quadriceps and hip flexors.

■ **SKILL LEVEL: All levels**

① Stand tall and start marching forward. Lift your knees to at least hip height.

② Forcefully bring your foot back down, using a flat-footed plant—don't bring your foot down so forcefully that you increase impact (you just don't want to let it float down).

③ Lift the opposite knee, then repeat for 20–50 meters.

BUILD YOUR RUNNING BODY

High Knees

High knees requires rapid nervous system recruitment of slow-twitch, intermediate, and fast-twitch muscle fibers in your legs and core.

■ **SKILL LEVEL: All Levels**

① Drive one knee upward, swinging your arms high, hands at face level. Stay on the balls of your feet throughout the drill.

② Forcefully bring your leg down, landing on the ball of your foot, while simultaneously beginning to drive your opposite knee upward.

③ Lift your knee high. Then repeat the drill for 20–60 meters.

Bounding

Bounding has you spring from one foot to the other. Imagine that you're Superman or Supergirl as you take off in flight, aiming for the sky.

■ **SKILL LEVEL: Intermediate, Advanced**

① Build into bounding with a couple of short hops from one foot to the other, then drive off the ball of one foot, leaping forward at about a 20–30° angle, getting some hang time in the air.

② Land on your opposite foot (don't skip!), quickly absorbing the impact and then bounding again. Repeat for 20–60 meters.

PLYOMETRICS

Although drills like high skipping, long skipping, and bounding all have plyometric components, actual plyometrics will further improve explosive recruitment of fibers, elastic recoil, and running economy. Rest 1–3 minutes between sets. Unlike with technique drills, you won't want to do strides between these. Make sure you're warmed up before attempting a plyometrics session.

Double-Leg Hops

Double-leg hops are a great introduction to plyometrics. This exercise is very demanding on your quads, glutes, hamstrings, calves, etc., so focus on form and don't skimp on recovery.

■ **SKILL LEVEL: Intermediate, Advanced**

① Stand up straight, feet hip-width apart, with your toes aimed forward or angled out slightly to each side. Now squat as you pull your arms down and behind you. Your quads should be almost parallel to the ground.

② Explode upward, leaping as high as you can.

③ Let your knees bend as you land, absorbing the force of this eccentric contraction (the goal of plyometrics is to marshal this force for the coming concentric contraction).

④ Explode upward again. Do 1–3 sets of 3–5 reps (maximum 10 reps), with 3–5 minutes of rest between sets.

Single-Leg Hops

Single-leg hops increase the force of the eccentric contraction when you land. You must do double-leg hops for several sessions before including these in your program.

■ SKILL LEVEL: Advanced

① Stand up straight, feet hip-width apart, with your toes aimed forward or angled out slightly to each side. Squat as you pull your arms down and behind you.

② Explode upward, leaping as high as you can.

③ Land on one foot, tucking the other slightly behind you. Let your landing knee bend, absorbing the downward eccentric force.

④ Leap upward off one foot. Swing one arm (or both) forward and above your head to aid the jump. Do 1–3 sets of 3–5 reps (maximum 10 reps), with 3–5 minutes of rest between sets.

Vertical Depth Jumps

The depth jump, like the double-leg hop, improves power and economy by marshaling the force of a concentric contraction of your quads and glutes.

■ **SKILL LEVEL: Intermediate, Advanced**

① Stand on a box or other platform—20–30 inches in height—with your feet at the front edge of the platform.

② Step (don't jump!) off the edge of the platform.

③ Land on both feet, letting your legs bend as you absorb the downward, concentric forces.

④ Rebound with an explosive leap upward. Some runners use a vertical leap marker to measure height. Do 1–3 sets of 3–5 reps (maximum 10 reps), with 3–5 minutes of rest between sets.

Single-Leg Depth Jumps

Single-leg depth jumps increase the force factor of double-leg depth jumps. These are perfect for sprinters, jumpers, and some middle-distance runners.

■ **SKILL LEVEL: Advanced**

① Stand on a box or other platform—20–30 inches in height—with your feet at the front edge of the platform.

② Step (don't jump!) off the edge of the platform.

③ Land on one foot, letting your leg bend as you absorb the downward, concentric forces. Tuck the other leg slightly behind you.

④ Rebound off that single leg with an explosive leap upward. Do 1–3 sets of 3–5 reps (maximum 10 reps), with 3–5 minutes of rest between sets.

Box Jumps

Box jumps are a great all-around workout for the lower body, enhancing nervous system recruitment of explosive fibers, improving elastic recoil, and increasing strength.

■ **SKILL LEVEL: Intermediate, Advanced**

① Stand in front of a box or other platform that's at least one foot high.

② Using both feet, jump up onto the platform.

③ Make sure both feet land squarely on the platform (for stability), then immediately jump backward to the start position, marshaling the eccentric force to jump up on the platform again. Do 1–3 sets of 5–10 reps, with 3–5 minutes of easy walking between sets.

Toe Taps

Toe taps develop quick and nimble legs and feet. Plus they're fun to do!

■ **SKILL LEVEL: All levels**

① Stand in front of a box or platform (1–3 feet high). Place one foot on the platform.

② Quickly drop the foot from the platform to the floor while lifting your opposite knee and tapping the top surface of the platform with your foot.

③ Just as quickly, drive your other knee back up, again tapping the top surface. Use a quick, high-step running motion for this drill. Repeat for 1–3 sets of 5–10 reps (each foot), with 3–5 minutes of easy walking between sets.

Lateral Barrier Jumps

These aren't for the beginner. You'll need some strength background (work The Runner 360 or a weight routine from Chapter 5). Lateral barrier jumps work hip flexors, extensors, abductors, and adductors. They're a great hip tune-up!

■ SKILL LEVEL: Advanced

① Stand to the side of a modest barrier (one foot in height or less).

② & ③ Using both feet, jump sideways over the barrier.

④ Land on the opposite side, letting your knees bend slightly to absorb the eccentric force.

⑤ & ⑥ Immediately repeat the motion going the opposite direction. Do 1–3 sets of 2–10 reps (each direction), with 3–5 minutes easy walking between sets.

Quick Hops

This drill increases foot speed, decreases foot-plant time, and delivers a plyometric burn to your quads. It's a good exercise for the end of a session of plyometrics—not the beginning.

■ SKILL LEVEL: Intermediate, Advanced

① Start with both feet hip-width apart and with a slight bend at the knees.

② Jump forward, landing as fast as you can. Don't jump higher than an inch or two. The object is speedy jumps, not distance. Keep going until you've covered 20–40 meters.

BALANCE AND PROPRIOCEPTION

Training for balance and proprioception is important for all runners, from fans of rugged trails to those who do all their running on the local track. Every runner makes an occasional incorrect step, and it's balance/proprioception training that teaches your body how to correct its position before injury occurs and to navigate any terrain. Begin training with simple balance exercises and then work up to the wobble board. Remember that barefoot running should be eased into slowly and then practiced sparingly (unless you're making a transition to barefoot running, in which case you should read Scott Douglas's book, *The Runner's World Complete Guide to Minimalism and Barefoot Running*).

Balance on One Leg

This is the simplest balance exercise of all. Close your eyes, and it becomes the simplest proprioceptive exercise, too! Beginners can wear their shoes. Advanced balancers (if you can balance on one foot for 30–60 seconds) will want to try this barefoot.

■ **SKILL LEVEL: All levels**

① Stand straight, knees slightly bent. Lift one foot off the floor and hold it. When you can't balance any longer, put the foot down. Work up to 30–60 seconds. For working proprioception, close your eyes during this exercise, but immediately open them when balance falters.

Variation When balancing itself becomes too easy, straighten your lifted leg behind you and bend down to touch your toes—do one set of 5–10 reps on each side.

Balance on One Leg with Medicine Ball

Adding object control and movement to your balancing act increases the demand on your nervous system.

■ **SKILL LEVEL: Intermediate, Advanced**

① Balance on one foot while holding a medicine ball (or other ball) in front of you.

② Remain balanced while moving the ball over your head.

③ Perform other movements with the ball, including touching your toes, holding it over each shoulder, and swinging it from side to side. Keep all movements smooth and controlled. There is no time limit for this exercise, so let fatigue be your guide.

Balance with Stability Trainer

Using a stability trainer (like the Thera-Band trainer pictured) adds instability to the surface you're standing on, requiring advanced nervous system adjustment—utilizing both balance and proprioception.

■ **SKILL LEVEL: Intermediate, Advanced**

① Balance on one foot while standing on a stability trainer. Use shoes for the first few sessions, then switch to bare feet. Work up to 30–60 seconds.

Variation If you're having any trouble (or anxiety) balancing on the trainer, do the exercise with a chair within easy grasp. If you try this exercise with closed eyes, definitely use the chair!

Two-Leg Balance on the Wobble Board

This simple balance exercise prepares your legs for the instability you're likely to encounter on trails and other uneven terrain.

■ **SKILL LEVEL: All levels**

① Stand with both feet centered on your wobble board and balance as long as you can, up to a minute. Keep your back straight, but use a slight bend in your knees—and be careful not to hyperextend them!

Variation As you become more proficient, balance on one foot. Remember to balance with your center of gravity situated over the center of the wobble board (for many exercisers, this will mean their heel, rather than their arch, is closer to the center).

Barefoot Running on Grass or Sand

Nothing feels better than running barefoot on the grass or sand. But be careful! If you're not accustomed to running barefoot, you'll need to start slow—no more than a mile, once or twice a week.

① Run easy over grass or soft sand. The uneven surface forces your body to rely on proprioceptive senses to navigate the terrain. If you're running on grass, watch out for potholes. If you're running on soft sand, be careful not to dig too deep, as you can strain tendons and ligaments in your feet.

Short Hill Sprints

Short hill sprints are the most effective workout for recruiting the maximum amount of muscle fiber types and muscle fibers in the minimum amount of time, for coordinating muscle fiber contraction and relaxation, and for triggering stride-length adaptations in muscle spindles. Runners who are deficient in nervous system training can shed between seconds and minutes from their race times with a single session of these sprints.

■ **SKILL LEVEL: Intermediate, Advanced**

① Find a hill that's steep, but not so steep that you can't maintain a rough approximation of your normal stride. Sprint uphill at 95 percent of max effort for 6–10 seconds. Do 4–8 reps. Walk down the hill for recovery, with additional rest creating 1–5-minute total recovery periods.

② Sprint down the hill at 85–95 percent of max effort. Downhill's eccentric contractions further challenge your nervous system, simultaneously creating protection against future quad soreness. Run 8–15 seconds (build into these reps more slowly than with uphill sprints, as you'll need to limit your pace to one in which you are stable and in control). Do 4–8 reps. Walk back up the hill for recovery, with additional rest creating 1–5-minute total recovery periods. But a word of caution: Don't overdo your initial downhill sessions; until your body adapts to this workout, there is a risk of injury.

Build Your Running Hormones

When many people think of hormones, they think of teenage romance, testosterone-fueled road rage, and anti-aging commercials touting gels, powders, and pills. Don't. Hormones are far more than fuel for emotional tempests and salve for midlife crises. They're an integral messaging system that governs your growth, mood, hunger, metabolism, immune system response, reproductive capability, and overall biological function. Without hormones, your muscles wouldn't get stronger, your cells wouldn't absorb nutrients, and your blood wouldn't have the RBCs it needs to transport oxygen throughout your body.

Hormonal balance is essential for healthy living. And learning how to arrange your training to elicit perfectly timed hormonal response is key to achieving peak fitness.

WHAT'S A HORMONE?

Hormones are chemical messengers within your body that govern all aspects of your biological function. Secreted by your *endocrine system* (endocrine glands are located in many tissues), hormones enter the bloodstream and are transported to target cells—muscles, organs, glands, bones, cartilage, and other tissues—where they affect reactions within those cells. While nervous system impulses travel rapidly along your neural network, hormones travel more slowly in your bloodstream; blood takes approximately one minute to make a full circuit of your body. Compounding this slow delivery, hormones often work in cascades (think of the board game Mouse Trap), with one hormone triggering the release of another and so on. Or, conversely, hormones can inhibit the secretion of other hormones. Also, unlike nervous system impulses, which elicit short-lived responses, hormonal impacts can last between minutes and days.

When you run, levels of exercise-related hormones begin to rise before your first step, as anticipation triggers a small release of *epinephrine* (adrenaline), which in turn stimulates the release of *glucagon*. Other hormones join in as your run begins, then slowly increase in volume until you reach an effort level of 50–75 percent of VO_2 max. A further increase in effort causes hormone levels to soar, as hormones play a major role in making fuel sources available to your muscles.

Hormones can be grouped into three types:

1. **Steroids:** These hormones are derived from cholesterol. Examples are *cortisol* and *testosterone*.
2. **Proteins and peptides:** Hormones in this group are created from chains of amino acids. Examples are *insulin* and *human growth hormone* (HGH or GH).
3. **Amines:** These hormones are derived from the amino acid tyrosine. Examples are epinephrine and *norepinephrine*, as well as the thyroid hormones *thyroxin* (T4) and *triiodothyronine* (T3).

When your hormones function properly, they help your body achieve *homeostasis*—they keep your body stable, its interval environment in balance, regardless of external conditions. Any deviation in your hormonal equilibrium can result in system-wide disruptions. That's why hormonal

BEGINNER'S GUIDELINE

Since running is a mostly *catabolic* exercise (it breaks muscle down) and resistance training is an *anabolic* activity (it releases hormones that build muscle and speed recovery), it's important to incorporate some resistance work at the outset of your training program.

get-fit-quick schemes—performance-enhancing drugs (PEDs) and supplements that contain precursors (substances that your body converts into hormones)—are especially dangerous. See the sidebar, "Gaming the system," for a rundown on hormonal misbehavior and its side effects.

TRAINING DISCUSSION

"Gaming the system"

It seems you can't turn on ESPN or read about sports without learning that another athlete—or group of athletes—has been accused, investigated, or banned for performance-enhancing drug (PED) use. Most non-stimulant PEDs are derived from hormones, and it's a testament to the power of hormones that their misuse has created a super race of bigger, faster, stronger, and, in the case of distance running, more indefatigable athletes than the world has ever seen.

It's long past the time when anyone could kid themselves that PEDs simply provide an edge to already-great athletes. PEDs turn non-athletes into athletes, average athletes into stars, and stars into superstars. A 1996 study published in the *New England Journal of Medicine* found that men who used steroids for ten weeks built three times as much muscle (thirteen pounds) as men who trained without PEDs (four pounds). Even scarier, men who used steroids but did *no training* for the same ten weeks gained seven pounds of muscle, almost twice that of those who trained clean. And studies on EPO (a red-blood-cell booster) have shown that just three months on the drug can boost VO_2 max by 8–12 percent and increase the time you can maintain 80 percent of VO_2 max (about half marathon effort for most runners) by 54 percent—in other words, a pace that you could run drug-free for a half marathon, you can run on EPO for twenty miles. Throw in some steroids and HGH, and you've got yourself a massive PR for the marathon.

If that seems like too much temptation for wannabe-stars to resist, it is. Consider:

► **2013:** To no one's surprise, fourteen Major League Baseball players were suspended for use of human growth hormone (HGH). Across the Atlantic (and then the Mediterranean), thirty-one Turkish track and field athletes were banned from competition for their use of anabolic steroids.

► **2012:** UCI, cycling's international governing body, stripped Lance Armstrong of his seven Tour de France titles for use of EPO, blood-doping, and other performance-enhancing drugs. In the process, pretty much the entire Tour peloton was implicated in the same type of doping. And in Kenya, German journalist Hajo Seppelt exposed widespread EPO use among Kenyan distance runners, long touted as super-runners who didn't need drugs, whose dominance was supposedly rooted in a lifetime of high-altitude training, barefoot running, and perfect ectomorph distance running bodies.

(continued)

TRAINING DISCUSSION

- ▶ **Top Ten Sprinters:** Of the top ten male 100-meter sprinters ever, based on time, seven have tested positive for PEDs. Another, Maurice Greene, was tied to a $10,000 wire transfer to a relative of notorious PED dealer Angel Heredia, according to a 2008 article in *The New York Times*. On the women's side, let's just say "Marion Jones" and leave it at that.

- ▶ **Masters runners:** At age forty and over, you'd think there'd be more important mid-life crises to fret over than diminishing athletic ability. Yet distance runner Eddy Helle-buyck, who doped his way to a 2:12:46 marathon at age forty-two, became the first American to be banned for EPO use. Not to be outdone, the men's age fifty-and-over world record-holder in the sprints, Val Barnwell, subsequently got himself a two-year ban for using testosterone. A half-dozen other masters athletes have followed suit, running the gamut of sprinters, distance runners, and field event performers.

It's no coincidence that any sport's PED abuser list looks like a ballot for that sport's hall of fame. PEDs work. They also do this: Risk the health of millions of competitors.

Lance Armstrong isn't the worst story of EPO use in cycling. The worst story is that since 1989, the year synthetic EPO was introduced, an estimated one hundred international racers have died in their sleep or dropped dead from heart attacks—not surprising, given how hard the heart struggles to pump blood thickened by increased red blood cells and decreased plasma volume (both effects of EPO), a life-threatening combination made worse by the extreme dehydration brought on by hours of daily training.

And PEDs don't have to kill you to hurt you. Use has been linked to shrunken testicles, impotence, tendon weakness (leading to tendon rupture), elevated bad cholesterol, liver toxicity, jaundice, liver cancer, hypertension, enlarged heart, increased risk of arteriosclerosis, and other cardiovascular threats (both heart and artery), not to mention anecdotal evidence of aggression, known as "roid rage." In men with prostate cancer, it speeds the tumor's growth. And HGH can enlarge your chin and forehead; like Barry Bonds, you'll need to get a bigger hat.

Worst of all, professional PED cheats pass on their legacy to young athletes. The Centers for Disease Control and Prevention (the CDC) has estimated that 3–6 percent of American high school students use steroids—that's five hundred thousand to one million boys and girls.

Gaming the system with PED use shouldn't be viewed as an inevitable consequence of competition, as nothing more than another stepping stone in an athlete's quest for trophies or the big bucks of professional sports. It should be seen for what it is: the attempt by a few unethical players to rob clean athletes of the right to compete on a level playing field. It also exposes young athletes to influences that reduce their chances of growing into healthy adults.

HORMONE TRAINING

Your body is expert at maintaining homeostasis. And it relies on hormones to do this. So you need to accept at the outset that the best endocrine system is a balanced endocrine system.

"The body doesn't make performance-enhancing drugs," says Dr. Jeffrey S. Brown, a nationally renowned endocrinologist who has treated twenty Olympic gold medalists and consults for both Nike and USA Track & Field. "It makes hormones to keep us normal. The body is so well-tuned that you can't overproduce unless you have a metabolic problem."

So does this mean that there's nothing you can do to improve hormonal function?

Not by a long shot.

While Dr. Brown stresses that a traditional approach to diet and exercise is the best way to keep your endocrine system healthy, coaches and exercise scientists, always looking for an edge, have been dabbling in natural (non-PED) hormone manipulation.

"If you change hormones at the right time, it can alter training adaptations and increase recovery," says exercise scientist and elite coach Steve Magness. Magness's methods include post-run resistance training and protein supplementation. "It's the timing that matters. You can get a short-term increase in several anabolic hormones. If [resistance training and protein supplementation] are done post–hard running session, which is catabolic, you should get an increase in recovery. You should get an increase in muscle repair."

Magness makes clear that this is a transient change. Your body eventually brings your hormonal levels back to homeostasis, which limits the anabolic effect but avoids the possible negative consequences of long-term hormonal imbalance.

Jay Johnson, an elite coach in Boulder, Colorado, with three national champions on his coaching résumé, agrees with Magness. "When you're out on a run," says Johnson, "everything you're doing is catabolic—it's breaking things down—and what [my athletes] are doing every moment from the end of the workout until we get into our cars are anabolic things."

This chapter's training will focus on those anabolic things. It will also cover altitude training for EPO, pre-workout stimulation for epinephrine, and a brief rundown of other important running hormones.

HUMAN GROWTH HORMONE (HGH OR GH)

Growth hormone is where adaptation to training begins. It promotes protein synthesis, muscle hypertrophy, bone density, and tendon and ligament strength, among other things—and helped determine your height during childhood and adolescence.

"You can organize your training around growth hormone," says Tom Cotner, a biology PhD and the distance coach for Seattle-based Club Northwest. "It serves as the trigger for adaptive response to training. It gets the muscle ready to import the building blocks—glucose and amino acids."

Dr. Brown, however, cautions against too great an optimism when training for HGH release. "The body has safety mechanisms," he says. "It will turn growth hormone production off after a certain amount of time." In other words, you can't trick your body into long-term overproduction of HGH. While weekend joggers get a large HGH release from a short run, fitter runners might have to go miles and miles to stimulate an equal dose.

Magness and Johnson aren't arguing for greater HGH release, however. They're arguing for better timing of the release that you do produce.

"If you do an afternoon run," says Johnson, "and you do your general strength right after the workout, you're going to have a different hormonal profile when you go to bed that night." Johnson thinks masters runners can especially benefit from post-run resistance training, "Because with age, your levels of testosterone and HGH are going to go down. It becomes that much harder to prevent injuries."

Magness champions protein spikes and recovery runs as ways to manage HGH release. "If you take a big spike of protein before bed," he says, "you'll get a huge spike in protein synthesis overnight. And overnight, when you're sleeping, is when a bunch of muscle repair and recovery goes on." Magness recommends 30 grams of protein before bed. He also suggests taking 15 grams of protein up to five times a day as a way to maintain an anabolic state. A 2006 Australian study on protein supplementation confirms Magness's hypothesis. The study found that weightlifters who consumed protein immediately before and after training saw significant increases in muscle size, strength, and glycogen stores, as well as decreases in body fat.

Magness also recommends recovery runs. "If you look at human growth hormone increases with easy distance runs," he says, "it takes roughly twenty-five minutes to get a significant increase. Maybe that's why people sometimes do a short shakeout of thirty minutes and feel better." Theoretically, breaking a daily longer run into a medium run and a short recovery run can increase the length of time that HGH is active in your body.

TESTOSTERONE

Testosterone increases muscle mass and bone density. In elevated levels, it can create larger muscle fibers and decrease recovery time after workouts. Often referred to as "male hormone,"

it's actually present in women, too, albeit at 10 percent the levels found in men.

Training recommendation

Training for HGH and testosterone release is a matter of timing. Your goal is to trigger release of the hormones when they can best contribute to adaptation and recovery. Moderate amounts of resistance training post-run can switch off the catabolic effect of running, leaving you in an anabolic state. To achieve this, try The Runner 360 (Chapter 5), Jay Johnson's Kettlebell Routine (see pages 232–234), or a 30-minute weight room session (Chapter 5). To make your run itself more anabolic, try Jay Johnson's Running Circuit (see pages 234–239). Protein supplementation can trigger protein synthesis (theoretically including HGH and testosterone release). Consume up to 15 grams of protein five times a day, including immediately after training. (This doesn't mean you should skip the post-run carbs, which you need for glycogen replacement!) Before bed, the amount can be increased to 30 grams. Don't exceed twice the daily RDA for protein, which is 56 grams for men and 46 for women. Also, be aware that catabolic effects aren't all bad; in fact, adaptation requires them. So beginning and intermediate runners, especially, should exercise caution in attempting to shut down catabolic effects—it's how we replace weak muscle fibers! Recovery runs are another option for stimulating HGH release.

Johnson believes that both post-run resistance training *and* intra-run strength circuits can effectively up-regulate testosterone (and HGH). For post-run training, he utilizes either a high-intensity

TRAINING DISCUSSION

"Growth hormone to the max"

Human growth hormone (HGH) stimulates your cells to grow, reproduce, regenerate, and recover. That's why athletes love it—and the more of it the better!

HGH is produced in the pituitary gland, which is the size of a pea and dangles from the hypothalamus, itself the size of an almond and located at the base of your brain. HGH is released when you exercise and during delta sleep (your deepest sleep). The more intense your training, the more HGH you'll produce—right up to the point where your body's need to preserve homeostasis shuts down production.

Increasing HGH production can be accomplished in three ways:

▶ **Running:** HGH production begins about ten minutes into a run, then shuts down after seventy-five minutes. Fartlek is especially beneficial for stimulating release.

▶ **Resistance training:** A few intense minutes *or* thirty to forty minutes of more moderate training are both good stimuli for release.

▶ **Protein supplementation:** Protein before and after training, as well as a good protein spike before bedtime, is thought to trigger higher levels of release.

Tom Cotner, a biology PhD and longtime distance coach for the Seattle-based Club Northwest, notes that there are also five easy ways to *decrease* HGH release:

1. **Sleep disturbance:** Anything that interrupts delta sleep interrupts HGH production.
2. **Poor nutrition:** It's especially important to consume enough calories.
3. **Injury:** HGH will shift its priority to healing any injury.
4. **Sickness:** Sickness lowers HGH release, especially if accompanied by a fever.
5. **Alcohol:** One drink decreases nocturnal HGH release by 30 percent. Two cuts it by 75–80 percent.

Stimulating maximum HGH requires you to do the right things—and avoid doing the wrong things.

---

kettlebell routine or lower-intensity strength training, noting that it takes about thirty minutes of the latter to equal the effect of three minutes of the former. For intra-run training, he uses running circuits that pair running with strength exercises (see photo instruction in this chapter). For less-experienced runners, these circuits extend the duration of workouts while simultaneously building the kind of strength that wards off injury.

Dr. Brown sounds a less optimistic note. "If you look at male hormone levels before, during, and after a very stressful run," he says, "they go down. The pituitary turns off the stimulation. To turn it back on, you have to recover. And the quicker you recover, the quicker you get male hormone levels back up."

Nevertheless, many of the world's top runners, including Mo Farah and Galen Rupp, the 2012 London Olympics gold and silver medalists at 10,000 meters, put their faith in post-run resistance training, performing intense strength and conditioning workouts within an hour of equally intense interval sessions on the track.

ERYTHROPOIETIN (EPO)

EPO stimulates your bone marrow to produce red blood cells. Red blood cells carry oxygen from your lungs to your cells, so more red blood cells means more oxygen for your muscles. A 2004 study by Genc, Koroglu, and Genc determined that EPO also plays "a critical role in the development, maintenance, protection, and repair of the nervous system." And a 2008 study from the University of Oxford found that administration of EPO improved cognitive function.

But when runners think about EPO, it's about the red blood cells. Numerous studies have confirmed increases in VO_2 max of 8–12 percent when *hematocrit* (percentage of total blood plasma volume composed of RBCs) is raised to a value of fifty—meaning 50 percent RBCs. And a 2007 study by Thomsen, et al., showed that a thirteen-week regimen of EPO supplementation increased time-to-exhaustion at 80 percent VO_2 max by more than 50 percent (see sidebar, "Gaming the system").

Still, Dr. Brown isn't sold on this aspect of EPO's performance impact. "The oxygen that gets to the muscle is actually dissolved oxygen in the plasma," he says. "You go from red blood cell to plasma to tissue. There's a homeostatic mechanism in the body that maintains oxygen levels in the plasma. And plasma is not affected by EPO."

Magness takes a more real-world view of EPO. "It works," he says, pointing out the enormous advantage it gives endurance athletes. A 2013 study found that EPO created a 5 percent improvement in the 3K times of Kenyan runners, long thought immune to benefits beyond what innate physiology and a heritage of high-altitude living had given them. Other studies have shown gains of 5–15 percent in aerobic performance. "It might not change the [oxygen-]carrying capacity to the muscle cell to a large degree, but it changes the feedback to the brain. If your brain senses that there's a higher red blood cell count, then that could be enough to affect the central governor [a theory of how the brain monitors fatigue and exertion]."

Training recommendation

Altitude training increases EPO levels, which will increase red blood cell volume in a runner who's not overly fatigued. Most runners benefit from at least three weeks at altitude; train easy the first week and make sure you get enough recovery between workouts. Some runners use altitude tents, which simulate the low-oxygen atmosphere found at 8,000–12,000 feet.

Altitude training is a natural way to increase EPO, and it's a staple of almost every elite distance runner's training program. You get your biggest increase in EPO during the first week at altitude. After that, EPO production levels out, although it still remains higher than normal. But translating that EPO spike into more RBCs requires enough "adaptive reserve" to fuel the process. Magness hypothesizes that runners who don't respond well to altitude might simply be tapped out, resource-wise, from the increased effort of training at higher elevations.

Whether EPO's effect on endurance is due to increased oxygen delivery, improved nervous system function, feedback to the central governor, or simply the psychological relief that comes from breathing more easily at sea level post-altitude training, there's no doubt that, for most runners, an increase in EPO is accompanied by an improvement in performance.

CORTISOL

Cortisol serves as both a catabolic agent and an anti-inflammatory. Where anabolic hormones (e.g., HGH and testosterone) promote tissue growth, catabolic hormones break down protein and fat. Of course, breaking down protein isn't always a bad thing. Cortisol, vital for muscle adaptation, breaks down weaker muscle tissue so that it can be replaced by stronger tissue. It also reduces inflammation by suppressing the immune system during high-intensity training. And it spares glycogen reserves by accelerating your use of fat.

So far, so good.

When athletes overtrain, however, their bodies can be overwhelmed by cortisol. Too much breakdown and not enough building lead to decreased performance. Long-term elevated levels of cortisol can lead to memory impairment, obesity, heart disease, depression, weight gain, insomnia, and night sweats, among other side effects.

You can use post-run anabolic training to switch off cortisol secretion. At the same time, it'd be a mistake to completely eliminate cortisol's positive impact on adaptation.

EPINEPHRINE (ADRENALINE)

Epinephrine increases heart rate, relaxes airways, constricts blood vessels in the skin (increasing blood flow to muscles), and stimulates the breakdown of muscle glycogen and fat. Known as the "fight or flight" hormone, it facilitates energy creation and prepares your body for action.

Anticipation of exercise is enough to raise your epinephrine levels, as anyone who's ever toed the line for a big race can verify. The trick is to bring a little of that same adrenaline rush to every hard workout. That's where coaches, training groups, and training schedules come into play. Looking forward to a hard workout with friends produces a lot more adrenaline than doing a solo slog along the same old trail. And an occasional pre-competition pep talk can do wonders for performance. "Win one for the Gipper," the halftime speech used by Knute Rockne to rally Notre Dame to a 1928 football victory over undefeated Army, may be a cliché, but it's also the template for good hormonal therapy.

Training recommendation

While pep talks from inspirational coaches and athletes are great, it's more practical to bring excitement to your runs the old-fashioned way: Run with groups, schedule 1–3 challenging workouts a week, and try to incorporate a variety of training.

INSULIN

Insulin directs your cells to take up glucose form the bloodstream and store it as glycogen in your muscles and liver. Too much insulin lowers your blood sugar (the pituitary gland's response is to release HGH, making insulin yet another prized PED for drug cheats). Insulin levels drop when blood glucose levels drop or when epinephrine levels rise.

GLUCAGON

Glucagon stimulates the liver to break down glycogen and release glucose when blood glucose levels fall. It also promotes fat-burning for aerobic energy. When you run, rising epinephrine levels stimulate the release of glucagon even before your glucose levels fall. This gives your body a head start on preparing fuels for your aerobic furnace. Glucagon's role in energy production makes it extremely valuable for longer races like the half marathon and marathon.

THYROID HORMONE (T4 AND T3)

Thyroxin (T4) and triiodothyronine (T3) are released from the thyroid gland. T4 is later converted to T3 within cells. Thyroid hormone plays a major role in determining metabolic rate and maintaining muscle, brain, bowel, and overall hormonal function. A malfunctioning thyroid can lead to hypothyroidism (under-secretion of T4) or hyperthyroidism (over-secretion of T4).

"With either too much or too little thyroid, your muscles don't contract normally," says Dr. Brown, who has treated many world-class athletes for thyroid dysfunction and claims that treatment brings them back to normal without conferring an advantage. "[Muscles] don't have the power to contract. So sprinters don't run as fast, jumpers don't jump as far, and distance runners' times get slower."

Alex Hutchinson, author of the *Runner's World* blog *Sweat Science*, isn't as comfortable with the high number of athletes currently on thyroid medication. He notes that a Spanish study on cyclists found that low-but-normal thyroid levels were associated with reduced performance. Is it ethical to increase those levels (to the high end of the "normal range") in order to increase performance? Hutchinson says "it pushes me closer to believing that WADA [the World Anti-Doping Agency] should be regulating thyroid medication use."

Also worth noting is that bodybuilders have long used thyroid medication, claiming that it both lowers body fat and increases the potency of injected HGH.

Training recommendation

A 2009 study suggests that calorie deficit is associated with thyroid dysfunction in athletes. So don't starve yourself. Diet sensibly and keep your available fuel levels high for training.

ENDORPHINS

Endorphins are responsible for the "runner's high"—a feeling of euphoria that runners sometimes experience during prolonged endurance training. The good news is that longtime runners become more sensitive to endorphins. The bad news is they also produce less and less of them.

ESTROGEN

Estrogen helps facilitate the breakdown of stored fat into fuel. Although known as a female sex hormone, estrogen is present in both sexes, albeit at lower levels in men.

HORMONES IN THE BALANCE

While the photo instruction for this chapter will detail some specific training for improving your anabolic hormonal profile, it's important that, in your daily life, you observe the two main tenets of hormonal balance:

▶ **Stay healthy:** Even a common cold will lead to a drop in hormone levels.
▶ **Eat right:** Get enough calories and don't completely eliminate cholesterol—you can't make steroid hormones without it.

With both your nervous system and endocrine system up to speed, there's no reasonable physiological request you can make of your running body that can't be delivered.

TRAINING RUNDOWN

Offsetting the catabolic effect of running involves performing anabolic training post-workout. Important training in this chapter's photo instruction includes:

▶ **Post-run kettlebell routine**
▶ **Running circuits**

Training from other chapters that affects your hormones includes:

▶ **The Runner 360 (Chapter 5)**
▶ **Resistance training (Chapter 5)**

To see exactly how these workouts can be incorporated into your overall training program, skip directly to Chapter 15: Build Your Training Schedule, where sample schedules are available for runners of all fitness levels and abilities.

Chapter 12: Build Your Running Hormones —
PHOTO INSTRUCTION

THE 95-SECOND KETTLEBELL ROUTINE

This 95-second routine was created by Coach Jay Johnson as an all-around strengthening routine and as a post-run anabolic stimulus. It requires moving fluidly from one kettlebell exercise to the next. It's advisable that you practice each exercise individually before putting all the exercises together. Also, pick a kettlebell weight that you can handle (i.e., start light) and be careful that the kettlebell never extends beyond the plane of your body (i.e., behind your head) when doing overhead presses and swings. When doing each exercise separately, allow 15–30 seconds of rest between exercises—or as much time as you need the first few times. When you put it all together, there is no rest between exercises, providing you with the kind of anabolic stimulus that will have your body building—rather than breaking down—during recovery. For more of Coach Johnson's routines and advice, go to: coachjayjohnson.com.

The following four exercises, from the Squat to the Single Arm Swing, are all part of the same continuous workout.

95-Second Kettlebell Routine

■ SKILL LEVEL: Intermediate, Advanced

Squat

① Begin from a standing position, feet hip-width apart, toes pointed slightly out. Hold the kettlebell at chest height.

② Move your hips backward as you lower your torso until your thighs are roughly parallel to the ground. Keep your heels on the ground. Don't lean forward too much. Reverse the motion to return to your starting position. Do 8–10 reps.

Squat to Press

① Stand with your feet hip-width apart, toes pointed slightly out. Hold the kettlebell at chest height.

② Move your hips backward as you lower your torso until your thighs are roughly parallel to the ground. Keep your heels on the ground. Don't lean forward too much.

③ Reverse the motion toward your starting position, but now press the kettlebell up and over your head in one smooth motion. Then drop straight back to the squat position. Do 8–10 reps.

Double Arm Swing

① Stand with your feet hip-width apart, toes pointed slightly out. Hold the kettlebell with both hands, letting it hang below your waist.

② Bend your legs as you lower the kettlebell between your legs.

③ Swing the kettlebell in one smooth motion over your head—don't let momentum carry the kettlebell beyond the plane of your body (i.e., behind your head). Then move straight back into instruction B for the next rep. Do 8–10 reps.

Single Arm Swing

① Stand with your feet hip-width apart—or slightly wider for this exercise, for increased stability—and your toes pointed slightly out. Hold the kettlebell with one hand, letting it hang below your waist.

② Bend your legs as you lower the kettlebell between your legs. Keep your arm straight.

③ Swing the kettlebell in one smooth motion over your head. There should be a straight line from your arm through the kettlebell. Switch arms at the bottom of the downswing (after performing all reps for one side). Do 8–10 reps with each arm.

RUNNING CIRCUIT

The running circuit workout requires that you run for a specified distance, stopping intermittently for quick sets of exercises. The object is to build running strength while keeping the workout anabolic (in a building phase) rather than catabolic (a breaking-down phase). The following running circuit was designed by Coach Jay Johnson. Each run/exercise segment of the workout includes the following:

1. A running repetition on the track (can be run from jogging to 10K pace, depending on current fitness) that lasts 500–700 meters, beginning at the track's general start line.

2. If 500 meters, walk back across infield to start line, stopping intermittently to perform strength exercises.

3. If 700 meters, jog 30 more meters, then do all four strength exercises for that segment. Then jog 70 meters back to start.

4. Perform all four segments during a single workout.

5. For alternative circuit exercises, go to: coachjayjohnson.com/2010/08/running-times-circuits-parts-1-2-and-3/

The following twenty exercises, from the Run Repetition #1 to the Scorpion, are all part of the same continuous workout.

Running Circuit

■ SKILL LEVEL: All levels

Run Repetition #1

The run-repetition segments of this workout should be determined by your fitness. This is meant to be a challenging workout, but it shouldn't be so hard that you can't complete the strength exercises that follow each run-repetition segment.

① Beginners start with 500 meters of easy running. Fitter runners can go 700 meters at tempo pace. Really fit runners can run 10K pace. (True newbies can start with 300 meters.)

Side Lunge

① Stand with feet hip-width apart. Step to your right. Sit back as you step—as if you were going to sit in a chair—while moving your weight toward your right leg. Keep your hands in front of your chest with your elbows wide. Do 10 reps, then repeat with your left leg.

Air Squat

① Stand straight, feet hip-width apart, toes pointed slightly out, arms at your sides. Bend your knees, pushing your hips back and lowering your torso until your thighs are parallel to the ground. As you squat, bring your arms up, extended in front of you (for balance). Do 10 reps.

Side Leg Lifts

① Lie on your side with your legs stacked. Either rest your head on one arm (your shoulder, hip, and feet in a line) or rest on your elbow (for the more flexible). Lift the top leg to 45° in a smooth motion, then bring it back down. Do 10–20 reps with each leg.

BUILD YOUR RUNNING BODY

Groaners

① Sit on the track with your hands behind you. Your feet are in front of you, with about a 90° bend at the knees. Now roll your knees laterally from side to side, touching the closest knee to the track. Do 10 reps (each side).

Run Repetition #2

① Repeat your same running repetition (as Run Repetition #1).

Front Lunge

① From a standing position, feet hip-width apart, step forward with your left foot until your knee is over your left ankle—you should have about a 90° angle at your knee. Move your arms in a running motion. Do 10 reps, then repeat with your right leg.

Wideouts

① Start with feet hip-width apart, a slight bend at the knees, hands held together at chest level with your elbows out. Now hop as you spread your legs wide (as pictured), as if you were avoiding a soccer ball kicked between your legs. Then hop to bring your legs back to the start position. Do 10 reps.

Prone Pedestal

① If you've ever done a push-up, this is your high-point, start position. On your hands and toes, arms extended, head in line with your spine. Don't raise your hips or sag. Eyes on the floor. Hold for 30 seconds.

Supine Pedestal

① This is the reverse of the prone pedestal. Face up, on your hands and heels, arms extended downward. Try not to sag. Hold for 30 seconds.

Run Repetition #3

① Repeat your same running repetition (as Run Repetition #1).

Backward Lunge

① From a standing position, take a big step backward with your right leg. Your left knee will be over your left ankle. Move your arms with a running motion. Alternate legs for 10 reps with each leg. You can either return to your starting position between reps or just keep moving backward.

Four O'Clock and Eight O'Clock Lunge

① From a standing position, take a big step back and to the side. If this was a clock, you'd be moving your right leg to the four o'clock position and your left leg to the eight o'clock position (with straight ahead being twelve o'clock). Your back foot should face sideways, perpendicular to your stationary front foot. Your back knee should finish over your back ankle. Your front leg remains straight. Do 5 reps with each leg.

Prone Pedestal Leg Raise

① Assume the prone pedestal position from your previous set of exercises. Using a smooth and continuous motion, raise and lower your right leg, lifting as high as is comfortable while trying to keep the leg straight (at this point in the workout, you'll probably struggle with this—that's okay!). Do 5 reps, then do 5 reps with your left leg.

Supine Pedestal Leg Raise

① Assume the supine pedestal position from your previous set of exercises. Using a smooth and continuous motion, raise and lower your right leg, lifting as high as is comfortable while trying to keep it straight. Keep a straight line from your shoulders through your hips and the lower leg. Do 5 reps, then do 5 reps with your left leg.

Run Repetition #4

① Repeat your same running repetition (as Run Repetition #1).

Burpees

① Start from a standing position.

② Drop into a squat with your hands on the track.

③ Kick your legs backward, forming the prone pedestal position. Then hop back to the squat position. Next, stand while raising your hands above your head (stand, don't jump). Do 10 reps.

Push-Ups

① Assume the supine pedestal position, hands spread slightly wider than shoulder width. Lower and raise your body by pushing against the track/ground. Start with 5 reps, then build up to more as fitness dictates.

Iron Cross

① Lie on your back with your arms extended laterally from your shoulders and your legs straight. Swing one leg over to the opposite side of your body, touching your foot to the track at hip height or higher. Return and perform the same motion with your opposite leg. Do 10 reps on each side.

Scorpion

① This exercise is the reverse of the Iron Cross. Lie on your belly, arms extended laterally from your shoulders. Swing one leg to the opposite side, bending at the knee and trying to touch your foot to the track as high as you can reach. Return and perform the same motion with your other leg. Do 10 reps on each side.

13

Build Your Running Brain

It's a sports cliché that success is 90 percent mental and 10 percent physical. But most of us don't really believe that. We know that we can't will ourselves to be as tall as Shaquille O'Neal, as tough as Ray Lewis, or as fast as Usain Bolt. And the previous eight chapters of Part Two of this book have made clear that improved physiology trumps positive thinking. Because of this, it's easy to dismiss the "90 percent mental" claim as hyperbole.

Only one problem with that: The cliché is 100 percent true.

It's not enough to spend weeks and months building your physiological running body. Before you can truly put that training to work, you'll need to pass a very important inspection. And your inspector is tough as nails. Tougher than the judge at a sentencing hearing. Tougher than a father giving his daughter's date the once-over before the high school prom. Tougher than a Military Training Instructor doing dormitory inspection during basic training. Your inspector is your brain. And your brain isn't about to let you harm your body just to run a PR. First, you'll have to convince it that your body's up to the challenge.

WHAT'S THE RUNNING BRAIN?

When we talk about your "running brain," we're talking about your brain's regulation of exercise and effort—not your physical brain parts. Specifically, we want to focus on fatigue, which is your brain's mechanism for limiting performance in training and racing.

For those who'd like a basic outline of the brain's physiology: It has about eighty-five billion neurons (we covered this in Chapter 11). It's composed of the cerebrum, cerebellum, and brain stem. And the cerebrum and cerebellum are covered by the *cerebral cortex*, which has two hemispheres containing bulges and grooves (gyri and sulci) and serves as the seat of human reasoning,

language, perception, etc.—and is gray, hence the term "gray matter."

But don't get bogged down in the anatomy. And don't expect this chapter to recommend calisthenics for your cerebral cortex or resistance training for your bulges and grooves. Instead, we'll explore some theories on why the brain creates sensations of fatigue and pain (while simultaneously dictating a reduction in the force your muscles can produce), and then we'll look at a few "tricks" for getting your brain to lighten up—to allow you to run a little faster, farther, and with less fatigue and discomfort.

We'll begin by looking at two general approaches to deciphering fatigue:

▶ **Theory of peripheral fatigue**
▶ **Theory of the Central Governor**

Then we'll look at a list of candidates for the exact cause of fatigue, and we'll also examine the brain's role (or lack of one) in each theory. Finally, we'll discuss some ways to lessen, delay, or disregard fatigue.

Be forewarned that the brain's role in running is a heavily debated topic among athletes, coaches, and physiologists. As of now, there are lots of studies, theories, and opinions, but there's little concrete evidence behind any of them. That's why we'll focus on real-world observations of how runners have affected their brains' regulation while training and racing.

BEGINNER'S GUIDELINE

Training your brain isn't about positive thoughts or fighting through pain. It's about performing the workouts that convince your brain you've earned the right to run a little harder, faster, and farther.

TRAINING DISCUSSION

"Is swishing and spitting the new carbo-loading?"

For most of us, the phrase "mind over matter" conjures images of Indian yogis levitating during deep meditation, Tony Robbins walking barefoot over hot coals, or Uri Geller bending a spoon with his mind—old tricks that we dismiss out of hand.

So when someone claims that simply swishing and then spitting out a carbohydrate or caffeine drink can improve your running performance, it seems reasonable to dismiss that as a trick, too. Except in this case, it's real.

A 2004 study found that cyclists who rinsed their mouths with sports drink for five seconds—and then spit it out—completed a forty-kilometer time trial a minute faster than cyclists who rinsed with a placebo. And a 2009 follow-up study documented a 3 percent performance improvement and included brain imaging that revealed post-swish activation of brain regions involved in reward and motor control. Finally, proving that more is better, a 2013 study showed that rinsing for ten seconds led to even greater improvement. The main takeaway points are these:

1. The cyclists' brains could tell the difference between real carbs and placebos.
2. Just the oral sensation of carbs was enough for the brain to increase muscle activation.
3. Improvement occurred even though carb depletion isn't a factor in forty-kilometer time trials.

In other words, the cyclists' brains were anticipating carb depletion—even though it hadn't occurred—so rewarded the promise of more carbs by freeing the cyclists to pedal harder.

A 2013 study conducted by a multinational quintet of authors, led by C. Martyn Beaven, produced similar results for both a caffeine drink and a combination caffeine-and-carb drink. Swishing caffeine improved sprinting ability, and a caffeine-and-carb rinse worked better than carbs alone.

What all these studies show is that there's more going on with fatigue than tired muscles. In the case of swishing and spitting, your brain is altering your immediate performance based on its belief that you've added an energy source for the near future.

But before you lobby the race director for your next 10K to set up spittoons at the start line, note that swishing and spitting only works if you're low on muscle glycogen. If you carbo-load ahead of time, swishing won't have much (or any) effect on your performance.

BRAIN TRAINING

Can the brain be trained? Most runners and coaches these days would answer, "Yes." But that hasn't always been the case. For decades, the brain was viewed as little more than a sensory relay station for fatiguing muscles—not as the arbiter of effort, pace, and exhaustion.

The *Peripheral Fatigue* model was the dominant theory of fatigue during the last century. In this model, fatigue is generated when muscles begin to fail, and, if allowed to continue, leads to a physiological "catastrophe"—acidosis, extreme body heat, etc.—that forces you to slow down or stop. It's worth noting that exercise physiology studies have traditionally been designed with this model in mind. Study participants perform an exercise task until fatigue forces them to quit (e.g., a treadmill test, in which speed and incline are increased at regular intervals until the participant is unable to continue). Measurements of the suspected agent of failure are taken before, during, and after the test. If measurements rise dramatically, it might be concluded that the agent did, in fact, cause failure. The problem with these tests is that real-world running doesn't proceed linearly to the point of failure. Instead, runners choose a pace that ensures they'll reach the finish, and they have the option of slowing down at any point during a run.

The *Central Governor* model, proposed in 1997 by Dr. Timothy Noakes (and later included in the fourth edition of his book, *Lore of Running*), rejects the peripheral fatigue model, instead proposing that fatigue is an emotion, generated by the brain as a means to protect your body. Your brain monitors feedback from all regions of your body during exercise. If your brain senses imminent danger from an effort level that might damage your organs, it decreases muscle fiber recruitment, thereby slowing you down. Noakes believes that the "end spurt" (picking up the pace for the last 10 percent of a race) proves that runners are never actually fatigued, that their brains hold back energy reserves until the finish line is near—when it's safe to increase effort.

Many runners and coaches opt for a third model: Your brain uses a combination of conscious and subconscious regulation to determine pace and to monitor fatigue. Indeed, as Samuele M. Marcora, a senior lecturer in Exercise Physiology at Bangor University in Wales, writes, "[The] end spurt is perfectly compatible with an effort-based decision-making model of exercise performance." Most athletes make conscious pace decisions and adjustments throughout a race. Just as Adrian Peterson of the NFL's Minnesota Vikings needs only a fraction of a second to choose his path through the defense, runners constantly monitor their environment (terrain, climate, competitors, etc.) and sensations of fatigue as they run, then make quick decisions on pacing, stride, and, most important, effort. At the end of a race, a conservative runner can increase effort—the end spurt—without collapsing. Runners who've been less mindful of their effort, however, are often *unable* to pick up the pace, a partial refutation of the Central Governor theory.

The training suggested in this chapter assumes both conscious and subconscious regulation of the many factors that affect fatigue. The goal is to train the brain to allow you to run harder, faster, and farther. Whether the fatigue being overcome is genuine physical discomfort or an "emotion" generated by the Central Governor doesn't change the benefit of convincing the brain to ignore it.

FATIGUE

Fatigue occurs when muscles being used for exercise show a progressive drop in performance accompanied by physiological and psychological discomfort. But there is genuine disagreement over the root cause of that reduced performance and subsequent (or, in the case of the Central Governor, anticipatory) fatigue. Let's look at a few of the candidates.

Acidosis

We discussed low pH in Chapter 9. Hydrogen ions formed during high-intensity energy production overwhelm your muscle fibers' buffering ability. The resulting acidosis has been linked to interference with calcium release within muscle fibers (necessary for muscular contraction), reduced ATP production, reduced ATP hydrolysis (release of energy from ATP), decreased force production, and decreased contraction velocity. A 1995 Australian study concluded, "Intracellular acidosis affects many aspects of muscle cell function[.]" And, as first noted in Chapter 9, a 2006 study by authors Knuth, Dave, Peters, and Fitts confirmed that "the fatigue-inducing effects of low pH" are significant in humans.

Leaky calcium channels

When Dr. Andrew Marks went looking for a cause of weakened cardiac muscle fibers in patients with congestive heart disease, he discovered damaged calcium channels—calcium is released within fibers as a prelude to contraction, then quickly pumped back into a storage area (the sarcoplasmic reticulum) so that the fibers can relax. Damaged calcium channels result in less forceful muscle contractions. In a 2008 study, Marks expanded his theory to skeletal muscle fibers. Mice forced to swim ninety minutes twice daily were given either a drug to shore up leaky calcium channels or a placebo. The mice that got the drug showed no decline in performance during weekly time trials to exhaustion. The mice who got the

placebo did. A subsequent test of trained cyclists—forced to exercise at near-maximum aerobic capacity for three hours, three days in a row—likewise revealed damaged calcium channels in skeletal muscle fibers, although ethical considerations prevented Marks from testing the unapproved drug on them (the calcium channels fully repaired themselves, however, after a few days). Since experiments with the mice were performed to exhaustion, it's unknown what effect leaky calcium channels have on real-world, submaximal exercise. (Note that Dr. Marks is not saying that having leaky calcium channels in skeletal muscle fibers due to exercise leads to damaged calcium channels in your heart; you'll recover quickly from changes in your skeletal muscle fibers—if all goes well, with stronger fibers than you had previously).

Body temperature

When your body temperature reaches a critical core temperature during exercise of 104 °F (40 °C), you stop running. But as Dr. Ross Tucker points out in an in-depth series on fatigue for his website, *The Science of Sport*, experiments based on heat-based failure are "set up to evaluate a 'forced' physiology leading to a distinct failure." Tucker explains that most humans *don't* exercise until their bodies reach 104 °F (106 °F for highly motivated athletes) because we have the option to *slow down*. Tucker had twelve trained cyclists perform 20K time trials in either hot or cool conditions. At 5K, cyclists in the hot conditions slowed down—even though their body temperatures remained almost identical (at that point) to cyclists in cool conditions—and their brain signaling to their muscles decreased. The cyclists didn't slow down because their body temperature rose; they slowed down in *anticipation* of a rising body temperature in the future—their *brains* slowed them down to avoid physiological catastrophe.

Depolarization

Triathlete, runner, and running-writer Matt Fitzgerald, who serves as a reliable harbinger of new running theories, has written that "muscles work kind of like batteries. They run on electricity, and, like batteries, they are most powerful when they are highly polarized." As you exercise at high intensity, however, the difference in positive charge between the inside of your muscle fibers and the space outside (the polarity) decreases. This *depolarization* makes it harder for nerve signals to penetrate your fibers, leading to weaker contractions. Interestingly, studies in 2001 and 2010 concluded that acidosis can counteract depolarization. In fact, the latter study found that lactate by itself protects against depolarization and "may reduce the importance of elevated extracellular K+ [positive charge] for the development of fatigue." Furthermore, lactate released to the bloodstream can mediate depolarization in muscle fibers throughout the body.

Ammonia

Raised ammonia levels are associated with liver disorders like cirrhosis, in which the liver can no longer adequately convert ammonia to urea. Too much ammonia also leads to diminished brain function and other toxic effects. Studies have found that extended and intense exercise can increase ammonia levels (through the removal of amino groups from adenosine monophosphate [AMP] and branched chain amino acids) within muscle fibers. A 2010 study by Wilkinson, Smeeton, and Watt warns, "Plasma concentrations of ammonia during exercise often achieve or exceed those measured in liver disease patients, resulting in increased cerebral uptake." Once ammonia crosses the blood-brain barrier, its toxic effect on neurons leads to reduced muscle fiber activation and sensations of fatigue.

Glycogen depletion

All runners know the phrase "hitting the wall." It's the moment fifteen to twenty miles into a marathon (or a long run) when glycogen stores run dry, forcing you to rely upon fats and protein. An average person stores about 300–400 grams (1,200–1,600 calories) of glycogen. But a trained, carbo-loaded athlete can store twice that much. A 2001 study, whose authors included Noakes (aforementioned creator of the Central Governor theory), found that while carbo-loaded cyclists and non-loaded cyclists started a time trial at the same pace, the non-loaded cyclists slowed down within a minute. Even more interesting, while the carbo-loaded cyclists rode the entire time trial 6 percent faster than the non-loaded cyclists, both groups finished with virtually the exact same amount of remaining muscle glycogen. In other words, they both chose paces that directly correlated to their relative levels of muscle glycogen.

Inorganic phosphate

When you burn ATP for energy, it splits into ADP and inorganic phosphate (Pi). While ADP and inorganic phosphate will be reassembled to produce more ATP, during intense exercise the production of ATP lags way behind its consumption. Ernest W. Maglischo, Ph.D., writes in a 2012 paper that "muscle calcium changes brought on by increases of inorganic phosphate and ADP may be major causative factors for muscular fatigue." And a 2012 review by Allen and Trajonovska argues that even moderate exercise leads to increased inorganic phosphate levels, resulting in reduced calcium release in muscle fibers, reduced activation of fibers, and fatigue.

Oxygen to the brain

That lightheaded feeling you get in the late stages of a race might be your brain running low on oxygen—up to 25 percent low, according to a 2010 study that blames low cerebral oxygenation for reduced muscle activation, diminished neural function, and fatigue. This conclusion has been echoed in numerous studies, but these studies have one thing in common: Participants exercise to failure. In a different 2010 study by Billaut, et al., runners were allowed to self-pace through a 5K time trial. This time, oxygen levels in the runners' brains remained within a range that didn't "hinder strenuous exercise performance," even as the runners rated their own efforts as maximal.

CNS fatigue

Although often overlooked, the central nervous system (CNS) undoubtedly plays a role in fatigue. A 1997 paper by Davis and Bailey in *Medicine & Science in Sports & Exercise* argues that "the unwillingness to generate and maintain adequate CNS drive to the working muscle is the most likely explanation of fatigue for most people during normal activities." The authors speculate that increases and decreases in certain neurotransmitters are to blame (with serotonin the probable top culprit), adding that cytokines and ammonia are also involved. A 2000 paper by Davis, Alderson, and Welsh on serotonin and central nervous system fatigue notes that serotonin levels "increase in several brain regions during prolonged exercise and reach a peak at fatigue." Serotonin is tied to lethargy, sleepiness, and altered mood.

Muscle and connective tissue damage

Another factor that's rarely discussed is the role of muscle and connective tissue damage in fatigue. Run long enough—or hard enough for long enough—and you'll reach a point where you feel every jarring step. And while you might not reach the point of physiological catastrophe that accompanies some other factors, there are times when beaten-down muscles and CT lead you to the inescapable conclusion: *I can't take another step.*

Afferent feedback

The theory of afferent (sensory) feedback suggests that all the above-listed factors in fatigue (and more) are reported via nerve impulses to your brain, which reacts by inhibiting your central motor drive (i.e., it activates less muscle). A 2013 study from the University of Utah had eight volunteers perform single-leg extensions (a quadriceps exercise) to exhaustion, testing each leg on a separate day. Both legs registered similar results. When the legs were subsequently re-tested consecutively on the same day, however, the time to exhaustion for the second leg tested was almost 50 percent shorter than for the first. The researchers concluded that afferent feedback from the first leg had inhibited performance in the second leg.

The Central Governor

The Central Governor theory, proposed by Dr. Timothy Noakes, has changed the way runners, coaches, and physiologists think about fatigue. Explaining the theory in a 2012 paper, Noakes writes, "The Central Governor Model of Exercise Regulation proposes that the brain regulates exercise performance by continuously modifying the number of motor units that are recruited in the exercising limbs." And it doesn't just do this in a reactive way (as with afferent feedback). Instead, the Central Governor (CG) anticipates danger to your body and acts preemptively to avoid it. At the start of a run, the CG picks your pace and effort within the first few seconds. Before making this decision, the CG considers your emotional state, motivation, experience, level of neurotransmitters, body temperature, etc. Once the run is under way, the CG continues to regulate performance based on oxygen in the blood and brain, glycogen levels, dehydration, and any other factor that could eventually prove dangerous to your vital organs.

"[There] are innumerable different 'homeostats,'" writes Dr. Tucker in a 2011 *Science of Sport* blog entry, explaining his mentor's theory, "all of which are monitored and regulated by the brain,

TRAINING DISCUSSION

"The age of Frankenstein"

If you've ever seen a Frankenstein movie, you'll shiver when you hear what a predominantly Brazilian research group did to ten cyclists in a 2013 study. They hooked up electrodes over the cyclists' temporal and insular cortexes, then zapped them with current for twenty minutes. The result? In a maximum incremental cycling test, the Frankenstein cyclists' peak power output increased 4 percent over cyclists receiving "sham stimulation." The Frankenstein cyclists also reported a more gradual rise in perceived effort. In other words, they rode harder and hurt less.

This isn't the first time that the insular cortex has been singled out as a prime actor in fatigue. Kai Lutz and a team from the University of Zurich performed a series of experiments, published in 2011, that identified the insular cortex as the brain structure that "might not only integrate and evaluate sensory information from the periphery [muscles], but also act in communication with the motor cortex . . . [This] is the first study to empirically demonstrate that muscle fatigue leads to changes in interaction between structures of a brain's neural network."

And, in 2012, researchers from the OptiBrain Center at the University of California, San Diego, revealed to *Scientific American* that their studies show that athletes who engage in a meditation technique called *mindfulness* are able to increase insular cortex activity, making them more physically self-aware and allowing them to react to feedback from their muscles (i.e., factors that cause fatigue) more quickly.

The insular cortex lies within the folds of the cerebral cortex and plays a role in consciousness, emotion, and bodily self-awareness. It's involved in heart rate and blood pressure (especially during exercise), regulating homeostasis, and evaluating pain. In sum, it's at the center of the interplay between brain, exercise, and fatigue.

And now you can zap your insular cortex with electricity to knock a big chunk of time off your next 5K or marathon. But before you go signing up for a series of electroshock treatments, be aware that other studies have had mixed results (with Alex Hutchinson reporting in his *Runner's World* blog that one researcher admitted seeing no performance boost at all).

So maybe stick to meditation for now. And a quick carbo swish and spit at the start line.

and then controlled by changes in exercise intensity. And that, in a nutshell, is the Central Governor theory."

Noakes argues that symptoms of fatigue are "entirely self-generated by each athlete's brain . . . As such they are illusionary." For Noakes, the illusion of fatigue exists solely to prevent athletes from risking a catastrophic biological failure. The winner of a running race is the athlete who best ignored the illusion. The other athletes accepted the illusion—and defeat.

TRAINING (TRICKING) THE BRAIN

The truth is that no one knows for sure what causes fatigue when you're running. The list above is a good start, but it's hardly comprehensive. For instance, we didn't even touch on dehydration (which demands much more than a paragraph; read Tucker, Dugas, and Fitzgerald's book, *The Runner's Body*, for the lowdown on dehydration). But you probably get the idea that there are many actors on this stage. And that the brain—whether it's limiting performance due to physiological failure or regulating performance to avoid physiological failure—is playing a huge role in stage direction.

So how do we train the brain?

The following simple training "tricks" will convince your brain to work with you, not against you, when you run:

1. **Take off your watch:** This is the easiest strategy of all—and the most difficult for many runners. Some runners can't conceive of running a mile untimed. But once you're familiar with your regular running routes, there's no reason to time every single run. Instead, stop worrying about the watch and start listening to your body. Become aware of your body's feedback, of the nuances that warn you of impending fatigue, of tension in your body, of poor breathing, or of inefficient form. Then try some repetitions (see 5K Road and Trail Reps, Chapter 7) or tempo runs, measured in time but not distance. Learn how to pace by effort. Note how various efforts feel, and pay attention to how fatigue builds through the course of those efforts. Experiment with subtle changes in pace. When you become more aware of your body's feedback, you'll find that you're able to anticipate problems before your brain steps in to correct them.

2. **Extended runs:** If you're having trouble increasing (or completing) your daily run, add 30–50 percent more distance to an outing. You'll suffer immensely in order to complete the run. But you'll be amazed how easy your regular run feels the next time out.

3. **The "down a quart" approach:** Your body adapts to increased stimulus. A full fuel and hydration belt may ease the fatigue of your daily run, but your body will respond better to the challenge of slight dehydration (up to 2 percent), reduced glycogen stores, and moderate discomfort. Your brain will likewise learn that you can survive while running "down a quart"—a lesson that will pay big dividends in races.

4. **Race-effort intervals:** Race effort intervals don't just prepare you physically for a race, they prepare you mentally, too. Just as sports like football and basketball "slow down" after you've played them awhile, your brain becomes familiar with race pace.

5. **Group workouts:** Want to surprise yourself with a monster workout or huge performance improvement? Try running with a group. When you focus on keeping pace with a group rather than obsessing over your own fatigue, your brain focuses more on pace and less on fatigue, too.

6. **Workouts with unspecified volume:** Some days, you need to run without a preconceived end point. Go exploring with friends on a distance run. Or run untimed, unmeasured repetitions with the goal of stopping when you've had enough, whatever "enough" turns out to be.

7. **Tune-up races:** Your brain will almost never allow you to run your first race after a significant break (from racing) as fast as your fitness should allow. Instead, it plays it safe. Tune-up races can serve as "rust-busters." It's not your body that's rusty. It's your brain. Like a protective parent, it thinks you're a child that needs strict boundaries. So schedule a tune-up race as a dress rehearsal for the real thing, show your brain that a hard effort won't kill you (or it), and don't be surprised when—as soon as a few days later—your brain rewards you with a race performance improvement of up to 5 percent or more!

8. **Matched time runs:** If you're going to run a half marathon or marathon, it's important that you do a run that approximates in time (*not pace or distance*) your goal for the race. Your brain needs to know that your body can keep exercising for the amount of time you intend to race.

9. **Negative split runs:** All training runs should be negative split runs. You should start slow, then build to your goal workout pace. Don't force your brain to put on the brakes by starting out too quickly! For marathon training, include some negative split long runs, where the second half of the run mimics the effort that will be required during your upcoming race: The first part of the run creates a watered-down version of the biomechanical fatigue and fuel shortage you'll face during an actual marathon; the negative split second half of the run familiarizes your brain with the force generation required to produce marathon pace when you're fatigued—all while sparing your body the extreme fatigue associated with an actual marathon race.

10. **Consistency:** Some days, maybe most days, your brain is going to tell you that you're too tired to run. Don't listen to it. Prove it wrong. The hardest part of a run is putting on your shoes and heading out the door. A mile into your run, you'll be fine. More importantly, your brain will discover that your body can run while fatigued—and will give you more leeway in the future.

And now a warning: When training the brain, it's a *big mistake* to train too hard, too fast, or for too long. Just as the items on the above list teach your brain to ease up on the reins, pushing too hard will convince your brain that you're a danger to your own body. So be patient. Be smart in your training. And show your brain that you can be trusted, that you've got the right stuff.

Training recommendation

Step one is to train every aspect of your running components as laid out in the previous component chapters. Whether a lack of physiological fitness is the direct cause of fatigue or an indirect stimulus for your Central Governor to create the illusion of fatigue, building a better running body is the remedy. For directly targeting your brain, begin by experimenting with the ten things on the above list, and then find your own boundaries—and exceed them.

TRAINING RUNDOWN

There is no photo instruction for this chapter; the applicable workouts have been illustrated in previous chapters. What you need to do now is convince your brain—by *doing those workouts*—that you've built a running body capable of achieving your running goals.

To see exactly how all the workouts from this book can be incorporated into your overall training program, see Chapter 15: Build Your Training Schedule, where sample schedules are available for runners of all abilities and fitness levels.

PART

3

Build Your Running Program— Principles and Schedules

14

Build Your Running Approach

Building your running body will be an individualized experience. You aren't a Ken or Barbie doll. You have a unique body type, your own mix of muscle fibers, your own fitness history, and your own fitness goals. But no matter who you are, where you live, or what motivates you to train, you *will* get fit, you *will* get faster, and you *will* stay healthy and injury-free—if you're willing to tackle each component of your running body and embrace a well-rounded training regimen.

WHAT'S A RUNNING APPROACH?

Your "running approach" is more than just your training schedule. It's the attitude and experience you bring to your training, the fitness goals you hope to achieve, and the lifestyle adjustments you're willing to accommodate. A runner who trains to be competitive will have a much different approach than a runner whose goal is all-around fitness. It's up to you to determine how much time to invest in your program. And it's up to you to decide what level of fitness best augments your lifestyle. While you're deciding, some factors you'll need to consider include:

▶ **Competitive versus non-competitive training**
▶ **Time management**
▶ **Sustainability**

Once you've made up your mind, you can choose the training schedule from Chapter 15 that best suits your approach. Or, using the knowledge you've gained from this book (coupled with your personal experience), you can fashion your own program. Training schedule in hand, you'll want to review some specific *principles of training* in order to get the most out of your workouts.

CHOOSING YOUR RUNNING APPROACH

When you choose a running approach, don't start by thinking about the training pieces—the running, drills, resistance training, stretching, and the rest of it. Instead, think about what you're trying to accomplish, and then make a realistic appraisal of how much room there is in your daily life for a training program that will get you there. Let's look at a few of the factors that should inform your decision.

Competitive versus non-competitive training

Why do you run? It was the first line of Chapter One. And it's the question you'll want to answer before settling on a training program.

If you're training for non-competitive reasons—for example, to lose weight, improve your health, or reduce stress—you might want your program to include more all-around exercises (e.g., resistance training and cross training) and less running-specific exercises (e.g., tempo and long repetitions). A benefit of non-competitive training is that there's more leeway with your schedule, since you aren't piggybacking adaptations one on top of another to peak for a race. Also, you're less likely to get injured on a schedule with lower volume and intensity. Instead of aches and pains, you'll feel stronger, springier, and more energetic during the day.

BEGINNER'S GUIDELINE

Fitness is a journey, not a destination. It is the incremental process of transforming both your mind and body into a healthier, stronger, and more resilient version of *you*. Choose a training schedule that you can maintain—one that compliments your life, rather than conflicts with it. Then be willing to adjust, to alter your training and your goals based upon feedback from your body.

TRAINING DISCUSSION

"Ten Mistakes Runners Make"

No one sets out to train incorrectly, yet it's training error that often sabotages our fitness goals. So that you can avoid some bumps in the road, here are ten mistakes that runners often make.

1. **Fast starts:** Going out too fast in workouts alters the workout. You train the wrong muscle fibers, engage the wrong energy systems, and wire the wrong neuromuscular pathways. Plus, it leads to shortened or aborted workouts.

2. **Medium runs:** Some runners think they need to prove their fitness during every workout. They run their easy runs too hard and are left too fatigued to excel during the hard ones. The result is a diet of medium runs that fails to garner the full benefits of either easy distance runs or speedwork.

3. **Speed limit:** Runners cannot live on mileage alone. Doing nothing but long distance leads to atrophy of faster muscle fibers, decreased nervous system efficiency, decreased muscle buffering capacity, and increased acidosis during races. Proper speedwork reverses and improves all those factors.

4. **Poor recovery:** Running damages muscle fibers and connective tissue, depletes fuel reserves and hormones, and fatigues your nervous system. Recovering takes time. Younger runners need two to four days between hard workouts. Older runners might need double that.

5. **Monster workouts:** Some runners believe more is better. More miles. More reps. More speed. The result is often a workout that is more physically taxing than a race. It risks injury, illness, and burnout. One monster workout can require up to two weeks of recovery.

6. **No adjustments:** Many runners refuse to alter a workout once it's started. But unpredictable variables like weather, fatigue, and allergies can affect your workout. Adjusting a workout on the fly allows you to get training benefits without risking overtraining.

7. **Cafeteria running:** *Runner's World*'s Scott Douglas coined this phrase to describe runners who treat training like a buffet, choosing the workouts they find most appealing from a dozen sources and then trying them all. This is like building a puzzle with pieces from several sets.

8. **Running fundamentalism:** Running fundamentalists cling to old training programs regardless of results. Things change: your body, your fitness, your experience, your age. What worked in year one of running won't work in year five—or year fifty.

(Continued)

9. **Injury block:** Studies confirm that 50–80 percent of runners will get injured in any given year. Many runners repress this fact, refusing to adopt injury-prevention routines, which take ten to fifteen minutes, three to four days per week. Unfortunately, injury-reversal routines generally take months.

10. **Goal fitness:** Many runners base their workouts on the fitness they'd like to have rather than the fitness they already possess. This is like buying a Porsche 918 Spyder ($845,000) in the belief that you'll soon be rich. Challenge your current fitness level; don't obliterate it.

If you want to run a race, but your goal is completion—not competition—you'll have to decide if you prefer a more well-rounded program or one with higher running volume. Either way, you'll need to include the type of race-specific training outlined in Chapter 24.

If you're training with competitive race goals in mind, you *must* include more volume and intensity in your training. You can expect residual fatigue during the day, some aches and pains, and a higher risk of injury. You'll also have less schedule flexibility, as each workout is linked inextricably to the next (and to the previous one). Skipping or changing workouts can sabotage weeks of training. Of course, you'll also discover the amazing potential that lies within your running body. And you'll feel great (sometimes euphoric) while you're running.

Time management

It does no good to map out an ambitious training program and then discover that you lack the time to complete the workouts. From the start, choose a training schedule that meshes with your daily commitments to family, career, social obligations, and community involvement. If you don't, you'll soon have to choose between your schedule and the rest of your life—and your life will win. Don't sabotage

yourself. And remember that a workout requires more than the time it takes to complete the exercise. For example, a sixty-minute run requires at least ten minutes to change into running gear pre-run, and then another twenty to thirty minutes post-run for showering and changing back into street clothes (and, if you're being very good, another ten to fifteen minutes for some post-run stretching and exercises). Don't try to squeeze square pegs into round holes. Plan your time wisely.

Sustainability

You'll want a training approach you can stick to long-term. Training too hard too soon almost always leads to injury, illness, or burnout. Your body can't adapt that quickly, and you won't be able to sustain your motivation. Plus, there's no rush. As a runner, you'll probably see improvement in both performance and overall fitness for at least a decade. That's right, a decade. And that's regardless of your age. But to see that improvement, you'll have to stay healthy and committed, and that means training at a manageable level. Everything good about running—the benefits for your body, health, mood, and social life—requires long-term participation. So pick your program the way you pick your friends, as an element of your life that you'll be happy to greet every day.

PRINCIPLES OF TRAINING

Once you've picked your running approach, there are some fundamental principles of training (and a few unbreakable rules, too) that you'll want to keep in mind:

Train with the body you have: You possess a distinct physiology and a unique potential. You can't build your body by training as if you were someone else.

Train with the fitness you have: Training too hard won't help you reach your fitness goal more quickly. Instead, you'll risk injury, illness, and burnout, and your fitness will suffer.

Training is a journey, not a destination: Fitness goals and race goals are just beacons. Steer for them and then keep going. As long as your fitness is improving, your training is on track.

Don't specialize: Until you've strengthened all the components of your running body, don't specialize. The training in this book will prepare you for *all* races from 5K to the marathon.

The 10 percent rule: The 10 percent rule recommends increasing training volume by no more than 10 percent per week. However, the 10 percent rule doesn't reflect how real runners train. Instead, use the three-week rule.

The three-week rule: It takes time for your body to adapt to increases in mileage and intensity. So after a significant jump in either, allow at least three weeks before your next increase.

The hard-easy rule: Hard days are followed by easy days, a few hard weeks are followed by an easy week, and a hard season is followed by a few very easy weeks.

Warm up: It takes ten to fifteen minutes of exercise (e.g., jogging, dynamic stretching, strides) for your body to become physiologically prepared for harder training.

Warm down: Although the value of a warm-down is debated in physiological circles, its value is *not* debated by coaches and athletes. Go with the coaches and athletes on this one.

Muscle fiber range: You'll need volume (distance) to train slow-twitch fibers and quality (reps, hills, drills, etc.) to train faster fibers. No single workout adequately trains all fibers.

The rule of repetitions: When running repetitions, always finish the workout knowing you could have run one or possibly two more reps if required. This protects against overtraining.

The value of hills: If you want to excel as a runner, you'll want to run hills: long hill runs, long hill repeats, and short uphill and downhill sprints.

The rule of specificity: The training you do in practice must match the activity in which you intend to compete. Biking is great but (by itself) won't make you a better runner.

Doubles: Running twice a day can benefit experienced runners (increased volume, extra HGH release, better running economy) but is generally too much for new runners.

Don't race workouts: A race is a 100 percent effort, and it requires a taper before and recovery after. A 100 percent workout requires the same.

For multiple 100 percent repetitions, see the next principle.

Better undertrained than overtrained: Undertrained, you'll feel good, and you can always improve. Overtrained, you'll feel like hell, and you'll need weeks of rest to recover.

The truth is that a conservative, patient approach to running will almost always yield positive results. That's because building your running body takes time. You can't do it with one workout. Or two. Or a dozen. It's going to take dozens of workouts to unlock your potential.

Shortcuts don't work.

Overtraining doesn't work.

Killer workouts and gung-ho boot camps won't do it.

If you remember one thing about training from this book, make it this: *There are no good workouts; there are only good training programs.*

Make your running approach one that slips easily into the life you're leading, is sustainable from Day One, and has the punch to satisfy your goals. Make it one you can stick to.

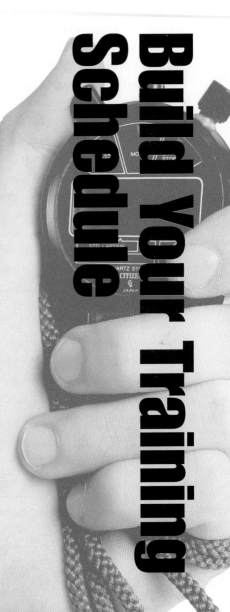

Build Your Training Schedule

Now that you've learned how the components of your running body work—and how to train them—as well as how to develop a program based on your own fitness goals, it's time to choose your training schedule. This chapter will offer sample schedules for six different training approaches (from non-competitive beginners to advanced competition-focused runners), as well as sample race-training schedules for 5K, 10K, half marathon, and marathon races.

Before you make a final decision about your training, consider the words of the late Dr. George Sheehan: "We are all an experiment of one." You have to pick a schedule that works for *your* fitness, *your* goals, and *your* life outside running. And you have to be willing to modify that schedule to meet your own individual requirements, using what you've learned in this book—and from your own experience—as your guide. If none of the schedules in this chapter work for you (either intact or as a starting point), then craft your own. Whichever path you choose, consider a few guidelines when embarking on your new fitness journey:

1. **Photo instruction:** Unless otherwise noted, all workouts in the schedules have entries in this book's photo instruction. Follow the instructions to make sure you get the full benefit of the workout.

2. **Volume/intensity:** Increasing the volume or intensity of individual workouts in the schedules is not advised.

3. **Warm-up/down:** For hard workouts, *always* include a warm-up and warm-down (cool-down).

4. **Pace:** If you don't know your pace for a workout (e.g., 5K pace), use the rule of repetitions (see previous chapter).

5. **Recovery:** Unless otherwise specified, use the recovery recommended in the photo instruction. Where there's a range, start with the high end (the longer recovery); use the lower end as your fitness improves.

6. **Suggested exercises:** Exercises for beginner's resistance training, technique drills, and plyometrics are included in the

schedules. After a few sessions, feel free to add or exclude exercises.

7. **Post-run:** Post-run routines and stretching are suggested for specific days, but you might prefer to schedule them for different days. As long as you're doing each a minimum of twice a week, you should be okay.

8. **Injury-prevention exercises:** If you're rehabbing from an injury or concerned about preventing one, add injury-specific exercises from the Injury Prevention table on page 377 to your post-run routine or resistance-training sessions.

9. **Rest:** If you need an easy day or a day off, take it.

10. **Missed workouts:** If you miss a workout, don't try to make it up—skip it.

11. **Additional workouts:** If you want to change workouts or add additional workouts (e.g., the Running Circuit from chapter 12), feel free, but remember that you'll have to eliminate a hard workout from the week in order to add a new hard workout—don't risk overtraining by running too many hard sessions in any given week.

12. **Racing:** Sample race-specific schedules have been included. If you want to race during the non-race schedules, do it! Just make sure to include a taper week before the race—and to schedule a reduced training load the following week. Then go back to your regular schedule.

Choose your schedule wisely. Good luck!

TRAINING SCHEDULES

12-WEEK TRAINING SCHEDULE FOR BEGINNING AND RETURNING RUNNERS—NON-COMPETITIVE

WEEK	SUNDAY	MONDAY	TUESDAY	WEDNESDAY	THURSDAY	FRIDAY	SATURDAY
1	OFF	Easy Walking [p. 47]: 10–15 minutes	OFF	Easy Walking [p. 47]: 10–15 minutes	OFF	Easy Walking [p. 47]: 10–15 minutes + Beginner's RT*	OFF or Easy Walking [p. 47]: 10–15 minutes
2	OFF	Easy Walking [p. 47]: 20 minutes	OFF	Brisk Walking [p. 47]: 15 minutes	OFF	Easy Walking [p. 47]: 20 minutes + Beginner's RT*	OFF or Easy Walking [p. 47]: 10–15 minutes
3	OFF	Brisk Walking [p. 47]: 15–20 minutes + Stretching**	OFF	Easy Walking [p. 47]: 20 minutes + Beginner's RT*	OFF	Walk/Jog [p. 48]:15–20 minutes + Beginner's RT* + Stretching**	OFF or Easy Walking [p. 47]: 20 minutes
4	OFF	Walk/Jog [p. 48]: 20 minutes + Stretching**	OFF	Easy Walking [p. 47]: 20 minutes + Beginner's RT*	OFF	Walk/Jog [p. 48]: 20 minutes + Beginner's RT* + Stretching**	OFF or Easy Walking [p. 47]: 20 minutes or XT†
5	OFF	Walk/Jog [p. 48]: 20 minutes + Stretching**	OFF	Easy Walking [p. 47]: 20 minutes + Beginner's RT*	OFF	Walk/Jog [p. 48]: 20 minutes + Beginner's RT* + Stretching**	OFF or Easy Walking [p. 47]: 20 minutes or XT†
6	OFF	Walk/Jog [p. 48]: 20 minutes + Stretching**	OFF	Easy Walking [p. 47]: 20 minutes + Beginner's RT*	OFF	Jog/Easy Run [p. 48]: 20 minutes + Beginner's RT* + Stretching**	OFF or Easy Walking [p. 47]: 20 minutes or XT†
7	OFF	Jog/Easy Run [p. 48]: 20–30 minutes + Stretching**	OFF	Walk/Jog [p. 48]: 20–30 minutes + The Runner 360 [p. 53] (1 set)	OFF	Jog/Easy Run [p. 48]: 20–30 minutes + Weight Room Routine [p. 59] + Stretching**	OFF or Walk/Jog [p. 48]: 20–30 minutes or XT†
8	OFF	Jog/Easy Run [p. 48]: 20–30 minutes + Stretching**	OFF	Walk/Jog [p. 48]: 20–30 minutes + The Runner 360 [p. 53] (1 set)	OFF	Jog/Easy Run [p. 48]: 20–30 minutes + Weight Room Routine [p. 59] + Stretching**	OFF or Walk/Jog [p. 48]: 20–30 minutes or XT†
9	OFF	Jog/Easy Run [p. 48]: 20–30 minutes + Stretching**	OFF	Jog/Easy Run [p. 48]: 15–20 minutes + Strides [p. 51] + The Runner 360 [p. 53] (1 set)	OFF	Easy Distance Run [p. 49]: 20–30 minutes + Weight Room Routine [p. 59] + Stretching**	OFF or Walk/Jog [p. 48]: 20–30 minutes or XT†

WEEK	SUNDAY	MONDAY	TUESDAY	WEDNESDAY	THURSDAY	FRIDAY	SATURDAY
10	OFF	Beginner's Fartlek [p. 49]: 10–15 minutes + Stretching**	OFF	Jog/Easy Run [p. 48]: 20–30 minutes + The Runner 360 [p. 53] (1 set)	OFF	Easy Distance Run [p. 49]: 20–30 minutes + Weight Room Routine [p. 59] + Stretching**	OFF *or Jog/ Easy Run* [p. 48]: 20–30 minutes *or* XT†
11	OFF	Long Run [p. 132]: 30–40 minutes + Strides [p. 51] + Stretching**	OFF	Jog/Easy Run [p. 48]: 20–30 minutes + The Runner 360 [p. 53] (1 set)	OFF	Easy Distance Run [p. 49]: 20–30 minutes + Weight Room Routine [p. 59] + Stretching**	OFF *or Jog/ Easy Run* [p. 48]: 20–30 minutes *or* XT†
12	OFF	Beginner's Fartlek [p. 49]: 15–20 minutes + Stretching**	OFF	Jog/Easy Run [p. 48]: 20–30 minutes + The Runner 360 [p. 53] (1 set)	OFF	Distance Run [p. 50]: 20–40 minutes + Weight Room Routine [p. 59] + Stretching**	OFF *or Jog/ Easy Run* [p. 48]: 20–30 minutes *or* XT†

TRAINING SCHEDULE NOTES:

*BEGINNER'S RT (Resistance Training)

Leg Lifts (1 set) [p. 60]; Russian Oblique Twise (1 set) [p. 61]; Side Leg Lifts (from Running Circuit) [p. 235]; Push–Ups (1 set) [p. 61]; Air Squat (1 set) [p. 235]; Bodyweight Lunge (1 set) [p. 64]; Heel Raises—Straight Knee (1 set) [p. 66]; Dumbbell Arm Swings (1 set) [p. 63]

NOTE: *Beginners should start with 1 set of each of the above exercises. Or you can do the Household Props routine (pages 107–110) as a substitution, but then don't progress to The Runner 360 or Weight Room Routine in this schedule.*

ONLY DO ONE TYPE OF STRETCHING: AIS [p. 104]; PNF [p. 70]; or Static [p. 76]

†XT = CROSS TRAIN (see pp. 153–163); If you choose to cross train, keep your workout aerobic and match the effort/duration of the prescribed run.

BUILD YOUR RUNNING BODY

12-WEEK TRAINING SCHEDULE FOR BEGINNING AND RETURNING RUNNERS—COMPETITIVE

WEEK	SUNDAY	MONDAY	TUESDAY	WEDNESDAY	THURSDAY	FRIDAY	SATURDAY
1	OFF	Easy Walking [p. 47]: 10–15 minutes	OFF	Easy Walking [p. 47]: 10–15 minutes	OFF	Easy Walking [p. 47]: 10–15 minutes + Beginner's RT*	OFF *or* Easy Walking [p. 47]: 10–15 minutes
2	OFF	Easy Walking [p. 47]: 20 minutes	OFF	Brisk Walking [p. 47]: 15 minutes	Easy Walking [p. 47]: 20 minutes + Stretching**	OFF	Walk/Jog [p. 48]: 20 minutes + Beginner's RT*
3	OFF	Walk/Jog [p. 48]: 20 minutes + Stretching**	OFF	Walk/Jog [p. 48]: 20 minutes	Easy Walking [p. 47]: 20 minutes + Beginner's RT*	OFF	Jog/Easy Run [p. 48]: 15–20 minutes + Beginner's RT*
4	OFF	Jog/Easy Run [p. 48]: 20 minutes + Strides [p. 51] + Stretching**	OFF *or* XT†	Jog/Easy Run [p. 48]: 20 minutes	Walk/Jog [p. 48]: 20 minutes + Beginner's RT* + Stretching**	OFF	Easy Distance Run [p. 49]: 20–30 minutes + Beginner's RT*
5	OFF	Jog/Easy Run [p. 48]: 20 minutes + Strides [p. 51] + Stretching**	OFF *or* XT†	Jog/Easy Run [p. 48]: 20 minutes	Walk/Jog [p. 48]: 20 minutes + Beginner's RT* + Stretching**	OFF	Easy Distance Run [p. 49]: 20–30 minutes + Beginner's RT*
6	OFF	Easy Distance Run [p. 49]: 20 minutes + Strides [p. 51] + Stretching**	OFF *or* XT†	Easy Distance Run [p. 49]: 20 minutes	Jog/Easy Run [p. 48]: 20 minutes + Beginner's RT* + Stretching**	OFF	Distance Run [p. 50]: 30 minutes + Beginner's RT*
7	OFF	Beginner's Fartlek [p. 49]: 10–25 minutes + Stretching**	OFF *or* XT†	Easy Distance Run [p. 49]: 20–30 minutes	Jog/Easy Run [p. 48]: 20 minutes + *either* Beginner's RT* *or* Post-Run Routine‡	OFF	Distance Run [p. 50]: 40 minutes + *either* Beginner's RT* *or* Post-Run Routine‡
8	OFF	5K Road & Trail Reps [p. 134]: 6 x 1 minute + Stretching**	OFF *or* XT†	Easy Distance Run [p. 49]: 20–30 minutes	Jog/Easy Run [p. 48]: 20 minutes + *either* Beginner's RT* *or* Post-Run Routine‡	OFF	Distance Run [p. 50]: 40 minutes + *either* Beginner's RT* *or* Post-Run Routine‡
9	OFF	5K Road & Trail Reps [p. 134]: 6 x 2 minutes + Stretching**	OFF *or* XT†	Distance Run [p. 50]: 20–30 minutes	Easy Distance Run [p. 49]: 20 minutes + *either* Beginner's RT* *or* Post-Run Routine‡	OFF	Long Run [p. 132]: 45–50 minutes + *either* Beginner's RT* *or* Post-Run Routine‡

WEEK	SUNDAY	MONDAY	TUESDAY	WEDNESDAY	THURSDAY	FRIDAY	SATURDAY
10	OFF	Slow Tempo [p. 130]: 1 x 10–15 minutes + Stretching**	OFF *or* XT†	Distance Run [p. 50]: 20–40 minutes	Hill Strides [p. 52] + *either* Beginner's RT* *or* Post-Run Routine‡	OFF *or* Easy Distance Run [p. 49]: 20–40 minutes	Long Run [p. 132]: 45–50 minutes + *either* Beginner's RT* *or* Post-Run Routine‡
11	OFF	5K Road & Trail Reps [p. 134]: 4 x 3 minutes + Stretching**	OFF *or* XT†	Distance Run [p. 50]: 20–40 minutes	Easy Distance Run [p. 49]: 20–30 minutes + Strides [p. 51] + *either* Beginner's RT* *or* Post-Run Routine‡	OFF *or* Easy Distance Run [p. 49]: 20–40 minutes	Long Run [p. 132]: 45–50 minutes + *either* Beginner's RT* *or* Post-Run Routine‡
12	OFF	5K Road & Trail Reps [p. 134]: 3 x 4 minutes + Stretching**	OFF *or* XT†	Distance Run [p. 50]: 20–40 minutes	Hill Strides [p. 52] + *either* Beginner's RT* *or* Post-Run Routine‡	OFF *or* Easy Distance Run [p. 49]: 20–40 minutes	Long Run [p. 132]: 50–60 minutes + *either* Beginner's RT* *or* Post-Run Routine‡

TRAINING SCHEDULE NOTES:

*BEGINNER'S RT (Resistance Training)

Leg Lifts (1 set) [p. 60]; Russian Oblique Twise (1 set) [p. 61]; Side Leg Lifts (from Running Circuit) [p. 235]; Push–Ups (1 set) [p. 61]; Air Squat (1 set) [p. 235]; Bodyweight Lunge (1 set) [p. 64]; Heel Raises—Straight Knee (1 set) [p. 66]; Dumbbell Arm Swings (1 set) [p. 63]

NOTE: *Beginners should start with 1 set of each of the above exercises. Or you can do the Household Props routine (pages 107–110) as a substitution, but then don't progress to The Runner 360 or Weight Room Routine in this schedule.*

**ONLY DO ONE TYPE OF STRETCHING: AIS [p. 104]; PNF [p. 70]; or Static [p. 76]

†XT = CROSS TRAIN (see pp. 158–163); If you choose to cross train, keep your workout aerobic and match the effort/duration of the prescribed run.

‡POST-RUN ROUTINE

Household Props [p. 107]; Weight Room [p. 59]; The Runner 360 [p. 53]; *Stretching (Choose 1 type: AIS [p. 104]; PNF [p. 70]; or Static [p. 76])*

NOTE: *Choose one of the three routines above; if Weight Room or Runner 360, add stretching.*

12-WEEK TRAINING SCHEDULE FOR INTERMEDIATE RUNNERS—
NON-COMPETITIVE

WEEK	SUNDAY	MONDAY	TUESDAY	WEDNESDAY	THURSDAY	FRIDAY	SATURDAY
1	OFF	Hill Run [p. 52]: 30–40 minutes	Easy Distance Run [p. 49]: 20–40 minutes + Post-Run Routine*	OFF or Distance Run [p. 50]: 20–40 minutes	Strides [p. 51] + Post-Run Routine*	OFF or Distance Run [p. 50]: 20–40 minutes or XT**	Long Run [p. 132]: 40–50 minutes + Post-Run Routine*
2	OFF	5K Road & Trail Reps [p. 134]: 8 x 1 minute	Easy Distance Run [p. 49]: 20–40 minutes + Post-Run Routine*	OFF or Distance Run [p. 50]: 20–40 minutes	Hill Strides [p. 52] + Post-Run Routine*	OFF or Distance Run [p. 50]: 20–40 minutes or XT**	Long Run [p. 132]: 40–50 minutes + Post-Run Routine*
3	OFF	Slow Tempo [p. 130]: 10–15 minutes	Easy Distance Run [p. 49]: 20–40 minutes + Post-Run Routine*	OFF or Distance Run [p. 50]: 20–40 minutes	Technique Drills†	OFF or Distance Run [p. 50]: 20–40 minutes or XT**	Long Run [p. 132]: 40–50 minutes + Post-Run Routine*
4	OFF	Hill Run [p. 52]: 30–40 minutes	Easy Distance Run [p. 49]: 20–40 minutes + Post-Run Routine*	OFF or Distance Run [p. 50]: 20–40 minutes	Strides [p. 51] + Post-Run Routine*	OFF or Distance Run [p. 50]: 20–40 minutes or XT**	Long Run [p. 132]: 50–60 minutes + Post-Run Routine*
5	OFF	5K Road & Trail Reps [p. 134]: 6 x 2 minutes	Easy Distance Run [p. 49]: 20–40 minutes + Post-Run Routine*	OFF or Distance Run [p. 50]: 20–40 minutes	Short Hill Sprints [p. 220]	OFF or Distance Run [p. 50]: 20–40 minutes or XT**	Long Run [p. 132]: 50–60 minutes + Post-Run Routine*
6	OFF	Slow Tempo [p. 130]: 2 x 10 minute	Easy Distance Run [p. 49]: 20–40 minutes+ Post-Run Routine*	OFF or Distance Run [p. 50]: 20–40 minutes	Technique Drills†	OFF or Distance Run [p. 50]: 20–40 minutes or XT**	Long Run [p. 132]: 50–60 minutes + Post-Run Routine*
7	OFF	Hill Run [p. 52]: 30–50 minutes	Easy Distance Run [p. 49]: 20–40 minutes + Post-Run Routine*	OFF or Distance Run [p. 50]: 20–40 minutes	Strides [p. 51] + Post-Run Routine*	OFF or Distance Run [p. 50]: 20–40 minutes or XT**	Long Run [p. 132]: 60–75 minutes + Post-Run Routine*
8	OFF	5K Road & Trail Reps [p. 134]: 4 x 3 minutes	Easy Distance Run [p. 49]: 20–40 minutes + Post-Run Routine*	OFF or Distance Run [p. 50]: 20–40 minutes	Hill Strides [p. 52] + Post-Run Routine*	OFF or Distance Run [p. 50]: 20–40 minutes or XT**	Long Run [p. 132]: 60–75 minutes + Post-Run Routine*
9	OFF	Slow Tempo [p. 130]: 15–20 minutes	Easy Distance Run [p. 49]: 20–40 minutes + Post-Run Routine*	OFF or Distance Run [p. 50]: 20–40 minutes	Plyometrics‡	OFF or Distance Run [p. 50]: 20–40 minutes or XT**	Long Run [p. 132]: 60–75 minutes + Post-Run Routine*

WEEK	SUNDAY	MONDAY	TUESDAY	WEDNESDAY	THURSDAY	FRIDAY	SATURDAY
10	OFF	Hill Run [p. 52]: 30–50 minutes	Easy Distance Run [p. 49]: 20–40 minutes + Post-Run Routine*	OFF *or* Distance Run [p. 50]: 20–40 minutes	Strides [p. 51] + Post-Run Routine*	OFF *or* Distance Run [p. 50]: 20–40 minutes *or* XT**	Long Run [p. 132]: 60–90 minutes + Post-Run Routine*
11	OFF	5K Road & Trail Reps [p. 134]: 4 x 3 minutes	Easy Distance Run [p. 49]: 20–40 minutes + Post-Run Routine*	OFF *or* Distance Run [p. 50]: 20–40 minutes	Short Hill Sprints [p. 220]	OFF *or* Distance Run [p. 50]: 20–40 minutes *or* XT**	Long Run [p. 132]: 60–90 minutes + Post-Run Routine*
12	OFF	Fast Tempo [p. 130]: 2 x 10 minutes	Easy Distance Run [p. 49]: 20–40 minutes + Post-Run Routine*	OFF *or* Distance Run [p. 50]: 20–40 minutes	Technique Drills†	OFF *or* Distance Run [p. 50]: 20–40 minutes *or* XT**	Long Run [p. 132]: 60–90 minutes + Post-Run Routine*

TRAINING SCHEDULE NOTES:

*POST-RUN ROUTINE
   Household Props [p. 107]; Weight Room [p. 59]; The Runner 360 [p. 53]; *Stretching (Choose 1 type: AIS [p. 104]; PNF [p. 70]; or Static [p. 76])*
   NOTE: *Choose one of the three routines above; if Weight Room or Runner 360, add stretching.*

**XT = CROSS TRAIN (see pp. 158–163); If you choose to cross train, keep your workout aerobic and match the effort/duration of the prescribed run.

†INT. NON–COMPETITION TECHNIQUE DRILLS
   Skipping [p. 208]; High Skipping [p. 208]; Flat–Footed Marching [p. 209]; High Knees [p. 210]; Quick Feet [p. 207]; Butt Kicks – Dynamic Flexibility [p. 206]

‡INTERMEDIATE PLYOMETRICS
   Double–Leg Hops [p. 211]; Box Jumps [p. 215]; Quick Hops [p. 216]

12-WEEK TRAINING SCHEDULE FOR INTERMEDIATE RUNNERS—COMPETITIVE

WEEK	SUNDAY	MONDAY	TUESDAY	WEDNESDAY	THURSDAY	FRIDAY	SATURDAY
1	OFF *or* Distance Run [p. 50]: 30–60 minutes *or* XT*	5K Road & Trail Reps [p. 134]: 8 x 1 minute	Easy Distance Run [p. 49]: 30–50 minutes + Post-Run Routine**	Distance Run [p. 50]: 30–50 minutes	Hill Strides [p. 52]	OFF *or* Easy Distance Run [p. 49]: 30–40 minutes *or* XT*	Long Run [p. 132]: 50–60 minutes + Post-Run Routine**
2	OFF *or* Distance Run [p. 50]: 30–60 minutes *or* XT*	5K Road & Trail Reps [p. 134]: 8 x 2 minutes	Easy Distance Run [p. 49]: 30–50 minutes + Post-Run Routine**	Distance Run [p. 50]: 30–50 minutes	Hill Repeats [p. 133]: 10–15 x 30 seconds	OFF *or* Easy Distance Run [p. 49]: 30–40 minutes *or* XT*	Long Run [p. 132]: 50–70 minutes + Post-Run Routine**
3	OFF *or* Distance Run [p. 50]: 30–60 minutes *or* XT*	5K Road & Trail Reps [p. 134]: 6 x 3 minutes	Easy Distance Run [p. 49]: 30–50 minutes + Post-Run Routine**	Distance Run [p. 50]: 30–50 minutes	Hill Repeats [p. 133]: 8–12 x 45 seconds	OFF *or* Easy Distance Run [p. 49]: 30–40 minutes *or* XT*	Long Run [p. 132]: 50–70 minutes + Post-Run Routine**
4	OFF *or* Distance Run [p. 50]: 30–60 minutes *or* XT*	Fast Tempo [p. 130]: 10–15 minutes	Easy Distance Run [p. 49]: 40–50 minutes + Post-Run Routine**	Distance Run [p. 50]: 40–60 minutes	Technique Drills†	OFF *or* Easy Distance Run [p. 49]: 40–50 minutes *or* XT*	Long Hill Run [p. 52]: 50–70 minutes + Post-Run Routine**
5	OFF *or* Distance Run [p. 50]: 30–60 minutes *or* XT*	5K Road & Trail Reps [p. 134]: 4 x 4 minutes	Easy Distance Run [p. 49]: 40–50 minutes + Post-Run Routine**	Distance Run [p. 50]: 40–60 minutes	Hill Repeats [p. 133]: 6–8 x 60 seconds	OFF *or* Easy Distance Run [p. 49]: 40–50 minutes *or* XT*	Long Run [p. 132]: 60–75 minutes + Post-Run Routine**
6	OFF *or* Distance Run [p. 50]: 30–60 minutes *or* XT*	5K Road & Trail Reps [p. 134]: 5 x 4 minutes	Easy Distance Run [p. 49]: 40–50 minutes + Post-Run Routine**	Distance Run [p. 50]: 40–60 minutes	Hill Repeats [p. 133]: 4–6 x 90 seconds	OFF *or* Easy Distance Run [p. 49]: 40–50 minutes *or* XT*	Long Run [p. 132]: 60–75 minutes + Post-Run Routine**
7	OFF *or* Distance Run [p. 50]: 30–60 minutes *or* XT*	Fast Tempo [p. 130]: 2 x 10 minutes (3-minute jog rest)	Easy Distance Run [p. 49]: 40–60 minutes + Post-Run Routine**	Distance Run [p. 50]: 50–60 minutes	Technique Drills†	OFF *or* Easy Distance Run [p. 49]: 40–60 minutes *or* XT*	Long Hill Run [p. 52]: 60–75 minutes + Post-Run Routine**
8	OFF *or* Distance Run [p. 50]: 30–60 minutes *or* XT*	5K Road & Trail Reps [p. 134]: 4 x 5 minutes	Easy Distance Run [p. 49]: 40–60 minutes + Post-Run Routine**	Distance Run [p. 50]: 50–60 minutes	Track Work [p. 125]: 12–16 x 200m, 3K pace (200m jog recovery)	OFF *or* Easy Distance Run [p. 49]: 40–60 minutes *or* XT*	Long Run [p. 132]: 60–90 minutes + Post-Run Routine**
9	OFF *or* Distance Run [p. 50]: 30–60 minutes *or* XT*	Track Work [p. 129]: 12–16 x 400m, 10K pace	Easy Distance Run [p. 49]: 40–60 minutes + Post-Run Routine**	Distance Run [p. 50]: 50–60 minutes	Hill Repeats [p. 133]: 6 x 90 seconds	OFF *or* Easy Distance Run [p. 49]: 40–60 minutes *or* XT*	Long Run [p. 132]: 60–90 minutes + Post-Run Routine**

WEEK	SUNDAY	MONDAY	TUESDAY	WEDNESDAY	THURSDAY	FRIDAY	SATURDAY
10	OFF *or* Distance Run [p. 50]: 30–60 minutes *or* XT*	Fast Tempo [p. 130]: 2 x 10 minutes (3-minute jog rest)	Easy Distance Run [p. 49]: 50–60 minutes + Post-Run Routine**	Distance Run [p. 50]: 50–60 minutes	Track Work [p. 124]: 12 x 200m, 1500m pace (200m jog recovery)	OFF *or* Easy Distance Run [p. 49]: 40–60 minutes *or* XT*	Long Hill Run [p.52]: 60–90 minutes + Post-Run Routine**
11	OFF *or* Distance Run [p. 50]: 30–60 minutes *or* XT*	Track Work [p. 127]: 12–16 x 400m, 5K pace	Easy Distance Run [p. 49]: 50–60 minutes + Post-Run Routine**	Distance Run [p. 50]: 50–60 minutes	Technique Drills†	OFF *or* Easy Distance Run [p. 49]: 40–60 minutes *or* XT*	Long Run [p. 132]: 60–120 minutes+ Post-Run Routine**
12	OFF *or* Distance Run [p. 50]: 30–60 minutes *or* XT*	Track Work [p. 127]: 5–6 x 1000m, 5K pace	Easy Distance Run [p. 49]: 50–60 minutes + Post-Run Routine**	Distance Run [p. 50]: 50–60 minutes	Hill Repeats [p. 133]: 4–6 x 90 seconds	OFF *or* Easy Distance Run [p. 49]: 40–60 minutes *or* XT*	Long Run [p. 132]: 60–120 minutes + Post-Run Routine**

TRAINING SCHEDULE NOTES:

*XT = **CROSS TRAIN** (see pp. 158–163); If you choose to cross train, keep your workout aerobic and match the effort/duration of the prescribed run.

POST-RUN ROUTINE

Household Props [p. 107]; Weight Room [p. 59]; The Runner 360 [p. 53]; *Stretching (Choose 1 type: AIS [p. 104]; PNF [p. 70]; or Static [p. 76])*

NOTE: *Choose one of the three routines above; if Weight Room or Runner 360, add stretching.*

†INT. NON–COMPETITION TECHNIQUE DRILLS

Skipping [p. 208]; High Skipping [p. 208]; Flat–Footed Marching [p. 209]; High Knees [p. 210]; Bounding [p. 210]; Quick Feet [p. 207]; Butt Kicks – Trigger Action [p. 206]; Butt Kicks – Dynamic Flexibility [p. 206]

12-WEEK TRAINING SCHEDULE FOR ADVANCED RUNNERS—COMPETITIVE

WEEK	SUNDAY	MONDAY	TUESDAY	WEDNESDAY	THURSDAY	FRIDAY	SATURDAY
1	*either* Distance Run [p. 50]: 60–70 minutes + Stretching* *or* OFF	5K Road & Trail Reps [p. 134]: 6 x 3 minutes	Easy Distance Run [p. 49]: 60–70 minutes + Post-Run Routine**	Distance Run [p. 50]: 60–75 minutes	Hill Repeats [p. 133]: 10–15 x 30 seconds	*either* Distance Run [p. 50]: 60–70 minutes + Post-Run Routine** *or* XT***	Long Run [p. 132]: 75–90 minutes
2	*either* Distance Run [p. 50]: 60–70 minutes + Stretching* *or* OFF	5K Road & Trail Reps [p. 134]: 5 x 4 minutes	Easy Distance Run [p. 49]: 60–70 minutes + Post-Run Routine**	Distance Run [p. 50]: 60–75 minutes	Hill Repeats [p. 133]: 8–12 x 45 seconds	*either* Distance Run [p. 50]: 60–70 minutes + Post-Run Routine** *or* XT***	Long Run [p. 132]: 75–90 minutes
3	*either* Distance Run [p. 50]: 60–70 minutes + Stretching* *or* OFF	Fast Tempo [p. 130]: 2 x 10 minutes (with 3 min. jog) *or* 15 minutes Fast Tempo [p. 130]	Easy Distance Run [p. 49]: 60–70 minutes + Post-Run Routine**	Distance Run [p. 50]: 60–75 minutes	Technique Drills†	*either* Distance Run [p. 50]: 60–70 minutes + Post-Run Routine** *or* XT***	Long Run [p. 132]: 75–90 minutes
4	*either* Distance Run [p. 50]: 60–70 minutes + Stretching* *or* OFF	5K Road & Trail Reps [p. 134]: 4 x 5 minutes	Easy Distance Run [p. 49]: 60–70 minutes + Post-Run Routine**	Distance Run [p. 50]: 60–75 minutes	Track Work [pp. 124–125]: 12–16 x 200m, 1500m–3K pace, start slower & finish faster (200m jog rest) + O2R‡	*either* Distance Run [p. 50]: 60–70 minutes + Post-Run Routine** *or* XT***	Long Hill Run [p. 132]: 75–90 minutes
5	*either* Distance Run [p. 50]: 60–70 minutes + Stretching* *or* OFF	Track Work [p. 127]: 16 x 400m, 5K pace	Easy Distance Run [p. 49]: 60–70 minutes + Post-Run Routine**	Distance Run [p. 50]: 60–75 minutes	Hill Repeats [p. 133]: 6–8 x 60 seconds + O2R‡	*either* Distance Run [p. 50]: 60–70 minutes + Post-Run Routine** *or* XT***	Long Run [p. 132]: 90–105 minutes
6	*either* Distance Run [p. 50]: 60–70 minutes + Stretching* *or* OFF	Fast Tempo [p. 130]: 2 x 10 minutes (with 3 min. jog) *or* 20 minutes Fast or Slow Tempo [p. 130]	Easy Distance Run [p. 49]: 60–70 minutes + Post-Run Routine**	Distance Run [p. 50]: 60–75 minutes	Short Hill Sprints [p. 220] + O2R‡	*either* Distance Run [p. 50]: 60–70 minutes + Post-Run Routine** *or* XT***	Long Run [p. 132]: 90–105 minutes
7	*either* Distance Run [p. 50]: 60–70 minutes + Stretching* *or* OFF	Track Work [p. 127]: 5–6 x 1000m, 5K pace + O2R‡	Easy Distance Run [p. 49]: 60–70 minutes + Post-Run Routine**	Distance Run [p. 50]: 60–75 minutes	Technique Drills† + O2R‡	*either* Distance Run [p. 50]: 60–70 minutes + Post-Run Routine** *or* XT***	Long Run [p. 132]: 90–105 minutes
8	*either* Distance Run [p. 50]: 60–70 minutes + Stretching* *or* OFF	Fast Tempo [p.130]: 2–3 x 10 minutes (with 3 min. jog) + O2R‡ *or* 20 minutes Fast Tempo + O2R‡	Easy Distance Run [p. 49]: 60–70 minutes + Post-Run Routine**	Distance Run [p. 50]: 60–75 minutes	Hill Repeats [p.133]: 4–6 x 90 seconds + O2R‡	*either* Distance Run [p. 50]: 60–70 minutes + Post-Run Routine** *or* XT***	Long Run [p. 132]: 90–120 minutes

BUILD YOUR RUNNING BODY

WEEK	SUNDAY	MONDAY	TUESDAY	WEDNESDAY	THURSDAY	FRIDAY	SATURDAY
9	*either* Distance Run [p. 50]: 60–70 minutes + Stretching* *or* OFF	Track Work [pp. 124–125]: 10 x 400m, 1500m–3K pace, start slower & finish faster + O2R‡	Easy Distance Run [p. 49]: 60–70 minutes + Post-Run Routine**	Distance Run [p. 50]: 60–75 minutes	Short Hill Sprints [p. 220] + O2R‡	*either* Distance Run [p. 50]: 60–70 minutes + Post-Run Routine** *or* XT***	Long Run [p. 132]: 90–120 minutes
10	*either* Distance Run [p. 50]: 60–70 minutes + Stretching* *or* OFF	Fast Tempo [p.130]: 2–3 x 10 minutes (with 3 min. jog) + O2R‡ *or* 20 minutes Fast Tempo + O2R‡	Easy Distance Run [p. 49]: 60–70 minutes + Post-Run Routine**	Distance Run [p. 50]: 60–75 minutes + O2R‡	Technique Drills† + O2R‡	*either* Distance Run [p. 50]: 60–70 minutes + Post-Run Routine** *or* XT***	Long Hill Run [p. 52]: 90–105 minutes
11	*either* Distance Run [p. 50]: 60–70 minutes + Stretching* *or* OFF	Blend Intervals [p. 149]: Sample Workout 2 + O2R‡	Easy Distance Run [p. 49]: 60–70 minutes + Post-Run Routine**	Distance Run [p. 50]: 60–75 minutes + O2R‡	Hill Repeats [p. 133]: 6 x 90 seconds + O2R‡	*either* Distance Run [p. 50]: 60–70 minutes + Post-Run Routine** *or* XT***	Long Run [p. 132]: 90–135 minutes
12	*either* Distance Run [p. 50]: 60–70 minutes + Stretching* *or* OFF	Track Work [p. 127]: 20 x 400m, 5K pace (with 1:1/2 recovery) + O2R‡	Easy Distance Run [p. 49]: 60–70 minutes + Post-Run Routine**	Distance Run [p. 50]: 60–75 minutes + O2R‡	Short Hill Sprints [p. 220] + O2R‡	*either* Distance Run [p. 50]: 60–70 minutes + Post-Run Routine** *or* XT***	Long Run [p. 132]: 90–135 minutes

TRAINING SCHEDULE NOTES:

*ONLY DO ONE TYPE OF STRETCHING: AIS [p. 104]; PNF [p. 70]; or Static [p. 76]

**POST-RUN ROUTINE
Household Props [p. 107]; Weight Room [p. 59]; The Runner 360 [p. 53]; *Stretching (Choose 1 type: AIS [p. 104]; PNF [p. 70]; or Static [p. 76])*
NOTE: *Choose one of the three routines above; if Weight Room or Runner 360, add stretching.*

***XT = CROSS TRAIN (see pp. 158–163); If you choose to cross train, keep your workout aerobic and match the effort/duration of the prescribed run.

†ADV. COMPETITION TECHNIQUE DRILLS
Skipping [p. 208]; High Skipping [p. 208]; Long Skipping [p. 209]; Flat–Footed Marching [p. 209]; High Knees [p. 210]; Bounding [p. 210]; Quick Feet [p. 207]; Carioca (optional) [p.207]; Butt Kicks – Trigger Action [p. 206]; Butt Kicks – Dynamic Flexibility [p. 206]

‡O2R = OPTIONAL 2ND RUN: 20–40 minutes (Easy Distance Run)

12-WEEK TRAINING SCHEDULE FOR TIME–CONSTRAINED RUNNERS—
INTERMEDIATE & ADVANCED

WEEK	SUNDAY	MONDAY	TUESDAY	WEDNESDAY	THURSDAY	FRIDAY	SATURDAY
1	OFF	5K Road & Trail Reps [p. 134]: 8 x 1 minute	OFF	Hill Strides [p. 52]	*either* Distance Run [p. 50]: 20–30 minutes + Post-Run Routine* *or* XT**	OFF	Long Run [p. 132]: 40–60 minutes + Post-Run Routine*
2	OFF	5K Road & Trail Reps [p. 134]: 6 x 2 minutes	OFF	Hill Repeats [p. 133]: 10 x 30 seconds	*either* Distance Run [p. 50]: 20–30 minutes + Post-Run Routine* *or* XT**	OFF	Long Run [p. 132]: 40–60 minutes + Post-Run Routine*
3	OFF	Slow Tempo [p. 130]: 15–20 minutes	OFF	Technique Drills†	*either* Distance Run [p. 50]: 20–30 minutes + Post-Run Routine* *or* XT**	OFF	Long Run [p. 132]: 40–60 minutes + Post-Run Routine*
4	OFF	HIIT [p. 145]: Gibala 8 x 60 seconds, 5K effort (75 seconds rest)	OFF	Hill Repeats [p. 133]: 8 x 45 seconds	*either* Distance Run [p. 50]: 20–30 minutes + Post-Run Routine* *or* XT**	OFF	Long Run [p. 132]: 40–60 minutes + Post-Run Routine*
5	OFF	5K Road & Trail Reps [p. 134]: 4 x 3 minutes	OFF	Plyometrics‡	*either* Distance Run [p. 50]: 20–30 minutes + Post-Run Routine* *or* XT**	OFF	Long Run [p. 132]: 40–60 minutes + Post-Run Routine*
6	OFF	Slow Tempo [p. 130]: 20 minutes	OFF	Technique Drills†	*either* Distance Run [p. 50]: 20–30 minutes + Post-Run Routine* *or* XT**	OFF	Long Run [p. 132]: 40–60 minutes + Post-Run Routine*
7	OFF	HIIT [p. 145]: Gibala 10 x 60 seconds, 5K effort (75 seconds rest)	OFF	Hill Repeats [p. 133]: 6 x 60 seconds	*either* Distance Run [p. 50]: 20–30 minutes + Post-Run Routine* *or* XT**	OFF	Long Run [p. 132]: 40–60 minutes + Post-Run Routine*
8	OFF	5K Road & Trail Reps [p. 134]: 3 x 4 minutes	OFF	Short Hill Sprints [p. 220]	*either* Distance Run [p. 50]: 20–30 minutes + Post-Run Routine* *or* XT**	OFF	Long Run [p. 132]: 40–60 minutes + Post-Run Routine*

BUILD YOUR RUNNING BODY

WEEK	SUNDAY	MONDAY	TUESDAY	WEDNESDAY	THURSDAY	FRIDAY	SATURDAY
9	OFF	Fast Tempo [p. 130]: 15–20 minutes	OFF	Technique Drills†	*either* Distance Run [p. 50]: 20–30 minutes + Post-Run Routine* or XT**	OFF	Long Run [p. 132]: 40–60 minutes + Post-Run Routine*
10	OFF	HIIT [p.145]: Gibala 12 x 60 seconds, 5K effort (75 seconds rest)	OFF	Hill Repeats [p.133]: 4 x 90 seconds	*either* Distance Run [p. 50]: 20–30 minutes + Post-Run Routine* or XT**	OFF	Long Run [p. 132]: 40–60 minutes + Post-Run Routine*
11	OFF	5K Road & Trail Reps [p. 134]: 2 x 5 minutes	OFF	Plyometrics‡	*either* Distance Run [p. 50]: 20–30 minutes + Post-Run Routine* or XT**	OFF	Long Run [p. 132]: 40–60 minutes + Post-Run Routine*
12	OFF	Fast Tempo [p. 130]: 20 minutes	OFF	Technique Drills†	*either* Distance Run [p. 50]: 20–30 minutes + Post-Run Routine* or XT**	OFF	Long Run [p. 132]: 40–60 minutes + Post-Run Routine*

TRAINING SCHEDULE NOTES:

*POST-RUN ROUTINE
Household Props [p. 107]; Weight Room [p. 59]; The Runner 360 [p. 53]; *Stretching (Choose 1 type: AIS [p. 104]; PNF [p. 70]; or Static [p. 76])*
NOTE: *Choose one of the three routines above; if Weight Room or Runner 360, add stretching.*

**XT = CROSS TRAIN (see pp. 158–163); If you choose to cross train, keep your workout aerobic and match the effort/duration of the prescribed run.

†TIME–CONSTRAINED TECHNIQUE DRILLS
Skipping [p. 208]; High Skipping [p. 208]; Flat–Footed Marching [p. 209]; High Knees [p. 210]; Bounding [p. 210]; Quick Feet [p. 207]; Butt Kicks – Dynamic Flexibility [p.206]

‡TIME–CONSTRAINED PLYOS
Double–Leg Hops [p. 211]; Box Jumps [p. 215]; Vertical Depth Jump (optional) [p. 213]; Toe Taps [p. 215]; Lateral Barrier Jumps (optional) [p. 216]; Quick Hops [p. 216]

6-WEEK TRAINING SCHEDULE FOR 5K RACE—INTERMEDIATE & ADVANCED

WEEK	SUNDAY	MONDAY	TUESDAY	WEDNESDAY	THURSDAY	FRIDAY	SATURDAY
1	OFF *or* Distance Run [p. 50]: 30–70 minutes	Fast Tempo [p. 130]: 2 x 10 minutes (with 3-minute jog rest) + O2R*	Easy Distance Run [p. 49]: 40–70 minutes + Post-Run Routine**	Distance Run [p. 50]: 50–75 minutes + O2R*	Track Work [pp. 124–125]: 12–16 x 200m, 1500m–3K pace, start slower & finish faster + O2R*	Distance Run [p. 50]: 30–70 minutes *or* XT†	Long Run [p. 132]: 60–120 minutes + Post-Run Routine**
2	OFF *or* Distance Run [p. 50]: 30–70 minutes	Track Work [p. 127]: 12–16 x 400m, 5K pace + O2R*	Easy Distance Run [p. 49]: 40–70 minutes + Post-Run Routine**	Distance Run [p. 50]: 50–75 minutes + O2R*	Hill Repeats [p. 133]: 6 x 90 seconds + O2R*	Distance Run [p. 50]: 30–70 minutes *or* XT†	Long Run [p. 132]: 60–75 minutes + Post-Run Routine**
3	OFF *or* Distance Run [p. 50]: 30–70 minutes	Road Intervals (not in book): 10–20 x 30 secs at 1500m–3K effort, with 1-minute jog recovery + O2R*	Easy Distance Run [p. 49]: 30–50 minutes + Post-Run Routine**	Easy Distance Run [p. 49]: 30–50 minutes + O2R*	Easy Distance Run [p. 49]: 25 minutes + Strides: 4–8 + Stretching‡	Jog/Easy Run [p. 48]: 20 minutes	Tune-Up Race: 5K RACE
4	OFF *or* Easy Distance Run [p. 50]: 30–70 minutes	Distance Run [p. 50]: 50–75 minutes + Post-Run Routine** + O2R*	Distance Run [p. 50]: 50–75 minutes *or* XT†	Fast Tempo [p. 130]: 2 x 10 minutes (with 3-minute jog rest) + O2R*	Easy Distance Run [p. 49]: 40–60 minutes	*either* Distance Run [p. 50]: 30–70 minutes + Post-Run Routine** *or* XT†	Long Run [p. 132]: 60–120 minutes
5	OFF *or* Distance Run [p. 50]: 30–70 minutes	Track Work [p. 129]: 4–6 x 1000m, Cruise Intervals (with 1:1 recovery based on time) + O2R*	Easy Distance Run [p. 49]: 40–70 minutes + Post-Run Routine**	Distance Run [p. 50]: 50–75 minutes + O2R*	Track Work [pp. 124–125]: 12 x 200m, 1500m–3K pace, start slower & finish faster + O2R*	Distance Run [p. 50]: 30–70 minutes *or* XT†	Long Run [p. 132]: 60–75 minutes + Post-Run Routine**
6	OFF *or* Distance Run [p. 50]: 30–70 minutes	Track Work [p. 127]: 6–12 x 400m, 5K pace + O2R*	Easy Distance Run [p. 49]: 30–50 minutes + Post-Run Routine**	Easy Distance Run [p. 49]: 30–50 minutes	Easy Distance Run [p. 49]: 25 minutes + Strides [p. 51]: 4–8 + Stretching‡	Jog/Easy Run [p. 48]: 20 minutes	Goal Race: 5K RACE

TRAINING SCHEDULE NOTES:

*O2R = OPTIONAL 2ND RUN: 20–40 minutes (Easy Distance Run)

**POST-RUN ROUTINE
  Household Props [p. 107]; Weight Room [p. 59]; The Runner 360 [p. 53]; *Stretching (Choose 1 type: AIS [p. 104]; PNF [p. 70]; or Static [p. 76])*
    NOTE: : *Choose one of the three routines above; if Weight Room or Runner 360, add stretching.*

†XT = CROSS TRAIN (see pp. 158–163); If you choose to cross train, keep your workout aerobic and match the effort/duration of the prescribed run.

‡ONLY DO ONE TYPE OF STRETCHING: AIS [p. 104]; PNF [p. 70], or Static [p. 76]

6-WEEK TRAINING SCHEDULE FOR 10K RACE—INTERMEDIATE & ADVANCED

WEEK	SUNDAY	MONDAY	TUESDAY	WEDNESDAY	THURSDAY	FRIDAY	SATURDAY
1	OFF or Distance Run [p. 50]: 30–70 minutes	Fast Tempo [p. 130]: 2 x 10 minutes (with 3-minute jog rest) + O2R*	Easy Distance Run [p. 49]: 40–70 minutes + Post-Run Routine**	Distance Run [p. 50]: 50–75 minutes + O2R*	Track Work [p. 124–125]: 12–16 x 200m, 1500m–3K pace, start slower & finish faster + O2R*	Distance Run [p. 50]: 30–70 minutes or XT†	Long Run [p. 132]: 60–120 minutes + Post-Run Routine**
2	OFF or Distance Run [p. 50]: 30–70 minutes	Track Work [p. 129]: 12–20 x 400m, 10K pace + O2R*	Easy Distance Run [p. 49]: 40–70 minutes + Post-Run Routine**	Distance Run [p. 50]: 50–75 minutes + O2R*	Hill Repeats [p. 133]: 6 x 90 seconds + O2R*	Distance Run [p. 50]: 30–70 minutes or XT†	Long Run [p. 132]: 60–75 minutes + Post-Run Routine**
3	OFF or Distance Run [p. 50]: 30–70 minutes	Road Intervals (not in book): 10–20 x 30 secs at 1500m–3K effort, with 1-minute jog recovery + O2R*	Easy Distance Run [p. 49]: 30–50 minutes + Post-Run Routine**	Easy Distance Run [p. 49]: 30–50 minutes + O2R*	Easy Distance Run [p. 49]: 25 minutes + Strides [p. 51]: 4–8 + Stretching‡	Jog/Easy Run [p. 48]: 20 minutes	Tune–Up Race: 5K RACE
4	OFF or Easy Distance Run [p. 50]: 30–70 minutes	Distance Run [p. 50]: 50–75 minutes + Post-Run Routine** + O2R*	Distance Run [p. 50]: 50–75 minutes or XT†	Fast Tempo [p. 130]: 2–3 x 10 minutes (with 3-minute jog rest) + O2R* or Fast Tempo: 20 minutes + O2R*	Easy Distance Run [p. 49]: 40–60 minutes	Distance Run [p. 50]: 30–70 minutes + Post-Run Routine**	Long Run [p. 132]: 60–120 minutes
5	OFF or Distance Run [p. 50]: 30–70 minutes	Track Work [p. 129]: 4–8 x 1000m, Cruise Intervals (with 1:1 recovery based upon time) + O2R*	Easy Distance Run [p. 49]: 40–75 minutes + Post-Run Routine**	Distance Run [p. 50]: 50–75 minutes + O2R*	Track Work [pp. 124–125]: 12 x 200m, 1500m–3K pace, start slower & finish faster + O2R*	Distance Run [p. 50]: 30–70 minutes or XT†	Long Run [p. 132]: 60–75 minutes + Post-Run Routine**
6	OFF or Distance Run [p. 50]: 30–70 minutes	Track Work [p. 129]: 8–16 x 400m, 10K pace + O2R*	Easy Distance Run [p. 49]: 30–50 minutes + Post-Run Routine**	Easy Distance Run [p. 49]: 30–50 minutes	Easy Distance Run [p. 49]: 25 minutes + Strides [p. 51]: 4–8 + Stretching‡	Jog/Easy Run [p. 48]: 20 minutes	Goal Race: 10K RACE

TRAINING SCHEDULE NOTES:

*O2R = OPTIONAL 2ND RUN: 20–40 minutes (Easy Distance Run)

**POST-RUN ROUTINE

Household Props [p. 107]; Weight Room [p. 59]; The Runner 360 [p. 53]; *Stretching (Choose 1 type: AIS [p. 104]; PNF [p. 70]; or Static [p. 76])*

NOTE: : *Choose one of the three routines above; if Weight Room or Runner 360, add stretching.*

†XT = CROSS TRAIN (see pp. 158–163); If you choose to cross train, keep your workout aerobic and match the effort/duration of the prescribed run.

‡ONLY DO ONE TYPE OF STRETCHING: AIS [p. 104]; PNF [p. 70], or Static [p. 76]

6-WEEK TRAINING SCHEDULE FOR HALF MARATHON—INTERMEDIATE & ADVANCED

WEEK	SUNDAY	MONDAY	TUESDAY	WEDNESDAY	THURSDAY	FRIDAY	SATURDAY
1	OFF *or* Distance Run [p. 50]: 30–70 minutes	Fast Tempo [p. 130]: 2 x 10 minutes (with 3-minute jog rest) + O2R* *or* Slow Tempo [p.130]: 20–30 minutes + O2R*	Easy Distance Run 124–130]: 40–70 minutes + Post-Run Routine**	Distance Run [p. 50]: 50–75 minutes + O2R*	Track Work [pp 124–125]: 12–16 x 200m, 1500m–3K pace, start slower & finish faster + O2R*	Distance Run [p. 50]: 30–70 minutes *or* XT†	Long Run [p. 132]: 60–120 minutes
2	OFF *or* Distance Run [p. 50]: 30–70 minutes	Track Work [p. 127]: 12–16 x 400m, 5K pace + O2R*	Easy Distance Run [p. 49]: 40–70 minutes + Post-Run Routine**	Distance Run [p. 50]: 50–75 minutes + O2R*	Hill Repeats [p. 133]: 6 x 90 seconds + O2R*	Distance Run [p. 50]: 30–70 minutes *or* XT†	Long Run [p. 132]: 75–135 minutes
3	OFF *or* Distance Run [p. 50]: 30–70 minutes	Fast Tempo [p. 130]: 2–3 x 10 minutes (with 3-minute jog rest) + O2R* *or* Fast Tempo: 20 minutes + O2R*	Easy Distance Run [p. 49]: 40–70 minutes + Post-Run Routine**	Distance Run [p. 50]: 50–75 minutes + O2R*	Road Intervals (not in book): 10–20 x 30 secs at 1500m–3K effort, with 1-minute jog recovery + O2R*	Distance Run [p. 50]: 30–70 minutes *or* XT†	Long Run [p. 132]: 90–150 minutes
4	OFF *or* Distance Run [p. 50]: 30–70 minutes	5K Road & Trail Reps [p. 134]: 6 x 3 minutes + O2R*	Easy Distance Run [p. 49]: 30–50 minutes + Post-Run Routine**	Easy Distance Run [p. 49]: 30–50 minutes + O2R*	Easy Distance Run [p. 49]: 25 minutes + Strides [p. 51]: 4–8 + Stretching‡	Jog/Easy Run [p. 48]: 20 minutes	Tune–Up Race: 5K RACE
5	OFF *or* Easy Distance Run [p. 49]: 30–70 minutes	Distance Run [p. 50]: 40–60 minutes	Distance Run [p. 50]: 40–60 minutes + Post-Run Routine**	Fast Tempo [p. 130]: 3 x 10 minutes (with 3-minute jog rest) + O2R*	Easy Distance Run [p. 49]: 40–60 minutes	Distance Run [p. 50]: 30–60 minutes + Post-Run Routine**	Long Run [p. 132]: 60–75 minutes + Strides [p. 51] (optional)
6	OFF *or* Distance Run [p. 50]: 30–70 minutes	Track Work [p. 127]: 6–12 x 400m, 5K pace + O2R*	Easy Distance Run [p. 49]: 30–50 minutes + Post-Run Routine**	Easy Distance Run [p. 49]: 30–50 minutes	Easy Distance Run [p. 49]: 25 minutes + Strides [p. 51]: 4–8 + Stretching‡	Jog/Easy Run [p. 48]: 20 minutes	Goal Race: HALF MARATHON

TRAINING SCHEDULE NOTES:

*O2R = OPTIONAL 2ND RUN: 20–40 minutes (Easy Distance Run)

**POST-RUN ROUTINE

  Household Props [p. 107]; Weight Room [p. 59]; The Runner 360 [p. 53]; *Stretching (Choose 1 type: AIS [p. 104]; PNF [p. 70]; or Static [p. 76])*

  NOTE: : *Choose one of the three routines above; if Weight Room or Runner 360, add stretching.*

†XT = CROSS TRAIN (see pp. 158–163); If you choose to cross train, keep your workout aerobic and match the effort/duration of the prescribed run.

‡ONLY DO ONE TYPE OF STRETCHING: AIS [p. 104]; PNF [p. 70], or Static [p. 76]

BUILD YOUR RUNNING BODY

8-WEEK TRAINING SCHEDULE FOR MARATHON—INTERMEDIATE & ADVANCED

WEEK	SUNDAY	MONDAY	TUESDAY	WEDNESDAY	THURSDAY	FRIDAY	SATURDAY
1	OFF or Distance Run [p. 50]: 30–70 minutes	Slow Tempo [p. 130]: 2 x 15 minutes (3-minute jog) + O2R*	Easy Distance Run [p. 49]: 40–70 minutes + Post-Run Routine**	Distance Run [p. 50]: 50–75 minutes + O2R*	Track Work [p. 125]: 16 x 200m, 3K pace + O2R*	either Distance Run [p. 50]: 30–70 minutes or XT† + Post-Run Routine**	Long Run [p. 132]: 90–135 minutes
2	OFF or Distance Run [p. 50]: 30–70 minutes	Track Work [p. 129]: 6–10 x 1000m, Cruise Intervals (with 1:1 recovery based on time) + O2R*	Easy Distance Run [p. 49]: 40–70 minutes + Post-Run Routine**	Distance Run [p. 50]: 50–75 minutes + O2R*	Hill Repeats [p. 133]: 6 x 90 seconds	Easy Distance Run [p. 49]: 30–70 minutes or XT†	Long Run [p. 132]: 105–150 minutes
3	OFF or Distance Run [p. 50]: 30–70 minutes	Track Work [p. 127]: 12–16 x 400m, 5K pace + O2R*	Easy Distance Run [p. 49]: 40–70 minutes + Post-Run Routine**	Distance Run [p. 50]: 50–75 minutes + O2R*	Easy Run [p. 48]: 30–50 minutes + Strides [p. 51]: 4–8 + Stretching‡	Easy Distance Run [p. 49]: 30–70 minutes or XT†	Slow Tempo [p.130]: 60 minutes
4	OFF or Distance Run [p. 50]: 30–70 minutes	Easy Distance Run [p. 49]: 30–70 minutes	Easy Distance Run [p. 49]: 40–70 minutes + Post-Run Routine** + O2R*	Distance Run [p. 50]: 50–75 minutes	Hill Repeats [p. 133]: 6 x 90 seconds + O2R*	Easy Distance Run [p. 49]: 30–70 minutes or XT†	Long Run [p. 132]: 120–180 minutes
5	OFF or Distance Run [p. 50]: 30–70 minutes	Fast Tempo [p. 130]: 3 x 10 minutes (with 3-minute jog rest) + O2R* or Slow Tempo [p. 130]: 30–40 minutes + O2R*	Easy Distance Run [p. 49]: 40–70 minutes + Post-Run Routine**	Distance Run [p. 50]: 50–75 minutes + O2R*	Track Work [p. 125]: 16 x 200m, 3K pace + O2R*	Easy Distance Run [p. 49]: 30–70 minutes or XT†	Long Run [p. 132]: 135–210 minutes
6	OFF or Distance Run [p. 50]: 30–70 minutes	Track Work [p. 127]: 6–12 x 400m, 5K pace + O2R*	Easy Distance Run [p. 49]: 30–50 minutes + Post-Run Routine**	Easy Distance Run [p. 49]: 30–50 minutes	Easy Run [p. 48]: 25 minutes + Strides [p. 51]: 4–8 + Stretching‡	Jog/Easy Run [p. 48]: 20 minutes	Tune-up Race: 5K RACE
7	OFF or Easy Distance Run [p. 49]: 30–70 minutes	Distance Run [p. 50]: 40–60 minutes	Distance Run [p. 50]: 40–60 minutes + Post-Run Routine**	Fast Tempo [p. 130]: 2 x 10 minutes (with 3-minute jog rest) + O2R*	Easy Distance Run [p. 49]: 40–60 minutes	Easy Distance Run [p. 49]: 40–60 minutes	Long Run [p.132]: 45–85 minutes + Strides [p. 51]: 4–8 + Stretching‡
8	OFF or Distance Run [p. 50]: 30–70 minutes	Distance Run [p. 50]: 40–70 minutes (option: Include 2–4 miles at Goal Marathon pace)	Easy Distance Run [p. 49]: 30–50 minutes + Post-Run Routine**	Easy Distance Run [p. 49]: 30–50 minutes	Easy Distance Run [p. 49]: 25 minutes + Strides [p.51]: 4–8 + Stretching‡ + Increase Carbs (see Chapter 19)	Rest & Travel + Increase Carbs (see Chapter 19)	Jog/Easy Run [p. 48]: 20 minutes + Increase Carbs (see Chapter 19)
9	Goal Race: MARATHON						

TRAINING SCHEDULE NOTES:

*O2R = OPTIONAL 2ND RUN: 20–40 minutes (Easy Distance Run)

**POST-RUN ROUTINE

Household Props [p. 107]; Weight Room [p. 59]; The Runner 360 [p. 53]; *Stretching (Choose 1 type: AIS [p. 104]; PNF [p. 70]; or Static [p. 76])*

NOTE: : *Choose one of the three routines above; if Weight Room or Runner 360, add stretching.*

†XT = CROSS TRAIN (see pp. 158–163); If you choose to cross train, keep your workout aerobic and match the effort/duration of the prescribed run.

‡ONLY DO ONE TYPE OF STRETCHING: AIS [p. 104]; PNF [p. 70], or Static [p. 76]

BUILD YOUR RUNNING BODY

Build Your Running Recovery

It's not the training you do that counts. It's the training from which your body can recover.

Many runners believe they get stronger during hard bouts of training. Not true. You get stronger while you're recovering from training. That's when muscle fibers are repaired, hormones are replaced, glycogen stores are replenished, mitochondria multiply, your nervous system reboots, and your cardiovascular system goes under construction, ready to be transformed into an oxygen superhighway. But the demands of recovery require more than plopping your butt on the couch post-run. Recovery is a multi-layered approach, combining both active and passive elements, that's aimed at generating physical improvement while simultaneously leaving you psychologically fresh—the better to maintain your motivation to train again.

WHAT'S RECOVERY?

Recovery is a low-key set of activities practiced in tandem with physical exertion. It's a mistake to think of recovery as a passive passage of time. Instead, you'll need to engage in activities that facilitate recovery. These can include stretching, post-run exercises, glycogen replacement, rehydration, recovery runs, stress-relieving activities, and complete rest and sleep, among others.

To understand recovery, it's important to first understand what happens during training.

Training is not a bank account. You aren't depositing workouts (distance, tempo, resistance training, etc.), into your training log, looking to withdraw them on race day. Instead, each workout applies a stimulus (your training) that

triggers an adaptation (improved fitness). As these adaptations accumulate, you begin to transform your running body, building a stronger and more durable you. But this transformation doesn't occur while you're training; it occurs while you recover. Without full recovery, you short-circuit your body's ability to adapt.

Proper recovery occurs on many levels when you're training:

▶ **Recovery between reps and sets (intervals, drills, resistance training, etc.)**
▶ **Recovery post-workout**
▶ **Recovery at night**
▶ **Recovery between hard workouts**
▶ **Recovery from the daily grind**
▶ **Recovery between race seasons**

Too many runners want to skip recovery and head straight into the next hard workout. They should heed the words of famed UCLA basketball coach John Wooden, who led the Bruins to ten NCAA titles, including seven in a row: "If you don't have time to do it right, when will you have time to do it over?"

THE MANY FACES OF RECOVERY

There are two factors that must be properly manipulated for every workout. One is the stimulus

BEGINNER'S GUIDELINE

Resist the urge to train harder than scheduled on days when you "feel good." If you're properly rested and recovered, you *should* feel good. That's the point of proper recovery. Feeling good is *not* a green light for running too hard. And running too hard will only ensure that you "feel bad" for your next workout—or your next few workouts.

(training) required to trigger the desired adaptation. The second is the recovery needed to ensure that the adaptation occurs. We've discussed many options for stimuli throughout this book. It's time to look at six important methods of recovery.

Recovery between repetitions

The recovery interval during repetitions is a tool for controlling the accumulation of fatigue; it allows you to complete another repetition at the workout's prescribed pace. Of course, manipulation of recovery intervals (shortening and lengthening them) also allows runners to shift a workout's focus to specific energy systems, muscle fibers, and other running components. And you'll recall that intervals as originally run (see chapters 4 and 7) utilized the recovery period to momentarily increase blood flow to the heart, thereby increasing stroke volume. By and large, however, recovery intervals simply control fatigue, allowing you to amass a greater volume of faster-pace training.

Recovery post-workout

The first fifteen to thirty minutes post-workout are critical. This is the time when your body requires your attention the most. It is important to establish a post-run routine that includes stretching (AIS or PNF if you have a rope or partner, static stretching if you don't) and some kind of strengthening—see the various routines from Chapter 5 and Chapter 6. It's not mandatory that you do a post-run routine every day; three to four days a week is adequate, and at least twice is essential. Follow your post-run routine (or your run on the days you don't do a post-run routine) by rehydrating and replacing your glycogen stores. You don't have to rehydrate all at once, but a glass or two of water will help return your body to homeostasis.

Carbohydrate intake (50–100 grams) during the immediate post-workout period can lead to glycogen replacement at 200–300 percent the normal rate. Include protein at a 4:1 ratio of carbs to protein if you desire.

Recovery at night

Sleep. It's what your body needs after a long day that includes training. A good night's sleep repairs cell damage, regenerates neurotransmitters, strengthens your immune system, improves flexibility, lowers stress, and keeps you fresh and alert. And a twelve-year study from Great Britain found that people who got between seven and nine hours of sleep live longer. Elite runners make sleep an essential part of their daily routine, logging nine hours per night, according to research by Martin Miller and Judd Biasiotto. That's more than an hour longer than the average person. While that much sleep might be more than a busy adult can schedule, you should target at least seven hours if you want to get the most out of your training.

Recovery between hard workouts

Recovery days allow your body to adapt to the training stimulus of a hard workout. This is when improvement occurs. Recovery days are also the time for your body to replace hormones, enzymes, and fuel, as well as to repair muscle fibers and connective tissue. Recovery gives your nervous system a chance to rejuvenate (a reboot, if you will). Easy running on recovery days provides a nice growth hormone and testosterone boost, too. See tables 16.1 and 16.2 for the approximate number of recovery days needed after both hard workouts and races (note that your recovery days will vary depending on your age and fitness).

Table 16.1
Number of Days Between
Hard Workouts

Runner's Age	Low Fitness	Medium Fitness	High Fitness
20	4.0	3.0	2.0
30	5.0	4.0	3.0
40	5.5	4.5	3.5
50	6.0	5.0	4.0
60	7.0	6.0	4.5
70	8.0	7.0	5.0
80	9.0	8.0	5.5

TABLE 16.1 offers the approximate number of days you should recovery between "hard" workouts (e.g., repetition training, long hill repeats, intense strength training, or fast tempo). Runners at different fitness levels require varying recovery.

Recovery from the daily grind

Don't forget to recover from the non-running elements of your daily life, too. Family, career, financial decisions, social and community obligations, driving, weather, errands and chores, noise, worry—they all take their toll. In Chapter One, we covered the damage stress can inflict on your body (e.g., inflammation, illness, increased blood pressure, and decreased bone and muscle density). While it's beating you up physically, stress is also lowering your motivation to train. So find an outlet for stress. Shoot some hoops. Read a book. Go to a movie. Go dancing. Write. Paint. Work in the garden. Take a vacation. Or there's always the old standby: sex. Rediscovering the joy in everyday life will make you a better runner—mostly because you'll actually feel like running.

Recovery between race seasons

Elite runners have race "seasons." But even less-competitive runners have versions of a season, usually revolving around a major goal race (e.g., a marathon) and the tune-up races that precede it. No matter how you define "season," you'll need a break when it's done. It's a law of physics that what goes up must come down. This applies to your fitness, too. Dr. Tom Cotner puts it this way: "If you don't take planned breaks, you find yourself taking unplanned breaks." So congratulate

Table 16.2
Number of Days Following a Race Before the Next Workout

Race Distance	Easy Workout	Medium Workout	Hard Workout	Age Adjustment	
				Age	Factor
800	1.0	2.0	3.0		
1500 (Mile)	1.0	2.0	3.0	20–29	1.0
3000/3200	1.0	2.5	4.0	30–39	1.1
5K	1.0	3.0	4.5	40–49	1.2
8K	1.0	4.0	6.0	50–59	1.3
10K	1.0	6.0	9.0	60–69	1.4
15K	1.0	7.0	11.0	70–79	1.5
Half Marathon	1.0	9.0	14.0	80–89	1.6
Marathon	1.0	17.0	26.0	90+	1.7+

TABLE 16.2 offers the approximate number of days following a race before you should attempt your next workout. An easy recovery or distance run is fine the day after a race. Medium workouts (e.g., slow tempo) require more recovery days. And hard workouts (e.g., 5K pace repetitions) require even longer recovery. The two columns on the right provide age adjustments. For instance, a fifty-year-old who'd raced a 5K would multiply 4.5 by 1.3, giving him/her approximately six days of recovery before the next hard workout.

yourself on a season well done, and then either take three weeks completely off (the Kenyans spend up to two months post-season doing nothing but lying on the couch and gaining weight) or lower your volume by 50 percent (or more)—in the latter case, take at least two days a week off and limit "hard" work to some strides a couple of times a week. Also, indulge in some alternative activities, like hiking or Frisbee. Ease up on the diet. Cheat a little on the stretching and strength routine. Give your body the break it deserves. If you're afraid you'll lose some of your conditioning—well, you will. But you'll be better for it, because you'll bounce back strong, one hundred percent ready to tackle a new program—body, mind, and spirit.

17

Build Your Running Injury Prevention

Wouldn't it be nice if no runner ever got injured? Sorry, not gonna happen. Studies confirm that between 50–80 percent of runners will suffer an injury during any given year. But studies also confirm that the majority of those injured runners failed to include injury-prevention routines in their training. By spending an extra ten to fifteen minutes (three to four times per week) on post-run stretching and exercises, you can lower your odds of suffering injuries. And when injuries do occur, you can use many of these same exercises to speed your recovery—or to limit the impact of the injuries so you can train through them.

WHAT'S A RUNNING INJURY?

In the introduction to his 2010 *Runner's World* article, "10 Laws of Injury Prevention," Amby Burfoot notes that "running injuries can be caused by being female, being male, being old, being young, pronating too much, pronating too little, training too much, and training too little."

In other words, running injuries occur when you run. Or when you do resistance training. Or technique drills. Or plyometrics. Or, for older runners, when you roll over in bed.

A running injury is damage or pain that occurs as a consequence of training. Injuries come in several forms:

▶ **Overload injuries:** These result from a sudden increase in volume, intensity, or both (e.g., excessive initial training that leads to DOMS). This is a common source of injuries among beginners.

▶ **Overuse injuries:** These result from repetition of a stress that irritates or damages tissue. For example, runner's knee (patella femoral pain syndrome) can occur when your kneecap tracks poorly in the femoral groove, irritating and damaging cartilage.

▶ **Chronic injuries:** These result from long-term repetition of an unmitigated stress, causing pain that simply won't go away,

oftentimes even with full rest. For example, Achilles tendinosis involves degenerative damage and microtears in the Achilles tendon caused by long-term overuse, and it requires specific strengthening exercises and therapeutic practices to overcome.

▶ **Accidents:** These could be spraining an ankle, jamming a toe, or straining a muscle, among other mishaps.

▶ **After-the-fact:** Fatigued muscle and battered connective tissue sometimes give way while engaged in activities post-training. For instance, quick or awkward movements, like springing up from a chair or slipping in the mud, can lead to calf and hamstring strains.

▶ **Cramping:** Post-workout cramps can lead to muscle strains, as any runner who's been jolted awake in the middle of the night by a spasmodic calf can attest.

▶ **Injuries from injuries:** The most maddening injuries are the ones that develop while trying to train through another injury. For example, compensating for injury on one side of your body (e.g., Achilles bursitis, plantar fasciitis, or hip pain) increases your risk of injury on the opposite side.

If you carefully parse the circumstances of the injuries listed above, you'll find one common

BEGINNER'S GUIDELINE

Injuries almost always occur in response to new physiological stress. Ramping up your training volume too quickly, introducing sharp increases in intensity, or making mechanical changes—like altering your stride—will create the kinds of physical overload that result in injury. Be like an ocean liner: Change tack gradually and reverse thrusters well ahead of perceived danger.

BUILD YOUR RUNNING BODY

cause that underpins *all* of the injuries: Runners' mistakes.

And the worst mistake we runners make is waiting to get injured before doing something about injuries. It's not possible to prevent all running injuries, but a simple post-run routine can go a long way toward lowering your risk. You'll want to include stretches and exercises that strengthen your body from core to toe—what's referred to as your *kinetic chain*. And you'll want to perform these exercises three to four times per week (two times at a minimum).

Warning: Acute and life-threatening injuries

Before reading about injury prevention and rehab, recognize that some injuries demand immediate, professional attention. If you suffer a sudden or severe injury while training—a sharp pain or debilitating incident—then you'll need a medical evaluation. In the case of heart arrhythmia, breathing difficulties, disorientation, sudden cessation of sweating (heat stroke), severe fever or headache, badly blurred vision, or other potentially life-threatening symptoms, you'll need *immediate* medical attention. You'll also need professional treatment for meniscus tears, stress fractures, torn tendons or ligaments, and other severe connective tissue damage. We could go on, but let's sum it up like this: If you suffer what seems to be a serious injury or set of symptoms, then run—don't walk—to your health professional.

INJURY PREVENTION TRAINING

Almost all athletes develop injuries at some point during their training. Injuries can be *acute* or *chronic*. Acute injuries (like ankle sprains and pulled hamstrings) result from specific, often traumatic incidents. Chronic injuries are injuries that develop over the course of time; IT band syndrome and Achilles tendinosis fall into this category. Injuries like plantar fasciitis and lower back pain can have either acute or chronic origins.

Acute injuries are simpler to treat, since the cause is known. If you step on a rock and tear your plantar fascia, the treatment begins with letting the plantar fascia heal. Chronic injuries are harder to diagnose because the cause is often unknown. For instance, if your plantar fascia becomes more painful over time—perhaps beginning with pain that feels like a stone bruise in your heel, then gradually sweeping across the bottom of your foot—the cause can be hard to pin down. Overpronation? Tight calves? Weak hips? Flat feet? Poor proprioception? Too much running on the track? Too much weight for squats, lunges, or cleans? Without knowing the cause of the injury, it can be difficult to design a rehab program to treat it.

There are other injuries, like general hip and knee pain, that can defy diagnosis. Go to four doctors, and you'll get four different opinions—and four different rehab routines.

This is why the best treatment is *injury prevention*. Anticipate the ambiguous nature of chronic injuries by strengthening your entire kinetic chain. This strengthening, in turn, will help guard against acute injuries. A well-rounded routine should include some or all of the following components:

- ▶ Stretching
- ▶ Strength training
- ▶ Wobble board
- ▶ Carbohydrate and protein supplementation
- ▶ Limited icing

These elements of injury prevention can be combined into a single post-run routine or divvied up into two routines that you alternate. Or they can even be performed as a separate workout altogether. For best results, each exercise, stretch, or other routine element should be performed a minimum of twice per week. And if you have a specific injury concern—if you've suffered an injury in the past or feel particularly susceptible to a new one (e.g., plantar fasciitis for masters runners)—use the table "Exercises to Prevent and Rehabilitate Running Injuries" on page 377 to identify specific exercises that will address that concern.

TWO COMMON PRACTICES TO AVOID

Equally as important as what to include in your injury prevention routine is what *not* to include:

Anti-inflammatories for muscle soreness: Inflammation is a necessary part of healing. Inflammation triggers specialized cells (neutrophils, macrophages, and monocytes) to clear away damaged muscle tissue. This paves the way for the creation of stronger, more durable muscle fibers. Interrupting the process derails your body's ability to recover and adapt.

Excessive antioxidant supplementation: The stimulus created by *free radicals* (oxygen molecules with an extra electron that cause damage to cells) triggers adaptations that make you a better runner. While including antioxidant-rich foods in your diet will limit exorbitant free radical formation and speed your recovery from exercise-induced inflammation, an overabundance of antioxidants, such as the excessive quantities found in many multivitamins and supplements, will inhibit both the stimulus and subsequent adaptations that lead to improved fitness.

STRETCHING

For most runners, a simple AIS routine (pages 104–106) will provide the most bang for their buck. AIS is quick, easy to perform, and provides the greatest increase in range of motion—improved range of motion can reduce the incidence of muscle and connective tissue injury as well as lessen the pain associated with tendinitis and bursitis. AIS curtails post-run stiffness, allowing even high-volume, high-intensity athletes to move more freely during daily activities. The only drawback for some runners is a decrease in explosive strength and power following AIS. PNF stretching (pages 70–75) is also effective for improving range of motion, but it takes longer to perform than AIS and requires a partner for best results. Post-run static stretching (pages 76–78) is effective for relieving stiffness. Pre-run static stretching results in temporary loss of explosive strength and power; nevertheless, it's grudgingly recommended for runners who've already practiced it long-term, due to the possibility of increased injury risk if it's stopped.

STRENGTH TRAINING

Running works some muscles more than others. That's a problem because muscle imbalance can lead to injury. It creates unequal tension between opposing muscles, puts pressure on tendons and ligaments, and reduces stride efficiency due to instability. You'll need to strengthen opposing muscles (e.g., quadriceps and hamstrings) and improve neuromuscular communication. For good full-body strengthening and balancing, The Runner 360 (pages 53–58) offers a dynamic routine. For greater strength gains, traditional weight room exercises (pages 59–69) will do the trick. For runners simply looking to stave off injury without building muscle, the Household Props routine (pages 107–110) can help keep you healthy.

WOBBLE BOARD

If you can, wobble. The wobble board is the single best training tool for fortifying your kinetic chain. The wobble board can help protect you from injury (from plantar fasciitis to *runner's knee*) or play a role in rehabilitation. Start with five reps of basic exercises (pages 91–92) and slowly increase the number each week. You can stop at ten reps, or you can push it as high as one hundred—though you'll want to do the minimum necessary to reap the rewards.

CARBOHYDRATE AND PROTEIN SUPPLEMENTATION

It's an old runner's trick: If you're suddenly heavy-legged and lethargic, eat lots of carbs and drink lots of water. A deficit in muscle glycogen (stored carbohydrates) can turn every run into a slog. By replenishing your glycogen, you should feel better in a few days. Protein supplementation can aid protein synthesis, which repairs damaged muscle. See Chapter 12 for more information on protein supplementation.

LIMITED ICING

Icing is part of the famous injury-treatment acronym: RICE (rest, ice, compression, elevation). RICE is great for acute injuries. But it's unwarranted for transient muscle soreness and inflammation (e.g., moderate cases of DOMS). "For most people, with normal training, you probably don't need to do anything about inflammation," says Jonathan Dugas, Ph.D., coauthor of the *Science of Sport* website. "Even during hard training, you don't need to do anything except follow the standard training process

of built-in rest periods." That's because icing, like anti-inflammatories, interrupts your body's normal healing cycle. On the other hand, icing is an integral part of dealing with chronic connective tissue injuries. Reducing post-workout inflammation is sometimes necessary if there is to be a next workout. But don't over-ice. Ten to fifteen minutes is enough. And quit if the surrounding tissue feels too cold. Freezing perfectly good tissue only adds a new injury to the old.

A FEW WORDS ABOUT CROSS TRAINING

Cross training is a popular tool for runners who are either recovering from injury or trying to train through chronic injuries. It's used to retain cardiovascular fitness, as well as some muscle and connective tissue strength, during periods when you're forced to reduce mileage. Since you don't train the exact same muscle fibers as running, however, expect to lose capillary, mitochondrial, and other cell-specific gains in those fibers not recruited (due to the *rule of specificity*, which we defined in Chapter 5). For this reason, it's best to pick cross training activities that most closely resemble running, including: pool running, the elliptical machine, ElliptiGO bicycles, treadmills, snowshoeing, and cross country skiing (see Chapter 9's photo instruction for a rundown on each).

See the Injury Prevention table on page 377 for a comprehensive list of common running injuries, including signs and symptoms for each injury, as well as a guide to workouts in this book that can prevent those injuries from occurring and, in many cases, help rehab them when they do occur (injuries that require immediate professional attention are noted).

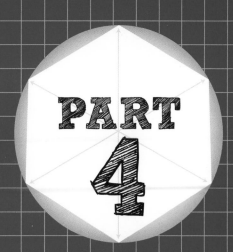

PART 4

Build Your Running Diet— Protein, Carbs, Calories, and Nutrition

18

Build Your Running Diet With Real Food

There's a strange sci-fi beauty to much of the processed food lining the aisles of the supermarket. Designed in labs and produced in factories, processed food offers the futuristic convenience of instant meals in packages. That said, it has no right to call itself food—or real food, at least. True, it can be put in your mouth, chewed, and digested, but it'd be a stretch to associate processed food with the kind of food nurtured with sunlight and soil. And most of its nutrients are but distant memories.

Processed food is food that has been taken from its original state, had the nutrients beaten out of it, and was then turned into something no longer recognizable as that which it once was. Think of an apple (a whole food), applesauce (slightly processed), and an Apple-Cinnamon Pop Tart (highly processed).

Real bodies need real food. A diet of artificial ingredients, preservatives, and indefensible amounts of added fats and sugars does not do a body good. Just look at the skyrocketing rates of obesity, diabetes, and cardiovascular disease.

For runners, real food is important for a number of reasons. Just as you wouldn't put a willy-nilly mixture of—hmmm—let's say paint, Kool-Aid, and baby oil into your car for gas, you shouldn't fuel your body with the toxic and empty ingredients that comprise processed food. There are complicated, physiological processes collaborating to build your running body, and those processes rely on the rich mix of nutrients found in real food.

NUTRITION DISCUSSION

"The Case of the Missing Nutrients"

When you compare whole foods with their processed offspring, you begin to see how much sugar, sodium, and fat are added, as well as how many nutrients get sacrificed.

Whole oat groats* versus instant oatmeal (per 150–160 calories)

	Fiber	Protein	Sugar
Oat Groats	5g	6g	1g
Instant Oatmeal	3g	4g	12g

Brown rice versus white rice (per 200 calories)

	Fiber	Potassium	Magnesium	Vitamin B6
Brown Rice	3.5g	84mg	21%	15%
White Rice	0.06g	55mg	4%	4%

Popcorn versus corn chips (per 160 calories)

	Fiber	Protein	Iron	Sodium	Fat
Popcorn	6g	6g	7%	3mg	1.5g
Corn Chips	1g	2g	0%	170mg	10g

Strawberry versus Strawberry Starburst candy (per 130 calories)

	Fiber	Potassium	Magnesium
Strawberry	7g	84mg	21%
Strawberry candy	0g	0mg	0%

(Nutrient values vary by brand; percentages refer to Percent Daily Values based on a 2,000-calorie diet.)

*Yes, "groats" sounds like a meal Charles Dickens would inflict upon his most pathetic of characters, but they can be delicious. See recipe page 303.

WHAT IS *REAL FOOD?*

Real food is food that hasn't had all the nutrients stripped from it, a process designed to ensure palatability for the masses and an eternal shelf life. For food manufacturers, this works. For your body, not so much. It's the difference between wheat berries—the whole grain from which flour is made—and white bread. While a 150-calorie serving of wheat berries has six grams of protein, six grams of dietary fiber, and 8 percent of the recommended daily amount for iron, among other nutrients, the same 150 calories of bread made from refined wheat has one gram of dietary fiber, half the protein, little iron, and thirty fewer nutrients. (See sidebar, "The Case of the Missing Nutrients," for more examples.)

WHAT ARE *SUPERFOODS?*

There is no legal definition for *superfoods*, but they are generally considered to be primarily plant-based foods that have exceptionally high values of antioxidants, vitamins, or other nutrients. They are often advertised as possessing the ability to fight disease, and they're described with words like "amazing" and "miracle." These dazzling, shiny, so-called "superfoods" are the hands-down darlings of the healthy-eating set, and neither food makers nor marketers have been shy about capitalizing on their fame.

Among superfoods' components, it's the antioxidants that get the most buzz. The National Institutes of Health describe antioxidants as "substances that may protect your cells against the effects of free radicals." *Free radicals* are molecules produced when the body breaks down food to produce energy (and by environmental pollutants like tobacco smoke and radiation).

In the 1990s, scientists first connected free-radical damage to the early stages of artery-clogging atherosclerosis. They hypothesized that free radicals might also be involved in a number of diseases and chronic conditions. Studies seemed to bear this out, revealing that people who consumed larger amounts of antioxidant-rich fruits and vegetables had a reduced risk for developing several chronic conditions.

Subsequent studies, however, have failed to confirm that antioxidants fight disease. Still, the Harvard School of Public Health has concluded that "abundant evidence suggests that eating whole fruits, vegetables, and whole grains—all rich in networks of antioxidants and their helper molecules—provides protection against many of these scourges of aging."

While superfoods may revel in the limelight, the important thing is that you eat a variety of fruits and vegetables, which by nature are already rich in antioxidants. You don't need exotic goji berries and trendy açai pulp—shipped long distance and generally costing a small fortune—when blueberries and red bell peppers will serve you just as well.

REAL FOOD VERSUS SUPPLEMENTS

Diet matters for runners. Whether we're trying to lose weight, defy aging, boost health, or lower our 5K time, we worry about nutrition. Unfortunately, we're also obsessed with miracle cures and the mythic fountain of youth. Just as we want to eat "superfoods," we want our nutrients concentrated into single, small doses. And the supplements industry is happy to oblige—happy to the tune of around $30 billion in sales annually, with half of all Americans indulging in pills, powders, or potions.

A dietary supplement is a product containing one or more dietary ingredients—vitamins, minerals, herbs or other botanicals, amino acids, etc.—that you add to your regular diet. Whey powder

NUTRITION DISCUSSION

"Eight simple superfoods for runners"

Picking the healthiest food for runners is like picking your favorite child. Most produce is loaded with healthy attributes. They're all just a little different. The items here are chosen for their running-specific benefits, availability, and ease of preparation. They're super-super!

1. **Almonds:** Almonds are a great source of calcium, magnesium, potassium, iron, protein, and fiber—the perfect storm of important nutrients for runners. They're also one of the best sources of alpha-tocopherol vitamin E, a potent antioxidant that provides a good defense against the oxidative stress (damage caused to cells by highly reactive groups of molecules known as free radicals), which can result from running.

2. **Beets:** Beets and beet juice possess an abundance of antioxidants, folate, and potassium. They are a great source of inorganic nitrate, which the body can convert to nitrite and then nitric acid, which positively affects blood flow, muscle contraction, neurotransmission, and other functions. One 2009 study showed that six days of beet juice consumption could lower blood pressure and improve physical performance during both moderate and intense exercise. And a 2013 study from the United Kingdom concluded that beet juice "increases plasma nitrite concentration, reduces blood pressure, and may positively influence the physiological responses to exercise."

3. **Blueberries:** A number of studies on blueberries have found numerous positive outcomes for health—too numerous, in fact, to list here. But two studies are of particular interest to runners. In the first, runners who ate a cup of blueberries daily had less inflammation and better immune health after long runs than a berry-free control group. In the second, elite athletes given polyphenols from blueberries burned fat longer post-exercise and increased their absorption of antioxidant compounds.

4. **Greek yogurt:** Yogurt is a great way to get calcium and tummy-loving probiotics (the "good bacteria" that keeps your gut a peaceful, healthy place) into your system. Thicker, creamier Greek yogurt offers twice the protein and half the sugar for the same number of calories as regular yogurt. Better yet, its nonfat version has a texture (unlike other nonfat dairy) that won't make you weep.

5. **Lentils:** Like other legumes, lentils are a great source of potassium, calcium, zinc, niacin, and vitamin K, and they're particularly rich in dietary fiber, lean protein, folate, and iron. Unlike other legumes, they don't require overnight soaking and long cooking times when you make them from scratch.

(Continued)

BUILD YOUR RUNNING BODY

BUILD YOUR RUNNING DIET—PROTEIN, CARBS, CALORIES, AND NUTRITION

6. **Red bell pepper:** Contrary to popular belief, it's red bell peppers, not oranges, that are the poster-child fruit for vitamin C. One half-cup of raw red sweet pepper contains 142 mg of vitamin C, twice as much as an orange, and for a mere 20 calories. Research credits vitamin C with alleviating muscle soreness and lowering heart rate during exercise, which leads to reduced perception of exertion and fatigue.

7. **Salmon:** Salmon packs a punch when it comes to nutrition. It's an excellent source of high-quality protein (30 grams per 4-ounce serving) and one of the world's best sources of omega-3 fats (essential fatty acids found in fish oil, plant oil, and algae oil). Omega-3 fats help regulate the body's inflammation response, and a 2006 study from Indiana University found that three weeks of fish oil supplementation reduced symptoms of exercise-induced asthma.

8. **Sweet potatoes:** If you like baked potatoes for the carbs, you might think about sweet potatoes as an occasional substitution. Both spuds are comparable in calories, carbs, protein, and fiber, but sweet potatoes offer nearly 20 percent more vitamin C and are packed with 380 percent of the daily-recommended value of vitamin A. With potassium, manganese, and copper to buoy muscle function, sweet potatoes should be a staple of every runner's diet.

shakes, vitamin pills, and açai berry juice are examples of supplements. Many Americans mistakenly believe that supplements pass rigorous government testing before they get put on the market. They don't. It took the FDA a decade to ban ephedra, even after thousands of adverse effects, including death.

For people who lack a full daily dose of nutrients in their diet, supplements might be helpful, but supplements are *not* a substitute for a well-rounded diet drawn from real food. The truth is that high doses of antioxidants, minerals, fiber, and other substances in pill form are not as effective at improving your health as the amounts found naturally in fruits, vegetables, whole grains, and other real food. Frankly, runners who want to eat healthy need to spend more time at the farmers' market and less at the pharmacy.

REAL PACKAGED FOOD

In a perfect world, we can all agree that the food on our table should be plucked directly from the soil and then, still warm from the sun, purchased during a leisurely stroll through the neighborhood farmers' market.

Now let's get real.

There's a reason packaged and processed food is so popular. The modern world moves fast. Most of us can barely keep our heads screwed on, let alone prepare fresh, nutritious meals from scratch three times a day. Throw in a training program, and the idea's absurd.

Which is where packaged food comes into play. First, we aren't talking about junky, processed food—cheesy mystery snacks that stain your fingers an otherworldly orange are out. But there are plenty of packaged foods that are healthy, making wholesome eating in a busy world possible. But first you must learn to distinguish between the good, the bad, and the unhealthy.

The produce aisle

If you stick to the produce aisle, it's almost impossible to go wrong. Although pre-cut and packaged produce is more expensive, it can be worth it. For example, skip the single head of lettuce and take advantage of pre-mixed salads that offer a variety of lettuces—each variety of leaf has a slightly different nutrient profile, making for a more dynamic meal.

In general, it's better to buy whole fruits and vegetables, but if buying pre-cut produce makes it likely that you'll eat more, then it's a good investment. (Keep in mind that there's a slight decrease in nutrients for cut vegetables, and they're usually subjected to a chlorine rinse—safe, but something to think about.)

When you can, buy produce that's local and in season. If you live in a productive agricultural region with a mild climate, this is a great way to ensure eating a variety of fruits and vegetables throughout the year. If you live in a more forbidding climate—say, winter in Maine—then frozen fruits and vegetables can serve as an alternative. While canned vegetables lose nutrients during the canning process (excluding tomatoes and pumpkin), frozen vegetables can be even more nutritionally robust than their fresh counterparts. This is because produce used for freezing is generally processed at its peak ripeness, a time when most fruits and vegetables are in their most nutrient-rich states.

Label logic

Most of us know that ingredients are listed on packages in the order of their predominance, from most to least. This is the way we check to see the relative proportions of those ingredients.

But there is a sneaky little trick that manufacturers often use. Since ingredients are listed individually, not in groups, something could contain three types of sugar—for example, corn syrup, cane sugar, and malt syrup—in seemingly small quantities toward the bottom of the list. But if you combine them into a group, *sugar*, they quickly move to the top of the list. Can you say, "Loophole"? When shopping packaged food, it pays to have a discerning eye.

The whole (grains) truth

We'll discuss whole grains in more detail in Chapter 19. For now, you need to know that the difference between refined grains and whole grains is key when discussing real food. When manufactures denude (strip) a grain of its bran, germ, and endosperm before processing it further into a baked good or snack item, it's pretty much finished as real food. Now it's just sad and empty. It's entered the realm of "things formerly known as food." The food industry covers up this transformation with deceptive—but legal—labeling claims. For instance, "made with wheat flour" doesn't mean that it's made with *whole wheat*. "Includes whole grains" could refer to 1 percent whole grains. And "seven grain" could be *seven hundred* grain and it wouldn't make a difference if they're not whole grains. Also, don't judge a loaf by its cover; bread tinged brown with molasses or topped with a flutter of oats might still be plain old white bread.

To crack this labeling code, simply scan the ingredients for the word "whole." If the first ingredient is grain (any grain!) preceded by "whole," then you've hit the jackpot. Whole wheat flour, whole oats, whole whatever—doesn't matter as long as the word "whole" is there. Fiber content is also a clue. Grain items containing at least three grams of fiber generally have whole grains.

Pass the salt

Salt tastes great and has its place in a proper diet. But adults in general shouldn't consume more than 2,300 mg of sodium per day. Compare that to the almost 3,500 mg (about 1½ teaspoons) that most Americans gulp down each day. How are you managing to eat a spoon and a half of salt each day? The answer is processed foods: canned foods, condiments, fast food, cured meats, and salty snacks account for 75 percent of our salt intake. Runners need salt, but not hypertension. So pass on the salt.

Trimming the trans fat

In 1957, the American Heart Association first raised the alarm that saturated fats (e.g.—butter and lard) were hard on the heart. By the 1970s, saturated fat's role in heart disease was confirmed, and food manufacturers turned to trans fats, assuming these fats were healthier since they were created from healthy vegetable oils through hydrogenation (hydrogen is added to vegetable oils, creating solid fats). Unwittingly, they had unleashed a monster.

Trans fat wasn't a hero come to the rescue. Instead, studies in the 1990s confirmed that trans fat decreased heart-happy good cholesterol *and* increased artery-clogging bad cholesterol. In the book, *Food Regulation: Law, Science, Policy, and Practice*, Walter Willet of the Harvard School of Public Health estimates that hydrogenated oils were at one time responsible for 30,000 heart-disease deaths per year, representing the "biggest food processing disaster in history."

Used in everything from muffins to microwave

NUTRITION DISCUSSION

"Real food sports drinks"

Many athletes rely on sports drinks for hydration, carbohydrates, and recovery. But few realize that there are healthy alternatives to the artificially flavored and colored brand names on the shelf. While trying "real food" sports drinks for the first time on race day isn't advised, it's worth experimenting with during a regular workout session.

- ▶ **Coconut water:** A 2012 study by Kalman, et al., found that coconut water works as well as sports drinks when it comes to rehydration and exercise performance. As a bonus, it's filled with nutrients! The only caution is that some runners experienced bloating and upset stomach.
- ▶ **Watermelon juice:** A 2013 study from Spain showed that men who drank watermelon juice before an intense stationary cycling test reported no leg soreness the following day. After drinking a placebo, however, they reported soreness. As an added benefit, subjects fueled by watermelon juice showed a lower heart rate, indicating better recovery. To make watermelon juice, blend seeded chunks of fruit in the blender and drink as is.
- ▶ **For the DIY set:** Yes, you can make your own. To 3½ cups water, add ¼ cup fruit juice, ¼ cup maple syrup or honey, and ¼ teaspoon salt. Mix, drink, endure.

popcorn to "healthy" margarine, trans fat was everywhere. But as of January 1, 2006, all packaged foods under the jurisdiction of the FDA must list the amount of trans fat on the label. Food manufacturers have begun to remove these fats from their products, but there are still plenty of foods that contain them. To be safe, check the ingredients for the words "partially hydrogenated" and "fractionated," which mean trans fat is present. If you see these ingredients on the label, leave the product on the shelf.

ORGANIC VERSUS CONVENTIONAL PRODUCE

A discussion of real food wouldn't be complete without acknowledging the debate between the merits of organic produce versus produce grown with pesticides. The latest large-scale study—a 2012 analysis of 237 studies on organic produce, meats, and dairy foods by Stanford researchers—concluded that organic foods don't offer a more advantageous nutrition profile than that of conventional produce. On the other hand, if you prefer to avoid consuming compounds designed to kill living things, then organic might be for you. Of course, the cost of organic produce can be prohibitive. If you're financially strapped, you can research which conventional crops are most likely to have pesticide residue, and then limit your purchases to organic versions of those crops. The consumer advocacy group Environmental Working Group compiles a yearly guide to inform shoppers about produce and pesticides. Their *Shopper's Guide to Pesticides in Produce*™ lists the year's "Dirty Dozen"—the twelve most contaminated fruits and vegetables—as well as a "Clean 15," representing produce that scores the lowest for pesticide residue. Be forewarned: Apples and oranges often appear in the Dirty Dozen. On the other hand, avocados and cabbage are regulars in the Clean 15.

A MATTER OF TRUST

The truth is that many of us no longer trust the food we eat to provide the nutrition our bodies require. So we buy supplements. We chase fads. We let misleading labels trick us into buying food that promises health but delivers empty calories. Real food will give you what supplements and an overload of empty calories can't: healthy carbs, proteins, and fats; enzymes; vitamins; minerals; and all the good stuff required to build your running body.

A note on *Build Your Running Body* recipes

These recipes were developed to be user-friendly. While baking is pretty much an exact science, cooking isn't. Measurements for salt and pepper will always say "season to taste," because some people hate salt or need to watch it, while others can't get enough. Likewise, an ingredient like jalapeño peppers can vary in its heat level, so they should be taste-tested and added accordingly. Also, become comfortable swapping ingredients. If the recipe says "cilantro," basil or mint or parsley will probably work, too. If the recipe says "almonds," ditto for hazelnuts. And feel free to use cow milk instead of the soy or coconut milk used frequently in these recipes. Ingredients will generally default to the least-refined option, but work with whatever you have on hand (e.g., we say "raw sugar," but maybe you only have white sugar). That said, nutrition is calculated based on the specified ingredients (note that nutritional values can vary depending on brand, and that calorie counts for recipes will sometimes differ from what the carb, protein, and fat intake predicts due to the presence of insoluble fiber and the practice of rounding the nutritional breakdown of each ingredient). Think of these recipes as a basic plan, then improvise to your mouth's content.

Best Oats and Groats Ever

When one encounters the word "groats," the natural instinct is to run away. But be brave. The unfortunately named groat is nothing more than a hulled grain (e.g., oat) generally used for breakfast cereal. Of all cereal grains, groats are the least processed. Steel-cut oats are whole oat groats that have been sliced. Rolled oats are oat groats that have been steamed, rolled, and flaked for easier cooking. Quick-cooking oats are rolled oats that have been chopped into smaller pieces. And instant oats are mashed and nearly powdered. In this recipe, we'll make groats and steel-cut oats that don't require the thirty to sixty minutes of standing-over-the-stove-stirring time—and taste good!

Overnight Oats or Groats— Slow Cooker Technique

▶ SERVES 8

6 to 8 cups water

2 cups steel-cut oats or groats

Fruit or sweetener, optional (see note on Additions)

Use 6 cups of water if the groats will cook for less than 8 hours, or 8 cups of water if they will cook for more than 8 hours (since this recipe calls for 6–8 cups, feel free to improvise—for example, 7 cups at 8 hours—depending on cooking time). Add the water, steel-cut oats, and fruit or sweetener, if desired; cover, and cook overnight on the lowest setting. Wake up to a nice warm bowl of oats.

Easy Morning Oats or Groats— Rice Cooker Technique

▶ SERVES 4

4 cups water

1 cup steel-cut oats or groats

Fruit or sweetener, optional (see note on Additions)

It's better to make smaller batches when using a rice cooker so that the mix doesn't bubble over. Add the water, steel-cut oats, and fruit or sweetener, if desired; cover, and cook while you're getting ready for the day—set the rice cooker to low for 30 minutes for steel-cut oats and 50 minutes for groats.

Additions: Add fresh or frozen fruit—blueberries, apples, pears—to the cooker to create a wonderful fruit-infused mush. Bananas make it extra creamy. Or try pumpkin for a fall treat. Dried fruits like cherries, cranberries, raisins, dates, and figs plump up and add a nice sweetness. For sweeteners, try honey, maple syrup, agave, or apple juice (in place of some water). If you want to add nuts, stir them in at the end, since they'll get soggy.

Per serving (rice cooker technique, with 1 cup blueberries and 1 banana added)

> **With groats:** 227 calories; 42 g carbs; 8 g protein; 3 g fat.

> **With steel-cut oats:** 187 calories; 39 g carbs; 7 g protein; 3 g fat.

Sweet Potato Fries

▶ **SERVES 4**

Sweet potatoes are a great food for runners, but their most popular presentation usually involves a mix of butter and sugar topped with marsh-mallows. The cure is this super-simple and seriously delicious method for baking them into healthy, crispy fries.

5 sweet potatoes, unpeeled, washed well and sliced into ¼-inch strips

1 tablespoon olive oil

Salt and pepper

Cayenne, curry powder, or paprika, optional

1. Preheat the oven to 450°F.

2. Toss the sweet potatoes with the olive oil, then season with salt and pepper. Add cayenne, if desired, to make the fries zesty, though they don't need it.

3. Spread them out in a single layer on a baking sheet. Bake, turning occasionally, until crispy and lightly browned, but still a bit tender, about 20 minutes.

Per serving: 159 calories; 30 g carbs; 3 g protein; 4 g fat.

Fresh Ginger Ale

▶ **24 SERVINGS**

Ginger has magical properties for runners. A 2010 study published in The Journal of Pain *concluded that the "daily consumption of raw and heat-treated ginger resulted in moderate-to-large reductions in muscle pain following exercise-induced muscle injury . . . and further demonstrate ginger's effectiveness as a pain reliever." Commercial sodas don't qualify as real food, but this recipe for ginger ale packs a pain-free punch that you won't get with a Coke.*

6-inch-long piece of fresh ginger

1 cup honey

3 cups water

1 cup sparkling or hot water

Ice

Juice of 1 lime, optional

Thinly slice the ginger (no need to peel if cleaned well) and mix with the honey and water in a saucepan. Simmer on low heat for about an hour. Allow the mixture to cool, then strain and put in a clean jar. Add 2 tablespoons of the ginger mixture to a glass of sparkling water, stir, add ice, and enjoy. The ginger mixture can also be added to a cup of hot water with lime juice to make a sweet, tart, and spicy tea.

Per serving: 45 calories; 12 g carbs.

Chocolate Beet Cake

▶ SERVES 8

Beets add a truckload of runner-friendly nutri-ents to this dessert, and their inherent moisture negates the need for butter. If you try really hard, you can taste beets, but mostly what you'll enjoy is a deep, earthy chocolate flavor.

1¾ cups cooked beets (about 3 beets)

2 cups unbleached all-purpose flour

1¼ cups raw sugar

¼ cup unsweetened cocoa powder

1½ teaspoons baking soda

¾ teaspoon salt

3 ounces bittersweet chocolate, chopped

1 large egg

¾ cup water

¼ cup mild olive oil or other vegetable oil

1 teaspoon pure vanilla extract

1. Some produce sections have packages of boiled beets, which make this a breeze. Other-wise: trim, peel, cut, and boil beets until very tender, about 30 minutes. Purée the beets in a food processor until smooth (or try a blender or cheese grater using the smallest shred size that will work.)

2. Preheat the oven to 350°F. Grease and flour well a 9-inch round cake pan (if you have parch-ment paper, line the bottom of the greased pan instead of using the flour, and grease again).

3. Stir together the remaining flour, sugar, co-coa powder, baking soda, and salt in a large bowl. Melt half the chocolate, and add to the flour mix-ture along with the egg, water, oil, vanilla, and beet purée. Stir in the unmelted chocolate.

4. Pour the batter into a pan, then bake for about 45 minutes or until a toothpick comes out clean. Cool on a wire rack for 20 minutes, remove from the pan, and leave out until completely cool.

Per serving: 345 calories; 57 g carbs; 5 g protein; 13 g fat.

SERVING SUGGESTIONS:

For chocolate glaze: This is based on a Martha Stew-art chocolate glaze, but with a healthy makeover. Bring ½ cup coconut milk and 1 teaspoon honey to a simmer in a small pan, then pour over 3 ounces of chopped bittersweet chocolate in a bowl to melt. Stir until smooth and shiny; let cool for 10 minutes and then pour over cake.

For beet chips: Make candied beets, or if you like a salty component with your sweets, use store-bought Terra beet chips.

For chocolate curls: Use a vegetable peeler and make long curls from the edge of a thick choco-late bar.

BUILD YOUR RUNNING BODY

Build Your Running Carbohydrates

 hummingbird's energy needs are so great that it would starve to death after a carbohydrate fast lasting only a few hours. If hummingbirds suddenly opted for a low-carb/high-protein diet, you'd find yourself dodging dead hummingbirds as they fell from the sky. Luckily, hummingbirds have better sense than that. You should, too. For runners, carbs are crucial.

Carbohydrates, also called *saccharides*, are one of the three macronutrients that fuel our bodies (proteins and fats are the other two). At the heart of every carbohydrate is a sugar molecule, which is a marriage of carbon, hydrogen, and oxygen (hence the name "carbohydrate"). Carbs are found in a wide variety of foods—beans, fruit, popcorn, potatoes, corn, cookies, pasta, pie, and just about everything else that isn't pure protein or fat. And while they come in a variety of forms, most are sugars—starches and fibers, two of the most common carbs, are basically chains of sugar molecules (some containing hundreds or even thousands of sugars).

Carbs are the main source of energy for your running body. It's no hyperbole to say that, without them, you'd be stuck on the couch.

WHAT ARE SACCHARIDES?

In order to understand carbohydrates, you'll need to put on your science cap and acquaint yourself with the saccharide family, consisting of four groups by which carbs are classified.

▶ **Monosaccharide:** The most basic units of biologically important carbohydrates, these are the simplest forms of sugar. They include glucose, galactose (found in milk and dairy products), fructose (found mostly in vegetables and fruit), and others. Monosaccharides link together to become polysaccharides.

▶ **Disaccharide:** When two monosaccharide molecules bond, they become disaccharides. Examples include lactose (glucose + galactose) found in milk, maltose (glucose + glucose) found in some vegetables and beer, and sucrose (glucose + fructose) found in table sugar.

▶ **Oligosaccharide:** These have three to ten monosaccharides bonded together. Examples are gentianose and stachynose (found in various plants) and raffinose (found in beans, cabbage, Brussels sprouts, and broccoli)—it's our inability to digest raffinose that gives us gas.

▶ **Polysaccharide:** Technically, disaccharides and oligosaccharides are polysaccharides, since they have more than one molecule, but the term is usually used to refer to chains of more than ten monosaccharides—and a polysaccharide can be made up of hundreds of thousands of monosaccharides. They include storage polysaccharides such as starch and glycogen, and structural polysaccharides like cellulose and chitin.

With that information in hand, it's time to discuss the difference between complex and simple carbohydrates.

COMPLEX VERSUS SIMPLE CARBOHYDRATES

In the good old days, carbohydrates were grouped into two categories: complex and simple. Simple carbohydrates included the mono- and disaccharides. Complex carbohydrates included all of the polysaccharides.

Complex carbohydrates, like those found in beans, starchy vegetables, and whole grain products, were considered healthier to eat than simple carbohydrates, such as those found in fruits, sweets, and refined grain products. Complex carbohydrates do, in fact, have more nutrients and more fiber, and they take longer to break down in the body. Simple carbohydrates offer little more than calories—the reason they're referred to as "empty calories."

NUTRITION DISCUSSION

"Top Ten recovery snacks"

Optimal post-workout recovery requires eating. Lucky you! And a big part of that recovery eating is getting enough carbs to replace burned glycogen. The golden rule of recovery is a 4:1 ratio of carbs to protein, although that ratio can be altered to reflect the specifics of your workout. Check the tables in Chapter 10 to get a better idea of what calories and macronutrients are most appropriate for each kind of workout. Then choose from the following list:

1. **Banana almond smoothie:** There are times post-workout that you just don't want to chew. For those days, a smoothie will do the trick. Blend until smooth: ½ cup low-fat vanilla yogurt, 1 banana, 1 tablespoon almond butter, ½ cup low-fat milk, and a handful of ice. *(1 serving: 335 calories; 45 g carbs; 14 g protein; 11 g fat.)*

2. **Clif Bar:** If you're not going straight home after a run, you'll need something in your bag. Clif Bars are a good packaged snack, using less-processed, mostly organic ingredients and employing the 4:1 carbs to protein ratio. *(1 Chocolate Brownie bar: 240 calories; 45 g carbs; 10 g protein; 4.5 g fat.)*

3. **Egg-and-avocado sandwich:** When recovery requires a little extra protein and fat, this quick sandwich can't be beat. Use two slices of toast, ¼ an avocado, and a sliced hard-boiled egg. Season with salt and pepper. *(1 serving: 360 calories; 55 g carbs; 18 g protein; 16 g fat.)*

4. **Banana and bagel:** The classic post-race freebie is also great for post-workout recovery. The nutritional value given here is for a Thomas whole-wheat bagel, but bagels vary widely when it comes to calories, so be alert. *(1 banana and bagel: 355 calories; 76 g carbs; 13 g protein; 2 g fat.)*

5. **Dried figs and goat cheese:** Sometimes post-workout you want a snack with pizzazz. For those days, figs and tangy goat cheese are just the thing! Dried figs are carb powerhouses, along with containing copious amounts of calcium, potassium, fiber, iron, and magnesium. *(6 dried figs, 1 tablespoon goat cheese: 380 calories; 60 g carbs; 12 g protein; 12 g fat.)*

6. **Chocolate milk:** Research confirms what runners have always known: Chocolate milk rocks! A 2011 study from the University of Texas at Austin found that low-fat chocolate milk provides recovery benefits for "serious and amateur athletes alike." Benefits included better body composition with more muscle and less fat, improved performance, and better overall fitness. *(8-ounce Horizon organic chocolate milk box: 150 calories; 22 g carbs; 8 g protein; 2.5 g fat.)*

(Continued)

7. **Cold pizza:** There's something to be said about heading straight to the refrigerator post-workout to indulge in cold leftovers. *(1 slice veggie pizza: 260 calories; 34 g carbs; 10 g protein; 9 g fat.)*

8. **Apple and cheese:** Sweet apples and salty cheese go together perfectly. While not super-high in carbs, it's a good snack when your recovery requires a boost of protein and fat. *(1 large apple, 1 ounce of cheese: 224 calories; 22 g carbs; 7 g protein; 9 g fat.)*

9. **Greek yogurt and granola:** Greek yogurt is one of the few dairy products where the no-fat version doesn't feel like a punishment—and buying a plain flavor allows you to sweeten to your liking. Add carbs by way of granola and honey. *(½ cup Greek yogurt, ½ cup granola, ½ tablespoon honey: 335 calories; 57 g carbs; 20 g protein; 5 g fat.)*

10. **Peanut butter and jelly sandwich:** Possibly the perfect training food, a PB&J post-run allows you to curl up in a ball and regress to childhood—although the adult might want to use natural peanut butter and all-fruit jelly. *(2 slices bread, 1 tablespoon peanut butter, 1 tablespoon jelly: 378 calories; 42 g carbs; 12 g protein; 18 g fat.)*

But this simple dichotomy doesn't tell the whole story. The digestive system aims to break down all carbs to single sugar molecules of glucose, your body's key source of energy. And that's where the glycemic index enters the picture, and where simplicity goes out the window.

THE GLYCEMIC INDEX AND GLYCEMIC LOADS

Your body turns carbohydrates into glucose, which subsequently enters your bloodstream and raises your blood sugar (glucose) levels. When blood sugar rises, the pancreas releases insulin, a hormone that directs cells in your muscles and liver to absorb the sugar (and store it as glycogen). When blood sugar levels drop, insulin release decreases, and when blood sugar falls to a certain point, the pancreas releases glucagon, a hormone that triggers the conversion of glycogen in the liver back into glucose, which is released into the bloodstream.

Problems arise when dramatically fluctuating blood sugar levels occur over a long period of time. This seesaw of glucose, insulin, and glucagon can lead to obesity, type 2 diabetes, heart disease, and other conditions. Currently, seventeen million Americans have type 2 diabetes, and millions more have insulin resistance and are at risk for diabetes.

There are ways to lower the risk of developing blood sugar–related conditions. For instance, natural carbohydrates (such as those found in fruits, vegetables, legumes, whole grains, etc.) enter the bloodstream more slowly compared to the carbs found in processed foods, leading to a gentler spike in insulin and blood sugar.

This is where the *glycemic index* (GI) comes into play. Carbs enter the bloodstream at different rates. The GI measures the rise in blood sugar triggered by different carbohydrates. Carbs that enter your blood quickly score a high GI. Those entering more slowly—because they take longer to break down—earn a low GI.

The GI doesn't take serving size into consideration, however, so it can be misleading. For example, watermelon has a high GI, but its actual glycemic load (the amount of carbohydrate in the food) is relatively low. For this reason, a food's *glycemic load* can be a better measure of a food's impact on blood sugar levels than GI. A unit of glycemic load is roughly equivalent to the effect one gram of glucose has on your blood sugar levels. With this in mind, a glycemic load of 20 or more is considered high, a load of 11 to 19 is considered medium, and a load of 10 or fewer units is scored as low.

But even though glycemic load may be a better way to estimate the impact of carbohydrates on blood sugar, it's GI that's used on a wider basis, with healthier carbs generally coming in with a lower GI. Some low GI foods include milk, yogurt, lentils, pasta, nuts, and northern-climate fruits like apples and oranges. Moderate GI foods include soft drinks, oats, and tropical fruits (e.g., bananas and mangos). High GI foods include refined bread, potatoes, sweetened breakfast cereals, and sports drinks—the latter good for quick blasts during endurance events but not so good for your body while watching TV.

Runners wondering how the GI affects their running should consider the following:

- ▶ **Low GI foods prior to a run:** Studies show that consuming low GI foods prior to training maintains blood sugar levels better than eating high GI foods. One study concluded that a low GI snack eaten fifteen minutes before running extended time to exhaustion by 23 percent.
- ▶ **Moderate-to-high GI foods during a run:** The rapidly digested carbs in sports drinks, gels, and energy bars offer a quick source of fuel during exercise.

NUTRITION DISCUSSION

"How to lower your glycemic load"

Moderate-to-high glycemic load foods have their place in a runner's diet, but, in general, low GL foods are better. Here's how to keep your glycemic load low:

- ▶ For breakfast cereal, choose oats, barley, or bran. Aim for the ones that are in their most natural state, as milling and grinding can raise the glycemic load dramatically.
- ▶ When you can, eat whole wheat bread.
- ▶ Indulge in lots of fresh fruit and vegetables.
- ▶ Pick whole fruit over fruit juice; if you do drink juice, get it with the pulp.
- ▶ Eat brown rice when you can.
- ▶ Eat whole wheat pasta when you can.
- ▶ Curb junk foods, processed foods, fast food, and foods with too many additives.

Healthy carbohydrate intake will lead to healthy energy production when you need it most.

- **High GI foods after you run:** High GI foods enable quick replenishment of burned glycogen stores. High GI foods have been shown to increase glycogen stores post-workout at a rate twice that of low GI foods.
- **The rest of the time:** Nearly all research concludes that low GI foods are better for maintaining good health.

HOW MANY CARBOHYDRATES DO YOU NEED?

The National Academy of Sciences has determined what percentage of your total daily caloric intake should come from carbohydrates, protein, and fat (i.e., your AMDRs: acceptable macronutrient distribution ranges). It's recommended that 45–65 percent of calories come from carbohydrates, 10–35 percent from protein, and 20–35 percent from fat. For a 2,000-calorie diet, that means consuming 225 to 325 grams of carbs every day.

Of course, athletes have higher carbohydrate and protein requirements than less-active people. See the charts in Chapter 10 for a breakdown of carbohydrate and fat use during various workouts. In general, the Academy of Nutrition and Dietetics recommends that endurance athletes get 2.3 to 5.5 grams of carbs for each pound of body weight. As you can see, that's a wide range. Then again, there's a wide range of carbohydrates burned between runners doing fifteen miles a week and those doing one hundred.

WHEN CARBS FAIL YOU

It's not surprising that when it comes to carbs—as with most things in life—one serving size doesn't fit all. While many athletes thrive on carbs, others have a few objections:

- **Weight gain:** Gram for gram, carbs have the same number of calories as protein (and less than half the calories of fat), but carb absorption is accompanied by a gain in water weight. In fact, your body absorbs about three grams of water for every gram of stored glycogen. So a runner with fully stocked glycogen stores can weigh five-plus pounds more than if his or her glycogen stores were mostly depleted. And the salt that accompanies many packaged and processed carb products can raise that number. Something to consider before carbo-loading for your next 5K.
- **Digestive distress:** Some of the best carbs have a double dose of fiber. Think beans, bran, and broccoli. An increase in fiber can lead to gas, cramps, bloating, and loose stools. You'll need to monitor what's going on downstairs and monitor fiber if things get rumbly.
- **Blood sugar changes:** Carbo-loading can affect your blood sugar levels. Runners with blood sugar issues should consult a doctor before scarfing down an increased volume of carbs.

While not opposed to carbs, ultra-runners sometimes favor a diet high in fat rather than carbs, since fat is a more plentiful stored-energy source and because energy needs at the paces at which they train and race can be met almost completely through fat-based aerobic energy production.

CARBOHYDRATE LOADING

Athletes have long known that carbs aid performance, but it wasn't until the 1960s that researchers from Sweden figured out how. They concluded that a diet high in carbs increased muscle glycogen, which provides 80–90 percent of your fuel for 5Ks and 60–70 percent for half marathons and marathons. Further research confirmed that a high-carb diet also boosted a runner's ability to absorb repeated heavy training loads. Thus, the relationship between runners and piles of steaming pasta was forever sealed. For more on carbo-loading, see the Chapter 10 sidebar, page 174, "Do carbo-loading and fat-loading work?"

THE FIBER FACTOR

Unlike other carbohydrates, fiber isn't broken down into sugar molecules by your body. Instead, it passes right through, undigested. But while it doesn't provide nutrients, it's essential for good health. Fiber helps regulate the body's use of sugars, and it slows down the digestive process, leading to a steadier supply of nutrients and a longer-lasting sensation of satiety. Ideally, adults should get 20 to 30 grams of fiber per day (i.e., roughly 14 grams per 1,000 calories consumed), though most Americans only get about 15 grams.

Of course, for all that's good about fiber, it can present problems for runners. Namely, it can lead to temporary gastrointestinal distress (not pleasant during a workout, a nightmare during a race). For this reason, runners have to be smart about fiber intake. Fiber takes about two hours to navigate its way through your body, so save fiber-rich foods for post-run, not before. Also, increase fiber in your diet in small increments. That way, your body can adjust. Start by adding whole wheat products, some fruits and vegetables, and beans as a replacement for meat.

THE SPECIAL RELATIONSHIP BETWEEN RUNNERS AND CARBS

If you run, you need carbs. It's that simple. Skimping on carbs is begging for sluggish runs, decreased strength, and muddled thinking. Remember that all intense training efforts are fueled by carbs. And running at mile race pace or faster, resistance training, plyometrics, drills, and most of the connective tissue exercises in the book are fueled *only* by carbs. So choose your carbs wisely, using the tips from this chapter, and then eat them.

Secret Healthy Pancakes

▶ **ABOUT 15 3-INCH PANCAKES**

For a carb-heavy meal, few things satisfy like yummy pancakes. The trick is to make them healthy without tasting like fried cardboard. The secret? A little miracle known as white whole wheat flour. Traditional flour is made with red wheat, but this is made with a lighter version, meaning less whole wheat flavor and color (if not found at your supermarket, check Bob's Red Mill and King Arthur Flour online). This recipe uses yogurt and milk instead of buttermilk, because who keeps fresh buttermilk in their fridge? But, naturally, feel free to swap it in.

1 cup white whole wheat flour

½ teaspoon baking powder

½ teaspoon baking soda

¼ cup raw sugar

1 cup low-fat plain yogurt

½ cup 2 percent milk

1 egg

1 tablespoon butter, melted

Butter for the pan

1. Stir the dry ingredients together in a large bowl; mix wet ingredients together in a separate bowl and then add to dry ingredients.

2. Lightly stir, leaving some lumps—pancake batter doesn't like to be over-stirred.

3. Place a skillet on medium heat and brush with butter. Pour the batter into the skillet and cook until small bubbles form in the pancake. Flip, cook, and place on a warm plate. Continue cooking until batter is gone.

Per pancake: 53 calories; 8 g carbs; 2 g protein; 1 g fat.

Linguine with Anchovies and Things

▶ **4 SERVINGS**

Whole wheat pasta plays well with big flavors, and this recipe is big on big. Based on tomatoes and other vibrant flavors, this quick recipe is also packed with salty things. So if you're watching your sodium (or find anchovies challenging), you can swap canned tuna and roasted red peppers for the anchovies and olives. But if you're looking for a salty meal (see Chapter 22 for why this might be the case) and you revel in savory anchovies, indulge in this as is.

1 pound whole wheat linguine

2 tablespoons olive oil

2 large cloves garlic, roughly chopped

Jalapeño, optional

3 large tomatoes, chopped

One 2-ounce tin of anchovies

⅓ cup Kalamata olives, chopped

2 tablespoons capers

Salt and pepper to taste

Sourdough croutons, fresh basil, or Parmesan for garnish, optional

1. Boil the pasta according to the instructions on the package.

2. While the pasta cooks, add the olive oil and garlic (and the jalapeño to taste, if using) to a large sauté pan, and heat on medium heat until sizzling. Add the tomatoes and olives, stirring occasionally. Cook until the tomatoes begin to soften and release their juice. Stir in the anchovies to taste (start with a few and see how many you can take) and the capers. Cook through until heated.

3. Strain pasta and toss with the sauce, season

with pepper and an extra sprinkle of olive oil if desired. Pasta topped with croutons adds a great crunchy texture, or finish with fresh basil and/or a few shavings of Parmesan.

Per serving: 514 calories; 84 g carbs; 17 g protein; 14 g fat.

Stuffed Tortilla Chiles with Feta, Corn, and Black Beans

▶ **4 SERVINGS**

This recipe began as a healthy makeover for chiles rellenos, then evolved into something entirely its own. It may not be the gloppy, saucy Mexican meal of your dreams, but it's fresh, bright, and spicy, and it hits all the right flavors, while being a fantastic source of carbs and protein, and still satisfying your every craving for Mexican food.

4 large chile peppers (Anaheim, poblano, and pasilla all work well)

1 medium onion, diced

1 cup corn off the cob

1 can black beans

1 cup feta cheese, crumbled

4 whole wheat flour tortillas

1 cup plain, nonfat Greek yogurt

1 cup salsa

¼ cup grated cheddar cheese for garnish

1. Roast peppers on a gas burner by turning up the flame and placing peppers directly on the grate. Turn with tongs until even black and burnt all over. If you don't have gas burners, place peppers under a broiler. When cool enough to handle, rub the charred skin off. This step can be skipped entirely, but it adds a nice smoky flavor.

2. Preheat the oven to 350°F. In a large bowl, stir together the onions, corn, beans, and feta cheese.

3. Make a slit in each pepper and remove the seeds, then stuff with the corn-and-bean mixture. Wrap each pepper with a tortilla so that the pepper seam is on the top and the tortilla seam is on the bottom. Nestle them together in a baking or casserole dish. Stir the salsa and yogurt together to make the sauce, then pour the sauce over and around the chiles. Sprinkle cheddar on top and bake for 30 minutes, or until golden on top and bubbling. Remove, let sit for 5 minutes, and serve.

> **TIP** This dish can be served with rice to boost the carb content even more.

Per serving: 445 calories; 67 g carbs; 26 g protein; 12 g fat.

Spicy Maple Hot Chocolate

▶ **1 SERVING**

Following a cool or rainy morning run, few snacks soothe like hot chocolate, which provides the same wallop of carbs and protein as its cooler cousin, chocolate milk (considered by many to be the best post-run recovery drink on the planet). This version takes its cues from south of the border, with a dash of cinnamon and a spicy kick. It doesn't lack for calories, making it perfect for runners who'd prefer to warm up before they chow down.

1 cup 2 percent milk

2 tablespoons unsweetened cocoa powder

2 tablespoons maple syrup

½ teaspoon vanilla extract

¼ teaspoon cinnamon

1 generous pinch of cayenne

1 pinch salt

Add all ingredients to a pot, then whisk over medium heat until well-combined and hot.

Per serving: 267 calories; 47 g carbs; 10 g protein; 6 g fat.

Proteins have been called the "building blocks of life"—and for good reason! Proteins are a part of every cell in your body. They are a major component of muscles, skin, organs, and glands. And they play a role in growth, digestion, tissue repair, immune system response, hormonal messaging, and a multitude of other bodily functions. For runners, protein is essential for muscle repair and recovery post-workout; the International Society of Sport Nutrition warns that inadequate protein increases your risk of injury while training. As enzymes, protein facilitates both aerobic and anaerobic energy production. As MCTs, it shuttles lactate and hydrogen ions out of your cells during intense running. And, as hemoglobin, it ferries the oxygen that makes human life possible. Carbohydrates and fat may fuel your running body, but it's protein that gives form and function to its engine.

WHAT ARE AMINO ACIDS?

Amino acids are themselves referred to as "building blocks," given that they're the building blocks of protein. They're the building blocks' building blocks. Officially, amino acids are a group of organic molecules that comprises a basic amino group, an acidic carboxyl group, and an organic R group (or side chain) that is specific to each amino acid. But you can just think of them as Legos—pieces that join together to create a nifty protein whole.

The US National Library of Medicine lists twenty-one amino acids used by your body to make proteins. Your body can synthesize twelve of them, but the remaining nine must be supplied by food. For this reason, the nine are called "essential amino acids"—as in, it's essential to get them through your diet. Unlike carbs and fats, your body can't store amino acids for future use, so you need to make essential amino acids a regular part of your daily nutrition. Not to panic, however, as most normal diets already include an adequate supply.

Amino acids fall into three groups:

▶ **Essential amino acids:** Your body can't produce these. They include histidine, isoleucine, leucine, lysine, methionine, phenylalanine, threonine, tryptophan, and valine.

▶ **Nonessential amino acids:** Your body produces these itself. They include alanine, asparagine, aspartic acid, and glutamic acid.

▶ **Conditional amino acids:** These normally nonessential amino acids can *become* essential during illness or stress. They include arginine, cysteine, glutamine, glycine, ornithine, proline, serine, and tyrosine.

COMPLETE PROTEINS VERSUS INCOMPLETE PROTEINS

While most of us think of animal sources when we think of protein, plant-based proteins are plentiful, too. It's just that most (not all) proteins from plants are *incomplete*. Protein sources are grouped according to a simple criteria: They either contain all the essential amino acids, or they don't.

A complete protein is also called a high-quality protein. It contains all the essential amino acids in optimal proportions for supporting biological functions in your body. Animal-based foods like meat, poultry, fish, milk, eggs, and cheese are complete protein sources.

An incomplete protein, on the other hand, doesn't contain sufficient amounts of all the essential amino acids. It may be missing one or more of the essential amino acids, or it might just be low in them. Most plant-based sources of protein—like vegetables and grains—are incomplete.

Fortunately, your body doesn't care if you get all your essential amino acids from a single source. It's perfectly happy to have you combine amino acids from multiple sources. This is good news for vegetarians, since few plant-based proteins are complete. But it's good news for meat-eaters, too: Although animal-based proteins are rich in essential amino acids, they're often accompanied by an unhealthy dose of saturated fat. Plant-based proteins are a healthy alternative, offering a variety of other important nutrients without a lot of fat.

NUTRITION DISCUSSION

"Protein powder: miracle shakes or marketing shakedown?"

Protein drinks are part of a sports-nutrition industry that accounts for about $3 billion a year in the United States alone, and they're the most popular supplement for teenage athletes. But are they beneficial? While protein powders are convenient—and according to packaging illustrations, a surefire recipe for the six-packiest abdominal muscles known to mankind—there is a growing body of research that counters the supplement industry's marketing machine. The supplement industry would like you to believe that a lack of protein is all that stands between you and a Mr. or Ms. Olympia title. (And maybe the industry has a sneaky point, given that a 2003 report from the International Olympic Committee found that almost 20 percent of supplements sold in the USA and UK were contaminated with banned, performance-enhancing substances.) But the reality is that most people—athletes and non-athletes alike—already get adequate protein in their diets. Mega-doses measuring many times the recommended daily amount simply give your body more protein than it knows what to do with.

In Chapter 12, "Build Your Running Hormones," we explained how protein intake could be manipulated to trigger a more sustained anabolic state—leading to faster recovery and better adaptation. But that's a far cry from burying your body in a mound of protein powder and hoping to emerge a champion.

Most runners should keep the following factors in mind:

▶ Protein supplements are expensive.
▶ They are not a whole food and lack a full array of nutrients.
▶ They often have artificial ingredients and sugar added to them.
▶ A 2010 *Consumer Reports* study found that 20 percent of tested supplements contained heavy metal (arsenic, cadmium, lead, and mercury) levels exceeding U.S. Pharmacopeia guidelines.

If you're going to use protein supplementation, use only an amount necessary to achieve the desired goal. If you aren't sure what that amount should be, put down the shake and read the rest of this chapter.

COMPLEMENTARY PROTEINS

Complementary proteins are two or more incomplete (plant) proteins that, when combined, result in a complete set of essential amino acids. For example, beans are low in methionine and cysteine, but high in lysine, while grains are low in lysine, but high in methionine and cysteine; eat them together, as many cultures have been doing for generations, and—*ta-da!*—you have a complete plant-based protein.

If you prefer a diet with low meat or no meat, you'll want to become familiar with complementary proteins. Experts previously believed that complementary proteins needed to be eaten at the same meal to successfully combine. But current opinion is that you can reap the full benefit by eating complementary proteins throughout the day. The one exception is protein eaten as part of post-workout recovery. Since this protein must be delivered within a specified window of time (fifteen to thirty minutes post-workout) in order to provide its needed benefit, you'll need to eat complementary proteins together.

Putting together complementary proteins requires you to play matchmaker. Rice and beans are the classic "complete protein" food marriage, but there are plenty of other options. You can pair legumes or dairy with grains, nuts, or seeds. Or you can pair dairy with legumes. Here are some pairings to get you started:

▶ Beans with corn or wheat tortillas
▶ Peanut butter on toast

▶ Whole wheat macaroni and cheese
▶ Bean dip with pretzels or tortilla chips
▶ Tofu with rice
▶ Hummus with whole wheat pita bread
▶ Peanut butter milkshake
▶ Grilled cheese sandwich
▶ Yogurt with nuts or granola
▶ Falafel sandwich
▶ Lentil or bean soup with rice, corn, or bread
▶ Whole grain cereal with milk
▶ Pizza or lasagna!
▶ Pasta salad with feta and chickpeas

Of course, half the fun is thinking up your own combinations. And a little complement will go a long way when it comes to meeting your protein needs.

HOW MUCH PROTEIN DO YOU NEED?

Most Americans get enough protein. But research suggests that athletes require more dietary protein than their couch-potato friends. The International Society of Sports Nutrition (ISSN) echoes this belief, writing in a 2007 commentary: "[The

NUTRITION DISCUSSION

"Quinoa: the superstar seed"

Quinoa (pronounced keh-NO-ah or KEEN-wah) is a relatively recent arrival to the American pantry, but this wee seed has been growing in the Andes and providing plant-based protein for thousands of years. Although grain-like, quinoa is a chenopod, coming from the same family as beets and chard (feel free to impress friends at cocktail parties with that tidbit). And this mild, nutty seed is a rock star of nutrition. Why? Because aside from being quite palatable and easy to prepare, it also contains all of the essential amino acids, something few grains and plants can claim. Of special interest to runners, it's particularly high in both lysine, an amino acid that's important for tissue growth and repair, and magnesium, a mineral linked to improved strength, as well as a reduced risk of type 2 diabetes.

USDA recommendation for] protein intake may be appropriate for non-exercising individuals, but it is likely not sufficient to offset the oxidation of protein/amino acids during exercise . . . nor is it sufficient to provide substrate for lean tissue accretion or for the repair of exercise induced muscle damage."

So what is the USDA's recommendation for protein intake? A measly, by athletes' standards, .8 grams of protein per kilogram (.36 grams per pound) of body weight per day. In contrast, the ISSN urges physically active people to consume 1 to 2 grams of protein per kilogram of body weight per day.

The ISSN breaks down protein need based on activity:

▶ **Endurance exercise:** You'll need 1.0 to 1.6 grams of protein per kilogram (.45 to .72 grams per pound) of body weight daily.
▶ **Intermittent exercise:** For activities that are high-intensity and intermittent in nature (e.g.,soccer, basketball, mixed martial arts, etc.), you'll need 1.4 to 1.7 grams of protein per kilogram (.64 to .77 grams per pound) of body weight daily. It's the increased intensity—and the accompanying increased stress on your muscles—that necessitates additional protein.
▶ **Strength/power exercise:** You'll need even more protein than for endurance sports and intermittent exercise, especially during the initial stages of training and/or during sharp increases in volume. Aim for a range of 1.6 to 2.0 grams of protein per kilogram (.72 to .90 grams per pound) of body weight daily.

To get a feel for the amount of protein in various foods, browse the following list, then try a few recipes steeped in healthy protein.

Food	Grams of Protein
Beef, ground, 85 percent lean, broiled, 3 ounces:	22.04
Beer, 12 fluid ounces:	1.63
Chickpeas, 1 cup:	14.53
Chicken, skinless, roasted, ½ breast:	26.68
Chocolate milk, 1 cup:	8.59
Clams, canned, 3 ounces:	20.61
Cottage cheese, 1 percent milkfat, 1 cup:	28.00
Cinnamon raisin bagel, 4-inch:	8.72
Lentils, cooked, 1 cup:	17.86
Halibut, cooked, ½ fillet:	35.84
Milkshake, vanilla, 16 fluid ounces:	11.22
Pretzels, hard, salted, 10 pretzels:	6.20
Pumpkin seeds, roasted, 1 ounce:	8.46
Refried beans, canned, 1 cup:	13.63
Trail mix, 1 cup:	20.73
Salmon, cooked, ½ fillet:	39.37
Soybeans, green, cooked, 1 cup:	22.23
Spinach, frozen, 1 cup:	7.62
Spinach soufflé, 1 cup:	10.73
Split pea soup, 1 cup:	16.35
Tofu, firm, ¼ block:	6.63
Tuna, yellow fin, cooked 3 ounces:	24.78
Tuna salad, 1 cup:	32.88
Turkey burger, 1 patty:	22.44
Turkey roast, light and dark, 3 ounces:	18.13
Veggie burger, 1 patty:	13.86
White beans, canned, 1 cup:	19.02

(Source: USDA National Nutrient Database for Standard Reference)

Peanut Butter Cup Smoothie

▶ **1 SERVING**

This is a great post-workout snack. One of the secrets to perfect smoothies is using frozen fruit instead of ice. Ice melts and dilutes the flavor and texture; frozen fruit doesn't. Frozen bananas in particular blend into a deliciously smooth and creamy consistency—it's worth peeling, slicing, and freezing some bananas so that you'll always be ready.

1 cup low-fat milk

1 cup nonfat vanilla Greek yogurt

1 frozen banana

2 tablespoons peanut butter

2 tablespoons cocoa powder

Add ingredients to blender, purée until smooth.

Per serving: 343 calories; 44 g carbs; 22 g protein; 11 g fat.

Modern Deviled Eggs Six Ways

▶ **SERVINGS VARY**

Although eggs get a bad rap for their cholesterol, the Harvard School of Public Health notes that eating unhealthy fats has a much larger effect on most people's cholesterol levels than eating food that contains cholesterol. In addition, eggs have nutrients that may help lower the risk for heart disease, including protein, vitamins B12 and D, riboflavin, and folate. Plus protein quality in an egg is so high that scientists often use eggs as the standard for measuring the protein quality of other foods. With that in mind, we present deviled eggs! But not the mayonnaisey classic. These recipes swap the mayo for ingredients that further boost the protein.

For any of the following, place six eggs in a single layer in a saucepan, then cover with cool water. Bring to a boil, cook for 1 minute (medium-sized eggs) or up to 2 minutes (jumbo-sized eggs). Turn off the heat, then let the eggs sit in hot water, covered, for 15 minutes. Remove the eggs from the pan, make a crack in each, and immerse them in cold water until cool. Peel, cut them in half, and place the yolks in a bowl. Then proceed to one of the following, depending on which variation you've chosen to prepare:

Wasabi + Sesame Eggs

Mash the 6 yolks with: ¼ cup plain nonfat Greek yogurt; 1½ teaspoons wasabi; 1 tablespoon sesame seeds; 1 tablespoon soy sauce. Stuff the eggs and top with minced pickled ginger.

Per egg: 82 calories; 1 g carbs; 8 g protein; 6 g fat.

Hummus Eggs

Mash the 6 yolks with: ½ cup hummus; 2 teaspoons olive oil; lemon, hot sauce, and salt to taste. Stuff the eggs and sprinkle with cayenne.

Per egg: 117 calories; 3 g carbs; 8 g protein; 9 g fat.

Salmon + Horseradish Eggs

Mash the 6 yolks with: ¼ cup nonfat Greek yogurt; 1 teaspoon prepared horseradish; ¼ cup minced smoked salmon; fresh dill, salt, and pepper to taste. Stuff the eggs and garnish with more fresh dill.

Per egg: 87 calories; 0 g carbs; 9 g protein; 6 g fat.

Guacamole Eggs

Mash the 6 yolks with: 1 medium avocado; 2 tablespoons salsa; lime and salt to taste. Stuff the eggs and garnish with chopped cilantro.

Per egg: 118 calories; 3 g carbs; 8 g protein; 9 g fat.

Eggs Tonnato

Mash the 6 yolks with: One 5-ounce can of tuna (in water), drained; 6 anchovies; 1 tablespoon capers; 1 tablespoon olive oil; lemon, salt, and pepper to taste. Stuff the eggs and garnish with a few capers.

Per egg: 112 calories; 0 g carbs; 11 g protein; 8 g fat.

Classic, Remixed

Mash 6 yolks with: 1/3 cup low-fat cottage cheese; 1 teaspoon Dijon mustard; sea salt to taste. Stuff the eggs and sprinkle with smoked paprika or cayenne.

Per egg: 91 calories; 1 g carbs; 8 g protein; 7 g fat.

Black Bean and Quinoa Burger

▶ **4 SERVINGS**

A big beef burger may yield more protein per patty than this healthy alternative, but it also yields more calories; per calorie, they actually have similar amounts of protein. And this non-meat option comes with great fiber, vitamins, and nutrients that are sorely lacking in its meaty cousin. Serve as you would a regular burger.

1 small onion

2 cloves garlic

1 can black beans, rinsed and drained

1 egg

1/4 cup roasted red peppers, diced

1/2 teaspoon smoked paprika

1/2 teaspoon cumin

1/2 cup cooked quinoa (follow package directions)

1/4 cup Parmesan cheese, grated

1/4 cup bread crumbs

Salt and pepper

1. Place the onion and garlic in a food processor and pulse until finely chopped. Add half the black beans, egg, red peppers, paprika, and cumin, and blend into a chunky paste.

2. Place the mixture in a large mixing bowl, then add the remaining black beans, quinoa, Parmesan, and bread crumbs. Season with salt and pepper, to taste—add red-pepper flakes or other favorite seasonings here if you like—and mix until well combined.

3. Divide the mixture into four portions and form into patties.

4. Bean burgers can be tricky to work with and respond well to being refrigerated for one hour prior to cooking to make them less likely to crumble. If you want to pan-cook or grill the patties, chill first; if you don't have chilling time, the baking method is for you.

5. To bake: Place the burgers on an oiled baking pan and bake for 20 minutes at 350°F. Flip, then bake them for another 10 minutes.

6. To pan-cook: Place the burgers on a hot oiled pan over medium-low heat and cook for 6 minutes per side, allowing them to get browned and crispy.

Per serving: 206 calories; 31 g carbs; 12 g protein; 5 g fat.

White Bean Blondies with Sea Salt

▶ **16 TWO-INCH SQUARES**

Beans aren't just for tacos and chili. In fact, Asian cultures have been using beans in desserts for ages (think red bean ice cream). Beans are a great way to add protein and fiber to your sweets. This recipe replaces butter, flour, and eggs with, yes, white beans. The result is a rich and gooey blondie with a lot of nutrients for a measly 200 calories.

1 can white beans

½ cup all-natural peanut butter

¼ cup pure maple syrup

2 tablespoons mild molasses

⅓ cup brown sugar

2 teaspoons vanilla

½ teaspoon salt

¼ teaspoon baking powder

¼ teaspoon baking soda

½ cup walnuts

½ cup semi-sweet chocolate chips

Sea salt

1. Preheat the oven to 350°F and lightly oil an 8×8-inch baking pan.

2. Rinse and drain the beans well, then add them, along with all the other ingredients (except the chocolate chips, walnuts, and salt) to a food processor. Purée until smooth.

3. Stir in the chocolate chips and walnuts, reserving a large handful of each. Pour the batter into a prepared pan and smooth the batter. Sprinkle the remaining chocolate and nuts on top, then finish with a sprinkle of sea salt.

4. Cook for 30 minutes or until the top is lightly browned and starting to crisp, and a toothpick inserted in the center comes out clean. Remove the pan from the oven, sprinkle with a little more sea salt, and allow to cool. Cut into 2-inch squares. At this point, they will be slightly on the gooey side; if you prefer them a little firmer, save them for the following day.

Per serving: 200 calories; 24 g carbs; 5 g protein; 9 g fat.

Does your inner Homer Simpson dream longingly of donuts? Do you find skim milk as appetizing as water infused with chalk? In a world without jean sizes, would you opt for potato chips over boiled kale? If you answered "yes" to any of these questions, congratulations! You like dietary fat, and that makes you a normal human being. The human fondness for fat is an evolutionary trait that helped steer our ancestors toward the energy-dense foods that they needed to survive.

In the modern age, however, with fat as readily available as packaged snacks in a mini-mart, it's important to temper evolution with a careful consideration of what kind of fat—and how much—you'll want to include in your diet.

WHAT ARE FATS?

Dietary fats are the third macronutrient (carbs and protein were the first two) that fuels your body. Consisting primarily of glycerides (with other lipids in minor quantities), fats comprise a large group of water-insoluble compounds. Fat has spent much of recent history as Public Enemy Number One, but that's an unfair assessment. Fat not only provides energy, it's essential to the proper function of your body.

Fat is the most concentrated source of dietary energy. It packs nine calories per gram, compared to four calories per gram for protein and carbohydrates. Fat also makes food taste good. Really good. And that's because we're hardwired to like it. Our taste for fat is thought to be a consequence of evolutionary pressures to select energy-dense foods necessary for survival. In fact, foods that are high in fat are instinctively more pleasing than low-energy-density fruits and vegetables. In Chapter 11 of *Fat Detection: Taste, Texture, and Post Ingestive Effects*, Andrew Dewnowski and Eva Almiron-Roig write: "The hedonic response to fat seems to be strongly linked to the endogenous opioid reward system." In other words, the brain rewards our choice of fat with a little blast of euphoria. French fries, please!

The problem is that our bodies developed this evolutionary craving for fat when it was scarce and hard to obtain. Nowadays, we're up to our ears in fatty foods, but abundance hasn't tempered our instinctive desire to keep eating it, and eating it, and eating it. The World Health Organization lists obesity and being overweight as the fifth-leading risk for global deaths, claiming at least 2.8 million lives each year. All told, one and a half billion adults in the world are overweight, with half a billion of those characterized as obese.

WHAT ARE THE BENEFITS OF FATS?

The argument can be made that we love fat too much, but it's inarguable that we need it. Fat stores energy, protects your vital organs, and helps proteins do their jobs. It keeps your skin and hair supple, helps you absorb important fat-soluble vitamins (A, D, E, and K), and triggers chemical reactions that help regulate growth, immune function, reproduction, and metabolism.

Fat also contains essential fatty acids—like the essential amino acids, these cannot be synthesized by your body and must be included in your diet. The two essential fatty acids, linoleic and linolenic acids, are required for ensuring proper brain function, keeping inflammation in check, and minimizing blood clotting.

Fat is the superstar when it comes to fueling low-to-moderate-intensity exercise, which includes the majority of your distance runs. (See Chapter 10 for more on lipolysis, the process by which fat is transformed into energy.)

Bottom line: Runners need fats. (Everyone does!) But there are good fats and bad fats. And then there are *really* bad fats. Being able to tell them apart and then develop a fat strategy is the key to including healthy fats in your diet.

UNSATURATED FATS

According to the Center for Science in the Public Interest, the average person now consumes 20 pounds more total fat per year than he or she did in 1970. And a recent report from the Department of Agriculture pegged daily American fat intake from added fats and oils at 645 calories—and that's *before* including fats naturally found in food. That's a lot of fat—so it's important to know which fats are "good" and which are "bad." All fats provide the same nine calories of energy per gram, but some fats have a chemical structure that makes them healthier.

Unsaturated fats have one or more double bonds in the fatty-acid chain and are considered to be good fats. Double bonds in unsaturated fats are carbon-to-carbon links that create "kinks" (bends) in the fatty-acid chain and pack fewer hydrogen molecules (i.e., they're less saturated with hydrogen); this makes them stack together less tightly than the un-kinked and more solid saturated fats. You can generally tell an unsaturated fat by its liquid consistency at room temperature (e.g., olive oil). Studies have found that unsaturated fats decrease levels of harmful low-density lipoprotein (LDL) cholesterol and increase levels of beneficial high-density lipoprotein (HDL) cholesterol. LDL cholesterol, or "bad" cholesterol (cue "boo hiss" sound effect), is a fatty substance that collects in arterial walls, contributing to the formation of plaques. An accumulation of these

NUTRITION DISCUSSION

"Five favorite fats"

To get the most out of your allotted daily fat calories, make them healthy LDL cholesterol-busting fats like these:

▶ **Avocados:** The 30 grams of fat that come packed in an avocado are monosaturated, meaning that an avocado is as good for you as it is delicious!

▶ **Eggs:** Given a bum rap when they were labeled cholesterol bombs, eggs are now thought to improve heart health. Current thinking is that it's the saturated fat content in food, not the dietary cholesterol, that leads to high LDL cholesterol levels—and an egg has only 1.5 grams of saturated fat. A phenomenal source of quality protein, eggs also have choline, an essential micronutrient that helps regulate the brain, nervous system, and cardiovascular system.

▶ **Olive oil:** Ever wonder why people in olive oil–rich Mediterranean countries live to be so old? Countless studies have concluded that olive oil can reduce the risk of heart disease, high blood pressure, and certain types of cancer. Include it as one of your daily fats—and may you live an exceedingly long life! (See Chapter 23 for more on the Mediterranean diet.)

▶ **Nuts:** Because nuts contain unsaturated fats, including omega-3 fatty acids, people who eat nuts are generally thinner, less likely to develop type 2 diabetes, and have a reduced risk of heart disease. You'd be nuts not to eat nuts.

▶ **Fatty fish:** Oily fish such as salmon, tuna, sardines, mackerel, and trout are chock-full of omega-3 fatty acids. The American Heart Association recommends eating at least two servings of fatty fish per week.

plaques leads to atherosclerosis, a disease characterized by narrowed arteries and increased risk of heart attack, stroke, and other significant health problems. HDL cholesterol, or "good" cholesterol ("Yay!"), is thought to grab bad cholesterol and whisk it away to the liver, where it can be properly disposed of.

Unsaturated fats come in two types:

▶ **Monounsaturated fats:** These contain one double bond. Eating foods rich in monounsaturated fats improves blood cholesterol levels and may benefit insulin levels and blood sugar control. Good sources include olive, peanut, and canola oils; avocados; nuts such as almonds, hazelnuts, and pecans; and seeds such as pumpkin and sesame.

▶ **Polyunsaturated fats:** These contain more than one double bond and are found primarily in plant-based foods and oils. Consuming foods rich in polyunsaturated fats improves blood cholesterol levels, decreasing risk of heart disease (and possibly of type 2 diabetes).

Polyunsaturated fats can be further broken down into two types:

1. **Omega-3 fatty acids:** These essential fatty acids appear to reduce inflammation and lower blood pressure. According to the Harvard School of Public Health, omega-3s also decrease the risk of coronary artery disease and stroke, protect against irregular heartbeats, and help control lupus and rheumatoid arthritis. Omega-3s are predominantly found in fatty fish (fish oil), but they can also be found in chia seeds, walnuts, leafy greens, and the oils from flaxseed, canola, and soybeans.

2. **Omega-6 polyunsaturated fatty acids:** These essential fatty acids (including linoleic acid) play a role in brain function, metabolism, reproduction, and the growth of bones, skin, and hair. Some Omega-6s have been associated with inflammation, although linoleic acid broken down several times to a final product (DGLA) actually reduces inflammation. Dietary sources include soybean oil, sunflower seed oil, most vegetable oils, eggs, nuts, cereal, coconut, and others.

SATURATED FATS

If you pay any attention to health or diet literature (or nutrition sound bites on the evening news), then you've heard bad things about saturated fats. The reason: Eating foods that contain them raises your level of "bad" LDL cholesterol. Not only that, but studies have found that some saturated fats found in dairy and meat—like palmitic acid and myristic acid—induce inflammation and damage your arteries. Saturated fats are generally solid at room temperature—for example, the marbled fat in a steak—and come primarily from animal sources, although they're also found in plant sources like palm oil, coconut oil, and cocoa butter.

But not all saturated fats live up to their bad reputation. Stearic acid, found in dark chocolate (and also meat), may be harmless. And coconut oil, long considered a bad fat, contains lauric acid, a fatty acid that actually *increases* levels of good HDL cholesterol, thereby reducing the risk of atherosclerosis.

Of course, it's still a good idea to avoid foods that are high in saturated fat. A rule of thumb when looking at a nutrition panel is that a Daily Value of 5 percent is low (although "0" is optimal) and 20 percent is high.

NUTRITION DISCUSSION

TRANS FAT

Trans fats (or *trans fatty acids*) are the result of hydrogenation, a process in which hydrogen is added to unsaturated fatty acids to make them more resistant to rancidity. Trans fats not only act as preservatives, they are also easier to spread and have a higher smoking point than unsaturated fats, which makes them easier to cook with. After being enthusiastically received by the processed-food industry at the turn of the twentieth century, they were added to a bevy of packaged foods, with Crisco introducing the first hydrogenated, all-vegetable oil shortening in 1911. While there were concerns dating to the 1950s about trans fat's connection to an increased rate of heart disease, it wasn't until the 1990s that the worst was confirmed. Trans fat was shown to raise bad LDL cholesterol, lower HDL cholesterol, increase the risk of heart disease and stroke, and possibly increase the risk of type 2 diabetes.

Despite efforts to reduce trans-fat consumption by way of label changes, reformulation of foods, and even state and local bans, trans-fatty acids are still found in many foods, including fried foods, vegetable shortenings, donuts, cookies, crackers, frozen pizzas, microwave popcorn, canned frosting, snack foods, margarines, and coffee creamers. And while trans-fat consumption has dropped, Americans still eat about 5.8 grams of trans fat per day. According to the Centers for Disease Control, further reducing trans-fat consumption could prevent 10,000–20,000 heart attacks and 3,000–7,000 coronary heart disease deaths per year in the United States.

RUNNING ON FAT

The world is rife with heated debates. The Rolling Stones versus the Beatles. Ginger versus Mary Ann. And, of course, the low-carb versus high-carb diet debate among runners.

Runners have long favored a high-carb, low-fat diet. Anything over 20 percent fat was rejected as inappropriate for the energy demands (including post-workout glycogen replacement) of running. But studies over the past two decades have many endurance athletes reevaluating this axiom of fueling. The new, low-carb view is this: During running (or any exercise), we utilize two main energy stores, muscle glycogen (carbohydrates) and fat; since glycogen is limited (as anyone who's bonked in a marathon can attest) and fat is virtually unlimited, the runner who trains his or her body to burn fat will last longer in an endurance event.

A 2000 study from the University of Buffalo compared twelve male and thirteen female runners who spent four weeks each on a 16 percent fat diet and then a 31 percent fat diet. In a test to exhaustion, the runners saw a 14 percent improvement in performance on the 31 percent fat diet compared to the 16 percent fat diet. VO_2 max wasn't affected by diet. A 2001 study by Venkatraman, et al., produced almost the same results. Fourteen experienced runners spent four weeks each on three successive diets: first a 15 percent fat diet, then a 30 percent fat diet, and finally a 40 percent fat diet. At 30 percent fat, the runners improved their times to exhaustion (at 80 percent of VO_2 max) over low-fat testing by 19 percent (women) and 24 percent (men). Their times at 40 percent fat were similar to those on the 30 percent fat diet.

In another study from the University of Buffalo, by Gerlach, et al., in 2008, a link was found between low fat consumption in female runners and injury risk. Fat intake was shown to correctly predict 64 percent of future injuries. The most common injuries were stress fractures, tendinitis, and iliotibial band syndrome. Deficiencies in the fat-soluble vitamins K and E were also recorded. The study concluded that female runners on low-fat diets (<30

percent) were 250 percent more likely to get injured. The study suggested that runners consume a 36 percent fat diet to avoid injury.

But before you jump on the fat bandwagon, consider that a 2004 study of elite Kenyan runners—the top distance runners in the world—found that their diets consisted of just 13.4 percent fat. And most of the world's top distance runners (5K through the marathon) eat a lot like the Kenyans do.

Bottom line: While ultra-runners and triathletes—or *anyone* competing for four hours or longer in an endurance event—would be wise to consider fat as a primary energy source (see Chapter 10 for more on fat-loading), the rest of us would do well to aim for a moderate amount of fat in our diets. If you do consider trying fat for a fuel, remember that it is slow to digest. It can take up to six hours before it's converted into usable energy. And don't forget that shorter races (5K and under) rely almost exclusively on carbohydrates.

HOW MUCH FAT CAN (SHOULD) YOU EAT?

Really, this is all you want to know anyway, right? Here are the most recent recommendations from the Dietary Guidelines for Americans:

▶ **Total Fat:** Limit total fat intake to 20 to 35 percent of your daily calories. Based on a 2,000-calorie-a-day diet, this amounts to about 44 to 78 grams of total fat a day.

▶ **Monosaturated fat:** No specific amount is recommended, but eat foods rich in this healthy fat while staying within your total fat allowance.

▶ **Polyunsaturated fat and omega-3 fatty acids:** Same as above.

▶ **Saturated fat:** Limit saturated fat to no more than 10 percent of your total calories.

Limit to 7 percent to further reduce your risk of heart disease. Based on a 2,000-calorie-a-day diet, a 10 percent limit amounts to about 22 grams of saturated fat a day, while 7 percent is about 15 grams. Saturated-fat intake counts toward your total daily allowance of fat.

▶ **Trans fat:** No specific amount is recommended, but the lower the better. The American Heart Association recommends limiting trans fat to no more than 1 percent of your total daily calories. For most people, this is less than 2 grams a day.

Of course, few runners training for a marathon—or even for their local 5K—are making do on 2,000 calories a day. So you'll have to adjust the above figures to match your personal calorie consumption. Injury-prone runners (or runners who are simply concerned about injuries) will want to aim for the high end of the recommended fat intake. On the other hand, runners prepping for an upcoming race that's marathon-length or shorter need to remember that carbohydrates will be their primary energy source; your body becomes most efficient at using the energy source it's accustomed to relying upon during training.

Cold Avocado Soup

▶ **4 SERVINGS**

This might best be described as a guacamole smoothie, but since that sounds gross, we'll instead put it in a bowl, use a spoon, and call it soup. Just like that, it goes from disgusting to delectable! It only takes a few minutes to prepare and will give you both a nice dash of protein and a healthy boost of fat.

3 or 4 ripe avocados, pitted and peeled (about 2 cups)

2 cups vegetable broth

1 cup nonfat Greek yogurt

½ cup cilantro, chopped

Salt

Cayenne or hot sauce

2 tablespoons fresh lime juice

Put the avocados, vegetable broth, yogurt, and half the cilantro in a blender. Purée until thick and creamy. Add salt, cayenne, and lime to taste. Chill for 2 hours. Taste again and adjust the seasonings, garnish with extra cilantro, and serve cold.

Per serving: 225 calories; 14 g carbs; 8 g protein; 17 g fat.

Sweet and Spicy Nuts

▶ **16 ¼-CUP SERVINGS**

Nuts are high in calories, so we're often warned to steer clear. But those calories come from healthy fats that our bodies need. Eating them in moderation is the key. Making them sweet and spicy like in this recipe is both a blessing and a curse—there's enough sweetness and kick to keep you from eating too many, but on the other hand, there's enough sweetness and kick that you may not be able to stop eating them. Be strong. And if you add a cup of dried cherries or other fruit to the mix, be extra strong!

2 egg whites

4 cups unsalted nuts of your choice (almonds, cashews, pistachios, pecans, you name it; can be roasted or raw)

½ cup raw (or brown) sugar

¾ teaspoon cayenne pepper (or more, depending on your heat preference)

1 teaspoon ground ginger

Sea salt to taste

1. Preheat the oven to 250°F.

2. Add the egg whites to a large bowl, add a dash of water, and stir until frothy. Add the remaining ingredients. Spread the mixture on a parchment-lined baking sheet (if you don't have parchment, just oil the baking sheet liberally).

3. Bake for 40 minutes, stirring occasionally. Remove from oven and reduce the oven temperature to 200°F, then return the sheet to the oven and cook for another 20 minutes or until crisp. Remove the sheet from the oven, stir again to dislodge the nuts before they stick, and let cool completely on the sheet.

Per serving: 260 calories; 21 g carbs; 7 g protein; 19 g fat.

BUILD YOUR RUNNING DIET—PROTEIN, CARBS, CALORIES, AND NUTRITION

Lemon Risotto with Avocado and Salmon

▶ 2 SERVINGS

The word "risotto" can bring to mind slaving over a stove—stirring, stirring, and stirring. And, yes, there is some stirring here, but it's not going to kill you. Risotto is typically made with Italian Arborio rice, but short grain rice works beautifully and, best yet, if you parboil the rice first for 20 minutes, the risotto only takes another 20 minutes after that. Be sure to use a vegetable stock with a flavor you like, since it will be a predominant taste in the rice. You may gasp at the fat content, but it's intentional—those grams are courtesy of health-promoting monounsaturated fats and the all-important fat from fish.

12 ounces salmon, divided into 2 pieces

1 cup short grain brown rice

2 large shallots (or 1 medium onion or large cleaned leek), diced

2 tablespoons olive oil

4 cups warm vegetable broth

Salt and pepper

1 lemon

Fresh mint, some leaves chopped, some leaves reserved whole for garnish

1 Haas avocado

⅔ cup green peas (frozen are great)

1. Boil the rice in water for 20 minutes, then drain in a colander.

2. Prepare the salmon. Place the cleaned filets on a broiler pan and rub with coarse sea salt and pepper.

3. Sauté the shallots in olive oil over medium until they start to soften, 3–4 minutes. Add parboiled rice and cook for a few minutes. Add ⅓ cup of the broth and stir until the liquid is absorbed. Repeat adding broth until it is all absorbed, about 20 minutes. Add a generous amount of salt and pepper and stir in the peas and chopped mint.

4. In between stirring, pat some sea salt on top of the salmon. Place the pan under the broiler on the upper rack and broil for 8–10 minutes, or until the fish has browned on top and cooked through.

5. Slice the lemon in half lengthwise and squeeze one half into the risotto. Use a zester or vegetable peeler to make lemon zest with the other half for garnish.

6. Plate the risotto, top with the salmon and avocado, scatter mint and lemon zest on top, and serve.

Per serving: 575 calories; 36 g carbs; 43 g protein; 26 g fat.

Tangerine and Almond Cake

▶ 8–10 SERVINGS

This slinky minx of a cake is a mix between a Tunisian citrus almond cake and Nigella Lawson's clementine cake—both lovely, flourless cakes that rely on almonds for their structure. It's a dense citrusy cake that resembles a steamed pudding. Although easy to make, it requires simmering tangerines for two hours, which is lovely for scenting the house but may be prohibitive time-wise for some—for those under time constraint, there's a quicker hack included in the instructions.

5 tangerines (or a quart of extra-pulp orange juice)

6 eggs

1 cup raw sugar

2 tablespoons honey

2⅓ cups thinly sliced almonds

1 teaspoon baking powder

1. Place the whole tangerines in a pot, cover with water, and bring to a boil. Reduce heat and simmer for 2 hours. Drain, let cool. Cut the tangerines in half and remove the seeds. For a shorter alternative to this step, take extra-pulp orange juice and strain the pulp out, reserving the juice. Add the juice back to the pulp until you have 16 ounces; this should work as a good equivalent.

2. Preheat the oven to 375°F. Lightly oil an 8-inch cake pan and line with parchment paper.

3. In a food processor, add the eggs, sugar, honey, almonds, and baking powder, and mix until the almonds are finely ground. Add the tangerines, peel and all, and process until smooth. The batter will be runnier than most cake batters, but that's fine.

4. Pour the batter into a pan and bake for 45 minutes. Remove from the oven and cover with aluminum foil to prevent the top from burning, then continue cooking for another 15 minutes. The cake is done when a toothpick inserted in the center comes out clean. Allow to cool, then serve.

Per serving: 345 calories; 36 g carbs; 11 g protein; 19 g fat.

For thousands of years, scurvy was the scourge of sailors, explorers, and people living in famine-afflicted and war-torn regions. One of the oldest diseases known to humankind—characterized by loose teeth, bleeding eyes, fever, convulsions, bone pain, malaise, and finally death—it cost one million seamen their lives during the seventeenth and eighteenth centuries and claimed 10,000 men as recently as the California Gold Rush. Yet, scurvy is also one of the simplest ailments to cure. It's a nutrient deficiency, a lack of vitamin C. An orange a day keeps scurvy away.

These days, we are inundated with research detailing the minutiae of every vitamin and mineral known to man. We are equally awash with marketing and media coercing us to purchase these vitamins and minerals. There's a magic-bullet supplement for everything that ails you, from osteoarthritis to cancer to the process of aging itself. It's hard to resist. Who doesn't dream of a Jetsons' diet in which everything we need is delivered in a perfectly proportioned, tidy little pill? Unfortunately, it's not 2062, and finding real nutrition hidden among supermarket shelves stacked high with supplements and processed foods sometimes seems like a treasure hunt. But fear not, matey! This chapter is your map.

NUTRITION DISCUSSION

"The scary side of supplements"

Athletes often attempt to fortify their diets with supplements. After all, it can't hurt, right? Set aside that kind of thinking in the faulty-logic file. Here's why:

- ▶ **Supplements aren't regulated:** Unlike food, prescription medication, and over-the-counter medicines, dietary supplements are not reviewed by the government before they're marketed. The FDA can only take action after unsafe supplements reach the shelves, and it's very difficult to remove them once they're there.
- ▶ **Some supplements are really prescription drugs:** Some supplement makers spike their supplements with prescription drugs. Since 2008, there have been 400 recalls of spiked products, most marketed for bodybuilding, sexual enhancement, and weight loss.
- ▶ **Supplements are strong:** Many contain active ingredients that have strong biological effects in the body, making them potentially harmful and even life-threatening.
- ▶ **Supplements can cause mineral and vitamin overdose:** Taking too many minerals or vitamins can create serious imbalances. For example, zinc supplements can reduce the absorption of iron, magnesium, copper, calcium, and chromium. And if you're eating fortified foods, like breakfast cereal and PowerBars, while taking a mineral supplement, you're almost certainly getting too much of something (and some people have adverse reactions to too much calcium or iron).
- ▶ **Supplements cause complaints:** *Consumer Reports* notes that between 2007 and 2012, the FDA received supplement-related complaints describing more than 10,300 serious outcomes, including 115 deaths and more than 2,100 hospitalizations, 1,000 serious injuries or illnesses, 900 emergency room visits, and 4,000 other medical events. On top of all that, the FDA suspects that most problems are never reported.

WHAT ARE NUTRIENTS?

Nutrients include *all* of the ingredients in food (plus water and oxygen!) that nourish your running body. We've already discussed protein, carbohydrates, and fats. In this chapter we'll focus on vitamins and minerals.

Vitamins

Vitamins are essential organic compounds (we get them from plants and animals) that function as regulators of protein, carbohydrate, and fat metabolism—and that play a critical role in growth, tissue maintenance, and, as noted earlier, disease prevention, among other functions. We use vitamins during energy production, but they are not sources of energy themselves.

Vitamins fall into two categories: fat-soluble and water-soluble. Fat-soluble vitamins (including A, D, E, and K) are absorbed with ingested dietary fat and are stored in moderate amounts in your body. They are vital to maintaining normal metabolic and biochemical functions. Water-soluble vitamins, on the other hand, need to dissolve in water before your body can absorb them. There are nine water-soluble vitamins, including C- and B-complex, which your body must use before they exit via urine.

Minerals

Minerals are inorganic elements that occur naturally. We get minerals from plants (which absorb minerals from water and soil), animals, dairy, fish, poultry, nuts, and a variety of food sources. They're important because they influence all aspects of energy metabolism. Your body requires large amounts of major minerals (e.g., calcium, potassium, and magnesium) and smaller amounts of trace minerals (e.g., chromium, iron, and zinc) to maintain health.

SUPPLEMENTS

As a species, we've done pretty well over the last few million years when it comes to food. We've learned to eat nutritious things, learned to avoid poisonous things, and somehow figured out how to cook and eat lobster and artichokes. Smart us!

But sometime during the last century the food industry galumphed into our collective healthy-eating conscious and sprinkled confuse-and-forget powder everywhere. The result is that three-fourths of world food sales now involve processed foods. We satisfy our desire for fruit with artificially colored high-fructose corn syrup concoctions, replace vegetables with snack foods, and refine away nutrient-rich grains until we're left with empty calories. What people eat is increasingly driven by a few multinational food companies, who seem bent on pushing fat, sugar, salt, and artificial additives on us—resulting in foods that are easy to produce, easy to ship, and, best of all, addictive. *Ka-ching!*

And thus, the supplement industry was born: We buy food that has had the nutrients processed out of it, and then we buy concentrated nutrients in pills. And somehow we think there's something healthy about that. Doesn't that seem a little odd?

Also, it's not as if supplements return all the nutrients removed by processing. Actual foods nourish better than supplements. Food contains health-protective substances such as phytochemicals, fiber, and compounds to protect against disease.

As a runner, you're specifically targeted by marketing strategies meant to convince you that top performance can only be achieved with supplements. And the marketing works: Research shows that 30–50 percent of elite and non-elite endurance athletes use supplements. Almost 100 percent of triathletes use them. That's a big boon for America's multi-billion-dollar supplements industry. But do supplements really work? Not according to the American College of Sports Medicine, which states emphatically: "[There] is no scientific evidence to support the general use of vitamin and mineral supplements to improve athletic performance. Only athletes with a defined nutrient deficiency or deficiencies will benefit from supplementation of the limiting nutrient."

VITAMINS AND MINERALS

Getting your nutrients from foods instead of pills requires some work. But don't worry. Eating is fun work! But first you'll need to know which nutrients are especially important for runners.

Vitamin B6

B6 plays a role in producing red blood cells, normalizing neural function, and metabolizing proteins—the latter making it important for building muscle. There are claims that B6 decreases joint pain and muscle fatigue after intense exercise, and a 2003 study found that patients with painful rheumatoid arthritis were low in B6. Although B6 deficiency is rare, birth control pills deplete B6; women on oral contraceptives should keep that in mind. If you use a B6 supplement, be aware that too much can lead to nerve damage.

> **Good sources:** *Baked potatoes, bananas, chicken, tuna, salmon, and fortified cereals.*

Vitamin B12

This "energy" vitamin has a reputation for delivering a quick boost, but it's main function is to keep your body's neurons and red blood cells healthy. Earning its rep, it's also essential for energy metabolism, and it plays a role in the replication of DNA. Most people get enough B12 in their food. Since it's found naturally in animal-based foods, however, strict vegans may become deficient.

> **Good sources:** *Animal products, dairy, and eggs. Many vegan products are fortified with it (check the labels).*

Vitamin C

Also known as ascorbic acid, vitamin C is important for its role as an antioxidant (protecting cells from damage caused by oxidation) and, of course, for preventing scurvy. For runners, it supports joints, reduces recovery times, and may speed recovery post–hard workout. Your body needs C to make collagen (connective tissue), improve absorption of iron from plant-based foods, and possibly boost the immune system.

> **Good sources:** *Red and green pepper, citrus fruits, kiwifruit, broccoli, strawberries, cantaloupe, baked potatoes, and tomatoes.*

Vitamin D

Vitamin D is calcium's best friend. Without D, absorption of calcium suffers, and so do your bones. Runners low in D have an increased risk of stress fracture. After Deena Kastor broke a bone in her foot during the Olympic marathon in Beijing, it was discovered that she was high in calcium but low in vitamin D. Vitamin D also helps muscles to move, nerves to send impulses, and the immune system to fight off bacteria and viruses. Few foods naturally contain D, so many of the foods you can buy are fortified with it. Your body also makes vitamin D when your skin is directly exposed to the sun. A 2009 study in the Archives of Internal Medicine found that only 23 percent of adolescents and adults in the United States had at least the minimum levels of vitamin D associated with good health. And a 2008 study from the Cooper

Clinic in Dallas reported that a statistically equivalent 75 percent of runners averaging twenty-plus miles a week had low vitamin D levels. If you're worried about your D level, ask your doctor for a test. It's also suggested that you get five to thirty minutes of sun exposure between 10:00 AM and 3:00 PM; the catch is that you can't use sunscreen, since sunscreen blocks the process (check with your doctor for risk factors!).

Good sources: *Wild salmon, tuna, mackerel, sardines, shrimp, eggs, beef liver, and irradiated mushrooms. Almost all milk in the USA is fortified with D, as are many breakfast cereals and some brands of orange juice.*

Vitamin K

You don't hear much about vitamin K, but it's another bone vitamin. People with higher levels of vitamin K have greater bone density, while low levels of vitamin K have been associated with osteoporosis. Research has shown that vitamin K improves bone health and reduces risk of bone fractures, particularly in postmenopausal women. For runners, studies suggest that vitamin K boosts bone health for both male and female athletes. In addition, a 2006 study by the American College of Rheumatology linked low blood plasma levels of vitamin K to an increased risk of osteoarthritis in both the hands and knees, with vitamin K theorized to have "several potential effects on articular cartilage and subchondral bone" that may thwart the development of the disease—one that has ended many a runner's days on the roads. To ensure that you don't become deficient in this vitamin, make sure to eat your leafy greens—kale, spinach, and collard greens are packed with it.

Good sources: *Dark leafy greens, broccoli, Brussels sprouts, prunes, asparagus, avocado, tuna, and blueberries.*

Calcium

Your body needs this essential mineral for bone strength. But it also uses calcium during muscle contraction, blood pressure regulation, nervous system function, hormone secretion, and enzyme regulation. For athletes, calcium maintains bone health, decreases the risk of stress fractures (if you're not getting enough calcium from your diet, your body swipes it from your bones) and may increase lean body mass. Menopausal women are often deficient, but calcium supplements might not be the answer. A 2012 study followed almost 24,000 adults for an average of eleven years, concluding that regular users of calcium supplements had an 86 percent increase in heart attack risk compared to those who didn't use supplements.

Good sources: *Milk, yogurt, and cheese are the best. Also, kale, broccoli, Chinese cabbage, canned sardines and salmon (with bones), and fortified sources such as some orange juices, cereals, soy and nut milks, and tofu. (See "10 foods for happy bones" in Chapter 6 for a list of foods particularly well-suited for bone health.)*

Iron

The World Health Organization lists iron deficiency as the number one nutritional disorder in the world. Iron gives blood its red color and is found in the hemoglobin that transports oxygen. It plays an important role in growth, immune function, metabolism, preventing anemia, and other vital functions. For runners, a deficiency can result in fatigue, poor performance, and reduced immune system function. On the other hand, excess iron can turn toxic and cause death. Although deficiency is not a severe problem in wealthy, industrialized countries, it does happen (more frequently among vegetarians and physically active women, the latter of whom are already at risk because of menstruation and a tendency to eat fewer calories, lowering iron intake from food). If you notice unexplained fatigue, you may want to request a blood test for iron.

Good sources: *See sidebar, "15 iron-packed food sources."*

Potassium

Potassium is an electrolyte that pairs up with sodium to regulate both your cell membrane potential (i.e., the sodium-potassium pump, critically important for both nerve and muscle function) and your fluid balance. Although abundant in most diets, potassium is depleted when you sweat. A potassium deficiency can leave you fatigued and with muscle weakness or cramping. Low levels can also affect glucose metabolism and lead to elevated blood sugar. Most sports drinks address potassium loss (e.g., Gatorade Endurance Formula has 140 mg of potassium). But take too much and potassium can upset fluid balance and may lead to abnormal and dangerous heart rhythms.

Good sources: *Bananas, baked potatoes, sweet potatoes, winter squash, milk, yogurt, cantaloupe, pinto beans, salmon, soy products, peas, prunes, and spinach.*

NUTRITION DISCUSSION

"15 iron-packed food sources"

Food has two types of iron: heme iron and non-heme iron. Heme iron is derived from hemoglobin and is found in animal-based foods, notably meat and mollusks. Non-heme iron is found in plant-based foods and isn't as easily absorbed as heme iron. Heme iron is absorbed two to three times more efficiently than non-heme iron. The RDA for iron in males aged eighteen and older is 8 mg daily; females aged nineteen to fifty should get 18 mg daily, and 8 mg daily for females fifty-one and older. Foods high in heme and non-heme iron:

1. Clams, canned, drained, 3 ounces: 23.8 mg
2. Fortified dry cereals, 1 ounce: 18 to 21.1 mg
3. Oysters, cooked, 3 ounces: 10.2 mg
4. Organ meats, cooked, 3 ounces: 5.2 to 9.9 mg
5. Fortified oatmeal, 1 packet: 4.9 to 8.1 mg
6. Soybeans, cooked, ½ cup: 4.4 mg
7. Pumpkin seeds, roasted, 1 ounce: 4.2 mg
8. White beans, canned, ½ cup: 3.9 mg
9. Blackstrap molasses, 1 tablespoon: 3.5 mg
10. Lentils, cooked, ½ cup: 3.3 mg
11. Spinach, cooked fresh, ½ cup: 3.2 mg
12. Beef, chuck, blade roast, 3 ounces: 3.1 mg
13. Beef, bottom round, 3 ounces: 2.8 mg
14. Kidney beans, cooked, ½ cup: 2.6 mg
15. Sardines, canned, 3 ounces: 2.5 mg

Sodium

We are constantly being alerted to the dangers of sodium—too much is linked to high blood pressure, and most Americans eat way too much of it. But at the same time, it's essential for regulating your body's fluid balance, which in turn helps control blood pressure and blood volume. Also, your muscles need it to function, and your nerves need it to fire. When you train, it's the major electrolyte in your sweat, and some people can lose as much as 3,000 mg per hour during an especially sweaty workout (keep in mind that the RDA is 2,300 mg). If you're a salty sweater—if you've noticed excessive dried salt on your skin after running in the heat—then you might consider a salty snack before or during a run. Sports drinks that contain sodium are an option as well. Endurance athletes who train more than five hours at a time should also consider a salty snack somewhere in the middle. Loss of salt during a run can trigger cramping, but it's also connected to hyponatremia, a rare and potentially fatal condition in which overhydration leads to low blood-sodium levels. Also called water intoxication, it usually results from drinking excessive amounts of plain water while sweating heavily (think endurance events).

Good sources: *Just about everything in the American diet. But aim for healthy sources like olives, tomato juice, low-fat cottage cheese, pretzels, and salted nuts.*

WATER

Just as a houseplant suffers the effects of too much or too little water, so do we (minus the root rot). Too little water leads to dehydration. And too much water can lead to hyponatremia (see above). Luckily, we can test our hydration status in two easy ways:

▶ **Color and amount of urine:** Clear and plentiful says hydrated. Dark and concentrated says dehydrated.

▶ **Body weight change:** Check the percentage of your body weight change before and after exercise. Well hydrated is -1 percent to +1 percent; minimal dehydration is -1 percent to -3 percent; significant dehydration is -3 percent to -5 percent; and serious dehydration is >-5 percent.

During training and competition, remember to drink to thirst. A little dehydrated is safe and will help you to achieve the full training stimulus and adaptation. That said, never push dehydration, and try to fully rehydrate within a couple of hours post-exercise.

SOME SUPPLEMENTAL INFORMATION

If increased nutrients are your goal, there are a few options that don't include pills, powders, or potions. Here are three:

1. **Figs:** Bananas and apples may win the popularity contest, but figs are like the quiet girl next door who turns out to be a salsa-dancing neurosurgeon. And dried figs are even more remarkable. Figs have a tremendous amount of fiber, a thousand times more calcium than other common fruits (by weight), 80 percent more potassium than bananas, more iron than most other fruits, and a potent blast of magnesium—all for around 30 calories a fig.

2. **Nutritional yeast:** Yes, for some this may sound more like a condition you'd want to avoid than something you'd willingly put into your mouth. But nutritional

yeast—grown on molasses, then deactivated and made into a powder—is the culinary salvation of legions of vegans. With its nutty, cheesy flavor, it adds a punch of umami (the savory fifth flavor) and is a good swap for Parmesan cheese. Vegans love its high-quality protein and B-complex vitamins—it's almost always fortified with B12. And it's delicious! Try it on popcorn, pizza, pesto, and on pasta in place of cheese.

3. **Epsom salt bath:** Many runners enjoy an occasional dunk in an Epsom salt bath, and it turns out it has nutritional value, too! Epsom salt consists of magnesium and sulfate, and soaking in an Epsom salt bath is a safe way to boost your body's levels of both (they're readily absorbed through the skin). Most Americans get less magnesium than recommended. Not good, since magnesium plays an important role in more than 300 enzyme systems regulating biochemical reactions in the body (e.g., protein synthesis, muscle and nerve function, and blood sugar control). So add two cups of Epsom salt to warm water and soak for at least twelve minutes, three times a week. *As with all supplements, please check with your doctor first.*

Banana Chia Breakfast Pudding

▶ **2 SERVINGS**

Yay, pudding for breakfast! You may know chia seeds from the "pets" that sprout chia from their terracotta forms, but the superfood era has promoted them from their ch-ch-ch-chia status to nutrition superstars. Rich in protein and omega-3 fatty acids, chia is also packed with phytochemicals, phosphorus, manganese, fiber, calcium, and vitamin C. In liquid, chia seeds expand and get gelatinous—and while that may sound off-putting, it means that when left to soak, they turn juice or milk into something very much like tapioca pudding.

¼ cup chia seeds

1 cup unsweetened almond milk (or milk of choice)

½ teaspoon pure vanilla extract

1 tablespoon honey

1 banana, sliced

1 cup fresh berries (for garnish)

Combine the chia seeds through the banana in a 1-quart jar and shake well; refrigerate overnight. Serve in bowls, top with berries, eat pudding for breakfast.

Per serving: 260 calories; 43 g carbs; 5 g protein; 12 g fat.

Kale, Kale, and Kale (Kale Three Ways)

Dark green and overwhelmingly healthy, kale was once a confirmed citizen of the Island of Misfit Vegetables. Then the leafy green was discovered by the foodie set and turned into a trendy and beloved vegetable. It's delicious! One of the few vegetables with significant calcium, and especially high in magnesium (one cup contains 40 percent of the RDA), kale also boasts nice amounts of vitamin A, as well as the phytochemicals lutein and zeaxanthin. Here are three ways to prepare this versatile vegetable:

1. Quick sauté

1 teaspoon olive oil

Fresh garlic, chopped

1 large bunch kale leaves, rinsed and thoroughly dried, ribs removed

Sea salt and freshly ground black pepper

Heat the olive oil in a large sauté pan, add the garlic, and sauté over medium-high heat until the garlic starts to sizzle and turn golden. Next, toss in a handful of kale leaves and stir a few times until they start to wilt. Continue tossing in a handful at a time. Adding them slowly will ensure that the water released cooks off before the next handful is thrown in, which will avoid sogginess. When all the kale is added, toss it with some sea salt and fresh pepper and serve.

2. Slow braise

1 teaspoon olive oil

1 clove garlic, minced

1 large bunch kale leaves, rinsed and chopped

1 cup vegetable stock

Kale revels in a long simmer. It has a lot of struc-ture, so it doesn't turn to mush, and its smoky flavors come out rich and mellow. Here's how to bring out the best of your kale: Sauté the garlic in olive oil, then add the kale, followed by the vege-table stock. Simmer over low-medium heat for 20 minutes, stirring occasionally and adding more stock if it becomes too dry. When it's ready, the stock should be reduced and all that remains is a tangle of moist, tender (but not disintegrating), delicious greens.

3. Oven roasted

1 bunch kale leaves, rinsed and dried, stems re-moved

1 teaspoon olive oil

Sea salt

Kale chips are definitely a "thing" now, but sadly, they're prohibitively expensive. So make oven-roasted kale, which is like kale chips, only with-out the thick coating of nutritional yeast, added flavors, and other assorted muck. In the simplest preparation, remove the stems from a bunch of kale, rinse and dry the leaves, spread them on a baking sheet, toss with the olive oil and some salt, and bake at 375°F for 15 minutes, turning occa-sionally and checking to make sure they don't burn. They're done when they're crispy, yet still tender, and slightly browned on the edges.

Per serving: 48 calories; 1 g carbs; 3 g protein; 4 g fat.

Wheat Berry Salad with Figs and Feta

▶ **4 SERVINGS**

Wheat berries are the kernels of whole grain wheat. They are a great source of potassium, phosphorus, fiber, protein, iron, and B vitamins—and the figs added to this dish elevate the nutri-ent levels even more. The grains have a nice nutty taste and a tender but chewy texture. It's often recommended that they should be soaked overnight, but it isn't necessary.

1½ cups hard wheat berries

½ teaspoon salt

2 stalks celery, chopped

1 tart, firm apple, diced

⅓ cup tart dried cherries

5 dried (or fresh) figs, chopped

¼ cup pine nuts

¾ cup feta cheese

1 tablespoon olive oil

Balsamic vinegar to taste

Rosemary for garnish

Freshly ground black pepper

1. In a sauce pan, combine the wheat berries, 5 cups of water, and ½ teaspoon of salt. Bring to a rolling boil, reduce heat, and cover and simmer for 50 minutes, or until tender. Alternatively, place the wheat berries, water, and salt in a slow cooker. Set the cooker on low and cook, covered, for at least 8 hours and up to 12 hours.

2. Drain the wheat berries, let them cool, and toss with the remaining ingredients. Letting the salad stand for 30 minutes allows the flavors to develop and brings it to a nice temperature for eating.

Per serving: 430 calories; 70 g carbs; 15 g protein; 12 g fat

Almond Cherry Pie Oat Bars

▶ **12 SERVINGS**

*Okay, we're not fooling anyone: These don't taste
like cherry pie. Even so, they're redolent of almonds
and cherries, wholesome, and the perfect choice for
a sweet packed with nutritional integrity.*

2 cups rolled oats

½ cup applesauce

2 tablespoons almond butter

¼ cup honey

¼ cup brown sugar

2 tablespoons cherry preserves

1 tablespoon mild vegetable oil

1 teaspoon sea salt

2 teaspoons almond extract

1 cup dried cherries

1 cup sliced almonds

½ cup semisweet chocolate chips

1. Preheat the oven to 350°F. In a large mixing
bowl, stir all the ingredients together.

2. Spread and pat the mixture down into an
oiled 8 × 9-inch baking pan.

3. Bake for 30 minutes, or until the top is golden
and the edges start to brown.

4. Remove, cool for 20 minutes, cut into 12
squares, allow them to cool completely, and
store in an airtight container.

Per serving: 65 calories; 41 g carbs; 5 g protein; 11
g fat.

23

Build Your Running Weight-Loss Program

Some people run to lose weight. Some people lose weight to run better. And some people run for the sole purpose of being able to eat more pie. Whatever your motivation, running and weight management are inextricably linked.

There isn't a perfect weight for every runner. That's a decision made by you and your running body. But whatever number you target as your goal or maintenance weight, it's important to pick a rational strategy for achieving that weight—and to understand the ramifications of exceeding that weight. After all, you wouldn't run a race with forty sticks of butter strapped to your waist, hips, and thighs. So why carry an extra ten pounds of body fat? (In fact, the calories in a stick of butter are roughly equivalent to a quarter-pound of body fat.) Healthy weight loss increases VO_2 max, reduces the impact forces weathered by your muscles and connective tissue, and improves running economy. Simply put, less weight—lost intelligently—will improve your endurance.

WHAT'S A HEALTHY WEIGHT?

Runners perform best when they are near the bottom of their healthy weight range. A quick way to gauge whether your weight is healthy is to check your Body Mass Index (BMI), keeping in mind that BMI doesn't account for frame and muscle mass—very muscular people have a high BMI. The National Institutes of Health provides the following calculation for determining BMI:

▶ Multiply your weight (in pounds) by 703.
▶ Divide the answer by your height in inches.
▶ Divide again by your height in inches.

Then check the following chart to see whether your weight is healthy for your height:

BMI	Classification
<18.5	Underweight
18.5–24.9	Healthy
25.0–29.9	Overweight
30.0–39.9	Obese
>40	Extreme or high risk obesity

Of course, just as muscular people have high BMIs, super-fit runners might discover that they

have a BMI on the low end. Double 2012 Olympic champion (5,000 and 10,000 meters) Mo Farah has a BMI of 21.1, while sprint star Usain Bolt tips the scales at 24.9. Some elite marathoners and ultra-marathoners fall into the "underweight" classification, scoring below 18.5, but most top-ranked marathoners yield marks between 19 and 21. What does this mean for you? It means that if you're otherwise healthy, a BMI anywhere in the 18.5 to 24.9 range is fine—and a little below or a little above probably isn't a cause for concern, either.

Another way to determine healthy weight is to check your body-fat percentage (if you have a skinfold caliper or a specialized water tank for hydrostatic weighing handy). The following chart from the American Council on Exercise offers body-fat ranges for several classifications ("essential fat" is the minimum percentage of fat required to remain healthy).

Classification	Men	Women
Essential fat	2–5%	10–13%
Athletes	6–13%	14–20%
Fitness	14–17%	21–24%
Average	18–24%	25–31%
Obese	25%+	32%+

Most runners, through experience, find a weight range in which they perform best. Training above this range leaves them sluggish. Training below this range robs them of strength and energy. In the meantime, it's important to understand *how* you lose weight.

LOSING A POUND A WEEK

For runners, losing a few "sticks of butter" isn't as easy as going on a juice cleanse, eating nothing

NUTRITION DISCUSSION

"8 healthy snack swaps"

Few things kill a diet faster than snacks. They tempt and lure. They hold a secret sway over us. It'd be easy to suggest keeping a stash of fruits and veggies on hand to thwart snack attacks, but let's be honest: Celery doesn't cut it when it's potato chips you crave. So here are some swaps that are wholesome, palatable stand-ins when raw carrots just won't do the trick.

- ▶ **Popped rice snacks for Doritos:** Popped rice snacks are not nutritionally perfect, but they're primarily made with whole grain brown rice, are flavorful, and are a superior choice to heavily processed tortilla chips.
- ▶ **Cereal bars for snack cakes:** Most cereal bars—with their caramel and peanut butter and chocolate chips—have way too much sugar to be considered a "health food," but they provide many more nutrients than vacuous, commercial snack cakes and can satisfy an urgent sweet tooth.
- ▶ **Good cookies for bad cookies:** If you have to have a cookie, that's understandable. Just don't reach for Oreos. Look for cookies with healthy ingredients like fruit, whole grains, and dark chocolate chips. A luscious oatmeal cookie with dried cherries and dark chocolate can go a long way toward nurturing both your cookie needs and your body.
- ▶ **Baked tortilla chips for fried ones:** It's easy to make baked tortilla chips: Cut corn tortillas into triangles, place them on a baking sheet, and bake at 350°F for about ten minutes, making sure they don't get too brown—they should still be slightly pliable. Not quite the salty, greasy chips you get from a Mexican restaurant, but with enough salsa and a bit of guacamole, you'll hardly notice the difference.
- ▶ **Popcorn for Cheetos:** Popcorn is a whole grain, so eat it to your heart's content. Your best bet is to cook it on the stovetop or in an air popper (microwave versions have added ingredients and fat). Add Parmesan or smoked paprika for decadence. If you add a tiny bit of olive oil or butter, you're still better off than if you'd chosen Cheetos.
- ▶ **Dark chocolate for candy bars:** The antioxidants in dark chocolate do a body good, which is more than can be said for a plain old candy bar. Aim for chocolate with a minimum of 35 percent cocoa, and don't eat more than 1.5 ounces. For increased satisfaction, look for dark chocolate–covered dried fruit, peanuts, pretzels, etc.

(Continued)

BUILD YOUR RUNNING BODY

► **Roasted seaweed snacks for chips:** One of the biggest surprise success stories in the snack food market has been that of roasted seaweed sheets, which can be purchased just about anywhere now. Even more surprising is how tasty and satisfying they are! You get all the crispy, salty *je ne sais quoi* of chips without the distressing calorie count from fat.

► **Frozen yogurt for ice cream:** Frozen yogurt may lack the deliriously creamy mouthfeel that fatty ice cream offers—but it comes close. Some frozen yogurt brands have the same amount of calories as ice cream, but others have significantly less. What frozen yogurt offers is a blast of calcium, lower saturated fat levels than ice cream, and all-important probiotics—giving frozen yogurt the healthy edge.

but bacon, or chowing down on all-you-can-eat cabbage soup. You need calories in order to train and nutrients to replace those lost during workouts. Crash diets lead to just that: a crash, as in bonk, nosedive, hit the wall. Losing too much weight or losing weight too quickly can be worse for your running body than having the extra weight in the first place. You'll need to lose weight strategically, with the aim to drop one to two pounds per week.

The mechanics of losing a pound per week is simple: There are 3,500 calories in a pound of body fat; therefore, a deficit of 3,500 calories will lead to the loss of one pound. You can create that deficit by caloric reduction (dieting) or by training (burning more calories). So to lose a pound a week, you need to consume 500 fewer calories than you burn per day, either by eating less or exercising more—or, better yet, through a combination of both.

Now the disclaimer: It's not really that simple. Your body has tricks up its sleeve. According to the "set point" theory, your body has a preferred weight that it attempts to maintain by lowering (and raising) your metabolism, thereby offsetting small calorie deficits or temporary, minor calorie excess (for an analogy, think about how your body maintains your body temperature regardless of air temperature). Changing your set point takes time and a long-term lifestyle adjustment. Of course, running can help instigate that change. As mentioned in Chapter 1, running has a unique relationship with weight loss, with runners losing almost twice as much weight as walkers from the same amount of exercise-induced calorie burn. This could indicate that the higher intensity of running has a more direct effect on your set point, giving you more weight loss bang for your calorie-burn buck. Bottom line: It takes a combination of reduced calories and increased activity to lose that pound a week while maintaining a diet healthy enough to support your running.

POPULAR DIET PLANS AND RUNNING

Although the handy-dandy 3,500-calorie-per-week trick is simple, not everyone is good at counting calories. Some need a well-defined diet plan. But which one? There are more than 70,000 diet books available on Amazon.com. Where does a runner even begin? Right here, that's where, with a rundown of five of the most popular diets and how they rate for people who pound the pavement.

Atkins and all the other pro-protein plans

When *Dr. Atkins' Diet Revolution* was unleashed in 1972, it suddenly seemed that the entire world was eating itself skinny on steak, eggs, and bacon. The plan (and its imitators) is based on the concept that carbohydrates are bad; by drastically reducing them and eating more protein and fat, we shift from the use of carbohydrates to burning stored fat (ketosis), thereby losing weight. Can you lose weight on the protein party-train? Yes. Is it healthy? No. Studies have found that low-carb diets increase heart attack risks. Is it good for runners? If you don't know the answer to that, you skipped Chapter 19 of this book. Please read it.

The Zone Diet

Enter the Zone (1995) was written by Dr. Barry Sears, a former bio-tech researcher at MIT, and promises great health benefits and a hot body, offering (in its subtitle) "a revolutionary life plan to put your body in total balance." Seriously, who wouldn't want that? *The Zone* preaches revamping your metabolism with a diet of 40 percent carbohydrates, 30 percent protein, and 30 percent fat. The diet's approach has some very good components, like its preference for vegetables, legumes, whole grains, and fruits, as well as its attempt to steer dieters away from simple carbohydrates. But while it's promoted as a diet for athletes, the limit on carbohydrates will prove prohibitive for most runners.

DASH diet

The National Heart, Lung, and Blood Institute created the DASH (Dietary Approaches to Stop Hypertension) diet to help prevent and control blood pressure. And the diet regularly takes the top spot in the annual diet rankings released by *U.S. News & World Report*. It's also recommended by the US Department of Agriculture (USDA) as an ideal overall eating plan. The DASH diet emphasizes fruits, vegetables, fat-free or low-fat dairy, whole grain products, fish, poultry, and nuts. It deemphasizes lean red meat, sweets, added sugars, and sugary beverages. Runners will like the way it favors foods rich in potassium, magnesium, and calcium. The goal of the diet is 55 percent carbohydrates, 18 percent protein, and 27 percent fat (in the neighborhood of a traditional 60 percent carbs, 15 percent protein, 25 percent fat running diet).

South Beach Diet

Cardiologist Arthur Agatston and dietician Marie Almo created the South Beach Diet in the early 1990s after watching their patients and clients gain weight on the then-recommended low-fat, high-carbohydrate diets. "We tried a different approach," says Dr. Agatston, "that emphasized the quality of the fats and carbohydrates, rather than the relative quantity . . . The basic principles of the South Beach Diet are good fats, good carbohydrates, lean sources of protein, and plenty of fiber." The diet plan is divided into three phases. Phase One eliminates "bad" carbohydrates, the source of cravings for sugary and refined foods. Phase Two introduces "good" carbohydrates and lasts until the dieter reaches his or her goal weight. Phase Three lasts for life and involves making healthy food choices. Runners might have trouble with the low-carb Phase One, but by Phase Three you can pick from all allowed foods and set your own carb-protein-fat ratio.

Weight Watchers

Weight Watchers works on a points-based system, although much of its success can be attributed to the community aspect of the program:

regular meetings, weekly weigh-ins with staff members, and lifetime memberships (LTMs) for those who meet and maintain their goal weight. Moreover, LTMs who continue to weigh in within two pounds (above or below) of their healthy goal weight are allowed to attend Weight Watchers meetings at no charge, an incentive that helps to keep LTMs connected with their weight-loss community for life. On Weight Watchers' *PointsPlus* plan, there are no food restrictions; instead, points are based on food content: calorie-dense foods with more fat and simple carbs have higher points totals, while protein- and fiber-rich foods get fewer. The plan encourages eating a wide variety of healthy foods, split between three meals plus snacks, and has enough flexibility to support a runner's fueling requirements. The diet also adheres to the macronutrient ratio established by the National Academy of Sciences: 45–65 percent carbohydrates, 10–35 percent proteins, and 20–35 percent fat.

THE ART OF AVOIDING FOOD

We live in an age of food avoidance. Gluten-free this. Fake-meat that. Nut-free these. Non-dairy those. But whatever reason fuels one's rejection of certain foods—allergy, disease, taste, wellness, ethics, neurosis—the question remains: Do meticulous dietary restrictions put some runners at a disadvantage? A suitable answer to that question can be supplied via three names: Scott Jurek, Amy Yoder Begley, and Tim VanOrden.

Jurek is one of the top ultra-runners in the world, having notched multiple victories in most elite trail and road events, including seven straight victories (1999–2005) at the Western States 100 Mile Endurance Run. He's been named *UltraRunning* magazine's Ultra-Runner of the Year three times. He's also a passionate vegan. Yoder

Begley is a two-time USA champion at 10,000 meters, an Olympian, and a sixteen-time NCAA All-American. She also has celiac disease and can't eat gluten. VanOrden is a two-time USA Masters Mountain Runner of the Year and has won USA Masters Trail Running titles at multiple distances, including 10K, 15K, half marathon, marathon, and 50K. And he's a raw vegan who fuels his running with plant-based food that hasn't been heated above 100°F (while most raw vegans allow food to be heated to 118°F, VanOrden believes that "foods begin to break down and lose nutritive value when subjected to temperatures over 100°F.")

The point: There are many ways to fuel a runner. Success is about making smart nutritional choices. If you stick to a proper macronutrient ratio and make sure you're getting enough calories and nutrients, you should be good to go. And go and go and go.

BENEFITS OF A MEDITERRANEAN DIET

As if living along the lovely Mediterranean coast wasn't enough, people from that region not only have beautiful food to eat, they also have a decreased risk of death from heart disease and cancer, as well as a reduced incidence of Parkinson's and Alzheimer's diseases. Welcome to the Mediterranean diet—not a meal and exercise plan, but instead an approach to eating inspired by the traditional dietary patterns of Italy, Greece, Spain, and Morocco.

Foods that make up this diet include vegetables, fruits, beans, whole grains, nuts, olives and olive oil, cheese, yogurt, fish, poultry, and eggs—all packed with micronutrients, antioxidants, vitamins, minerals, and fiber. Most of the foods in the diet are fresh, seasonal whole foods. Meat, sugar, sodium, and processed foods are kept to a minimum. There is no limit on healthy fats (you

NUTRITION DISCUSSION

"Sly sugars"

Food manufacturers like to sneak sugar into places where, quite frankly, sugar just doesn't belong (a Dunkin Donuts bran muffin with 40 grams of added sugar comes to mind). The American Heart Association recommends no more than 100 calories of added sugar daily for women and 150 calories for men. Since nutrition labels don't differentiate between added sugar and natural sugar (e.g., sugar from fruit), you need to do some label sleuthing to ferret out added sugars. These are the names by which these sly sugars may be creeping into your food:

- Barley malt
- Beet sugar
- Brown sugar
- Cane juice crystals
- Cane sugar
- Caramel
- Corn sweetener
- Corn syrup
- Corn syrup solids
- Confectioner's sugar
- Carob syrup
- Castor sugar
- Date sugar
- Demerara sugar
- Dextran
- Dextrose
- Evaporated cane juice
- Fructose
- Fruit juice
- Fruit juice concentrate
- Glucose
- Glucose solids
- Golden sugar
- Golden syrup

- Grape sugar
- High-fructose corn syrup
- Honey
- Icing sugar
- Invert sugar
- Maltodextrin
- Maltose
- Malt syrup
- Mannitol
- Maple syrup
- Molasses
- Muscovado sugar
- Palm sugar
- Raw sugar
- Refiner's syrup
- Rice syrup
- Sorbitol
- Sorghum syrup
- Sucrose
- Sugar
- Syrup
- Treacle
- Turbinado sugar
- Yellow sugar

may indulge your love of olive oil with reckless abandon), and moderate consumption of wine is allowed.

For runners, it's the best of all worlds. If you're looking to lose weight, a switch away from processed foods to nutrient-dense food will help you achieve that 3,500-calories-per-week reduction. Plus you can customize your macronutrient ratio of carbs-protein-fat to what works best for you. With very few empty calories, the Mediterranean diet is sound, sensual, delicious real food in which every element offers some kind of nutritional whizbang. It's the real-world summation of all the nutritional ideas put forth in the previous five chapters. And it is, quite possibly, the best way to build your running body.

NUTRITION DISCUSSION

"Eat like a Greek granny, run like a champ"

The basics of the Mediterranean diet are pretty simple. Keep these guidelines—based on suggestions from the Mayo Clinic—in mind. Your running body will thank you.

▶ Produce, produce, produce: Vegetables and fruit (fresh and whole are best) should be eaten at every meal—for snacks, too.

▶ Switch to whole grains for all your baked goods, cereal, pasta, and rice.

▶ Don't shy away from nuts, just practice moderation. Although they're high-calorie, they are loaded with healthy fats and protein.

▶ Rebuff the butter, fall in love with olive oil. The more you eat olive oil, the more you will love its rich flavor (and you're allowed to use it liberally!).

▶ Play with herbs and spices. Not only do they boost flavor, most have health benefits all their own.

▶ Eat fish at least twice a week: Fresh or water-packed tuna, salmon, trout, mackerel, and herring are healthy choices. If you're concerned about mercury, visit the "Health" section of nrdc.org for more information.

▶ Skip the red meat. You don't have to give it up, just limit it to a few times a month. When you do eat it, choose a lean cut and small portions. Avoid sausage, bacon, and other processed meats.

▶ Opt for low-fat dairy. Use low-fat milk and nonfat Greek yogurt, and try sorbet instead of ice cream.

Roasted Asparagus with Poached Eggs

▶ 2 SERVINGS

This really couldn't be easier, and it's way more satisfying than 200 calories has any right to be. Among vegetables, asparagus is the leading supplier of folic acid and a good source of potassium, thiamin, and vitamin B6. It is also one of the richest sources of rutin, which strengthens capillary walls. Eggs are an excellent source of protein, choline, lutein, and zeaxanthin.

20 spears asparagus

1 teaspoon olive oil

4 eggs

Salt and pepper to taste

Truffle oil, shaved Parmesan cheese, or fresh herbs, optional

1. Preheat oven to 400°F.

2. Snap off the rough ends from asparagus stalks (save them for soup) and toss the spears in olive oil. Spread out on a baking sheet and sprinkle with salt and pepper. Bake for 20 minutes, turning occasionally, until they begin to brown lightly and look slightly wilted, but still have body left to them.

3. While the asparagus cooks, poach the eggs. There are many methods for poached eggs, and each cook will swear by theirs and theirs alone. If you have a favorite, use that. If not, play around with the methods available and see what works best for you. We like a simple method using a pot with at least three inches of gently boiling water; break the eggs into a cup and gently slide them into the water and boil for 3 to 4 minutes. If you're afraid of poaching eggs, simple fried eggs will work just as well. Even scrambled eggs will do in a pinch—you can't go wrong.

4. Remove the asparagus from the oven, divide onto two plates, and top with two eggs each. Salt and pepper to your liking. Add the truffle oil, parmesan cheese, or herbs, if desired.

Per serving: 190 calories; 6 g carbs; 16 g protein; 12 g fat.

Custom Homemade Hummus

▶ 8 SERVINGS

Hummus has taken over the dip world. It seems there are a thousand different flavors at the supermarket to choose from—so don't, because it's really fun to make your own, and you can customize it to your heart's content, making 100 calories' worth of nutrient-loaded, flavorful spread. First off is the basic recipe, then some ideas for different ways to enhance it.

1 can chickpeas

2 garlic cloves

3 tablespoons tahini (sesame paste)

2 lemons

1 tablespoon olive oil

Salt to taste

Drain the chickpeas, saving the juice and setting it to the side. Add the chickpeas, along with all remaining ingredients, to a food processor. Pulse until you have a paste, adding reserved liquid until you achieve a nice hummus texture—smooth, thick, and spreadable.

Per ¼ cup: 100 calories; 11 g carbs; 4 g protein; 6 g fat.

ADDITIONS

Try including these with the other ingredients above before the reserved chickpea liquid is added to the food processor.

Roasted red peppers and jalapeño; garnish with fresh cilantro.

Fresh ginger and mint; garnish with pomegranate seeds.

Miso paste and wasabi; garnish with sesame seeds.

Anchovies and sundried tomatoes; garnish with fresh oregano.

Black olives and capers; garnish with fresh parsley.

Wild Mushroom Lasagna

▶ **MAKES 6 AMPLE PORTIONS**

Yes, we have lasagna in the weight loss section! While that may seem wrong on many levels, it really isn't. By using whole wheat pasta, the dish is already healthier and heartier than regular lasagna (and whole wheat tastes great with mushrooms!). This recipe swaps the mounds of mozzarella and ricotta for some lower-fat alternatives.

Olive oil

1 12-ounce package whole wheat lasagna noodles

1 large garlic clove

1 tablespoon olive oil

2 pounds mixed mushrooms (white, portabello, shiitake, etc.), sliced

Salt and pepper to taste

1½ cups part-skim ricotta

1½ cups nonfat Greek yogurt

1 cup crumbled goat cheese

1 cup grated fresh Parmesan cheese

1. Preheat the oven to 375°F.

2. Cook the noodles according to the instructions on its package, then set aside.

3. Mince the garlic and add to a large sauté pan with olive oil. Cook on medium-high heat until sizzling. Add the mushrooms (in several batches if your pan isn't large enough), and salt to taste as you go along. Sauté, stirring frequently, until the mushrooms have released their juices and are slightly dry.

4. Stir the ricotta and yogurt together in a separate bowl.

5. Add a little olive oil to the bottom of an 8 × 12-inch baking dish (if you only have an 8 × 8 or 9 × 13, don't sweat it; you can make it all fit one way or the other). Place a layer of noodles down, followed by ⅓ of the ricotta mixture, ⅓ of the mushrooms, and ⅓ of the goat cheese. Repeat until all the ingredients have been used, ending with a layer of noodles and topping it all with the Parmesan.

6. Bake for 45 minutes, or until browned and bubbly; let sit for 15 minutes. Serve with roasted kale (page 343).

Per serving: 393 calories; 33 g carbs; 26 g protein; 17 g fat.

BUILD YOUR RUNNING DIET—PROTEIN, CARBS, CALORIES, AND NUTRITION

Butternut (or Pumpkin) Pudding

▶ **4 SERVINGS**

Every autumn it happens: All manner of food items begin to have "pumpkin" attached to them—coffee, muffins, beer, donuts, cakes, martinis, you name it. So why not a rich, custardy pudding? This recipe calls for butternut squash because it's easier to handle when cooking from scratch (and the taste is nearly indistinguishable from pumpkin), but if desired you can make the recipe easier by using canned pumpkin puree. Both squashes are loaded with impressive amounts of vitamin A, vitamin C, vitamin B6, potassium, and folate.

1¾ cups butternut squash puree (or one 15-ounce can of pumpkin puree)

1⅓ cups coconut milk

3 tablespoons cornstarch

2 tablespoons maple syrup

1 tablespoon molasses

¼ cup raw sugar

½ teaspoon cinnamon

½ teaspoon nutmeg

½ teaspoon salt

1. If using fresh butternut squash: Peel with a vegetable peeler, cut it in half lengthwise, remove the seeds, and dice into cubes. Boil for 15–20 minutes or until soft, then puree in a blender or food processor until smooth. (There will be extra; you can use it in soup.)

2. Whisk all the ingredients until combined well and smooth.

3. Add to a medium pot and cook on medium-low heat, stirring, until thickened, about 8 minutes.

4. Transfer to a serving bowl or individual serving cups and refrigerate until set, overnight, or at least 1½ hours.

Per serving: 248 calories; 35 g carbs; 3 g protein; 11 g fat.

PART 5

Build
Your Race
Strategy

24

Build Your Race Approach

The first thing you need to understand about a race is this: A race is nothing more than a run in which you give a 100 percent effort. In fact, you could stand all alone at the start line on a track, wait for someone to yell, *Go!*, and run all-out until you dropped. You'd probably last about two hundred meters, halfway around the track—if you're lucky. Then your lungs would burn, your legs would seize, and you'd stagger to a stop with your hands on your knees (or your forehead on the track's surface), wondering what ever possessed you to think racing was a good idea. But you would have done it. You would have raced.

Building a race approach is nothing more than teaching your body how to stretch those 200 meters into a 5K, or a half marathon, or a marathon. It's about shifting your focus from improved fitness to race fitness. It's about preparing mentally for the specific challenge of your race. And this is the best part: With a proper race approach, you'll feel *much* better finishing your first 5K or half marathon than you would racing that 200 meters on Day One.

WHAT'S A RACE APPROACH?

Some runners train to race. Others race to add mileposts and purpose to their training. Many never race at all. A race is not a required outcome of training. It's a choice. But if you make that choice—whether your goal is to complete a specific distance, compete for PRs and age-group medals, or simply to share the community experience—you'll need a plan.

The difference between a training run and a race is this: You'll run a little harder or a little farther (or both) in a race. It's a mistake to treat racing as intrinsically different from normal training. In a race, you'll push yourself a little beyond what you do in normal training runs—but *not* beyond what you've trained your running body to handle. In fact, with a proper race approach, you'll discover that the actual race isn't so much a challenge as it is an opportunity to do what you're not allowed to do in normal training: to redline your powerfully rebuilt running body.

The challenge for a properly trained runner isn't the race; it's the preparation.

Two race approaches

While the training schedules provided in this book prepare your running body to race *any* distance, you'll want to make a few modifications in order to ensure the best race experience. Step one is to establish your race goal. Most runners race with one of two goals in mind:

- ▶ **Completion:** You want to finish a distance that represents a challenge to your fitness (e.g., completing a half marathon).
- ▶ **Competition**: You want to run fast and compete against other runners.

Each race goal (and each variation on each of those) demands a slightly different training approach.

Training for completion

Training to complete a race distance is often the goal for new runners, as well as for experienced runners looking for a new challenge (e.g., a regular 10K competitor testing the marathon distance). If this is you, there are three principles to keep in mind:

BEGINNER'S GUIDELINE

For many runners, the first racing mistake occurs long before race day. It happens when they run 100 percent in workouts. Don't do that. Your body doesn't know the difference between 100 percent in training and 100 percent in a race. And it has a limited capacity for 100 percent efforts. Runners who go all-out in workouts run out of race capacity long before they toe an actual race start line.

1. Allow adequate time to prepare for the race. While a few weeks might be all you need to prep your body for a 5K, you'll need a few months for a marathon.

2. Race preparation is incremental. Gradually introduce greater duration and intensity into your training so that the race is merely a small increase in both.

3. Don't overdo it. Training too hard leads to injury, illness, and burnout.

With those principles in mind, you'll need to include the following specific adjustments in your training:

▶ **Increase your long run:** Your long run must be progressively lengthened until it's close to the length of your goal race. For a 5K, you'll need to build up to 2–3 miles. For longer races, like a marathon, you might need to use *time* as your measuring stick rather than distance. While a sub-three-hour marathoner should build up to 20–22 miles, slower runners can't run that far (time-wise) without risking injury. Instead, these runners should cap their long run at 3.5 hours (2.5 hours if you're new to the sport). That's a safe duration, and slower runners can add a *negative split long run* (see below) to mimic the increased effort required over a marathon's final miles.

▶ **Practice race intensity:** If you think your race pace will be faster than your normal distance pace, you'll need to spend some time training at faster paces.
  - *Shorter races:* Add a few sessions of repetitions at race pace.
  - *Longer races:* Include negative split long runs—in this workout, you run the first half of your long run at your regular distance pace and the second half a little faster.
    - *Marathon only:* A variation of the negative split long run is to run several miles (e.g., miles 12–18 of a 20-mile long run) at goal marathon pace. Exercise scientist and coach Greg McMillan takes this a step farther with "fast-finish long runs," in which you gradually increase your pace over the final 30–90 minutes of your run, finishing at near-maximum effort.
  - ▶ **Tune-up races:** See the guidelines that follow later in this chapter.

In 2012, there were more than fifteen million race finishers (at all race distances) in the United States. There's no reason you can't be a race finisher, too.

Training for competition

Competitive racing requires race-specific preparation. You'll need to prepare, body and mind, for a 100 percent effort. Specific training must include:

▶ **Equal duration:** For shorter races (i.e., half marathon or less), you'll need to include distance runs that are at least as long as your goal race. For the marathon, you should include runs that match the *duration* (up to 3.5 hours), not necessarily the distance of the race.

▶ **Equal effort:** Whatever the race distance, you'll need to run repetitions (or tempo) at your expected race effort.

▶ **Goal pace:** As race week draws near, you'll want to shift your focus from repetitions and tempo at race effort to goal race pace. This increases race economy (running efficiency) at race pace and teaches you the physiological and sensory cues that will keep you on pace.

- ▶ **Speed work:** Repetitions at faster-than-race pace (e.g., 200-meter reps at 1500-meter pace while training for a 5K) increase anaerobic enzymes, recruit a wider range of muscle fibers, and make race pace itself feel "slower" and more manageable.
- ▶ **The warm-up:** Now is the time to develop a standard warm-up routine. Use it before every hard workout (e.g., repetitions, hill repeats, or drills) so that, come race day, its familiarity can help settle pre-race jitters and boost confidence.
- ▶ **Tune-up races:** See the guidelines that follow later in this chapter.

Training to race competitively isn't guesswork. You build your running body with solid training. Then you fine-tune it with race-specific workouts. The work is completed before you toe the start line.

Tapering

Regardless of your race goal, you'll want to *taper* in the days or weeks leading up to your race. Tapering is a period of reduced training that allows your muscles and connective tissue to heal more fully. It also gives your body a chance to restock levels of muscle glycogen, hormones, enzymes, and neurotransmitters. Tapering for a 5K might only require a few days, while tapering for a marathon traditionally requires three weeks. Even then, different athletes will find that different tapers work best for them. Some options include:

- ▶ **Traditional 5K taper:** Eliminate (or reduce) your long run the weekend before the race. Do a single repetition workout 4–6 days preceding the race, maintaining normal

repetition intensity but decreasing the volume of reps by 33–50 percent. Then reduce your mileage until the race, adding one session of 8–10 strides 2–3 days out. Run easy or skip running the day before the race.

- ▶ **Traditional marathon taper:** The marathon taper begins three weeks out, following your last (and longest) long run.
  - *Three weeks out*—Reduce both mileage and *quality work* (i.e., harder workouts like repetitions and fast tempo) by 20–30 percent. Maintain normal effort during workouts. Finish the week with a run that's 50 percent the length of the previous week's long run.
  - *Two weeks out*—Reduce mileage and quality work another 20–30 percent. Maintain normal effort. Your last hard quality workout should be run 10 days out from your marathon. Finish the week with a run that's no more than 40 percent the length of your last long run.
  - *One week out*—Reduce your mileage to as little as 25 percent of normal volume. Some runners will include 2–4 miles at marathon pace during their Monday run. Rest completely for 1–2 days before the race. Increase carbohydrates to 70 percent of your diet for 2–3 days before racing.
- ▶ **Reduced taper:** Some runners find that a traditional taper of 40–60 percent leaves them susceptible to colds, allergy attacks, and a feeling of staleness come race day. For these runners, a reduced taper of only 20–25 percent—beginning 2–3 days out for the 5K and 2–3 weeks out for the marathon—provides better results.

TRAINING DISCUSSION

"Race Jitters"

We all get nervous immediately before a race. But *race jitters*, that irrational panic that grips so many runners, isn't limited to race day. The following race jitters can infect the final weeks before a race, compromising your training and leading to subpar race performance.

▶ **Phantom injury:** You're suddenly overwhelmed with minor injuries, from tendinitis to lower-back tightness to flare-ups of bursitis. *Can you really be that injured?* Yes, you can. They're the normal aches and pains that accompany hard training. It's just that you usually ignore them—you ignore them, that is, until race anxiety turns you into a hypochondriac and amplifies every tiny tingle into something it's not: an actual injury. Don't fret; these phantom injuries will disappear once the race is under way.

▶ **Leaving your race in your workout:** With race day fast approaching, you lose confidence in your fitness and decide to run a time trial or an all-out session of intervals to test your conditioning. Stop. Do not pass GO. A 100 percent workout is a race, and you'll deplete your body of the resources you need for the real race.

▶ **Second-guessing syndrome:** With the race a week away, you decide you've prepared incorrectly. You should have done more tempo. Or intervals. Or drills. You wonder if you should run these workouts before race day. Relax. There's nothing you can do in a week to get faster—and *lots* you can do to sabotage your race. If adjustments are in order, make them *after* the race.

▶ **Training through a race:** You lessen race anxiety by treating the race as a workout. You won't taper for it, won't worry about proper rest and nutrition, and won't go easy the next day. *Don't do this.* A race is a 100 percent effort no matter what you do before and after. Without proper tapering and recovery strategies, you risk overloading your body with an effort it can't handle.

▶ **Waiting until *top shape*:** Afraid of embarrassing yourself, you refuse to race until you've reached "top shape." One problem: Racing is an integral part of getting into top shape. It trains your brain. It stresses your running body in a way that workouts don't. Besides, "top shape" describes a utopian future that, for most runners, rarely, if ever, arrives.

▶ **Food for thought:** You decide to improve your racing through diet. Smart, if you're talking about long-term, healthy eating choices. Not so smart if you mean radical changes in diet during race week. New foods can lead to equally new gastrointestinal reactions. Changes in diet need to be tested long before race week—lest carboloading become carbo-unloading during the race.

(Continued)

BUILD YOUR RUNNING BODY

▶ **Changes in routine:** You change your daily routine to be better rested and prepared for your race. You skip work, opt out of chores, avoid stairs, and stretch continuously. "Most great performances come when you're not trying to do it," says coach Jack Daniels. He's right. Stick to your routine. And have faith in your training—and yourself.

Ultimately, the best way to deal with race jitters is to stick to your pre-jitters plan.

One caveat to tapering: Newer runners who are still improving their fitness every week are sometimes better off skipping the taper and simply resting the day before the race.

PERIODIZATION

You might have heard seasoned runners talking about *periodization of training*. In periodization, training is separated into distinct phases. For many athletes, this begins with a *base training* phase, in which aerobic conditioning and improvements in muscle and connective tissue strength take place. Following base training, some athletes insert a pre-season *strength-building* phase, with a focus on hills, drills, and anaerobic training. Others move straight to a *competition* phase, during which they run races, often building toward a major race goal. Lastly, there's a *recovery* phase, during which runners take a break from hard training, either through complete rest or by significantly reducing the volume of their training. While periodization works well for elite athletes with defined seasons, most runners compete throughout the year and function best with a more general, less-seasonal training approach.

TUNE-UP RACES

Tune-up races are essential for achieving top performances in goal races. The 100 percent effort level of a race provides a physiological stimulus that you don't get through training, and it also trains your brain to allow even harder efforts in the future. Beyond that, tune-up races serve as dress rehearsals for all the mundane aspects of racing, including parking, delayed start times, shortages of porta-potties, etc. Finally, they give you feedback on your fitness, allowing you to make minor adjustments in your training. Different race distances require different tune-up strategies.

5K and 10K

For these two popular race distances, you'll probably tune up with a 5K. While it's best to tune up with a race that's shorter than your goal race, there are few road races shorter than 5K. If you can't find a tune-up race, then some tune-up substitutes might include: a 1500-meter or mile time trial; 5×1000 meters at goal pace, with a 400-meter jog recovery; 2×1 mile at 5K pace, with a 400-meter recovery interval.

BUILD YOUR RUNNING BODY

Half marathon

Both the 8K and 10K distances are appropriate as half marathon tune-up races. If you race farther than 10K (e.g., 15K), you might consider limiting yourself to a fast tempo effort for the tune-up race. Tune-up race substitutes can include: a 20–30 minute fast tempo run; 3×2 miles (3200 meters) at race effort, with a 3–4 minute recovery; or a 5K–10K (3–6 mile) time trial.

Marathon

All distances from 5K to the half marathon make for good marathon tune-up races. A half marathon should be run well in advance of the marathon (five or six weeks). You can run a 5K as close as one week out from your marathon. Tune-up race substitutes can include: 60 minutes at slow tempo pace; a 13-mile run at marathon effort; and time trials at 5K to 10 miles.

With a proper race approach, you can prepare your body and mind for race day. All that's left is to run.

Build Your Race

It's race day. You've done your training. Done your taper. Eaten right. Hydrated. All that's left is to run the race. Every year, millions of runners toe the line at races across America and around the world. And now you're one of them, asking yourself what separates those runners who race well and achieve their goals from those who bonk and fail. It's not genetics. It's not talent. It's two things: Training, and knowing how to race. You've got the first down pat. And the second is easy. It's just a matter of knowing what to do—and, more important, what *not* to do.

WHAT'S A RACE?

As explained in Chapter 24, a race is a 100 percent effort. The specific challenge of a race is not physiological. It's psychological. Anyone can run themselves to exhaustion. The trick is to spread your 100 percent effort evenly over your entire race distance. Sound easy? In the abstract, maybe, but at an actual race, not so much. You'll have adrenaline coursing through your veins and a sea of equally excited running peers all around you. There'll be the excruciating wait at the start line and then the full-body jolt when the gun fires (or the air horn sounds). There will be people cheering, runners sprinting off the start line, pushing and shoving, and the instinctive urge just to *go go go* with the herd . . . in that moment, you'll need a plan that you've rehearsed, and you'll need the confidence to carry it out.

RACE STRATEGY

A running race is quite possibly the simplest athletic competition known to humans. And the best race strategy is equally simple. You pick a pace that you're confident you can maintain. You make in-race adjustments based upon feedback from your body (something you've rehearsed during numerous long runs and interval sessions). And as the finish banner comes into view, you expend all the energy you have left to cross the line 100 percent spent.

In practice, however, it's remarkably difficult to carry out this strategy.

It doesn't take a genius to figure out that there's a maximum pace you can maintain from start to finish. But it takes a disciplined runner to block out distractions—other competitors, cheering spectators, your own inner voice—in order to stay on pace. Following a few basic guidelines can make the task easier:

▶ **Accelerate without sprinting:** Accelerate forcefully off the start line to your expected pace (and no faster), but don't sprint—sprinting the first 100 meters almost ensures that you'll crawl the final 100. If you change pace during the race, do it gradually. Sprints—and all overzealous pace adjustments—carry far too great an energy cost.

▶ **No bumping:** Don't get involved in jostling with other runners. It wastes time. It's stupid. And you'll regret your involvement in unsportsmanlike behavior later—guaranteed.

▶ **Maintain consistent effort:** Run the entire race (excluding the kick) at a consistent effort, what coach Jack Daniels labels "even intensity." This doesn't mean your effort

BEGINNER'S GUIDELINE

The best race strategy is to aim for a "good" race, not a great one. Trying to run a great race invites disaster; it encourages you to go out too fast and to ignore feedback from your body. In contrast, trying to run a good race invites confidence. You run the pace for which you prepared. You reach the race's midpoint feeling strong—*and it's amazing what you can accomplish in the second half of a race when you're fit and feeling strong.*

BUILD YOUR RACE STRATEGY

will feel the same throughout the race. The first part will feel easy, the latter stages won't. But your effort should drain your resources at a consistent rate, resulting in a pace you can maintain.

▶ **Take legal shortcuts:** Run tangents (the shortest distance possible) during the race. Hug curves. Don't zigzag when passing other runners. And when crossing from one side of the road to the other in preparation for an upcoming turn, remember that the shortest distance between two points is a straight line.

▶ **Draft:** Running just behind a competitor or on their shoulder gives you two advantages. Physiologically, you save 4–8 seconds per mile (lowered wind resistance lets you run faster at the same energy cost). Psychologically, you let someone else shoulder the stress of setting the pace.

▶ **Take inventory:** Constantly monitor your energy and fatigue levels. Ask yourself, "Can I finish the race at this effort?" If yes, then keep it up. If no, then back off before you sabotage your race.

▶ **Shorten the suffering:** Maintaining a correct, consistent effort allows you to delay the onset of heavy fatigue (hence, suffering). You shorten the period you have to hurt. If you're hurting by the halfway point of a race, it's hard to finish strong.

▶ **Kick late:** Refrain from kicking until you're certain you can maintain the effort through the finish line. If you run out of kick before the finish, you'll lose more time crawling to the line than you gained picking up the pace.

▶ **Run your own race:** It's a cliché for a reason. Everyone in the race brings their own fitness, talent, and race strategy. Someone else's might work for them. It won't work for you.

▶ **Run the race you have in you that day:** Not every race will bring a PR. If you aren't hitting your targeted splits and can't increase your pace, forget the PR and run as strongly as you can. If nothing else, you'll get valuable feedback that you can apply to your training.

Follow these guidelines, and you'll race well. And on some days, you'll even race great.

EFFORT VERSUS PACE

We've talked a lot about both "effort" and "pace" in this chapter, and you might be wondering if they represent different strategies, if they're flip sides of the same coin, or if they're separate concepts that are utilized together while racing.

The answer is: All of the above.

First, let's look at what each approach represents:

1. **Pace:** You predict your goal pace, train at that pace, and then attempt to match that pace during the race (for a table on pace for four race distances from 5K through the marathon, based on time per mile, see table 25.1 at the end of this chapter).

2. **Effort:** You utilize workouts to learn what your effort feels like for different race distances and how that "feel" changes as you fatigue. You then draw on that experience to closely monitor fatigue levels—and the accompanying expenditure of resources—throughout a race.

Runners choose which of the two they prefer to follow more closely during a race. But let's get one thing straight: This isn't a case of the

TRAINING DISCUSSION

"Mistakes runners make"

Experience tells us that very few runners will achieve a perfectly paced race from start to finish. Too many runners abandon their race plans when excitement—or anxiety—takes hold. And when that happens, mistakes get made:

▶ **Changing your warm-up on race day:** You see Olympic 5,000- and 10,000-meter champion Mo Farah doing a mini-interval session as part of *his* warm-up and decide you need to do the same. Don't. There's something remarkably calming about repeating the same progression of jogging, strides, and stretches that you've practiced before hard workouts. Besides, you'll feel like a dope when Mo pulls on his sweats, and you realize he's there as a spectator.

▶ **Going out too fast:** The laws of physiology apply to races, just like they do to workouts. You wouldn't run the first mile of a 10-mile run at mile race pace, and you can't run the first mile of a 5K at mile race pace, either. At that pace, you'll only last, well, a mile.

▶ **Running an uneven pace:** Elite Kenyan distance runners are famous for setting a scorching early race pace, launching vicious surges, and covering every move from their opponents. So if you're an elite Kenyan distance runner, stop reading. Everyone else: Stop behaving like elite Kenyan distance runners! There is one finish line in a race, and it's at the finish. The best strategy for getting there the fastest is to run with an even effort.

▶ **Engaging in mid-race mini-battles:** Refer to the previous mistake—*there is one finish line in a race, and it's at the finish.* Battling back and forth with someone during a race only ensures that someone else has a better chance of beating both of you.

▶ **Overthinking the race:** Don't get so caught up in pace calculations, weather reports, course specifics, gear checklists, or concerns about the competition that you lose track of the race itself. It's counterproductive to overthink a race. There are simply too many variables that can't be predicted—like tripping at the start, having your shoe come untied, or taking a wrong turn. Have confidence in your ability to adjust on the fly. And be willing to accept that your 100 percent effort will be enough. Some runners can't. Successful runners do.

▶ **Overanalyzing an unsatisfactory performance:** You'll learn something from every race you run. But that doesn't mean that every race is a microcosm of all that's right or wrong with your training. Sometimes a bad race is just a bad race. So learn from the race, make training adjustments that are warranted, and move on.

You'll never run a perfect race. But avoiding unnecessary, costly, and self-destructive mistakes is a good first step in running a satisfactory one.

BUILD YOUR RACE STRATEGY

Hatfields and the McCoys. It's true that a majority of runners fall into one camp or the other—and the vast majority of those opt to race by pace—but it's equally true that, regardless of which camp runners choose, they invariably use aspects of both approaches during a race.

Pace racing involves predicting your finish time and then trying to run splits (e.g., your predicted time for each mile of a 5K) that represent an even breakdown of that time. For example, an 18:48 5K is exactly six-minute-mile pace, so you'd aim for 6:00 for your first mile, 12:00 for two miles, and 18:00 for three miles. To train for that pace, you'd run repetitions at six-minute-mile pace (e.g., 12 × 400 meters in ninety seconds, with an easy 200-meter recovery jog). By rehearsing at race pace, you both improve your running economy at that pace and become consciously familiar with sensory cues (especially visual) that allow you to recognize that pace in a race. The drawback to pace racing is twofold. First, your body might not be ready for that exact pace come race day; on a bad day, it's too fast, while on a good day, it might limit your performance. Second, the race course, weather, competition, and other variables might alter the practiced pace; maintaining your predicted pace on an uphill mile or during extreme heat would be a far harder effort than a flat mile practiced in good conditions.

Effort racing involves choosing an exertion level right off the start line that you assume will drain your energy resources at a consistent rate. You utilize both internal and external cues (i.e., feedback from your body and a sensory assessment of terrain, weather, etc.) to adjust the intensity of your effort as required. Your pace might slow during a hill climb, but your expenditure of energy remains roughly consistent. This doesn't mean that your effort will always feel the same. Your effort will feel easier at the start of the race than at its conclusion. The drawback to effort-based racing is that it requires tremendous experience—both in workouts that are based on effort and in races themselves. Newer runners often misread the easier effort required for the first third of a race as a green light to increase their intensity. And experienced runners can sometimes be lulled into slower performances as they attempt to elude fatigue.

Practical racers often use a combination of both approaches. They'll include workouts based on both effort (road and trail repetitions, fartlek, tempo) and pace (track repetitions, time trials, tune-up races). And they'll use effort to guide their exertion in a race, even as they use splits to reassess that effort.

Beginning and less-experienced runners should probably stick with racing by pace until they've become more familiar with what their running bodies can—and cannot—do.

THE PERFECT RACE

There is no perfect race. And no perfect race strategy. The approach favored by this book is the one put forward in this chapter: even intensity, confidence in your training, adherence to your race plan, and running the race you have in you on that day. There are, of course, other approaches. American distance legend Steve Prefontaine (known affectionately as "Pre" to his fans), who died tragically in a car accident in 1975 at the peak of his running career, famously said: "A lot of people run a race to see who is fastest. I run to see who has the most guts, who can punish himself into exhausting pace, and then at the end, punish himself even more." He also said, "Somebody may beat me, but they are going to have to bleed to do it."

But that was Pre. And there's a reason he's a legend.

For most of us, a race is not so much a contest to see who can suffer the most as it is a training milepost. It's a celebration of improved fitness and the athletic community we've joined.

After the race, we take what we learned, train some more, and then race again.

That's how we get better. That's how we build our running body.

No one is born a perfect runner. And none of us will become one. But through incremental steps, we can become better runners. And that's the beauty of this sport: There are no shortcuts, nothing is given to us; we earn every mile, and we earn every result.

Table 25.1
Pace Table: 4:00–15:59 per mile

Pace	5K	10K	½ Mar.	Mar.
4:00	12:26	24:51	52:26	1:44:53
4:05	12:41	25:22	53:32	1:47:04
4:10	12:57	25:53	54:37	1:49:15
4:15	13:12	26:24	55:43	1:51:26
4:20	13:28	26:56	56:48	1:53:37
4:25	13:43	27:27	57:54	1:55:48
4:30	13:59	27:58	59:00	1:57:59
4:35	14:14	28:29	1:00:05	2:00:10
4:40	14:30	29:00	1:01:11	2:02:21
4:45	14:45	29:31	1:02:16	2:04:32
4:50	15:01	30:02	1:03:22	2:06:43
4:55	15:17	30:33	1:04:27	2:08:55
5:00	15:32	31:04	1:05:33	2:11:06
5:05	15:48	31:35	1:06:38	2:13:17
5:10	16:03	32:06	1:07:44	2:15:28
5:15	16:19	32:37	1:08:49	2:17:39
5:20	16:34	33:08	1:09:55	2:19:50
5:25	16:50	33:39	1:11:01	2:22:01
5:30	17:05	34:11	1:12:06	2:24:12
5:35	17:21	34:42	1:13:12	2:26:23
5:40	17:36	35:13	1:14:17	2:28:34
5:45	17:52	35:44	1:15:23	2:30:45
5:50	18:07	36:15	1:16:28	2:32:57
5:55	18:23	36:46	1:17:34	2:35:08
6:00	18:38	37:17	1:18:39	2:37:19
6:05	18:54	37:48	1:19:45	2:39:30
6:10	19:10	38:19	1:20:50	2:41:41
6:15	19:25	38:50	1:21:56	2:43:52
6:20	19:41	39:21	1:23:02	2:46:03
6:25	19:56	39:52	1:24:07	2:48:14
6:30	20:12	40:23	1:25:13	2:50:25
6:35	20:27	40:54	1:26:18	2:52:36
6:40	20:43	41:25	1:27:24	2:54:48
6:45	20:58	41:57	1:28:29	2:56:59
6:50	21:14	42:28	1:29:35	2:59:10
6:55	21:29	42:59	1:30:40	3:01:21
7:00	21:45	43:30	1:31:46	3:03:32
7:05	22:00	44:01	1:32:51	3:05:43
7:10	22:16	44:32	1:33:57	3:07:54
7:15	22:31	45:03	1:35:03	3:10:05
7:20	22:47	45:34	1:36:08	3:12:16
7:25	23:03	46:05	1:37:14	3:14:27
7:30	23:18	46:36	1:38:19	3:16:38
7:35	23:34	47:07	1:39:25	3:18:50
7:40	23:49	47:38	1:40:30	3:21:01
7:45	24:05	48:09	1:41:36	3:23:12
7:50	24:20	48:40	1:42:41	3:25:23
7:55	24:36	49:12	1:43:47	3:27:34
8:00	24:51	49:43	1:44:53	3:29:45
8:05	25:07	50:14	1:45:58	3:31:56
8:10	25:22	50:45	1:47:04	3:34:07
8:15	25:38	51:16	1:48:09	3:36:18
8:20	25:53	51:47	1:49:15	3:38:29
8:25	26:09	52:18	1:50:20	3:40:40
8:30	26:24	52:49	1:51:26	3:42:52

Pace	5K	10K	½ Mar.	Mar.
8:35	26:40	53:20	1:52:31	3:45:03
8:40	26:56	53:51	1:53:37	3:47:14
8:45	27:11	54:22	1:54:42	3:49:25
8:50	27:27	54:53	1:55:48	3:51:36
8:55	27:42	55:24	1:56:54	3:53:47
9:00	27:58	55:55	1:57:59	3:55:58
9:05	28:13	56:26	1:59:05	3:58:09
9:10	28:29	56:58	2:00:10	4:00:20
9:15	28:44	57:29	2:01:16	4:02:31
9:20	29:00	58:00	2:02:21	4:04:43
9:25	29:15	58:31	2:03:27	4:06:54
9:30	29:31	59:02	2:04:32	4:09:05
9:35	29:46	59:33	2:05:38	4:11:16
9:40	30:02	1:00:04	2:06:43	4:13:27
9:45	30:18	1:00:35	2:07:49	4:15:38
9:50	30:33	1:01:06	2:08:55	4:17:49
9:55	30:49	1:01:37	2:10:00	4:20:00
10:00	31:04	1:02:08	2:11:06	4:22:11
10:05	31:20	1:02:39	2:12:11	4:24:22
10:10	31:35	1:03:10	2:13:17	4:26:33
10:15	31:51	1:03:41	2:14:22	4:28:45
10:20	32:06	1:04:13	2:15:28	4:30:56
10:25	32:22	1:04:44	2:16:33	4:33:07
10:30	32:37	1:05:15	2:17:39	4:35:18
10:35	32:53	1:05:46	2:18:44	4:37:29
10:40	33:08	1:06:17	2:19:50	4:39:40
10:45	33:24	1:06:48	2:20:56	4:41:51
10:50	33:39	1:07:19	2:22:01	4:44:02
10:55	33:55	1:07:50	2:23:07	4:46:13
11:00	34:11	1:08:21	2:24:12	4:48:24
11:05	34:26	1:08:52	2:25:18	4:50:35
11:10	34:42	1:09:23	2:26:23	4:52:47
11:15	34:57	1:09:54	2:27:29	4:54:58
11:20	35:13	1:10:25	2:28:34	4:57:09
11:25	35:28	1:10:56	2:29:40	4:59:20
11:30	35:44	1:11:27	2:30:45	5:01:31
11:35	35:59	1:11:59	2:31:51	5:03:42
11:40	36:15	1:12:30	2:32:57	5:05:53

11:45	36:30	1:13:01	2:34:02	5:08:04
11:50	36:46	1:13:32	2:35:08	5:10:15
11:55	37:01	1:14:03	2:36:13	5:12:26
12:00	37:17	1:14:34	2:37:19	5:14:37
12:05	37:32	1:15:05	2:38:24	5:16:49
12:10	37:48	1:15:36	2:39:30	5:19:00
12:15	38:04	1:16:07	2:40:35	5:21:11
12:20	38:19	1:16:38	2:41:41	5:23:22
12:25	38:35	1:17:09	2:42:46	5:25:33
12:30	38:50	1:17:40	2:43:52	5:27:44
12:35	39:06	1:18:11	2:44:58	5:29:55
12:40	39:21	1:18:42	2:46:03	5:32:06
12:45	39:37	1:19:13	2:47:09	5:34:17
12:50	39:52	1:19:45	2:48:14	5:36:28
12:55	40:08	1:20:16	2:49:20	5:38:40
13:00	40:23	1:20:47	2:50:25	5:40:51
13:05	40:39	1:21:18	2:51:31	5:43:02
13:10	40:54	1:21:49	2:52:36	5:45:13
13:15	41:10	1:22:20	2:53:42	5:47:24
13:20	41:25	1:22:51	2:54:48	5:49:35
13:25	41:41	1:23:22	2:55:53	5:51:46
13:30	41:57	1:23:53	2:56:59	5:53:57
13:35	42:12	1:24:24	2:58:04	5:56:08
13:40	42:28	1:24:55	2:59:10	5:58:19
13:45	42:43	1:25:26	3:00:15	6:00:30
13:50	42:59	1:25:57	3:01:21	6:02:42
13:55	43:14	1:26:28	3:02:26	6:04:53
14:00	43:30	1:27:00	3:03:32	6:07:04
14:05	43:45	1:27:31	3:04:37	6:09:15
14:10	44:01	1:28:02	3:05:43	6:11:26
14:15	44:16	1:28:33	3:06:49	6:13:37
14:20	44:32	1:29:04	3:07:54	6:15:48
14:25	44:47	1:29:35	3:09:00	6:17:59
14:30	45:03	1:30:06	3:10:05	6:20:10
14:35	45:18	1:30:37	3:11:11	6:22:21
14:40	45:34	1:31:08	3:12:16	6:24:32
14:45	45:50	1:31:39	3:13:22	6:26:44
14:50	46:05	1:32:10	3:14:27	6:28:55
14:55	46:21	1:32:41	3:15:33	6:31:06

Pace	5K	10K	½ Mar.	Mar.
15:00	46:36	1:33:12	3:16:38	6:33:17
15:05	46:52	1:33:43	3:17:44	6:35:28
15:10	47:07	1:34:14	3:18:50	6:37:39
15:15	47:23	1:34:46	3:19:55	6:39:50
15:20	47:38	1:35:17	3:21:01	6:42:01
15:25	47:54	1:35:48	3:22:06	6:44:12

15:30	48:09	1:36:19	3:23:12	6:46:23
15:35	48:25	1:36:50	3:24:17	6:48:35
15:40	48:40	1:37:21	3:25:23	6:50:46
15:45	48:56	1:37:52	3:26:28	6:52:57
15:50	49:12	1:38:23	3:27:34	6:55:08
15:55	49:27	1:38:54	3:28:39	6:57:19
15:59	49:39	1:39:19	3:29:32	6:59:04

To use this table, find your 5K, 10K, half marathon, or marathon time on the table. Your pace per mile for that race pace appears in the left-hand column, beneath the heading "Pace."

Note: All times in italics indicate performances that are faster than the current world records for those distances.

INJURY PREVENTION

The table below suggests exercises to prevent and rehabilitate specific running-related injuries (though you should only use these exercises for rehabilitation after clearance from a medical professional). Note that a full-body strengthening and injury-prevention program should always be your first option. If injuries come on suddenly and are accompanied by sharp or severe pain, restricted movement, high fever, or other critical warning signs, consult a health professional immediately. Also note that you should consult a physician regarding dose and duration of use before including ibuprofen as part of your prevention or rehabilitation routine.

Excercises to Prevent and Rehabilitate Running Injuries

Injury	Description	Exercises	Page	Notes
Achilles Bursitis	Pain on the rear of your heel caused by an inflamed bursa (lies between Achilles tendon and heel bone).	AIS – Calves (gastrocnemius)	105	Icing post-run may reduce chronic inflammation.
		Heel Dips, performed on flat surface (e.g., floor)	109	
Achilles Tendinitis	Overuse injury accompanied by painful inflammation in the Achilles tendon.	AIS – Calves (gastrocnemius)	105	Icing and elevation may help. Short-term use of heel lifts and ibuprofen can provide temporary relief. Consider foot subtalar joint alignment assessment by orthopedist, podiatrist, or physical therapist.
		Wobble Board – Forward & Backward	91	
Achilles Tendinosis	Degenerative damage in the Achilles tendon producing chronic pain without inflammation.	Heel Dips	109	Don't ice or use anti-inflammatories, as tendinosis doesn't involve inflammation. Consider foot subtalar joint alignment assessment by orthopedist, podiatrist, or physical therapist.
		AIS – Calves (gastrocnemius)	105	
		Wobble Board – Forward & Backward	91	
ACL Injury (anterior cruciate ligament)	Sprain or tear of ligaments in the middle of your knee that connect your femur to your tibia.	Walkout/Jogout	94	See a health professional immediately if an ACL injury is suspected.
		Backward Walkout/Jogout	95	
		Jumpouts	95	
		Jumpouts – Sideways	96	

Injury	Description	Exercises	Page	Notes
Ankle Sprain	Pain, inflammation, discoloration, and reduced mobility of the ankle due to torn (or partially torn) ligaments.	Balance on One Leg	217	See a health professional if an ankle sprain is suspected.
		Balance with Stability Trainer	218	
		Wobble Board – Forward & Backward	91	
		Wobble Board – Side to Side	92	
		Wobble Board – Around the Clock	92	
		Ankle Eversion	98	
		Ankle Inversion	98	
Black Toenails	Painful, discolored (black) toenails. The toenail is lifted from its bed (by fluid or blood buildup) and generally falls off.			Accompanying redness indicates infection; see a health professional. Otherwise, the pain should diminish on its own. For prevention, always make sure there is ample room in the toebox of your shoe.
Blisters	A sometimes painful bubble of fluid trapped beneath the skin caused by friction and irritation.			Use a sterilized needle or pin to puncture the blister at its outside edge. Drain. Use strips of moleskin or other raised padding around the outside of the blister, covered by gauze and tape, to prevent re-irritation during running.
Calf Tightness & Strains	Pain and tightness in your calves, usually following more intense running (e.g., reps, hills, or drills).	Calf – Foam Roller	101	If pain is severe, ice for 10–15 minutes. Use either AIS or PNF stretching, not both.
		Heel Raises – Straight Knee	66	
		AIS – Calves (gastrocnemius)	105	
		PNF – Calf Stretch #1	71	
		PNF – Calf Stretch #2	72	
Chafing	Painful irritation of the skin caused by the rubbing of skin against skin or fabric.			Reduce friction by applying Vaseline or another lubricant to the affected area. Products are available (check your local running store) that won't stain your clothes. Band-Aids on the nipples can prevent pain and bleeding. Or carry a tube of Chapstick for quick application on problem areas.
Cold Lungs	Painful lungs from running in extreme cold.			A balaclava or neck warmer worn over your mouth can keep inhaled air warmer and moist. Your lungs won't freeze (air is sufficiently warmed by the time it reaches your lungs), but your air passages might suffer without some protection in extreme cold and dry air.

Injury	Description	Exercises	Page	Notes
Compartment Syndrome	Severe pain in the lower leg that begins while exercising and persists afterward, caused by pressure build-up in muscles that are restricted from expanding by connective tissue (bone, fascia).			Seek advice from a health professional. If diagosis is confirmed, either rest or surgery will be required.
DOMS (delayed onset muscle soreness)	Muscular pain following changes in training intensity or duration. Thought to be caused by eccentric muscle contractions.	Easy Distance Run	49	Ibuprofen, icing, and massage can provide pain relief but may delay repair and recovery. Run easy distance until DOMS improves, or try complete rest.
Groin Strain	Pain in the groin or inner thigh area, especially when lifting your knee, that can come on either suddenly or gradually.	PNF Hip Flexors Stretch	74	Pain can come from straining any of five adductor muscles or damage to associated CT. Ice and ibuprofen can temporarily relieve symptoms. Prevention and rehab involves stretching and strengthening exercises.
		PNF Quadriceps Stretch	74	
		PNF Hip Adductor Stretch	73	
		Leg Swings: Forward & Backward (dynamic stretching)	75	
		Monster Walk	94	
		Hip Adduction (resistance band)	96	
		Side Steps (resistance tubing or band)	93	
Hamstring Tightness & Strains	Pain or tightness in your hamstring, often restricting movement.	The Runner 360	53	Severe hamstring injuries require time off (up to several weeks). Ibuprofen and icing at outset will help with pain management. Resistance training is the best preventative medicine. Do PNF or AIS, not both.
		Hamstring – Foam Roller	101	
		Bodyweight Lunge	64	
		Air Squat	65	
		Heel Raises – Bent Knee	67	
		PNF Hamstring Stretch	70	
		PNF Hip Adductor Stretch	73	
		Hamstring – AIS	104	
Heat Exhaustion	Overheating due to high temperatures, high humidity, or hard training, leading to cramps, nausea, headache, and weakness.			Heat exhaustion can progress to heat stroke, which is a life-threatening condition. Stop training, get in a cool environment, and rehydrate.

Injury	Description	Exercises	Page	Notes
Heat Stroke	A life-threatening condition caused by prolonged exposure to extreme heat or humidity or by exercising in that heat. The National Institutes of Health lists these symptoms: Fever (>104 °F); dry, hot, red skin; confusion; rapid, shallow breathing; rapid, weak pulse; seizures; and unconsciousness. Heat stroke can cause damage to the brain and other organs, and can lead to shock or even death.			The NIH recommends: Someone with suspected heat stroke should lie down in a cool place with his or her feet lifted 12 inches; apply cool, wet cloths to the person's skin; if the person is conscious and alert, give sports drinks or a salted beverage (1 teaspoon salt per quart) to sip; Call 911 at the first sign of heat stroke.
"Heavy" Legs	Your legs feel heavy and nonresponsive. Your energy levels are low, and your motivation is sapped. Heavy legs usually results from acute or long-term overtraining.	Easy Distance Run	49	For rejuvenating "heavy" or "dead" legs, easy distance running is the best cure. A long run (at a very slow pace) can be very therapeutic. Sometimes, complete rest is required. Rehydration and carbo-loading can sometimes reverse symptoms.
		The Long Run	132	
Hip Pain & Instability	Nonspecific pain in your hip area.	The Runner 360	53	Unless you experience sharp pain, icing isn't advised, as hip pain often radiates, making it hard to locate the specific origin. General strengthening is the best prevention and remedy; perform either The Runner 360 or the various weight room exercises. Stretching exercises will help increase range of motion and lessen tension.
		Step-Ups	63	
		Step-Downs	109	
		Lunge Clock	100	
		Air Squat	65	
		Deadlift	69	
		Side Steps	93	
		Monster Walk	94	
		Hip Adduction (resistance band)	96	
		PNF Hip Adductor Stretch	73	
		Gluteals – AIS	106	
		Leg Swings – Forward & Backward	75	
		Leg Swings – Sideways	76	
Hip Bursitis, aka Trochanteric Bursitis	Pain and inflammation on the outside of your hip, located at the bony protuberance of your femur.	Leg Lifts	60	Icing and ibuprofen can provide temporary relief. Prevention and rehab requires core and stability training.
		Russian Oblique Twist	61	
		Sidewinder Plank with Leg Lift (from The Runner 360)	55	
		Windshield Wipers (from The Runner 360)	57	

Injury	Description	Exercises	Page	Notes
IT Band Syndrome	Pain on either the outside of your knee or the outside of your hip generated by a tight IT Band (iliotibial band), often with weak hip abductors as an underlying cause.	IT Band Stretch	78	Icing and ibuprofen can provide temporary relief, but longterm prevention and recovery requires both loosening (stretching) the IT band and strengthening your hip abductors.
		IT Band – Foam Roller	102	
		Wobble – Side to Side	92	
		Wobble – Around the Clock	92	
		Side Steps	93	
		Side Leg Lift (from Running Circuit)	235	
Knee Pain (general- -see below for "Runner's Knee")	Generalized, sharp knee pain that can occur on the front of the knee without an obvious inciting incident or structural impairment (no visible swelling or damage).	Step-Ups	63	Pain in the knee that is hard to diagnose might result from damage to pain nerves themselves (from poor mechanics). Prevention and rehab requires strengthening the hips and quads.
		Step-Downs	109	
		Side Steps	93	
		Side Leg Lift (from Running Circuit)	235	
		Hip Adduction (resistance band)	96	
Lethargy (loss of motivation)	You feel annoyance or dread in anticipation of an upcoming workout. You have no desire to train at all.			Mental burnout is the first sign of physical burnout. You've probably been overtraining. Take an easy week or, if required, take some time off completely (at least a few days). Rehydration and carbo-loading can sometimes reverse symptoms.
Lower Back Pain & Stiffness	Pain or stiffness in the lower back, often affecting your stride and making it hard to perform everyday activities.	Marching Bridge (The Runner 360)	58	For lower back tightness, try the Daydreamer for a quick fix. Use all exercises to strengthen, loosen, and maintain flexibility.
		Russian Oblique Twist	61	
		PNF Hip Flexors Stretch	74	
		Lower Back – Foam Roller	103	
		Trunk Extensors (Lower Back) – AIS	106	
		The Daydreamer	110	
MCL and LCL Damage (collateral ligaments)	Pain and swelling on the side(s) of your knee, often accompanied by instability. Usually results from a blow or force that moves the knee sideways.	Step-Ups	63	See a health professional if a sprain or tear of the MCL or LCL is suspected. Strengthen surrounding muscles (especially your quadriceps) for prevention.
		Bodyweight Lunge	64	
		Air Squat	65	
		Wobble – Side to Side	92	
		Wobble – Around the Clock	92	

Injury	Description	Exercises	Page	Notes
Meniscus Tear	Pain at the side or center of your knee, accompanied by swelling, usually following a twisting motion (with your foot stationary) that damages one of the pads of fibrocartilage cushioning your knee.			See a health professional if a meniscus tear is suspected. Symptoms include: a popping sensation at the time of injury, swelling that gets worse, or your knee's catching or feeling unstable.
Morton's Neuroma	Painful, burning sensation on the bottom of your foot beneath your third and fourth toes, sometimes radiating to the small toe and toward the second toe.			Caused by inflammation of a nerve between the third and fourth toe. Ice and ibuprofen can provide some temporary relief. A shoe with plenty of room in the toe box might help (tight shoes can contribute to the problem). Insoles with extra padding beneath the affected area are suggested. Toe spacers (special socks or home-made gauze/fabric wedges that spread the toes) can provide relief. Surgery is sometimes necessary, so see a health professional.
Muscle Cramps	Sudden, involuntary, and sustained contraction of a muscle that causes pain and doesn't relax.	Hamstring (static stretch)	76	When cramps occur, use static stretching to overcome the cramp, with the stretch held long enough to negate the stretch reflex, thereby loosening the muscle; hold the stretch until the muscle relaxes. Also try weightbearing ankle dorsiflexion (e.g., pulling toes/ forefoot up while in a standing position).
		Calf (static stretch)	78	
Osteoarthritis	Pain, swelling, and immobility in a joint (for runners, usually knee or hip) caused by loss of cartilage.			Most osteoarthritis is genetic, with age and trauma also acting as factors; running doesn't cause it. Masters runners should consider getting an x-ray to check on cartilage thickness; if thinning has occurred, you'll be able to make informed training and racing choices that better allow you to remain physically active.
Pes anserine bursitis (medial knee)	Pain on the inside (medial) part of the lower knee (located a couple of inches lower than the level of the kneecap).	Hamstring – AIS	104	Icing (10–15 minutes) and ibuprofen can relieve initial symptoms. Prevention and rehab should include stretching (especially the hamstring) and strengthening exercises.
		PNF Hip Adductor Stretch	73	
		Step-Downs	109	
		Lunge Clock	100	
		Air Squat	65	

Injury	Description	Exercises	Page	Notes
Piriformis Syndrome	Sharp pain, tingling, or numbness that originates slightly above the center-middle portion of your glute (buttock) and can travel down the buttocks and into your hamstring.	Glutes – Foam Roller	103	Caused by the piriformis muscle compressing the sciatic nerve. Treatment can initially include icing and ibuprofen to reduce inflammation of the piriformis. Prevention and rehab requires strengthening hip abductors, increasing range of motion of hip flexors, and relaxing hip adductors and lower back.
		Lower Back – Foam Roller	103	
		PNF Glute Stretch	72	
		PNF Hip Adductor Stretch	73	
		Quadriceps (static stretch)	77	
		Gluteals – AIS	106	
		Leg Swings – Forward & Backward	75	
		Leg Swings – Sideways	76	
		Flat-Footed Marching	209	
		Side Steps	93	
		Sidewinder Plank with Leg Lift (from The Runner 360)	55	
Plantar Fasciitis	Pain that can be felt: in the heel, where it's often mistaken for a heel bruise; at the point where the heel meets the arch; along the arch; or elsewhere throughout the foot.	Towel Toe Curls	107	Plantar fasciitis can stop your running in its tracks, then linger for months (or years). Icing and ibuprofen can provide temporary relief. Onset can be sudden, with an inciting incident, or gradual (over the course of weeks). Consider foot subtalar joint alignment assessment by orthopedist, podiatrist, or physical therapist.
		Big Toe Taps	108	
		Foot Work	107	
		AIS – Calves (gastrocnemius)	105	
		Wobble – Forward & Backward	91	
		Wobble – Side to Side	92	
Plica Syndrome (knee)	Pain, sometimes accompanied by inflammation and a snapping sensation, on the inside (medial) part of the knee.	Step-Ups	63	Initial treatmeant with ice and ibuprofen can reduce inflammation. Gait (stride) problems are associated with this injury, so hip and quadriceps strengthening are advised.
		Step-Downs	109	
		Side Steps	93	
		Side Leg Lift (from Running Circuit)	235	
		Hip Adduction (resistance band)	96	
		Hamstring – AIS	104	
		Quadriceps – AIS	105	

Injury	Description	Exercises	Page	Notes
Pulled Muscle (general)	A "pulled muscle" is another term for a muscle strain. It involves pain, tightness, and sometimes immobility and discoloration (bruising).	The Runner 360	53	Ice and ibuprofen can be used to treat initial pain and inflammation. Preventive strategies should include regular resistance training and stretching.
		Runner's Weight Room Routine	59	
		Foam Roller massage	101–103	
		AIS Stretching	104	
		PNF Stretching	70	
Quadriceps Pain	Aching, painful quadriceps (front thigh) muscles that aren't related to an inciting incident (in contrast to DOMS, which results an from overtraining incident). Pain can become both chronic and intense enough to restrict running—and may even make walking up and down stairs painful.	Downhill Running	52	Icing and ibuprofen can provide some temporary relief. Many runners use either downhill running at tempo effort or downhill sprints to prevent and cure this condition; the eccentric contractions trigger beneficial adaptations.
		Short Hill Sprints (downhill)	220	
		PNF Quadriceps Stretch	74	
		Quadriceps – AIS	105	
		Quadriceps – Foam Roller	102	
		Butt Kicks – Dynamic Flexibility	206	
Runner's Knee, aka Patellofemoral Pain Syndrome, aka Chondromalacia	Knee pain caused by cartilage irritation or deterioration beneath your kneecap (patella).	The Runner 360	53	Ice and ibuprofen can be used to treat initial inflammation. Strengthen your hips and thighs to help your patella track better.
		Runner's Weight Room Routine	59	
		Monster Walk	94	
Sciatica	Pain, tingling ("pins and needles"), and/or numbness that is usually felt in the lower back, buttocks, and hamstring, but can radiate down through the calves and feet. It can be incapacitating.	Glutes – Foam Roller	103	Caused by irritation of the sciatic nerve (see "Piriformis"). Treatment by chiropractors provides relief to many runners. A core muscle strength and stability exercise program designed by a physical therapist might be warranted. Reducing inflammation and tension helps. Complete rest isn't always effective.
		Lower Back – Foam Roller	103	
		Gluteals – AIS	106	
		PNF Hip Flexors Stretch	74	
Shin Splints (medial) – aka Medical Tibial Stress Sydrome (MTSS)	Sharp pain along the inside (medial location) of your shins.	Ankle Inversion	98	Icing and ibuprofen can provide temporary relief. Consider foot subtalar joint alignment assessment by orthopedist, podiatrist, or physical therapist.
		Ankle Plantarflexion	97	
		Foot Work	107	
Shin Splints – Front (outside of shin)	Sharp pain along the outside (front) of your shins.	Ankle Dorsiflexion	97	Icing and ibuprofen can provide temporary relief.
		Seated Toe Taps	108	
		Foot Work	107	

Injury	Description	Exercises	Page	Notes
Side Stitches	A sharp pain just beneath the rib cage—usually on the right side, but can occur on the left as well. Although the cause isn't fully understood, a spasmodic diaphragm is suspected.	Leg Lifts	60	Adequate hydration and good fitness are a primary defense. Four-step breathing can relieve symptoms: Breath in twice in succession (in sync with two strides) to fill your lungs maximally, then purse your lips (like blowing out a candle) and blow out intensely for two more strides. Repeat 10–20 times. If all else fails, ibuprofen taken 2 hours before a race can help prevent stitches, but consult a doctor before taking any medication during exercise.
Sports Hernia	An injury to your core muscles (obliques), leading to chronic pain in the lower abdomen, groin, and (in males) the testicles.	Russian Oblique Twist	61	An injury/tear to the abdominal wall that doesn't produce the bulge seen in a traditional hernia. Prevention includes strengthening of your obliques (side abdominals). Recovery may require surgery.
		Scorpion Fighter (from The Runner 360)	55	
		Sidewinder Plank with Leg Lift (from The Runner 360)	55	
		Leg Lifts	60	
Stress Fracture (tibia)	Sharp pain alongside your shins (feels like severe shin splints) that hurts from the first step until the last.	The Runner 360	53	If you suspect you have a stress fracture, see a podiatrist, orthopedist, or other health professional. Prevention includes all-around strength training, limiting yourself to gradual increases in mileage and intensity of training, and doing specific exercises to strengthen surrounding lower leg muscles.
		Ankle Inversion	98	
		Ankle Plantarflexion	97	
		Seated Toe Taps	108	
		Foot Work	107	
Stress Fracture (metatarsal)	Sharp pain in your foot. You might feel pain over a wide area of your foot, but if you apply pressure directly to the spot of the fracture, the pain will become sharp and intense.			If you suspect you have a metatarsal stress fracture, see a podiatrist, orthopedist, or other health professional. You might need to wear a cast or walking boot. Prevention includes proper footwear (with suitable arch support), limiting yourself to gradual increases in mileage and intensity of training, and avoidance of rushed adaptation to barefoot running (or to shoes meant to mimic barefoot running). If you suffer a metatarsal stress fracture, you'll need to take 1–3 months off from training.

Injury	Description	Exercises	Page	Notes
Stress Fracture (other)	Sharp pain in other areas of the foot, and in the fibula, femur (especially in women), pelvis, etc.			If you suspect you have a stress fracture, see a podiatrist, orthopedist, or other health professional. Stress fractures in some areas heal more slowly than in others, and some stress fractures indicate other underlying medical problems.

BUILD YOUR RUNNING BODY

ACHILLES TENDINITIS

An overuse injury of the Achilles tendon that is accompanied by painful inflammation.

ACHILLES TENDINOSIS

Degenerative damage of the Achilles tendon at the cellular level that produces chronic pain without inflammation. The cause of most Achilles tendon pain.

ACHILLES TENDON

The tendon on the back of the lower leg connecting the calf muscles (gastrocnemius, soleus, and plantaris) to the heel bone (calcaneus).

ACHILLES TENDON TEAR/RUPTURE

An acute injury that occurs when the Achilles tendon tears partially or fully ruptures. In the case of rupture, pain is often described as a sudden snap, like getting shot in the back on the heel, and results in immediate limping and some incapacitation.

ACIDOSIS

A pH of less than 7.0 within muscle fibers, caused by the buildup of hydrogen ions created during anaerobic energy production. Acidosis is theorized to cause fatigue and pain when running at high intensities and can lead to a state of near-incapacitation.

ACTIN

One of two myofilaments within muscle fibers that work together to shorten (contract) the fiber. Actin is the "thin" filament that theoretically slides over myosin (the "thick" filament) during muscle contraction.

ACUTE INJURY

An injury that occurs as the result of a single event, usually traumatic, and that requires immediate treatment (e.g., muscle strains, fractures, and sprained ankles).

AEROBIC

Refers to a process that requires oxygen.

AEROBIC ENERGY

Energy produced by aerobic processes. In cells, aerobic energy is produced by tiny organelles called mitochondria.

AEROBIC ENZYMES

Proteins that increase the efficiency of chemical reactions within mitochondria, thereby improving mitochondria's ability to produce aerobic energy.

AFFERENT FEEDBACK

Messages sent from sensory nerves to the central nervous system in response to external stimuli.

AGE GRADING

A scoring system for races in which each runner's finish time is scored as a percentage of the maximum performance expected at that runner's age, with 100 percent being the top predicted score. In age-grading, the maximum performance for each age is determined by a curve of all age-group world records for the race distance.

AIS (ACTIVE ISOLATED STRETCHING)

A stretching technique that utilizes contracted opposing muscles to move a muscle into a stretched position, then requires assistance (e.g., pulling on a rope) to slightly increase the stretch. To avoid the stretch reflex, AIS movements are never maintained (or held) at full range of motion for longer than two seconds.

ALKALINE

A pH above 7.0. The opposite of acidic.

ALTITUDE TENT

A commercially available tent that simulates the low-oxygen atmosphere found at 8,000 to 12,000 feet.

ALVEOLI

Tiny air sacs in the lungs where carbon dioxide and oxygen are exchanged. Alveoli are surrounded by small blood vessels called capillaries, which help facilitate the exchange.

AMINO ACIDS

The building blocks of protein. A group of organic molecules that are comprised of a basic amino group, an acidic carboxyl group, and an organic R group (or side chain) that is specific to each amino acid. The human body uses twenty-one amino acids, only twelve of which it can produce itself.

ANAEROBIC

A process that doesn't require oxygen.

ANAEROBIC ENERGY

Energy created without the use of oxygen by the glycolytic and phosphagen systems. In muscle fibers, anaerobic energy production takes place in the sarcoplasm.

ANAEROBIC ENZYMES

Enzymes that break down the carbohydrates that fuel glycolysis. Without enzymes, glycolysis would not occur.

ANTERIOR CRUCIATE LIGAMENT

One of a pair of ligaments that sit in the middle of the knee and connect the femur (thigh bone) to the tibia (shin bone). The cruciate ligaments stabilize the tibia's forward and backward motion, and they also help stabilize rotation in the joint.

ANTIOXIDANTS

Molecules (e.g., vitamins C and E) that can counteract the effects of free radicals, safely donating electrons to them and stopping the free-radical chain reaction that can damage cells.

AORTA

The largest artery in the body, through which oxygenated blood is first pumped out of the heart.

ARTERY

A large blood vessel that carries oxygenated blood away from the heart (except for the pulmonary arteries, which carry deoxygenated blood from the heart to the lungs).

ARTICULAR CARTILAGE

The smooth coating on the surface ends of bones that allows bones to glide over one another and provides a flexible cushion within the joint.

ATP (ADENOSINE TRIPHOSPHATE)

ATP is the end product of both aerobic and anaerobic energy production. It provides the energy for all physical movement. Each molecule of ATP is recycled by the human body approximately 500–750 times per day.

ATRIUM

One of the two upper chambers of the heart. The right atrium receives deoxygenated blood from the body; the left atrium receives oxygenated blood from the lungs.

AXON

A long nerve fiber that transmits messages from the nerve cell body to the axon terminal, where messages cross a synapse to other neurons, muscles, or glands.

BAREFOOT RUNNING

Running without shoes. Championed as a more natural way to run, it has advocates who contend that it makes running healthier and more efficient, but studies have failed to find support for this hypothesis.

BASE TRAINING

A period of training in which aerobic conditioning and improved muscular and connective tissue strengthening are targeted.

BODY HEAT

Energy created as a by-product of ATP production. Body heat is created when energy is released during the breakdown of carbs, fats, and protein to create ATP, as well as when ATP is used to power muscle contractions. Up to 75 percent of the energy produced is not captured and escapes the body as heat.

BONE

Rigid connective tissue that forms the skeletal structure of the body. Bone is a living tissue that undergoes constant renewal.

BONE REMODELING

The process by which bone is broken down and replaced. During bone remodeling, cells called osteoclasts remove old, damaged tissue while osteoblasts create new bone. This cycle can take 3–4 months.

BONK

To run out of energy in an endurance competition. Bonking is typically the result of depleted muscle glycogen, excessive fatigue, severe dehydration, or extreme body temperature.

BUFFERS

Substances that neutralize the effects of hydrogen ions (acidic pH) within muscle fibers. Examples are phosphates, bicarbonate, and some proteins.

CALVES

The gastrocnemius and soleus, the large muscles on the backs of your lower legs.

CAPILLARIES

The smallest blood vessels in the human body. Capillaries are fed by arterioles (which

are fed by arteries), and then feed into venules, which drain into veins.

CAPILLARIZATION

The increased growth of capillaries surrounding muscle fibers.

CAPILLARY BEDS

The zone between your bloodstream and cells
where oxygen, carbon dioxide, nutrients, and
cellular waste products are exchanged.

CARBOHYDRATES

Also called saccharides, one of the three macronutrients. Carbohydrates are built upon
simple sugar molecules containing carbon,
hydrogen, and oxygen.

CARBO-LOADING

Increasing carbohydrate consumption and
decreasing fat and protein consumption prior
to competing in endurance events in an effort
to boost muscle glycogen stores. Modern
sports drinks, gels, and other glycogen replacement strategies have reduced the importance of carbo-loading.

CARDIAC MUSCLE

Specialized muscle found in the heart. Cardiac muscle can beat (contract and relax)
nonstop for a lifetime.

CARDIAC OUTPUT

The amount of blood that a heart can pump
in one minute, determined by a combination
of stroke volume and heart rate.

CARDIO

Jargon for "cardiovascular system training,"
the term has become synonymous with endurance training of all kinds.

CARDIOVASCULAR SYSTEM

A blood distribution network composed of
the heart, blood, and blood vessels, which
transports oxygen, nutrients, hormones,
waste products, etc. throughout the body.

CARTILAGE

A tough connective tissue. All bones begin as
cartilage in the womb. In adults, cartilage is
found in the ears, the nose, the bronchial
tubes, the ribs, and between joints.

CENTRAL GOVERNOR

A theory on the cause of fatigue. Proposed by
Dr. Timothy Noakes in 1997, it hypothesizes
that fatigue is an emotion generated by the
brain as a means to protect the body during
exercise. The Central Governor anticipates
physiological "catastrophe" (damage to your
body) from overexertion during physical activity and reduces muscle fiber activation,
thereby limiting exertion.

CENTRAL NERVOUS SYSTEM (CNS)

The brain and spinal cord.

CEREBRAL CORTEX

"Gray matter." The cerebral cortex is the out-
ermost layer of the brain and is associated
with higher brain functions that include reasoning, language, and perception.

CHRONIC INJURY

Pain, inflammation, or incapacitation that generally results from overuse, muscle imbalance,
improper footwear, or improper technique

over an extended period of time. Examples are IT band syndrome, Achilles tendinosis, and non-acute cases of plantar fasciitis.

COLLAGEN FIBER

Tough, flexible fibers that are a primary component of connective tissue, especially tendons and ligaments.

COMPLEMENTARY PROTEINS

A combination of two or more sources of incomplete (plant) proteins that results in a full set of essential amino acids.

COMPLETE PROTEIN

Also called high-quality protein, a protein that contains all the essential amino acids in optimal proportions for supporting biological functions in the body.

CONDITIONAL AMINO ACID

A nonessential amino acid that can become essential during illness or stress.

CONNECTIVE TISSUE

Tissue that connects the body's muscles, organs, blood vessels, nerves, and all other tissues together—surrounding, supporting, strengthening, cushioning, protecting, and storing energy for them.

CONTRACTION VELOCITY

The time it takes a muscle fiber to reach peak contraction (to shorten).

CONVECTION

In running, the process by which heat transferred from muscles to the blood is diffused into the air. At air temperatures greater than 98.6°F, the average human body will absorb heat from the air.

CONVERSATIONAL PACE

A pace at which a conversation can be maintained while running. Considered the mark of a safe, aerobic pace, it is the favored pace for all regular and easy distance runs.

CORE

Muscles of the belly, groin, hips, mid-back, and lower back that strengthen and stabilize posture, position, and movement during athletic activity.

CORI CYCLE

The process by which lactate is converted to glucose in the liver.

CORTISOL

A hormone that serves as a catabolic agent and an anti-inflammatory. In running, cortisol breaks down weaker muscle tissue so that it can be replaced by stronger tissue, reduces inflammation during high-intensity training, and spares glycogen by accelerating the use of fat.

CREATINE PHOSPHATE

Also known as phosphocreatine, creatine phosphate is the fuel source for the phosphagen system.

CROSS EDUCATION

Strength gains that occur in an untrained limb when its opposite is trained.

CRUISE INTERVALS

Repetitions (usually 400–2,000 meters) that

are run at an effort equivalent to what a runner could maintain for an hour all-out. Often used as an alternative to tempo runs.

DEPOLARIZATION

A decrease in the difference in charge between the inside of muscle fibers and the space outside. One theory of fatigue suggests that depolarization leads to weaker muscle contractions.

DIFFUSION

The process by which substances (liquids, gases, and solids) move from an area of high concentration to an area of lower concentration.

DISTANCE

Short for "distance running," it refers to a workout from a few to many miles at a steady, submaximal pace—often referred to as a "conversational pace." Distance accounts for the majority of volume in an endurance runner's training program.

DRAFTING

Running just behind or on the shoulder of other runners to gain a physiological and psychological edge.

DYNAMIC STRETCHING

Controlled movements that bring muscles to their full range of motion (without exceeding their natural range of motion or holding the muscle in that position). Examples include leg swings, high-knee drills, butt-kick drills, and any other activity that simultaneously works and stretches the muscle. Shown to consistently improve performance, it is the best stretching activity pre-workout or pre-competition.

DYNAMOMETER (HAND)

An instrument for measuring grip strength, which is helpful for monitoring nervous system fatigue (when fatigue goes up, grip strength goes down).

ECCENTRIC MUSCLE CONTRACTIONS

Muscle contractions that occur when muscles are forced to contract and stretch (i.e., shorten and lengthen) at the same time. For example, when you run, your quadriceps muscles both contract and relax when your foot touches down.

ECTOMORPH

A body type common among elite distance runners. Features include long thin limbs, flat chest, equal shoulder and hip width, and low body fat.

ELASTIC FIBERS

Fibers composed of elastin proteins that can stretch up to 1.5 times their length. They are found in connective tissues like skin and fascia, and to a lesser degree in tendons and ligaments.

ELASTIC RECOIL

The ability of connective tissue to store energy each time it's stretched, and then to release that energy in response to muscle contraction and shortening of the connective tissue. Recoil can provide up to 50 percent of the propulsive force for a running stride.

ELECTRON TRANSPORT CHAIN

Part of the aerobic energy system within

mitochondria. The electron transport chain receives electrons from NADH and FADH2 produced by the Krebs cycle, triggering a series of reactions that creates the majority of aerobically produced ATP and ends with oxygen acting as the final electron acceptor in the chain.

ENDOCRINE GLAND

A gland that secretes hormones.

ENDOCRINE SYSTEM

The system that produces chemical messengers called hormones. Endocrine glands are found in many tissues.

ENDORPHINS

Hormones secreted by the pituitary gland and the hypothalamus during exercise. They are responsible for the "runner's high," the feeling of euphoria that runners sometimes experience during endurance training.

ENDOSYMBIOTIC THEORY

The theory that mitochondria are the evolved remnants of a bacterial invasion that occurred more than one billion years ago. It suggests that such an invasion made human life possible.

ENERGY PATHWAY

One of the aerobic or anaerobic processes for creating ATP from food (carbohydrates, fats, and proteins). The three energy systems—glycolytic, phosphagen, and aerobic—and the various steps within each.

EPINEPHRINE

Also called "adrenaline," a hormone that increases heart rate, relaxes airways, constricts blood vessels in the skin, and stimulates the breakdown of muscle glycogen and fat for energy production.

ERYTHROPOIETIN (EPO)

A hormone that stimulates bone marrow to produce red blood cells; it also improves nervous system and cognitive function. In its synthetic form, a widely used performance-enhancing drug that improves endurance performance by 5–15 percent. EPO is banned by WADA and has been linked to numerous athlete deaths.

ESSENTIAL AMINO ACID

An amino acid that the body cannot produce on its own, and which must therefore be obtained from food.

ESSENTIAL FATTY ACID

A fatty acid that cannot be synthesized by the human body and must be included in the diet.

ESTROGEN

Known as "female sex hormone," estrogen is actually found in both sexes, but with lower volumes in males. In running, it facilitates the breakdown of stored fat into fuel.

EXTRACELLULAR MATRIX

The distinctive mix of fibers, proteins, carbohydrates, minerals, salts, fluids, and other elements that surrounds connective tissue cells and provides structural support.

FASCIA

Connective tissue that surrounds and

penetrates every muscle, nerve, organ, bone, structure, cavity, and tissue in the body. Composed of collagen and elastic fibers, it appears as membrane, sheet, cord, and gristle.

FASCICLE

Columns of muscle fibers that are banded together to form skeletal muscles.

FAST GLYCOLYSIS

The anaerobic energy pathway most people think of when they discuss anaerobic energy production. Fast glycolysis uses the two pyruvate molecules created by glycolysis to produce lactate and NAD+, allowing glycolysis to cycle again quicky, generating ATP up to one hundred times faster than aerobic energy production. Fast glycolysis is only capable of one minute of full-capacity energy production.

FAST-TWITCH MUSCLE FIBER

One of the three human muscle fibers. These large fibers contract faster and more forcefully than both slow-twitch and intermediate fast-twitch fibers. Especially useful for sprints, jumps, and other activities that require short bursts of power. Technically referred to as Type IIx muscle fiber.

FATIGUE

A reduced ability to generate muscular force when attempting to maintain or increase effort. Multiple theories have been proposed, from acidosis to leaky calcium cells, but the exact cause of fatigue remains unclear.

FAT-LOADING

Increasing the percentage of fat in an athlete's diet in preparation for endurance events lasting more than four hours. Sticking to a high-fat diet for 7–10 days before a competition can increase the rate at which an athlete burns fat by as much as 50 percent.

FATS

One of three macronutrients (along with carbohydrates and proteins). The most concentrated source of dietary energy, with nine calories per gram, versus four each for carbs and protein. Fats consist primarily of glycerides, with other lipids in minor quantities.

FEMUR

The thigh bone. The largest bone in the human body, the femur can support up to thirty times the weight of the human body.

FIBER CONVERSION

Conversion of one type of muscle fiber into another as a result of training or inactivity. Most "conversion" is thought to occur due to fibers taking on the characteristics of other fibers (i.e., they don't actually transform into the new fiber type, with the full physiological properties of those fibers).

FIBROCARTILAGE

Dense connective tissue that makes up the lateral and medial menisci (in knees), as well as the discs that cushion vertebrae and numerous joints. Your body often repairs damaged articular cartilage with fibrocartilage, which has tremendous tensile strength and resilience.

FIGHT-OR-FLIGHT RESPONSE

A reaction to a perceived danger that induces an immediate nervous system and endocrine system response, preparing the body to either "fight" or to flee the danger. The resulting increase in strength and speed is useful for athletes who are preparing for competition.

FOREFOOT AND MID-FOOT STRIKE

Landing on the forefoot or mid-foot during each running stride. Believed by minimalist and barefoot running advocates to result in fewer running injuries due to reduced impact forces.

FREE RADICAL

An atom or molecule with an odd, unpaired number of electrons that typically forms when oxygen interacts with other molecules during metabolism. Free radicals damage molecules by attempting to "steal" their electrons, often triggering a chain reaction that harms the cell.

GAP JUNCTIONS

Tiny cylindrical channels that allow the electrical impulse from a nerve to jump the synaptic gap to the target tissue.

GLUCAGON

A hormone that stimulates the liver to break down glycogen and release glucose when blood glucose levels drop. Glucagon promotes fat-burning and is valuable in longer races.

GLUCOSE

The form of carbohydrate most often used by humans for energy production. Glucose is used as a substrate for glycolysis, which serves as a first step in both aerobic and anaerobic energy production (via the glycolytic system) within muscle fibers.

GLYCEMIC INDEX (GI)

A measure of the rise in blood sugar. Blood sugar levels rise based on the speed at which glucose enters the bloodstream, with glucose itself having a GI of 100.

GLYCEMIC LOAD (GL)

An estimation of the rise in blood sugar levels following the ingestion of carbohydrates, with one unit of GL roughly equivalent to the effect of one gram of glucose.

GLYCOLYSIS

A multi-step chemical reaction within cells that produces two or three ATP molecules plus two molecules of pyruvate. The pyruvate can either be recycled to produce anaerobic energy or shuttled to mitochondria to produce aerobic energy.

GLYCOLYTIC SYSTEM

An anaerobic energy system (or pathway) that resides in the sarcoplasm and relies upon glycolysis. Glycolysis produces two or three ATP molecules anaerobically, at which point it becomes either "fast" glycolysis or "slow" glycolysis.

HALF-LIFE

The length of time it takes for an amount of something (e.g., number of capillaries gained through training) to fall to half its original number or volume.

HAMSTRINGS

In common usage, the large muscles on the back of the upper leg (the biceps femoris, semimembranosus, and semitendinosus). Technically, hamstrings are the tendons that connect these muscles to the tibia and fibula, and can be felt (and seen) on the back of the knee.

HEART RATE

The number of times that the heart beats in one minute.

HEAT EXHAUSTION

In running, a heat-related illness usually caused by exposure to high temperatures (especially when accompanied by high humidity), resulting in dehydration or salt depletion.

HEAT STROKE

A life-threatening heat illness defined as having a body temperature in excess of 104–106°F (40–41°C). Untreated, it can lead to damage of several organs, including the brain, heart, and kidneys.

HEEL DIPS

An eccentric calf exercise that involves rising up on the balls of the feet and then slowly lowering one heel either to or below floor level. Usually performed on platforms, steps, etc., it is the only known reliable treatment for Achilles tendinosis.

HEEL STRIKE

Landing on the heel of the foot during each running stride.

HEMATOCRIT

The percentage of total blood plasma volume that is composed of red blood cells.

HIP ABDUCTORS

Muscles that help move the leg away from the body. They include the gluteus medius and the gluteus minimus.

HIP ADDUCTORS

Muscles that help move the legs back toward the midline of the body. They include the adductor brevis, adductor longus, adductor magnus, pectineus, and gracilis.

HIP EXTENSORS

Muscles that increase the angle between the thigh and the torso (i.e., backward leg swings). They include the gluteus maximus and the hamstrings.

HIP FLEXORS

Muscles that decrease the angle between the thigh and the torso (i.e., muscles that lift the knee). They include the psoas major, iliacus, rectus femoris, and sartorius.

HITTING THE WALL

The moment in a long race when competitors run out of muscle glycogen and must then rely on fat sources for energy, necessitating a slower pace and resulting in increased fatigue.

HOMEOSTASIS

The body's ability to maintain a stable and balanced internal environment, regardless of external conditions.

HORMONES

Chemical messengers within the body that govern all aspects of biological function.

HUMAN GROWTH HORMONE (HGH OR GH)

A hormone released from the pituitary gland that promotes protein synthesis, muscle hypertrophy, bone density, and tendon and ligament strength, among other things. Involved in athletic performance improvement, it is a widely abused performance-enhancing drug banned by WADA.

HYDROGEN IONS

Protons that accumulate in muscle fibers during anaerobic energy production, leading to acidosis. Hydrogen ions are also an essential component of the electron transport chain (aerobic energy production).

HYPERTHYROIDISM

A hormonal disorder caused by excess production of the thyroid hormone in the thyroid gland.

HYPERTROPHY

With respect to muscles, an increase in size. This can occur due to an increase in the sarcoplasmic volume of the muscle fiber or from an increase in myofilaments and myofibrils within muscle fibers.

HYPONATREMIA

A life-threatening condition in which sodium concentration in the blood drops dangerously low. In runners, this is usually caused by overhydrating (drinking too much water) before and during races.

HYPOTHYROIDISM

A hormonal disorder caused by deficient production of the thyroid hormone in the thyroid gland.

IMPULSES

Electrochemical messages sent by neurons. These messages can travel between two and 390 feet per second.

INCOMPLETE PROTEIN

A protein that is either missing one or more of the essential amino acids or is too low in them.

INORGANIC PHOSPHATE

Also known as "Pi," one of the products of ATP consumption. During intense exercise, more ATP is consumed than produced, leading to an increase in inorganic phosphate, which has been postulated as a cause of fatigue.

INSULAR CORTEX

A portion of the brain that lies within the folds of the cerebral cortex and plays a role in consciousness, emotion, and bodily self-awareness. The insular cortex has been identified by some studies as a major actor in the experience of fatigue.

INSULIN

A hormone that directs cells to take up glucose from the bloodstream and store it as glycogen in the muscles and liver.

INTERMEDIATE FAST-TWITCH MUSCLE FIBER

Muscle fibers that are larger than slow-twitch fibers and smaller than fast-twitch fibers, and which possess characteristics of both. They can function aerobically or anaerobically and are capable of being trained to produce both endurance and speed, making them perfect for middle-distance running. Technically referred to as Type IIa muscle fibers.

INTERVAL

The rest period following a repetition during a repetition or interval workout. Also used as an alternative term for "repetition."

INTERVAL TRAINING

Repetitions with rest intervals. Pace will vary depending on the training goal.

INVERTED PYRAMID TRAINING

A training approach practiced by runners

whose race goal is completion. Training begins with small volume and limited intensity, then gradually builds toward the expected volume and intensity of the race.

JARGON

Terms and phrases specific to a singular activity or group (e.g., in running, "PR" refers to a runner's personal record).

JOINT SPACE

The area separating bones in a joint, which is filled by cartilage. Loss of cartilage narrows the joint space and can lead to osteoarthritis.

KICK (IN A RACE)

The final finishing sprint in a race or, as used in the Central Governor model of fatigue, an increased effort (pace) over the final 10 percent of a race.

KINETIC CHAIN

The interconnected chain of muscles, nerves, connective tissue, and other structural components of the body that work together to move joints and create body movement.

KINETIC ENERGY

Energy possessed due to motion.

KREBS CYCLE

Also called the citric acid cycle, the Krebs cycle is part of aerobic energy production and occurs in the mitochondria. The two pyruvate molecules formed during slow glycolysis are converted into acetyl CoA and carbon dioxide; the acetyl CoA molecules enter the Krebs cycle, generating a total of two ATP molecules.

LACTATE

An end-product of anaerobic fast glycolysis that can be used as a carbohydrate fuel for aerobic energy production by the cell, adjacent cells, or distant cells. Once released into the bloodstream, it can also be converted to glucose by the liver through the Cori cycle.

LACTATE SHUTTLE

The process by which lactate is moved into mitochondria (within the cell), out of the cell, and between cells. Once outside the cell, lactate can travel to adjacent muscle fibers or into the bloodstream, where it's transported to distant muscles, organs (e.g., the heart and brain), or to the liver.

LACTIC ACID

Running's "bogeyman," long thought to be the cause of fatigue, pain, and even DOMS. Currently, physiologists disagree over the role of lactic acid in energy production. Recent theory suggests that lactic acid is never produced in human muscle fibers, but some physiologists still argue that it's formed briefly before immediately splitting into lactate and hydrogen ions.

LATERAL COLLATERAL LIGAMENT

One of a pair of ligaments that stretch vertically along the inside (medial collateral ligament) and outside (lateral collateral ligament) of the knee, controlling the joint's sideways motion. Damage to these ligaments disrupts the stability of the knee.

LEFT VENTRICLE

The lower left chamber of the heart, which receives oxygenated blood from the left atrium and pumps that oxygenated blood into the aorta.

LIGAMENT

Connective tissue that connects bone to bone, thereby stabilizing joints.

LIGAMENT LAXITY

Elongated ligaments, usually as a result of repeated ligament trauma, that can create joint instability. Sometimes referred to as "loose joints."

LIPOLYSIS

The breakdown of fats to fuel aerobic energy production. Although slower than carbohydrate-fueled ATP production, lipolysis provides a larger return of ATP, with a single palmitate fatty acid producing 129 molecules of ATP.

"LISTEN TO YOUR BODY"

The slogan of Dr. George Sheehan, running's late physician-philosopher, who believed that a runner's body provides valuable feedback on fitness, fatigue, injury, and more, as long as the runner is willing to consciously recognize and respond to it.

MAGIC BULLET

A one-stop solution for remedying a previously divisive, troubling, or limiting issue. In running, magic-bullet remedies (e.g., barefoot running or stride adjustment) promise improved fitness, performance, or injury reduction, ignoring the extremely complex physiology and psychology involved in running.

MASTERS COMPETITORS

In track and field, athletes age 35 and older. In road racing and cross country within the United States, athletes age 40 and over. Internationally, masters road racing is open to athletes age 35 and over.

MAXIMUM HEART RATE

The maximum number of times the heart can beat in one minute. A general guideline for estimating maximum heart rate is to use the formula: 220 minus a person's age. Maximum heart rate is determined by genetics and cannot be influenced by training.

MEDIAL COLLATERAL LIGAMENT

One of a pair of ligaments that stretch vertically along the inside (medial collateral ligament) and outside (lateral collateral ligament) of the knee, controlling the sideways motion of the knee. Damage to these ligaments disrupts the stability of the knee.

MENISCUS

Pads of fibrocartilage that provide shock absorption and structural support for the knees. Treatment for adult meniscus tears usually requires surgery to repair or remove the affected cartilage.

META-ANALYSIS

A review of multiple studies, experiments, or papers on a similar topic that looks for shared and statistically relevant patterns and outcomes.

MILEAGE

The total amount of miles that a runner logs, typically measured by the week. Most runners include all running in their "mileage," including warm-ups, warm-downs, distance runs, strides, repetitions, jogging intervals between repetitions, etc. Some runners, however, only count "quality" miles, excluding warm-ups, warm-downs, jogging, and recovery runs.

MINERALS

Inorganic elements that act as cofactors for enzymes and influence all aspects of energy metabolism.

MINIMALISM

An approach to shoe design—and training—that emphasizes a return to a more natural stride. Minimalist shoes bring the foot closer to the ground, have a reduced difference between heel and forefoot height, are lightweight and flexible, and have a wider toe box. (Some minimalist shoes, like Vibram FiveFingers, mimic barefoot running.)

MITOCHONDRIA

Microscopic structures within cells that use substrates and oxygen to produce aerobic energy.

MITOCHONDRIAL BIOGENESIS

The process by which mitochondria increase in volume within muscle fibers, including both the total number of all mitochondria and the size of individual mitochondria. Specific training (e.g., tempo runs) can stimulate increased mitochondrial biogenesis.

MONOCARBOXYLATE TRANSPORT PROTEINS (MCTS)

Specialized transport proteins that move lactate (and hydrogen ions). Within cells, MCTs move lactate to mitochondria or help push it out of the cell. MCTs can also import lactate from outside the cell for use as fuel.

MOTOR NEURONS

Neurons in the spinal cord that control muscles. Each motor neuron controls a specific group of muscle fibers within a single muscle.

MOTOR UNIT

A motor neuron and all the muscle fibers it controls. All muscle fibers within a motor unit must be of the same fiber type, and they all fire simultaneously.

MUSCLE

See entries for cardiac muscle, smooth muscle, and skeletal muscle.

MUSCLE BALANCE

Complimentary (balanced) strength, flexibility, coordination, and fitness found in opposing muscles (e.g., hamstrings and quadriceps).

MUSCLE FIBER LADDER

The theoretical process by which human muscle fibers are recruited. Slow-twitch fibers are recruited first. As force requirements increase, intermediate fast-twitch fibers are added. Finally, beginning at about 65 percent maximum force, fast-twitch fibers are recruited. Slower fibers remain active as faster fibers are recruited.

MUSCLE FIBER TYPE

A muscle fiber's designation as slow-twitch, intermediate fast-twitch, or fast-twitch, as well as its possession of the characteristics of that specific type of fiber.

MUSCLE SPINDLE

Stretch receptors (sensory organs) located within muscles that line up parallel to muscle fibers. They sense changes in the length of muscles and, in runners, limit stride length through the stretch reflex, which forces muscles to contract in order to avoid injury from overstretching.

MUSCULOTENDINOUS ZONE (MUSCLE-TENDON ZONE)

The area where muscle gradually gives way to tendon, and where muscle fibers and tendons merge, operating as a de facto muscle-tendon unit.

MYOFILAMENTS

Protein filaments within muscle fibers, generally referring to actin and myosin, which according to the "sliding filament theory" interact to create muscle fiber—and hence muscle—contraction.

MYOSIN

One of two myofilaments within muscle fibers that work together to shorten (contract) the fiber. Myosin is the "thick" filament that actin (the "thin" filament) theoretically slides over during muscle contraction.

MYOTENDINOUS JUNCTION

The point at which individual muscle fibers meet tendon. It is considered the muscle's weak link (the spot where most muscle strains occur).

NERVOUS SYSTEM

One of two principal communications networks in the body (the other is the endocrine system), composed of the central nervous system and the peripheral nervous system.

NEURAL PATHWAY

The path that a nerve impulse follows. Some simple pathways, like reflexes, are hard-wired. Others, like those involved in a runner's stride, develop in response to training. A goal of training is to improve neural-pathway efficiency.

NEURON

A nerve cell.

NEUROTRANSMITTERS

Chemicals released by neurons that are used to communicate messages across the synapse.

NONESSENTIAL AMINO ACID

An amino acid that can be synthesized by the human body.

NOREPINEPHRINE

Also known as "noradrenaline," a hormone and neurotransmitter that is active in the fight-or-flight response, raising heart rate, blood flow to skeletal muscle, and glucose levels in the blood.

NUTRIENTS

All the components of food—plus water and oxygen—that nourish the body.

ORGANELLES

Tiny parts of cells, analogous to organs in the human body.

OSTEOARTHRITIS

A degenerative joint disease in which the joint space can narrow to the point of bone-on-bone contact, leaving the joint inflamed, painful, less mobile, and partially disabled.

Osteoarthritis is linked to cartilage damage, age, and genetics.

OSTEOBLASTS

Cells that repair damaged bone by laying down new bone and filling cavities left by osteoclasts.

OSTEOCLASTS

Cells that dig out old, damaged tissue from bone, leaving tiny cavities.

OVERTRAINING

Training that includes too much volume, too much intensity, or both. Overtraining leads to aches and pains, chronic fatigue, mental burnout, and/or a sudden drop in running performance. Severe cases require 6–12 weeks of rest to ensure full recovery.

OXYGEN TRANSPORT SYSTEM

The cardiovascular system, which extracts oxygen from your lungs and then transports it to your skeletal and cardiac muscle cells. It includes the heart, blood, and blood vessels.

PALMITATE

A common fatty acid that accounts for 10–20 percent of dietary fat intake.

PERIODIZATION

The separation of training into distinct phases, often including a base-training phase, a strength-building phase, a competition phase, and a recovery phase.

PERIPHERAL FATIGUE THEORY

A theory of fatigue which argues that fatigue is generated when muscles begin to fail during athletic activity. If allowed to build,

fatigue leads to a physiological "catastrophe" (acidosis, overheating, etc.) that forces the athlete to slow down or stop.

PERIPHERAL NERVOUS SYSTEM (PNS)

All of the nerves outside the central nervous system. It includes sensory neurons that relay messages from all corners of the body back to the central nervous system, reporting stimuli received from the senses.

pH

In running physiology, the measurement of hydrogen ions in the body. More hydrogen ions result in an acidic pH (below 7.0), while fewer create an alkaline pH (above 7.0). The human body prefers a slightly alkaline pH (7.35–7.45 on a scale of 1–14).

PHOSPHAGEN SYSTEM

An anaerobic energy system that relies on creatine phosphate as its fuel source and serves as the human body's first responder when muscle fiber ATP levels fall. This system can operate at maximum capacity for up to ten seconds and provides the majority of energy for very short sprints, jumps, and heavy lifts.

PLACEBO EFFECT

Improvement or perception of improvement in health, performance, or behavior derived from the belief in the efficacy of a treatment rather than from any actual direct benefit of medication, treatment, training, etc. The classic example is a patient who recovers from a disorder after being prescribed sugar pills.

PLYOMETRICS

Explosive exercises that use forced eccentric contractions to trigger powerful concentric contractions (e.g., depth jumps from a box). Less-intense jumping exercises and drills are also considered plyometrics, although the greatest adaptations result from the quickest transitions from landing to jumping.

PNF (PROPRIOCEPTIVE NEUROMUSCULAR FACILITATION) STRETCHING

A stretching technique that requires a muscle be stretched to its maximum range of motion, then restrained during a 5–8 second contraction, and then moved to a position of increased stretch.

POSE METHOD

A technique for altering running form that teaches vertical alignment of the head, shoulder, and hips, high cadence, shorter and quicker steps, forefoot landing, and a slight forward lean so that the runner "falls," using gravity to fuel forward motion.

POSTERIOR CRUCIATE LIGAMENT

One of a pair of ligaments that sit in the middle of the knee and connect the femur (thigh bone) to the tibia (shin bone). The cruciate ligaments stabilize the tibia's forward and backward motion and also help to stabilize rotation in the joint.

POWERHOUSES OF THE CELL

Mitochondria.

PR (PERSONAL RECORD)

Also called a PB (personal best), a personal record refers to the best time ever recorded by a runner for a particular distance—or for a particular distance at a particular age. PRs are specific to the type of race being run; for

example, a PR for a track race doesn't double as a PR for a road race.

PROCESSED FOOD

Food that has been changed from its original state, often sacrificing nutrients and other beneficial characteristics.

PROPRIOCEPTION

The nervous system's ability to track the body's position in space relative to the outside world and to adjust accordingly. Composed of a network of sensory nerves located in muscles, ligaments, organs, and the inner ear.

PROTEIN

One of three macronutrients (along with carbohydrates and fats). Composed of amino acids, protein is part of every cell in the human body, and it is a major component of skin, muscles, organs, and glands.

PROTON

A hydrogen ion.

PYRUVATE

A molecule produced by glycolysis that can be cycled through "fast" glycolysis, yielding lactate and NAD+, or shuttled to the mitochondria through "slow" glycolysis to serve as a substrate for aerobic energy production.

QUADRICEPS

The large muscle group on the front of the upper leg, composed of the rectus femoris, vastus lateralis, vastus medialis, and vastus intermedius.

BUILD YOUR RUNNING BODY

RATE CODING

The rate at which nerve impulses are sent from motor neurons to muscle fibers. An increase in rate coding can increase both the force and duration of muscle contraction.

REAL FOOD

Food that hasn't had its nutrients stripped from it through processing.

RECOVERY

A low-key set of activities practiced in tandem with physical exertion. Recovery actitivities can include stretching, post-run exercises, glycogen replacement, rehydration, recovery runs, stress-relieving activites, and complete rest and sleep, among other things. Recovery is required for adaptation from training to occur.

RECRUIT (MUSCLE FIBERS)

Activate muscle fibers.

RECRUITMENT PATTERNS

Neural pathways that determine how muscle fibers are recruited during activity. In running, training leads to the development of more efficient neural pathways, as well as better recruitment of all fiber types.

RED BLOOD CELLS (RBCS)

Red blood cells carry 98 percent of the oxygen that the body uses and also transport carbon dioxide back to the lungs. RBCs usually live 120 days, but they live only 70 days in trained athletes.

REDUCED INHIBITION

Decrease in resistance from opposing muscles when muscles contract. When a muscle contracts, its opposite muscle must relax (e.g., biceps and triceps). Even the slight failure of an opposing muscle to fully relax results in reduced performance.

REPETITION

One of several repeated efforts at a set distance, usually with a set goal pace, as part of a repetition or interval workout. Repetitions range between 150 meters and two miles (in rare cases, longer than that), and are separated by rest intervals of standing, walking, or jogging to allow recovery before the next repetition.

RESPIRATORY SYSTEM

The system that provides oxygen to the blood and carries away carbon dioxide. It consists of the lungs, air passageways, and muscles that aid respiration (breathing).

RUNNER'S KNEE

Also referred to as "patellofemoral pain syndrome" and "chondromalacia," knee pain that's caused by the irritation or deterioration of cartilage beneath the kneecap.

RUNNING ECONOMY

A measurement of fitness based on how efficiently a runner uses oxygen at a given running speed. Running economy is determined by multiple factors, including genetics and nervous system efficiency, and is especially important at submaximal running speeds.

SA NODE (SINOATRIAL NODE)

A specialized group of cells in the upper right atrium. These cells deliver the electrical impulse that first causes both atriums to contract, pushing blood into the lower ventricles, and then causes the ventricles to contract, pushing deoxygenated blood toward the lungs and oxygenated blood into the aorta. The firing rate of the SA node determines heart rate.

SACCHARIDES

Carbohydrates.

SARCOPLASM

The gel-like filler of a muscle fiber (equivalent to the cytoplasm of other cells).

SCIENCE-Y

Terms and concepts from science that aren't familiar to the general public, sometimes giving the impression that the subject matter is more complex than it really is.

SIZE PRINCIPLE

In physical activity, the process whereby force production is increased by recruiting a greater number of muscle fibers and by recruiting larger (faster) muscle fibers.

SKELETAL MUSCLE

Muscle that moves the body and accounts for a third of human body mass. Examples of skeletal muscle include biceps, hamstrings, abdominals, and calves.

SLOW GLYCOLYSIS

One of two pathways for pyruvate molecules produced by glycolysis (the other pathway is "fast" glycolysis). Pyruvate is shuttled to the mitochondria to fuel aerobic energy production.

SLOW-TWITCH MUSCLE FIBER

Small muscle fibers that contract more slowly and less forcefully than intermediate

fast-twitch and fast-twitch fibers. Dense with capillaries and mitochondria, these fibers' high capacity for aerobic energy production makes them perfect for endurance sports. Technically referred to as Type I muscle fibers.

SMOOTH MUSCLE

One of three human muscle types, smooth muscle controls involuntary functions like digestion and blood pressure, and can be found in the stomach, intestines, and blood vessels (among other locations).

SPECIFICITY OF TRAINING RULE

The requirement that an athlete train specific muscle fibers in the exact way that they'll be used during competition (e.g., distance running and race pace repetitions to prepare for a 10K race).

SPEED WORK

A general term referencing shorter, intense running repetitions. Examples include 200-meter repetitions at 800-meter race pace, 400-meter repetitions at mile race pace, and short hill sprints at 90–95 percent effort.

SPLIT

The time for a fraction of a race; for example, a 400-meter split in a 1500-meter race, or a mile split in a 10K race. Also, the time for a single repetition during a repetition/interval workout.

SPRAINED ANKLES

Overstretched or torn ligament (or ligaments) in the ankle, often leading to joint instability.

STATIC STRETCHING

Moving a muscle to the end of its full range of

motion and then holding the position for a predetermined period of time (usually 30–60 seconds). Static stretching is used to reduce stiffness post-run, but has been shown to reduce power pre-workout.

STEROID HORMONES

Hormones derived from cholesterol (e.g., testosterone, cortisol).

STRETCH REFLEX

An involuntary muscular contraction that occurs during overstretching or when a stretch is held at maximum range of motion for longer than two seconds.

STROKE VOLUME

The amount of blood pumped from your right or left ventricle with each beat. In running, it almost always refers to blood pumped from the left ventricle.

SUBMAXIMAL RUNNING SPEED

Any running effort below 100 percent of VO_2 max.

SUBSTRATE

In energy systems, the fuels that are associated with each energy pathway (e.g., carbohydrates, specifically glucose and glycogen, for glycolysis).

SUCKING WIND

Slang for breathing exceptionally hard during a training or race effort.

SUMMATION

Increased contraction force in a muscle due to an increased rate of neural impulses instructing the muscle fibers to contract.

SUPERFOODS

Primarily plant-based foods with high values of antioxidants, vitamins, or other nutrients. Superfoods are commonly marketed as disease-fighting and anti-aging, claims largely unsubstantiated by research data.

SYNAPSE (SYNAPTIC CLEFT, SYNAPTIC GAP)

A small space that separates a neuron from other neurons and muscle cells, across which neurons send signals to communicate messages.

TABATA INTERVALS

A workout composed of twenty-second all-out repetitions followed by ten-second rest intervals. Based on a 1996 bicycle ergometer study by exercise physiologist Izumi Tabata, Tabata intervals have been shown to improve VO_2 max by increasing anaerobic capacity, but they have a negligible impact on cardiovascular development.

TAPERING

Reducing training volume in the days or weeks before a race, which allows the body to fully repair muscles and connective tissue, as well as restock muscle glycogen stores, hormones, enzymes, and neurotransmitters.

TEMPO

Sustained fast running (10–40 minutes) at a pace you could maintain for at least an hour—often performed at half marathon or marathon pace.

TENDON

A connective tissue that connects muscle to bone. Tendons transmit the force generated by muscles to move joints, which in turn moves the body.

TENDON STIFFNESS

A measurement of the amount of force it takes to stretch a tendon. Important for elastic recoil, in which greater force leads to greater recoil. A stretch beyond 4–6 percent is dangerous.

TESTOSTERONE

A hormone that increases muscle mass and bone density. It is often referred to as the "male hormone," although women have approximately 10 percent the levels of men. Testosterone is a widely abused performance-enhancing drug banned by WADA.

TETANUS

A sustained muscle contraction. When the increased rate of neural impulses (rate coding) reaches maximum summation (the maximum contraction force for those muscle fibers), the muscle is in a state of tetanus.

THYROID HORMONE

A general term that refers to the thyroid hormones, although thyroid hormone replacement therapy usually involves treatment with T4 only. (See following entry.)

THYROXIN (T4)

The form of thyroid hormone with the highest concentration in the blood. Thyroxin is converted to T3 in cells, and is vital to the metabolism of all cells in the body. See *hyperthyroidism* and *hypothyroidism* for disorders related to this hormone.

TIBIA

The shin bone. The large, supporting bone in the lower leg connecting the knee to the ankle bones.

TIME TRIAL

An all-out effort at a specified distance—usually either a race distance or a portion of a race distance. Runners use time trials to prepare for races, as well as to gauge their fitness.

TRAINING ADAPTATION

Physiological or psychological changes that occur in response to training stimuli (workouts). Improved fitness results from an accumulation of training adaptations.

TRAINING STIMULUS

A workout or activity that challenges current fitness. When the training stress is greater than what is normally encountered, the body responds by growing stronger, given adequate recovery.

TRIIODOTHYRONINE (T3)

The more potent form of thyroid hormone. T3 circulates in the bloodstream at only one-fortieth the volume of T4. Only about one-fifth of T3 is produced in the thyroid gland, with most created outside the thyroid gland through conversion of T4.

UNSATURATED FATS

Fats that have one or more double bonds in the fatty-acid chain. Unsaturated fats are considered "good" fats, as they decrease harmful LDL cholesterol levels and increase beneficial HDL cholesterol levels. They are usually liquid at room temperature (e.g., olive oil).

VEIN

Large blood vessels that carry deoxygenated blood toward the heart (except for the pulmonary veins, which carry oxygenated blood from the lungs to the left atrium).

VENTRICLE

One of the two lower chambers of the heart. The right ventricle pumps deoxygenated blood toward the lungs. The left ventricle receives oxygenated blood from the left atrium and pumps it into the aorta.

VENULES

Small blood vessels that receive deoxygenated blood from capillaries and transport it to veins, which then carry this blood back to the heart.

VIBRAM FIVEFINGERS

A minimalist shoe that includes toe sleeves. Research has shown increased bone damage in runners transitioning to this shoe.

VISCOSITY

Resistance. In muscles, viscosity can be reduced by performing a warm-up (which improves neural messaging to muscles, increases temperature and suppleness in muscles, and stimulates release of lubricating synovial fluid at the joints, etc.). In the case of blood, viscosity refers to thickness based on a higher red blood cell count or reduced plasma volume, creating greater resistance in blood vessels; this can be caused naturally by dehydration or stimulated unnaturally by the use of EPO, among other triggers.

VITAMINS

Essential organic compounds that play a critical role in the regulation of metabolism, growth, tissue maintenance, and disease prevention, among other things. Vitamins are not themselves sources of energy, and they must be obtained through diet (with the exception of a very few nonessential vitamins like vitamin D and biotin, which can be produced within your body).

VO$_2$ MAX

The maximum amount of oxygen that a human body can consume in one minute.

WADA

World Anti-Doping Agency

FURTHER READING

Build Your Running Body was itself built upon a wide-ranging foundation of magazine, journal, book, and internet research.

A few of the books that were used countless times in the course of writing *Build Your Running Body* (and which have sprouted hundreds of post-it notes in the process) include:

Daniels, J. (2005). *Daniels' Running Formula, Second Edition.* Champaign, IL: Human Kinetics.

Galloway, J. (2002). *Galloway's Book On Running, Second Edition.* Bolinas, CA: Shelter Publications.

Hutchinson, PhD, A. (2011). *Which Comes First, Cardio or Weights?: Fitness Myths, Training Truths, and Other Surprising Discoveries from the Science of Exercise.* New York, NY: Harper.

Martin, D. E., & Coe, P. N. (1997). *Better Training for Distance Runners, Second Edition.* Champaign, IL: Human Kinetics.

Noakes, T. D. (2002). *Lore of Running, Fourth Edition.* Champaign, IL: Human Kinetics.

Tucker, R., Dugas, J., & Fitzgerald, M. (2009). *Runner's World, The Runner's Body: How the Latest Exercise Science Can Help You Run Stronger, Longer, and Faster.* Emmaus, PA: Rodale.

For those of you interested in keeping abreast of the latest in training advice and exercise science, the following websites—all of which were bookmarked and visited regularly in the course of preparing this manuscript—provide a wealth of up-to-date information coupled with insightful commentary:

The Science of Sport, by Ross Tucker, PhD, and Jonathan Dugas, PhD
www.sportsscientists.com

Sweat Science, by Alex Hutchinson, PhD
www.runnersworld.com/sweat-science

The Science of Running, by Steve Magness
www.scienceofrunning.com

Runner's World
www.runnersworld.com

Running Times
www.runnersworld.com/running-times-home

Finally, *Build Your Running Body* utilized hundreds of magazine and journal articles. The following list presents some of the most interesting and salient articles from the bunch, grouped by chapter, so that you can go to the source for topics about which you'd like to know more:

Chapter 1: Build Your Running Motivation

Chakravarty, E., Hubert, H., Lingala, V., & Fries, J. (2008). Reduced Disability and Mortality among Aging Runners: a 21-year Longitudinal Study. *Archives of Internal Medicine*, 168(15), 1638–1646.

Williams, P. (2013). Greater weight loss from run-

...g than walking during a 6.2-yr prospective follow-up. *Med Sci Sports Exerc*, 45(4), 706–713.

Chapter 2: Build Your Running History

Bramble, D., & Lieberman, D. (2004, November 18). Endurance running and the evolution of Homo. *Nature*, 432, 345–352.

Chapter 3: Build Your Running Gear

Dengate, J. (n.d.). *Jeff Dengate articles*. Retrieved from Runner's World: www.runnersworld.com/person/jeff-dengate

Chapter 5: Build Your Running Muscles

Simic, L., Sarabon, N., & Markovic, G. (2013, March). Does pre-exercise static stretching inhibit maximal muscular performance? A meta-analytical review. *Scand J Med Sci Sports*, 23(2), 131–148. doi:10.1111/j.1600-0838.2012.01444.x

Chapter 6: Build Your Running Connective Tissue

Williams, P. (2013, July). Effects of running and walking on osteoarthritis and hip replacement risk. *Med Sci Sports Exerc*, 45(7), 1292–1297. doi:10.1249/MSS.0b013e3182885f26

van der Plas, A., de Jonge, S., de Vos, R., van der Heide, H., Verhaar, J., Weir, A., & Tol, J. (2012, March 1). A 5-year follow-up study of Alfredson's heel-drop exercise programme in chronic midportion Achilles tendinopathy. *Br J Sports Med*, 46(3), 214–218. doi:10.1136/bjsports-2011-090035

Heinemeier, K., Schjerling, P., Heinemeier, J., Magnusson, S., & Kjaer, M. (2013, May). Lack of tissue renewal in human adult Achilles tendon is revealed by nuclear bomb 14C. *FASEB J*, 27(5), 2074–2079. doi:10.1096/fj.12-225599

Dhillon, M., Bali, K., & Prabhakar, S. (2011, Jul–Aug). Proprioception in anterior cruciate ligament deficient knees and its relevance in anterior cruciate ligament reconstruction. *Indian J Orthop*, 45(4), 294–300. doi:10.4103/0019-5413.80320

Lieberman, D., Venkadesan, M., Werbel, W., Daoud, A., D'Andrea, S., Davis, I., . . . Pitsiladis, Y. (2010, January 28). Foot strike patterns and collision forces in habitually barefoot versus shod runners. *Nature*, 463, 531–535. doi:10.1038/nature08723

Ridge, S., Johnson, A., Mitchell, U., Hunter, I., Robinson, E., Rich, B., & Brown, S. (2013, July). Foot bone marrow edema after a 10-wk transition to minimalist running shoes. *Med Sci Sports Exerc*, 45(7), 1363–1368. doi:10.1249/MSS.0b013e3182874769

Franz, J., Wierzbinski, C., & Kram, R. (2012, August). Metabolic cost of running barefoot versus shod: is lighter better? *Med Sci Sports Exerc*, 44(8), 1519–1525. doi:10.1249/MSS.0b013e3182514a88

Chapter 7: Build Your Running Cardiovascular System

Kim, J., Malhotra, R., Chiampas, G., d'Hemecourt, P., Troyanos, C., Cianca, J., . . . Baggish, A. (2012). Cardiac Arrest during Long-Distance Running Races. *New England Journal of Medicine*, 366, 130–140. doi:10.1056/NEJMoa1106468

Williams, P., & Franklin, B. (2013, June 7). *Reduced Incidence of Cardiac Arrhythmias in Walkers and Runners*. (C. Earnest, Ed.) doi:10.1371/journal.pone.0065302

Deloukas, P., Kanoni, S., Willenborg, C., Farrall, M., Assimes, T., Thompson, J., . . . Weang, K. H. (2013). Large-scale association analysis identifies new risk loci for coronary artery disease. *Nature Genetics*, 45, 25–33. doi:10.1038/ng.2480

Garret, A., Creasy, R., Rehrer, N., Patterson, M., & Cotter, J. (2012, May). Effectiveness of short-term heat acclimation for highly trained athletes. *Eur J Appl Physiol*, 112(5), 1827–1837. doi:10.1007/s00421-011-2153-3

Gething, A., Williams, M., & Davies, B. (2004, December). Inspiratory resistive loading improves cycling capacity: a placebo controlled trial. *Br J Sports Med*, 38(6), 730–736. doi:10.136/bjsm.2003.007518

Chapter 8: Build Your Running Powerhouses

Marguilis, L., & Sagan, D. (1997). *Microcosmos: Four Billion Years of Microbial Evolution*. Berkeley, CA: University of California Press.

Holloszy, J. (2008). Regulation by Exercises of Skeletal Muscle Content of Mitochondria and GLUT4. *Journal of Physiology and Pharmacology*, 59(Suppl 7), 5–18. Retrieved from http://www.jpp.krakow.pl/

Terjung, R. (1995). *SSE #54: Muscle Adaptations to Aerobic Training*. Retrieved from Sports Science Exchange: http://www.gssiweb.org/Article/sse-54-muscle-adaptations-to-aerobic-training

Gibala, M., Little, J., Macdonald, M., & Hawley, J. (2012, March 1). Physiological adaptations to low-volume, high-intensity interval training in health and disease. *J Physiol*, 590(Pt 5), 1077–1084. doi:10.1113/jphysiol.2011.224725

Chapter 9: Balance Your Running pH

Costill, D., Barnett, A., Sharp, R., Fink, W., & Katz, A. (1983). Leg muscle pH following sprint running. *Med Sci Sports Exerc*, 15(4), 325–329.

Knuth, S., Dave, H., Peters, J., & Fitts, R. (2006, September 15). Low cell pH depresses peak power in rat skeletal muscle fibres at both 30 degrees C and 15 degrees C: implications for muscle fatigue. *J Physiol*, 575(Pt 3), 887–899.

Maglischo, E. (2012). Does Lactic Acid Cause Muscular Fatigue? *Journal of the International Society of Swimming Coaching*, 2(2), 4–40.

Robergs, R., Ghiasvand, F., & Parker, D. (2004, September 1). Biochemistry of exercise-induced metabolic acidosis. *American Journal of Physiology – Regulatory, Integrative and Comparative Physiology*, 287(3), R502-R516. doi:10.1152/ajpregu.00114.2004

Brooks, G. (2009, December 1). Cell-cell and intracellular lactate shuttles. *The Journal of Physiology*, 587(23), 5591–5600. doi:10.1113/jphysiol.2009.178350

McKenna, M., & Hargreaves, M. (2008, January). Resolving fatigue mechanisms determining exercise performance: integrative physiology at its finest! *Journal of Applied Physiology*, 104(1), 286–287. doi:10.1152/japplphysiol.01139.2007

Chapter 10: Build Your Running Energy System

Buono, M., & Kolkhorst, F. (2001, June 1). Estimating ATP resynthesis during a marathon run: a method to introduce metabolism. *Adv Physiol Educ*, 25(2), 70–71.

Rauch, H., Hawley, J., Noakes, T., & Dennis, S. (1998, July). Fuel metabolism during ultra-endurance exercise. *Pflügers Archiv European Journal of Physiology*, 436(2), 211–219.

Ahlborg, G., & Felig, P. (1982, January). Lactate and Glucose Exchange across the Forearm, Legs, and Splanchnic Bed during and after Prolonged Leg Exercise. *J. Clin. Invest.*, 69, 45–54.

Ahlborg, G., Wahren, J., & Felig, P. (1986, March). Splanchnic and Peripheral Glucose and Lactate Metabolism During and After Prolonged Arm Exercise. *J. Clin. Invest.*, 77, 690–699.

Jansson, E., & Kaijser, L. (1987, March). Substrate utilization and enzymes in skeletal muscle of extremely endurance-trained men. *J Appl Physiol*, 62(3), 999–1005.

Duffield, R., Dawson, B., & Goodman, C. (2004, September). Energy system contribution to

100-m and 200-m track running events. *J Sci Med Sport*, 7(3), 302–313.

Duffield, R., Dawson, B., & Goodman, C. (2005, March). Energy system contribution to 400-metre and 800-metre track running. *J Sports Sci*, 23(3), 299–307.

Chapter 11: Build Your Running Nervous System

Farndon, J. (2009, September 16). *Nerve Signalling: Tracing the Wiring of Life*. Retrieved from Nobelprize.org: http://www.nobelprize.org/educational/medicine/nerve_signaling/overview/

Lee, M., & Carroll, T. (2007). Cross education: possible mechanisms for the contralateral effects of unilateral resistance training. *Sports Med*, 37(1), 1–14.

Hill, D. J. (2013, July 15). *Boston Dynamics' Humanoid Robot, ATLAS, In Latest Video*. Retrieved from Singularity HUB: http://singularityhub.com/2013/07/15/ready-boston-dynamics-humanoid-robot-atlas-in-latest-video/

Oliveira, A., Silva, P. L., Gizzi, L., Farina, D., & et al. (2013, March 18). *Effects of Perturbations to Balance on Neuromechanics of Fast Changes in Direction during Locomotion*. (A. Lucia, Ed.) doi:10.1371/journal.pone.0059029

McHugh, M., Tyler, T., Mirabella, M., Mullaney, M., & Nicholas, S. (2007, August). The Effectiveness of a Balance Training Intervention in Reducing the Incidence of Noncontact Ankle Sprains in High School Football Players. *Am J Sports Med*, 35(8), 1289–1294. doi:10.1177/0363546507300059

Saunders, P., Pyne, D., Telford, R., & Hawley, J. (2004). Factors Affecting Running Economy in Trained Distance Runners. *Sports Med*, 34(7), 465–485.

Dallam, G., Wilber, R., Jadelis, K., Fletcher, G., & Romanov, N. (2005, July). Effect of a global alteration of running technique on kinematics and economy. *J Sports Sci*, 23(7), 757–764.

Turner, A., Owings, M., & Schwane, J. (2003, February). Improvement in running economy after 6 weeks of plyometric training. *J Strength Cond Res*, 17(1), 60–67.

Berryman, N., Maurel, D., & Bosquet, L. (2010, July). Effect of Plyometric vs. Dynamic Weight Training on the Energy Cost of Running. *Journal of Strength & Conditioning Research*, 24(7), 1818–1825. doi:10.1519/JSC.0b013e3181def1f5

Chapter 12: Build Your Running Hormones

Bhasin, S., Storer, T., Berman, N., Callegari, C., Clevenger, B., Phillips, J., . . . Casaburi, R. (1996, July 4). The Effects of Supraphysiologic Doses of Testosterone on Muscle Size and Strength in Normal Men. *N Engl J Med*, 335, 1–7. doi:10.1056/NEJM199607043350101

Lundby, C., & Olsen, N. (2011, March 15). Effects of recombinant human erythropoietin in normal humans. *J Physiol*, 589(Pt 6), 1265–1271. doi:10.1113/jphysiol.2010.195917

Thomsen, J., Rentsch, R., Robach, P., Calbet, J., Boushel, R., Rasmussen, P., . . . Lundby, C. (2007, November). Prolonged administration of recombinant human erythropoietin increases submaximal performance more than maximal aerobic capacity. *Eur J Appl Physiol*, 101(4), 481–486.

Chapter 13: Build Your Running Brain

Carter, J., Jeukendrup, A., & Jones, D. (2004, December). The effect of carbohydrate mouth rinse on 1-h cycle time trial performance. *Med Sci Sports Exerc*, 36(12), 2107–2111. doi:10.1249/01.MSS.0000147585.65709.6F

Chambers, E., Bridge, M., & Jones, D. (2009, April 15). Carbohydrate sensing in the human mouth: effects on exercise performance and brain activity. *Journal of Physiology*, 587, 1779–1794. doi:10.1113/jphysiol.2008.164285

Sinclair, J., Bottoms, L., Flynn, C., Bradley, E., Alexander, G., McCullagh, S., . . . Hurst, H. (2013, April 11). The effect of different durations of carbohydrate mouth rinse on cycling performance. *Eur J Sport Sci*, 259–64. doi:10.1080/1746 1391.2013.785599

Marcora, S. M. (2008, September 26). The end-spurt does not require a subconscious intelligent system. Retrieved from BMJGroup Blogs: http://blogs.bmj.com/bjsm/the-end-spurt-does-not-require-a-subconscious-intelligent-system/

Bellinger, A., Reiken, S., Dura, M., Murphy, P., Deng, S.-X., Landry, D., . . . Marks, A. (2008, February 12). Remodeling of ryanodine receptor complex causes "leaky" channels: A molecular mechanism for decreased exercise capacity. *Proc Natl Acad Sci USA*, 105(6), 2198–2202. doi:10.1073/pnas.0711074105

de Paoli, F., Ørtenblad, N., Pedersen, T., Jørgensen, R., & Nielsen, O. (2010, December 1). Lactate per se improves the excitability of depolarized rat skeletal muscle by reducing the Cl-conductance. *J Physiol*, 588(Pt 23), 4785–4794. doi:10.1113/jphysiol.2010.196568

Wilkinson, D., Smeeton, N., & Watt, P. (2010, July). Ammonia metabolism, the brain and fatigue; revisiting the link. *Prog Neurobiol*, 91(3), 200–219. doi:10.1016/j.pneurobio.2010.01.012

Rauch, H., Gibson, A., Lambert, E., & Noakes, T. (2005). A signalling role for muscle glycogen in the regulation of pace during prolonged exercise. *Br J Sports Med*, 39, 34–38. doi:10.1136/bjsm.2003.010645

Allen, D., & Trajanovska, S. (2012). The multiple roles of phosphate in muscle fatigue. *Front Physiol*, 3, 463. doi:10.3389/fphys.2012.00463

Davis, J., Alderson, N., & Welsh, R. (2000, August). Serotonin and central nervous system fatigue: nutritional considerations. *Am J Clin Nutr*, 72(2), 573s–578s.

Amann, M., Venturelli, M., Ives, S., McDaniel, J., Layec, G., Rossman, M., & Richardson, R. (2013). Peripheral fatigue limits endurance exercise via a sensory feedback-mediated reduction in spinal motoneuronal output. *J Appl Physiol*, 115, 355–364. doi:10.1152/japplphysiol.00049.2013

Noakes, T. (2012). Fatigue is a Brain-Derived Emotion that Regulates the Exercise Behavior to Ensure the Protection of Whole Body Homeostasis. *Front Physiol*, 3, 82. doi:10.3389/fphys.2012.00082

Okano, A., Fontes, E., Montenegro, R., de Tarso Veras Farinatti, P., Cyrino, E. L., Bikson, M., & Noakes, T. (2013, February 27). Brain stimulation modulates the autonomic nervous system, rating of perceived exertion and performance during maximal exercise. *Br J Sports Med*, doi:10.1136/bjsports-2012-091658

Upson, S. (2012, July 24). A Single Brain Structure May Give Winners That Extra Physical Edge. Retrieved from *Scientific American*: http://www.scientificamerican.com/article/olympics-insula-gives-edge/

Chapter 14: Build Your Training Approach

Magness, S. (2008). Training. Retrieved from The Science of Running: http://magstraining.tripod.com/training.html

Chapter 18: Build Your Running Diet with Real Food

Wylie, L., Kelly, J., Bailey, S., Blackwell, J., Skiba, P., Winyard, P., . . . Jones, A. (1985, August 1). Beetroot juice and exercise: pharmacodynamic and dose-response relationships. *J Apple Physiol*, 115(3), 325–336. doi:10.1152/japplphysiol.00372.2013

Mickleborough, T., Lindley, M., Ionescu, A., & Fly, A. (2006, January). Protective Effect of Fish Oil Supplementation on Exercise-Induced

Bronchoconstriction in Asthma. *Chest Journal*, 129(1), 39–49.

Tarazona-Díaz, M., Alacid, F., Carrasco, M., Martinez, I., & Aguayo, E. (2013). Watermelon Juice: Potential Functional Drink for Sore Muscle Relief in Athletes. *J. Agric. Food Chem.*, 61(31), 7522–7528. doi:10.1021/jf400964r

Smith-Spangler, C., Brandeau, M., Hunter, G., Bavinger, J., Pearson, M., Eschback, P., . . . Bravata, D. (2012). Are Organic Foods Safer or Healthier Than Conventional Alternatives?: A Systematic Review. *Ann Intern Med.*, 157(5), 348–366. doi:10.7326/0003-4819-157-5-201209040-00007

Chapter 19: Build Your Running Carbohydrates

Ferguson-Stegall, L., McCleave, E., Ding, Z., Doerner III, P., Liu, Y., Wang, B., . . . Ivy, J. (2011). Aerobic Exercise Training Adaptations Are Increased by Postexercise Carbohydrate-Protein Supplementation. *Journal of Nutrition and Metabolism*, 2011. doi:10.1155/2011/623182

Chapter 20: Build Your Running Protein

Campbell, B., Kreider, R., Ziegenfuss, T., La Bounty, P., Roberts, M., Burke, D., . . . Antonio, J. (2007). International Society of Sports Nutrition position stand: protein and exercise. *Journal of the International Society of Sports Nutrition*, 4, 8. doi:10.1186/1550-2783-4-8

Consumer Reports. (2010, July). Alert: Protein Drinks: You Don't Need the Extra Protein or the Heavy Metals Our Tests Found. *Consumer Reports*, 75(7), 24–27. Retrieved from http://www.consumerreports.org/cro/2012/04/protein-drinks/index.htm

Chapter 21: Build Your Running Fats

Horvath, P., Eagen, C., Fisher, N., Leddy, J., & Pendergast, D. (2000, February). The effects of varying dietary fat on performance and metabolism in trained male and female runners. *J Am Coll Nutr*, 19(1), 52–60.

Gerlach, K., Burton, H., Dorn, J., Leddy, J., & Horvath, P. (2008). Fat intake and injury in female runners. *Journal of the International Society of Sports Nutrition*, 5(1). doi:10.1186/1550-2783-5-1

Talbott, S. (2013, September 10). *Supplement Use Amongst Endurance Athletes*. Retrieved from Competitor: http://running.competitor.com/2013/09/nutrition/supplement-use-amongst-endurance-athletes_17360

Chapter 22: Build Your Running Nutrients

Ginde, A., Liu, M., & Camargo, Jr., C. (2009, March 23). Demographic differences and trends of vitamin D insufficiency in the US population, 1988–2004. *Arch Intern Med*, 169(6), 626–632. doi:10.1001/archinternmed.2008.604

Bolland, M., Grey, A., Avenell, A., Gamble, G., & Reid, I. (2011, April 19). Calcium supplements with or without vitamin D and risk of cardiovascular events: reanalysis of the Women's Health Initiative limited access dataset and meta-analysis. *BMJ*, 342, d2040. doi:10.1136/bmj.d2040

Chapter 25: Build Your Race

Rapoport, B. (2010). Metabolic Factors Limiting Performance in Marathon Runners. *PLoS Comput Biol*, 6(10). doi:10.1371/journal.pcbi.1000960

ACKNOWLEDGMENTS

Creating this book required the direct and indirect efforts of so many people—for starters, the literally hundreds of coaches, athletes, scientists, and others who contributed innovations to the sport—that listing them would fill another book. So the authors wish to thank them en masse.

Next, we'd like to thank Matthew Lore, president and publisher for The Experiment, for his early enthusiasm for the book and, obviously, for publishing it. We'd also like to thank Nicholas Cizek, our editor, for his skill, guidance, and patience.

And speaking of early enthusiasm, a heartfelt thank-you to our agent, David Vigliano, for seeing something unique in the original book outline, then helping us to mold that outline into a proposal. Thanks also to Matthew Carlini and the rest of Vigliano Associates.

This book grew out of articles and columns first published by *Running Times* magazine, so we'd like to thank the magazine and its editor-in-chief, Jonathan Beverly, for permission to borrow ideas, passages, descriptions, quotes, and even the book's title from those pieces.

Big thanks, too, to Stuart Calderwood, our copy editor, for smoothing out bumps in the manuscript and for appending a marathon-long list of production notes.

This book's photo instruction wouldn't have been possible without the enthusiasm and sponsorship of Nike, with special thanks to Kevin Paulk and Vida Rabizadeh; Thera-band, with special thanks to Chrissy Foster; AquaJogger, with special thanks to Steve Bergstrom; Classic Kickboxing in Pasadena, CA, with special thanks to Mauricio Gonzales; Anytime Fitness in La Cañada, CA; and PowerLung, with special thanks to Carolyn Morse.

We'd also like to thank Bill Greene and Sports Tutor for allowing us to use their warehouse and grounds for multiple photo shoots—and for letting us leave up the lighting, background sheets, floor mats, etc. for the long weeks it took to finish the job.

The injury-prevention routines, exercises, and photo shoots wouldn't have been possible without the advice, input, and oversight of Michael P. Parkinson, PT, and Bianca Guzman, MPT (who also donated her time as a model). Also contributing to the shoots and exercises were Phil Wharton (whartonhealth.com) and CB Richards.

The book drew heavily on interviews conducted with Steve Magness (scienceofrunning.com); Jay Johnson (coachjayjohson.com); Jeff Dengate (runnersworld.com/person/jeff-dengate); Christopher B. Scott, Ph.D. (usm.maine.edu/ehss/chris-scott); Sean Wade (kenyanway.com); Alex Hutchinson, Ph.D.; Robert Montgomery, Ph.D.; Tom Cotner, Ph.D.; Jeff Gaudette (runnersconnect.net); Jeff Sneed; and Roger Sayre.

We also mined interviews previously conducted for Pete Magill's *Running Times* articles and columns, including those with Dr. Jeffrey S. Brown (houstonendocrinology.com); Jonathan Dugas, Ph.D.; Joe Rubio (runningwarehouse.com); Dr. James Fries, of the Stanford School of Medicine; and Richard L. Rupp, DPM.

This book used photo instruction as its centerpiece, a theme that couldn't have worked without the time and dedication of our wonderful models: Eddie Andre, Sean Brosnan, Christian Cushing-murray, Jessica Cushing-murray, Kathleen Cushing-murray, Nathaniel Cushing-murray, Rebecca Cushing-murray, Zachary Cushing-murray, Emii, Callie Greene, Sean Magill, Matt Nelson, Jessica Ng, Grace Padilla, Jacques Sallberg, Angie Stewart, and Tanya Zeferjahn.

A big thanks to Ed Murphy and the Cal Coast Track Club for creating our race pace tables. And to John Gardiner, Rob Arsenault, and other members of the Cal Coast Track Club for providing numerous suggestions for the lists that appear in this book (from running fads to race jitters).

Thanks, too, to Liz Palmer for her advice on strength workouts, Fred Raimondi for advice on photo editing, John Fell for shooting the food photos for Part 4, the American College of Sports Medicine (ACSM) for allowing use of their formulas in creating some of the book's tables, the American Council on Exercise for permission to reprint their chart, "Percent Body Fat Norms for Men and Women" (Copyright © [2011], American Council on Exercise; All rights reserved; Reprinted by permission), and Scott Douglas for his valuable feedback on early drafts of this project.

Finally, we'd like to offer our deepest thanks to two very special participants in this project. First, a big thank-you to Andy DiConti, who was instrumental in designing the format for this book's component chapters and worked tirelessly to bring the project to fruition. Second, we owe an enormous debt of gratitude to photographer Diana Hernandez, whose offer to do a two-day shoot turned into a thousand hours of shoot prep, photography (those two shoots grew to a dozen), and photo editing—not to mention additional work proofreading and providing thoughtful edits.

INDEX

Page numbers in *italics* refer to tables and charts.

BUILD YOUR RUNNING BODY

BUILD YOUR RUNNING BODY

BUILD YOUR RUNNING BODY

Pete Magill is a senior writer and columnist for *Running Times* magazine and the 2013 USA Masters Cross Country Runner of the Year. He is the fastest-ever American distance runner over age 50 in the 5K and 10K. He lives in South Pasadena, California.

Thomas Schwartz runs the popular website TheRunZone.com. His personal training website is RunningPRs.com. He is an exercise physiologist and coach in Meridian, Idaho.

Melissa Breyer is the coauthor of *True Food* and is a Green Living columnist for Discovery Channel's Treehugger.com. She lives in Brooklyn, New York.